THE CLUSTER

OF

SPIRITUAL SONGS,

DIVINE HYMNS,

AND

SACRED POEMS;

BEING CHIEFLY

A COLLECTION.

BY JESSE MERCER,
Minister of the Gospel at Powelton, Georgia.

"Let the word of Christ dwell in you richly, in all wisdom; teaching and admonishing one another in Psalms, and Hymns, and Spiritual Songs, singing with grace in your hearts to the Lord."——*Paul.*

THIRD EDITION, REVISED.

PRINTED FOR THE PROPRIETOR,
BY WILLIAM W. WOODWARD,
Philadelphia.

1823.

Copy slightly larger than actual size.

Barbara Baldwin Richards
Decatur, Georgia

JESSE MERCER

The Cluster of Jesse Mercer

by

C. Ray Brewster

RENAISSANCE PRESS

MACON, GEORGIA—1983

© Copyright 1983 by C. Ray Brewster

All rights reserved.
For further information, write: RENAISSANCE PRESS,
P.O. Box 7063, Macon, GA 31209.

Library of Congress Catalog Card Number 83-62474
ISBN 0-914707-01-9

Printed at Braun-Brumfield, Inc.
Ann Arbor, Michigan

To EMMA BRONSON MILLER,
whose faith matched that of Jesse Mercer
and whose musical talent exceeded his.

The Cluster of Jesse Mercer

CONTENTS

Preface		xi
CHAPTER ONE	THE LIFE AND TIMES OF JESSE MERCER	1
CHAPTER TWO	AN INTRODUCTION TO MERCER'S *Cluster*	15
CHAPTER THREE	HYMN TEXTS FROM *The Cluster*	47
CHAPTER FOUR	A SAMPLE OF TUNES FOR *The Cluster*	161
CHAPTER FIVE	A GENERAL INDEX OF *The Cluster*	199
CHAPTER SIX	A LIST OF MERCER'S WRITINGS	215

Preface

To the question, why such a publication as this, one answer immediately presents itself; nothing, so far as we know, has been republished on the subject since the 1835 edition that Jesse Mercer himself compiled, edited, and published. That the *kairos* is right may be indicated by celebration of Mercer University's Sesquicentennial, marking the founding of the institution named after the compiler of this hymnbook. Alex Haley's *Roots*, and many another recently published book, lends evidence to a general interest among Americans for rediscovering their heritage. For the philosophically-minded the present work may afford a standpoint of reference whereby the values and goals of our present-day society and life in the churches may be compared. It should be sufficient to offer the purpose as praise to God, presenting in a new-old idiom a musical oblation to the Almighty, which is probably the way Mercer himself would have wished his efforts remembered. The title page of his 1810 edition of *The Cluster* points simply to three Biblical passages from David, Isaiah, and Paul: "Sing us one of the Songs of Zion," "Now will I sing to my well beloved a Song," and "Speaking to yourselves in Spiritual Songs." Its general preface explictly states the purpose hoped for: "... it is now submitted to a pious Public, whose GOOD TO SEEK is a duty and privilege, AND TO EFFECT, a glory much desired by theirs, in bonds of dearest relation," (Signed, JESSE MERCER, dated March 20, 1810.)

The presentation here offered constitutes a selection of almost half the hymn texts published by Mercer, as taken from the several editions from 1810 to 1835. Although no tunes and no music are found in *The Cluster*, explicit mention of tune-names by Mercer, forty or so with some repeats, permits the inclusion of a section, a sort of sampling, with notation and melodies. This is important because texts and tunes have a way of linking together in holistic fashion with affecting influences upon the singers. In a few cases tunes have been associated with hymn texts, even though no indication of tune-name is found in *The Cluster*.

We have tried to organize the materials to let Mercer's *Cluster* speak for itself. Where analysis does come into the picture it is guided by an effort to remain true to implications and developments based upon Mercer's own judgments. Except for some indexing, selected bibliography, and a brief indication of sources used, the four main parts of this book are: (1) hymn texts from *The Cluster*; (2) twenty-seven tunes that are associated with particular hymns; (3) a calendar of events from the life and times of Jesse Mercer; and (4) a short introduction to *The Cluster*, written by the present author.

The treatment of these materials is not exhaustive nor complete. It is a beginning; and it is hoped that a few of the paths charted now will lead to further determinations not arrived at here. There has been a conscious concern to make evident a distinction between the more assured judgments and the considerable amount of guesswork attendant upon any study of what New World Americans view as "ancient hymnbooks."

Complex would be the present writer's attempt to know the basis upon which his selection of texts was made. It has been largely a random one, inexact and with a tendency to favor the American influences, even though we can say for sure that half the almost seven hundred hymns considered are derived from the British Isles. The present selection owes something to these criteria: the allowing for a variety of metrical choices; a proportional representation from each of the topical theological classifications; a balance between hymns traceable to known authors and those remaining unknown; a conscious selection of hymns with choruses attached (indicating greater congregational participation); and a tipping of the hat to hymns that have become favorites to the present author during a two year period of work on *The Cluster*. All the hymns that can be identified as having been composed by Jesse Mercer himself obviously have been included. It is to be noted that seventeen hymn texts from the 1810 edition are not carried over to later editions. They have been placed in an appendix, leaving the reader to decide why Mercer dropped these. For the most part, later editions merely added to the choices of an earlier day.

Dangerous as it is to the cause of good manners in acknowledging specific names of persons for whom the author feels a profound sense of gratitude, we take the risk: Harold L. McManus, Chairman of the Christianity Department, Mercer University; Howard P. Giddens, who made unexpectedly a gift of his personal edition of the *Cluster* to the author; Mr. Robert Byrd, Manuscripts Department, Duke University; and Mrs. Mary Overby, Curator, Special Collections, Stetson Library, Mercer University, without whose gentle prodding, wry humor, and enduring patience this present offering would not have come to pass. To members of the Georgia Baptist Historical Society is owed a great debt, especially Robert G. Gardner, Charles O. Walker, J. R. Huddlestun, Waldo Harris, and Edmond D. Keith. To those zealous, gentle, lovers of music, who continue to sing each Sunday and keep alive the old songs: Raymond Hamrick, John Garst, and Hugh McGraw. Quietly and efficiently as librarians, Mrs. Corawayne Wright of Wesleyan College and

Mrs. Frances Shepherd of Mercer University contributed significantly to the accomplishment of our task. Our gratitude extends as well to two other librarians, Ray Rowland of Augusta College, who guided us to the 1810 *Cluster* in the Rare Books Room, Duke University, and to Mercer University's chief librarian, Daniel Lamar Metts, Jr.

Macon, Georgia
July, 1983   C. Ray Brewster

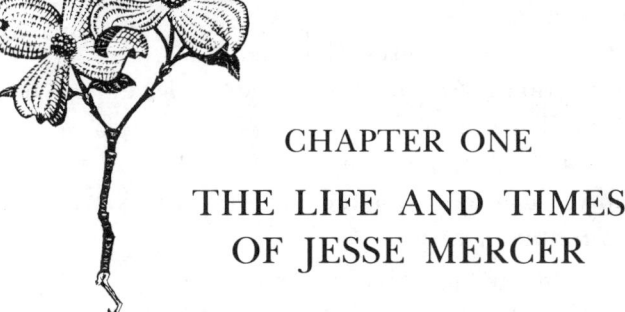

CHAPTER ONE
THE LIFE AND TIMES OF JESSE MERCER

For the reader's understanding of the historical and cultural context in which editions of *The Cluster* first appeared C. D. Mallary's *Memoirs of Elder Jesse Mercer* is the best source for study. The writings of Adiel Sherwood and Jesse Mercer himself should be consulted, along with the minutes of the Georgia Association and the Georgia Baptist Convention. Shortened accounts by B. D. Ragsdale and Spright Dowell are also helpful.

In the present work we offer a selection of events from the life and times of Jesse Mercer between the time of his birth (1769) and his death (1841), which will allow readers the opportunity at a quick glance to observe some of the external yet personal happenings related to the compiler and composer of *The Cluster*. The events pertain mostly to the state of Georgia, but some relate wider regional, national, and world happenings of note. Publication dates of a few hymnbooks are sprinkled in during the present listing with a more careful and extended listing supplied elsewhere in this volume. A more comprehensive bibliography of the writings of Jesse Mercer is included in our present work. (Cf. Chapter Six.)

EVENTS FROM THE LIFE AND TIMES OF JESSE MERCER, 1769–1841

1769 Dec. 16. Birth of Jesse Mercer in Halifax, County, N.C., son of Silas and Dorcas Mercer. Eldest of eight children: Ann, Mary (died in infancy), Daniel, Mourning (died in infancy), Hermon, Mount Moriah, Joshua.
1770 Death of George Whitefield.
1772 Spring, Kiokee Baptist Church constituted.

1773   New Savannah Georgia Baptist Church established by E. Botsford.
1773   Dec. Boston Tea Party.
1774   Sept. First Continental Congress, Philadelphia.
1775   Silas Mercer, previously Anglican, immersed by Alexander Scott.
1776   Archibald Bulloch becomes first president of Georgia.
1776   July 4. Declaration of Independence.
1777   Wilkes County organized from Indian territories.
1777   Feb. First Constitution of Georgia.
1777   Mar. Button Gwinnett, president of Georgia.
1777   May. Under new Constitution Treutlin becomes first governor of Georgia.
1778   British capture Savannah.
1779   Jan. 27. Silas Mercer at the Battle of Burke County Jail.
1779   Jan. Augusta captured by the British.
1779   Mar. British regain authority in Georgia.
1780   Jan. Washington, Georgia, established.
1780   Heard's Fort, Wilkes County, becomes temporary capital of Georgia.
1782   Capital moves to Augusta. John Martin, governor.
1782   Feb.-Mar. Cherokee Indians defeated by Elijah Clarke.
1782   July. British give up Savannah.
1782   July. Georgia General Assembly reconvenes in Savannah.
1783   Jan. Lyman Hall elected governor of Georgia.
1783   May. North Georgia land ceded by Cherokee Indians.
1783   June. Fishing Creek Church formed in Wilkes County.
1783   Sept. 3. Treaty of Paris signed by U.S. and Britain.
1784   The Georgia Association formed at Kiokee with Daniel Marshall as moderator. Jesse Mercer present as a delegate (and in attendance from 1784–1839).
1784   Oct. Georgia legislature supports "Public Duties of Religion."
1784   Nov. Daniel Marshall dies.
1785   Feb. Act to support churches with tax monies passes in the Georgia General Assembly.
1785   Charter granted to Franklin College (University of Georgia).
1785   Hymnbook: Daniel Read, AMERICAN SONG BOOK.

1785	State capital moves to Augusta.
1785	May. Phillip's Mill Church established.
1785	Silas Mercer helps establish Whatley's Mill Church, twelve miles east of Greensboro (later named Bethesda).
1785	May. Remonstrance of the Georgia Baptist Association, a protest by Silas Mercer and others against the use of taxes for Church of England ministers.
1786	Virginia Statute of Religious Freedom.
1786	July. Powel's Creek Church (Powelton) constituted with the help of Silas Mercer.
1787	Hymnbook: John Rippon, A SELECTION OF HYMNS ("Selection of Hymns from the best authors, intended to be an Appendix to Dr. Watts' Psalms and Hymns").
1787	Till 1805. Second "Great Awakening" in the U.S.
1787	July 1. Jesse Mercer relates his conversion experience at Phillips' Mill Church.
1787	July 8. Jesse Mercer baptized.
1788	Georgia ratifies the U.S. Constitution.
1788	First Negro Baptist Church organized in Savannah by Abraham Marshall.
1788	Death of Charles Wesley.
1788	Jan. 31. Jesse Mercer marries Sabrina Chivers, daughter of Joel and Sarah H. Chivers, born May 16, 1772.
1788	Hutton's Fork Church organized (later, Sardis). Jesse Mercer, minister, 1788–1817.
1789	A new Georgia Constitution is written.
1789	Nov. 7. Jesse Mercer ordained at Phillips' Mill Church with Silas Mercer and Sanders Walker members of the presbytery.
1790	Population of Georgia: ca. 83,000.
1790	Silas and Jesse Mercer sent as messengers to the Charleston Association.
1790	Hymnbook: PHILADELPHIA COLLECTION.
1791	Silas Mercer and Jeremiah Walker debates on the merits of free will and free grace.
1791	Death of John Wesley.
1792	Jesse Mercer receives ten pounds from the General Committee for the Charleston Baptist Educational Fund.

1792	Number of churches in the Georgia Association: 56.
1793	Silas Mercer establishes an academy (Salem Academy) in his home.
1793	Eli Whitney invents the cotton gin.
1793	Silas and Jesse Mercer make a preaching tour in N.C.
1793	At the Georgia Association Abraham Marshall argues in favor of a law to prevent further importation of slaves.
1793	Indian Creek (later, Bethany) formed as a church. Jesse Mercer, minister, 1793–1796.
1793	Hymnbook: Daniel Read, COLUMBIAN HARMONY.
1794	Hephzibah Association formed.
1795	Silas Mercer participates in a review of the 1789 Georgia Constitution.
1795	Oct. Silas Mercer elected moderator, Jesse Mercer, clerk, of the Georgia Association, Shoal Creek meeting-house (Jesse Mercer, clerk, 1795–1816).
1795	Louisville becomes state capital of Georgia.
1795	Yazoo Land Act passed by the Georgia legislature.
1796	Yazoo Act is nullified.
1796	Treaty with the Indians.
1796	Aug. 1. Death of Silas Mercer at age 52.
1796	Jesse and Daniel Mercer take charge of Salem Academy with Jesse Mercer as preceptor.
1796	Till 1827. Jesse Mercer, minister of Phillips' Mill Church.
1796	Till 1827. Jesse Mercer, minister at Bethesda Church (formerly called Whatley's Mill).
1796	Till 1835. Jesse Mercer, minister at Powelton Church (formerly called Powel's Creek).
1797	Population of the U.S.: ca. 4,900,000.
1797	Oct. 14. Jesse Mercer preaches Introductory sermon (Isaiah 13:4), Baptist meeting.
1798	Jesse Mercer travels in northern states of the U.S.
1798	Jesse Mercer writes the section on religious liberty at the state convention to revise the Georgia Constitution.
1798	Dec. 1. Birth of first daughter, Miriam, to Jesse and Sabrina Mercer.
1799	May. Sarepta Association formed.
1799	Jesse Mercer travels 3000 miles on a preaching tour in S.C., N.C. and Va.

1799	Sept. 21. Death of daughter, Miriam, at age 9 months and 21 days.
1799	Hymnbook: Joshua Smith, DIVINE HYMNS (9th Edition).
1800	Population of Georgia: ca. 163,000.
1800	Great Revival begins at Logan County, Ky., signalling the start of camp meetings and "camp spiritual songs. Leaders: McCready, Hodges, Rankin, and the McGee brothers.
1800	Library of Congress established in Washington, D.C.
1800	Death of Rev. John Springer, first Presbyterian minister ordained in Georgia and teacher of Jesse Mercer in the academy.
1801	Till 1809. The Jeffersonian presidency.
1801	May. First Powelton conference (Powel's Creek).
1801	Opening of Franklin College (University of Georgia).
1801	Jesse Mercer: Circular letter of the Georgia Association.
1801	Tripoli declares war on the U.S.
1802	May. Second Powelton conference (consideration of Indian missions).
1802	May-June. Beginning of the ANALYTICAL REPOSITORY, edited by Henry Holcombe of Savannah (first Baptist periodical in the South).
1802	Revival at Powel's Creek Church.
1803	Apr. Purchase of the Louisiana Territory from France.
1803	Apr. Third Powelton conference.
1803	May. Formation of "The General Committee of Georgia Baptists," with three goals: (1) to help itinerant preachers; (2) to encourage Indian missions, and (3) to establish a college.
1804	May. Lewis and Clark Expedition through the Northwest.
1804	Hymnbook: Jeremiah Ingalls, CHRISTIAN HARMONY.
1804	Plans laid at Kiokee Church to establish "The Baptist College of Georgia.
1805	Apr. 13. Birth of a second daughter, also named "Miriam," to Jesse and Sabrina Mercer.
1805	Hymnbook: Stephen Jenks, DELIGHTS IN HARMONY.
	Jesse Mercer: Circular concerned with discipline.
1806	Mt. Enon Academy begins its planning stage.
1806	Georgia legislature denies Baptists a charter for a college.
1806	Jesse Mercer becomes vice president for Mt. Enon Academy with Henry Holcombe, president.

1807	Sept. Charter for Mt. Enon Academy granted and begins, Richmond County.
1807	Jesse Mercer: Discourse on Matt. 5: 46, for the General Committee of the Georgia Baptists.
1808	Jan. Act prohibiting the importation of African slaves.
1809	Till 1817. The Madison presidency.
1810	Hymnbook: John Wyeth, REPOSITORY OF SACRED MUSIC.
1810	Jesse Mercer issues THE CLUSTER OF SPIRITUAL SONGS, printed by Hobby and Bunce, Augusta, Ga. (3rd Edition, Revised, with 183 hymn texts).
1810	The General Committee of Georgia Baptists dissolves.
1811	Mt. Enon Academy fails when Henry Holcombe moves to Philadelphia.
1811	Jesse Mercer: Circular on "the reasons, briefly, which lead us to deem Pedobaptist administration, though in the proper mode, invalid."
1812	President Madison recommends war with Britain.
1812	War of 1812 (till 1814) between the U.S. and Britain. Georgia Baptists pass a resolution supporting the war.
1812	Newall, Judson, Rice, Nott, and Hall sail for India as missionaries.
1812	Hymnbook: John Newton, OLNEY HYMNS IN THREE BOOKS (with William Cowper).
1813	Summer. Luther Rice returns to the U.S.
1813	Oct. Jesse Mercer: Introductory sermon at Fishing Creek Church, Wilkes County (Gen. 24: 56).
1813	Dec. Formation of the Savannah Baptist Society for Foreign Missions.
1814	May 18. The Triennial Baptist Convention organized at Philadelphia.
1814	Treaty of Ghent.
1814	Aug. White House and Washington, D.C., burned by the British.
1814	Dec. 15. Death of Miriam, second daughter of Jesse and Sabrina Mercer, at age nine years and eight months.
1814	Jesse Mercer: presents Circular concerned with "Savannah Baptist Society for Foreign Missions."
1814	(or, early 1815). Powelton Academy begins.
1815	Georgia Association relates itself to the Baptist Board of Foreign Missions with Jesse Mercer, chairman.

The Life And Times Of Jesse Mercer

- 1815 May 5. Establishment of "The Powelton Baptist Society for Foreign Missions" with Jesse Mercer, president.
- 1815 Battle of Waterloo.
- 1815 Death of Rev. Andrew Fuller, Scotch theologian.
- 1816 Jesse Mercer runs for senator in Georgia legislature, but is defeated.
- 1816 Till 1839. Jesse Mercer, moderator of the Georgia Association.
- 1816 Jesse Mercer: Circular on Christian duties (regarding the overcoming of church disorders).
- 1817 Beginning of controversy between Missions and Anti-missions factions (lasting till 1837).
- 1817 Hymnbook: "WINCHELL'S WATTS" (Arrangement of Watts with a Supplement).
- 1817 Till 1825. Monroe presidency.
- 1817 Jesse Mercer preaches the funeral sermon of Gov. Peter Early.
- 1817 Jesse Mercer gives charge to John Mason Peck at the General Convention (Second Triennial) in Philadelphia. An enlarged edition of THE CLUSTER published.
- 1817 Fighting erupts between Seminole Indians and South Georgians.
- 1817 Nov. 17. William Rabun, a lifelong friend of Jesse Mercer, becomes governor of Georgia and serves as song-leader in Mercer's Powelton church, even while governor.
- 1818 Whatley's Mill Church changed name to "Bethesda" and a brick meeting-house built.
- 1818 Sept. 7. Mrs. Dorcas Mercer (widow of Silas and mother of Jesse) dies.
- 1818 Oct. Adiel Sherwood arrives in Savannah.
- 1818 Nov. Jesse Mercer helps constitute church in Eatonton.
- 1819 Steamship Savannah crosses the Atlantic (first to cross).
- 1819 June. Adiel Sherwood visits Jesse Mercer.
- 1819 Adiel Sherwood organizes the first Baptist Sunday School in Georgia (Trail Creek Baptist Church-Athens).
- 1819 Florida territory sold by Spain to the U.S.
- 1819 Fall. Jesse Mercer sick; reported as dead.
- 1819 Jesse Mercer gives the Funeral Oration for Gov. William Rabun (2 Sam. 3: 38).
- 1820 Great fire in Savannah.
- 1820 Jan. Jesse Mercer takes charge of Eatonton Church.

1820 Mar. 18. Jesse Mercer preaches a funeral sermon.
1820 Mar. 20. Ordination of Adiel Sherwood at Bethesda during meeting of the Mission Board of the Georgia Association (Jesse Mercer on the presbytery).
1820 Jesse Mercer attends the General Convention, Philadelphia. Another edition of THE CLUSTER published.
1820 Plan for Indian Reform with Jesse Mercer, corresponding secretary (The Board of Trustees of the cooperating Baptist Associations for instructing and evangelizing the Creek Indians).
1820 Oct. 23. Resolution by Adiel Sherwood for organizing a "General Meeting of Correspondence" passes in the Sarepta Association.
1821 Opening of the first public high school in the U.S. (Boston).
1821 Jesse Mercer and Adiel Sherwood organize a church at Greensboro.
1821 Jesse Mercer: Circular on "Unity of the churches."
1822 Till 1824. "Accounts" book of Jesse Mercer shows sale of THE CLUSTER and other items.
1822 Columbian College established in Washington, D.C.
1822 Luther Rice begins the periodical, THE COLUMBIAN STAR.
1822 June. Organization of the Georgia Baptist Convention. Jesse Mercer becomes president of the General Baptist Association for the State of Georgia (during a meeting at the Powelton Church). Jesse Mercer gives discourse: 1 Thess. 2:3.
1822 Santa Fe Trail blazed, opening the Southwest.
1823 City of Macon established.
1823 Jesse Mercer represents the Georgia State Convention at the S.C. Baptist State Convention.
1823 Dec. Monroe Doctrine enunciated.
1823 New edition of THE CLUSTER, 3rd Edition, Revised.
1823 Aug. Jesse Mercer and Adiel Sherwood preach through an interpreter to the Indians in the Valley Towns on the Hiwassee river.
1824 The Flint River and the Yellow River Associations organized; the former, missionary Baptist, and the latter eventually becoming Primitive Baptist.
1825 Population of the U.S.: ca. 11,250,000.
1825 Till 1829. Presidency of John Quincy Adams.
1825 Georgia receives lands ceded by the Creek Indians.

1825	Jesse Mercer: "An Exposition of the first 17 verses of the 12th chapter of Revelation" (read to the Convention).
1825	May 29. Jesse Mercer gives the missionary sermon at Eatonton.
1825	June-Nov. Jesse Mercer ill.
1826	Mar. Jesse Mercer preaches the missionary sermon at the General Association, Augusta, Ga.
1826	Jesse Mercer preaches a sermon at the Triennial Convention of Foreign Missions, New York (Matthew 28: 19). Another edition of THE CLUSTER published.
1826	Sept. 23. Mercer's wife, Sabrina, dies at Andersonville, S.C., on return to Georgia from the Triennial Convention.
1827	Till 1828. General prosperity among Georgia Baptists, including 270 baptized at Bethesda from March to October.
1827	Cherokee Indians organize a Baptist church at Tinsawattee, Cherokee County.
1827	Mar. Jesse Mercer helps to establish a church at Washington, Ga., a branch of Phillips' Mill church.
1827	Jesse Mercer writes a letter of concern about the Tinsawattee School (appearing in the BAPTIST MAGAZINE).
1827	Dec. 11. Marriage of Jesse Mercer to Mrs. Nancy Simons (widow of Captain Abram Simons), born Oct. 30, 1772, daughter of John and Lucy Mills of Virginia.
1828	Creek Indians forbidden to enter Georgia without a special pass.
1828	Georgia State Temperance Society organizes.
1828	First passenger railroad train begins service from Baltimore.
1828	Oct. 10–13. At Shiloh in Greene County, Jesse Mercer, J. Armstrong, and J. P. Marshall prepare the Circular and Constitution.
1829	Dissension becomes prevalent among Georgia Baptists.
1829	Mar. Jesse Mercer: "Dissertation on the Prerequisites to Ordination" (given at Milledgeville).
1829	At the Georgia Baptist Convention Josiah Penfield, a jeweler from Savannah, offers a gift of $2,500.00, to be matched, for the aid of the poor who would study for the ministry (instrumental in founding of Mercer University).
1829	Gold discovered in White County, Georgia.
1829	Sept. Controversy involving Jesse Mercer's use of "cogniac brandy"; dialogue with W. T. Brantly.
1830	Webster-Hayne debates on states' rights.

1830　Jesse Mercer becomes president of the Baptist Board of Foreign Missions and serves until 1841.

1830　Jesse Mercer: Circular on "the Scriptural Meaning and Manner of Ordination" (for the Convention meeting at Bethesda).

1830　Jesse Mercer writes "Ten Letters on Atonement" in a controversy with Rev. Cyrus White.

1831　Reaping machine invented by Cyrus McCormick.

1831　Apr. 7–9. Introductory sermon by Jesse Mercer (Eph. 4: 11–13), meeting at Buckhead, Burke County. At the same meeting Adiel Sherwood gives his motion urging Baptists toward education. Circular presented by Jesse Mercer on "the importance of a more elevated standard of Christian morality, among the churches and ministers of our denomination."

1831　Oct. Jesse Mercer preaches the Introductory sermon (John 16: 7–10) at the Georgia Association at Aberdeen, Columbia County.

1831　Sept. Three Presbyterian missionaries arrested by Georgia officials for unauthorized preaching in Indian territories.

1832　Jesse Mercer defends Georgia laws by writing a letter: "Imprisonment of Missionaries to the Cherokees."

1832　Cherokee Land Lottery.

1832　Jesse Mercer gives $1000 to erect the president's home at Mercer Institute.

1832　Adiel Sherwood operates a manual labor school in his home near Eatonton, Ga.

1832　Jesse Mercer gives a New Testament to his wife, Nancy.

1832　Aug. Executive Committee of Georgia Baptists visits Sherwood's school.

1833　Jan. 14. Opening of Mercer Institute at Penfield, Georgia.

1833　American Anti-Slavery Society founded.

1833　Jesse Mercer resists pressure to run for governor of Georgia.

1833　May 10–13. Jesse Mercer: "A dissertation on the resemblances and differences between church authority and that of an Association" (meeting at McDonough).

1833　Jesse Mercer: "An essay on the Lord's Supper, being an attempt to run the analogy between it and the Passover" (using as text, 1 Cor. 5:7, 8).

1833　Jesse Mercer buys THE COLUMBIAN STAR AND CHRISTIAN INDEX and changes the name to THE CHRISTIAN INDEX AND BAPTIST MISCELLANY (first issue from Washington, Ga., Sat., Sept. 14).

1833	THE CHRISTIAN INDEX publishes Jesse Mercer's "Essay on the Independence of the Churches."
1834	May 11. Jesse Mercer: "Knowledge indispensable to a Minister of God," based on 2 Cor. 6: 4, 6 (at the Georgia Baptist Convention meeting at Indian Creek, Morgan County).
1834	Aug. Jesse Mercer writes on education in THE CHRISTIAN INDEX.
1834	Aug. 15. Jesse Mercer writes "The Prefatory Notice" to Rev. John Sladen's "The Doctrine of Particular Election."
1835	Hymnbook: William Walker, SOUTHERN HARMONY.
1835	Jesse Mercer travels by the steamboat, "WILLIAM GIBBONS," from Charleston to Richmond to attend the Triennial Convention; he preaches the Introductory sermon.
1835	New edition of THE CLUSTER published.
1835	Jesse Mercer receives the D.D. from Brown University.
1835	Jesse Mercer makes a substantial gift to the Baptist Board of Foreign Missions.
1835	Jesse Mercer resigns from Phillips' Church and is succeeded by Rev. W. H. Stokes.
1835	Presbyterians secure a charter for Oglethorpe University, to be located in Midway, near Milledgeville.
1836	Texas declares its independence from Mexico during the Battle of the Alamo.
1836	Hymnbook: Linsley and Davis, SELECT HYMNS.
1836	Apr. 29-May 3. Jesse Mercer attends Georgia Baptist Convention at Talbotton, Ga.
1836	May 1. Central Association gives a silver medal to Jesse Mercer.
1836	Publication by Jesse Mercer of a HISTORY OF THE GEORGIA ASSOCIATION (with co-editing by W. H. Stokes).
1836	Jesse Mercer preaches at Eatonton, "A Sermon on Ministerial Union."
1836	Feb. 11-Apr. 21. Jesse Mercer gives five theological replies to "H" in THE CHRISTIAN INDEX.
1836	July. Meeting of ministers at Forsyth, where articles of faith are adopted; Jesse Mercer gives an address.
1836	Oct.-Nov. Another meeting of ministers convened to address strife and dissension among Baptists in Georgia.
1837	Till 1841. Van Buren presidency.
1837	Hymnbook: Allen and Carden, MISSOURI HARMONY.

1837	Ocmulgee Association votes to become Primitive Baptist.
1837	Great depression hits the U.S. economy.
1837	Summer. "Father Mercer" delivers a sermon at Clark's Station, Wilkes County (James 4: 12).
1837	Jesse Mercer participates in the writing of "A Review of a Report by a Committee appointed to reply to reasons assigned by certain churches for seceding from the Flint River Association."
1837	Oct. 24–26. Jesse Mercer attends ministers' meeting at Eatonton.
1837	Oct. 31. Abandonment of plans for a "Southern Baptist College" at Washington, Ga.
1838	May. Mrs. Nancy Mercer stricken with palsy.
1838	July. C. D. Mallary declines offer of the presidency of Mercer University and B. M. Sanders accepts temporarily (first meeting of the Board of Trustees after the addition of the "College").
1838	Jesse Mercer writes on the subject of atonement.
1838	Cherokee Indians forcefully removed from Georgia.
1838	Oct. Jesse Mercer: "Sermon on the Importance of Ministerial Union" (John 17: 11), given at Harmony in Eatonton.
1839	First "Normal School" organized in Massachusetts.
1839	Jan. Jesse Mercer writes on Towaliga problems in THE PRIMITIVE BAPTIST.
1839	May. Nancy Mercer's sickness worsens (now an entire paralytic).
1839	Nov. Jesse Mercer gives essay: "The Cause of Missionary Societies the cause of God" (at Powelton).
1840	Spring. Anti-slavery Convention meets in New York.
1840	May. Jesse Mercer gives THE CHRISTIAN INDEX to the Georgia Baptist Convention.
1840	Jesse Mercer writes to the Georgia Association at Bethesda reporting on the sickness of his wife and himself and their inability to attend the Association (THE CHRISTIAN INDEX, Nov. 26).
1840	Oct. 21. Jesse Mercer writes to Lucius Bolles on the subject of abolition.
1841	Population of the U.S.: ca. 17,700,000.
1841	Feb. 12. In THE CHRISTIAN INDEX Jesse Mercer writes about the problem of union and missions in the context of abolition.
1841	Mar. Jesse Mercer: "The Forgiveness of Sins" (three articles in THE CHRISTIAN INDEX).

1841 Jesse Mercer writes on Revelation: "Hear what the Spirit saith unto the Churches" (THE CHRISTIAN INDEX).
1841 Friday, May 21. Death of Nancy Mercer.
1841 Jesse Mercer writes on the "division of South from the North" in THE CHRISTIAN INDEX.
1841 June 20. Jesse Mercer preaches at Washington, Wilkes County: 1 Sam. 12; 23. (Cf. THE CHRISTIAN INDEX, July 23, 1841.)
1841 Sept. 6. Jesse Mercer's death at the home of his friend, James Carter, eight miles north of Indian Springs, Butts County, Ga. and burial at Penfield.

END

CHAPTER TWO

AN INTRODUCTION TO MERCER'S *CLUSTER*

> Wave your tall heads, ye lofty pines,
>   To him that bids you grow,
> Sweet clusters bend the fruitful vines,
>   On evry thankful bough.
>   "Hallelujah," URANIA, 1761.

That Jesse Mercer, the man for whom Mercer University is named, compiled and edited an early American hymbook is a surprise to many. A certain *kairos*, or fitting time, seemed to make the first third of the nineteenth century a ripe moment for the birth and propagation of *The Cluster of Spiritual Songs*, which by the year 1810 had already seen three editions. It is not precisely known when the first printings were made, though it was probably about the turn of the century. As hymns on individual sheets or loosely gathered into unbound groupings, the first *Cluster* likely appeared; and between the ages of 31 and 66 this man of the cloth toiled to produce and to distribute this hymnbook. It need not be doubted that Hobby and Bunce, printers located in Augusta, Georgia, were its first publishers; though Philadelphia was to become the scene for later publications. An 1810 edition, residing in the Rare Book Room of Duke University, contains 183 hymn texts with no music included; and by 1835 the collection had increased to nearly 700 (more than 700 if rejected hymns are added) hymn selections under the longer title, *The Cluster of Spiritual Songs, Divine Hymns and Sacred Poems*. It is rather astonishing that so little has been written of this man's personal labors in producing a significant hymnbook.

C. D. Mallary, B. D. Ragsdale, and Spright Dowell have amply noted the pecuniary gifts made by Mercer and his vocational activities as Baptist minister, leader in Baptist foreign missions, editor of *The Chris-*

tian Index, and founder of the Georgia Baptist Convention; but *The Cluster* is scarcely mentioned. Its early publication and distribution influenced later collections of hymns by its example; and the selection of hymns insured a continuing connection with Great Britain and Baptist beginnings there. Yet Mercer's purpose was to provide a hymnbook and practical handbook for believers as they praised God in Christ for the redemption of their souls.

Heralding the publication of a new edition of *The Cluster* in 1829, W. T. Brantly of Philadelphia pointed out:

> A great proportion of the Hymns are of a standard character, and such as occur in most of our judicious selections, whilst many others come under the denomination of SPIRITUAL SONGS, and are adapted to Society meetings and the private circle.[1]

Over 33,000 copies had earlier been printed, says Brantly, meeting with "uncommon success and popularity." According to Dowell, no less than seven editions of *The Cluster* were printed, the first three having been issued prior to 1817 and not copyrighted.[2] Those of 1817, 1823, 1826, 1829, and 1835 were properly registered and copyrighted.

It is hoped that the present undertaking will fill to a small degree the vacancy of knowledge regarding *The Cluster* and will serve to introduce the general reader to certain important aspects of Mercer's hymnbook. Special attention will be given to the sources used in selection, placement and organization of the hymns, the criteria influencing Mercer in his choice of hymn texts, and the compiler himself as a composer of hymns. A special analysis which considers sociological methods and factors will relate *The Cluster* to our own times.

I

First, the matter of sources. In the third edition issued in 1823 one finds 664 texts of hymns with no music or tunes included. (Certain tune names do appear with a few individual texts, e.g. "Lenox," the most popular of those in *The Cluster*.) A section, "Sacred Poems," was added at the back, increasing the total number of entries to 677. The enlarged fourth and fifth editions made available 14 more hymns, along with a new topical index; so that 691 separate entries emerged in 1829 and 1835. The present study will take into account all 691 items, although a few of the poems are not appropriate for a translation into hymns, e.g., Benjamin Moseley's *The Character, Death, etc. of the Rev. Silas Mercer* (677).[3]

A search through Julian's *Dictionary of Hymnology* results in an identification of almost half the authors of hymns contained in *The Cluster*.[4] Instead of titles, "first lines" supply the indexed information. We have been able to validate at least 52 hymns contributed by Isaac Watts, the most of any one composer in Mercer's collection. (See the appendix for an index of hymns by authors.) From the Wesleys have come 30 hymns; John Newton, 29; Anne Steele, 19; and Benjamin Beddome, 18. Of the top five, Steele and Beddome were Baptists. Doddridge, Hart, S. Medley, Fawcett, S. Stennett, and Toplady account for 59 texts; and three English poets—Addison, Pope, and Cowper—have hymns represented. At least five compositions have come from the hand of Jesse Mercer. Approximately seventy authors have been authenticated with the help of Julian's *Dictionary*.[5] With this incomplete examination one is yet able to discern that the sources are mostly limited to Britain (to England for the most part, though a few from Scotland and Wales appear), that practically all come from the eighteenth and nineteenth centuries, and that virtually all were written originally in the English language (John Wesley's translations of Moravian hymns being the chief exception). The language, phrases, metaphors, and rhyming patterns of the 1611 King James Version of the Bible are apparent in the great majority of those listed. One may surmise that of the half whose authorship has not been authenticated, most were written at a later time and were derived from American composers. Though it is probably tenuous to make the judgment, a summary glance at the themes and language of the unidentified hymn texts would seem to suggest this conclusion. We shall have more to say later about the Calvinistic and Evangelical influences, along with central Baptist convictions, which present themselves in the substance of the hymns.

II

How did Jesse Mercer arrange and organize his hymnbook? Why was there no greater inclusion of Old Testament Psalms? What reasons lie behind the diminishment of sections for "special occasions," which previous collections contained? These and other questions lie closely beside another: what criteria determined his selection and arrangement? We must consider these issues together; and in the absence of any explanation from the compiler himself, the answers must be derived from studying *The Cluster* itself. In other words, considerable subjective components will be in operation along with those objective lines that may be nailed down. The index which Mercer placed at the close of his hymnbook is not very helpful; and a number of errors occur, e.g., incorrect pagination and inaccuracies of sequence in the alphabetical order. It is confusing to have the page numbering in Arabic and the individual hymns listed under Roman numerals. A subheading or caption is included with each hymn, giving a bare hint of the subject, e.g., "The Joys of a Revival long sought" (277) or "The New Jerusalem described and Desired" (284). Scanty mention of tune names, "Bunker's Hill" and "America," for instance, may offer an association of the hymn text with the New World, yet tell nothing of the source of the text or the organization of the hymns. Mercer usually took the exact words of captions from the sources he used in collecting hymns for his *Cluster*, books such as Winchell's *Watts* (1817), Rippon's *Selections* (1787), *Olney Hymns* (1779), and the various hymnbooks by the Wesleys. Yet he has supplied us with no index of the subheadings or captions.

There is an explicit organizational scheme to be observed in *The Cluster*. According to "the experience of real Christians," Mercer carefully placed in a certain order his hymns. A reflection of this scheme will demonstrate that he gave as much thought to the order as does a good minister preparing the dramatic turns in a worship service. By thumbing through *The Cluster*, observing the top margins, one may detect sections that are given in explicit words. For the sake of convenience the present writer has prepared an index, which should be consulted at this point in the examination.[6] Mercer did not include any such general index on one page; but he might easily have done it, since the various items do appear throughout the hymnbook. Mercer was an active participant in the later Evangelical movement which included earlier no less a theologian than Jonathan Edwards and later, George Whitefield and the Wesleys. Experimental or experiential Christianity meant the personal participation of the believer in practical exercises of his faith. Part of this was a reaction to the dry and arid formalism in religion that had turned enthusiastic Christians into lukewarm believers. Hymn 60 indicates this: "I'm tir'd of visits, modes and forms . . . vain delights and empty stuff." The conversion experience was to be followed by "growth in grace," a life-long development. This was *existential*, to use a modern term, an intimate "I-Thou" encounter of the believer with the resurrected Christ. For the Evangelicals it was Christ's reign that was the greatest glory, somewhat in contrast to their forebears, the Puritans, who emphasized God the Creator and His activities as sovereign Governor, and in contradistinction to later "social gospellers," who spoke chiefly of the immanence of the Spirit in establishing a just society. The centrality of Christ is second to no other conviction in the organizing of Mercer's hymnbook; and the manner, means, and substance of his presentation reflect the influence of moderate Calvinists such as Andrew Fuller.

CHART: A TOPICAL COMPARISON OF THE 1810 and 1823 EDITIONS OF JESSE MERCER'S *Cluster*

1810 EDITION	No. of Hymns	1823 EDITION	No. of Hymns
On Free Grace	12	On Free Grace	56
Glories of the Redeemer	18	Christ Crucified	49
Conversion and Conviction	12	The Glories of Christ	55
Lively Exercises of Religion	10	Missions	20
Christian Exercises	28	Warning & Invitation	42
Christians Encouraged and Cautioned	25	Conviction & Conversion	28
Perseverance in Grace	13	Believers' Baptism	16
Sinners Invited and Warned	14	Christian Exercises	288
Ministers Grieved and Comforted	3	Joy and Praise	79
The Parting of Christian Brethren	3	Prayer and Praise	18
Backsliders Returning	4	Faith and Prayer	20
Imputed Righteousness	2	Prayer	83
The Latter-Day Glory	1	Conflict	23
Christian Pastorals	5	Hope & Encouragement	20
Believer's Baptism	5	Morning Devotions	22
Christ Crucified	13	Evening Devotions	12
Death the Effect of Sin	4	Backslidings Lamented	11
The Last Judgment	10	Christians Encountered	34
The Everlasting Song	1	Imputed Righteousness	6
		Perseverance In Grace	21
		Death	33
		Judgment	16
Total =	183	Total =	664

This comparison reveals that the 1823 edition is well over three times larger than the 1810 edition in total number of hymn texts; and that the greatest change came with an expansion of the topic "Christian Exercises." Of the 183 hymn texts in the 1810 edition, seventeen were dropped by Mercer and not carried over into the later editions. The topics, based primarily on theological and faith judgments, remain the same in the editions from 1823 to 1835.

Since the value of this comparison is to show changes in the theological arrangement, we have chosen to omit the appendices and miscellaneous poems, which include more hymns but without categorization under topics.

The section (1810 ed.) on "Christian Pastorals" indicates Mercer's interest, similar to that of Watts and others, in Christianizing the Old Testament Psalms. No topical sections appear for "Temperance," "National Hymns," "Church Calendar," or special historical occasions, although other hymnbooks in use during Mercer's time do often include these.

Jesse Mercer was a Calvinist in theology; and since theology was important for arranging the order of his hymnbook, it will be useful to delve briefly into what his Calvinism meant. A well-known acrostic will provide a frame of reference, even though it is too rigid, static, and wooden. It comes from the Synod of Dort, 1618, where the Arminians were put to flight and fits the word "tulip," indeed, was called the "tulip theology." *T* - Total Depravity; *U* - Unconditioned Election; *L* - Limited Atonement; *I* - Irresistible Grace; *P* - Perseverance in Grace. Mercer more than once differed in arguments with the theology of the Wesleys on the point of *limited atonement*, the reason being that Jesus died only for the elect, according to Mercer's view. That his own theology was close to the "tulip theology" is to be noted in the résumé he gave in his *History of the Georgia Association* (page 409) of Brother Joseph Roberts:

> In doctrine, bro Roberts was sound and evangelical. His views were in accord with the faith of the Baptists in the State, and as we think, with the Scriptures of truth. The theme of his preaching was *free grace*. man's depravity from the fall of Adam, Regeneration and Faith by the operation and influence of the Holy Spirit, and the Perseverance through grace to Eternal Life. He was also a practical preacher—urging to a prompt discharge of every Christian duty, by present motives of gratitude.

What Calvinism meant to Mercer has relevance to the general question: was *The Cluster* an American hymnbook? It is generally agreed that the Calvinist theology was most influential of the theologies transported across the Atlantic, for good or ill. Many in America today look with negative judgments upon that influence, particularly those tending toward a Unitarian faith or a position of ethical humanistic faith. With Calvinism many modern Americans associate a stifling of the human spirit, being a prude, manifesting a down-in-the-mouth legalism about all pleasures, whether they be drinking any kind or amount of alcohol or the enjoyment of sex. Dancing, attending theaters, even playing the fiddle, have been among those pleasures condemned by some. The words, "predestination," "election," and "foreknowledge" convey to many the worst sort of fatalism. And to these Americans a totalitarian God seems worse than the terrible image of "Big Brother" promised for 1984. For many present-day Americans the perception of Calvinism is likened to that weight-losing diet which says "if it tastes good, spit it out." What John Calvin really said or meant does not matter; the perception among the majority of Americans today is something like that described above.

Jesse Mercer was not ashamed to be depicted as a Calvinist. He would turn the sword of Calvin in the other direction. Our frantic lives would seem to him vapid and empty, full of meaningless activity or inactivity, loose and amorphous, and lacking commitment to any great cause. The manner in which we face death and die would be tragic and abominable to him. He would view the idolatries of the present-life, or this-worldly life, as grotesque and sinful. Hopelessness with respect to life after death would remove zest and affirmation for present-day living. He might well join in agreeing with the wry sarcasm that rudely suggests today, "If you ask a Methodist or a Baptist who he is and he says he is a Methodist or a Baptist, then you have to ask him who he is."

The Calvinistic theology espoused by Jesse Mercer found expression in the outburst of evangelical Christianity in the America of 1800. *Sola gratia, sola Christus* united Calvinists, Lutherans, and Baptists against a works-righteousness which denied Christ's triumph of grace. The faith and the life of living persons and communities of believers took precedence over any doctrinal statement, hence the Baptist rejection of creeds as an adequate statement of faith. Redemption was actual and occurred in this-life; it did not have to await a future existence. The "sweetness of Christ" included knowledge as well as the witness of love in both the earlier "Great Awakening" of Edwards, Whitefield, and the Wesleys and in the later manifestations of the same Spirit that became evident in America's experience. Christ's redemption in the actual life of an early American demonstrated itself in head and heart, in knowledge and in the affections. As Christ's death on the Cross was an objective action in history, so the continuing action of the Holy Spirit, as resurrected Lord, was understood by Mercer and others caught up in the Evangelical revivals as not self-induced but as coming from above. Though personal, it was not individual in the sense that community was lost. The same sort of experience happened in the lives of more than one person. The experience could be shared and compared. Perhaps the spirit and actualization expressed in joy was the Evangelical equivalent of that "blessed assurance" felt in Calvinistic circles. For history, as for nature, Christ touched down in an earthly manner. The intimacy of nature and grace has been expressed in this way: healing is not only a parable of redemption; it is redemption (cf. 124). The work of Christ in the believer or the church community is more than a "redemption in principle." It is actual salvation within time and history. The glory and the action of redemption came from Christ; yet Mercer and other Evangelicals could claim Christ's death for his own, saying with the Apostle: "It is no longer I who live, but Christ who lives in me." (Galatians 2:20.) A person did not lose his identity or selfhood by turning his life over to the Holy Spirit, yet the community of the Holy Spirit was in intimate relationship to the believer's core of existence. Paul gave consent to the Resurrected Lord acting in him and upon him but he did not give away his freedom nor his responsibility as a person. Not that one can do his own boasting in having "found it" or "possessed it." Nevertheless, actual redemption and godly bliss begin now, begin in the present, earthly life and do not wait until a life only after death. For death or for life in this transient earthly existence, faith in Christ was sufficient. If God the Father were to be known through Christ's smile as loving, then the happiness of heaven overwhelmed any desire in the believer to remain on earth in a this-worldly fashion. The Evangelicals went beyond those Calvinists who placed great emphasis upon an "intra-worldly asceticism." But the ambivalence remained. One need only think of the worldly activities in which Mercer was engaged; and he was not atypical among Evangelicals who never tired of speaking of this-life as a "thorny maze" or "barren desert," not to be compared with that which lay ahead in heaven's bliss.

Without foundation is the charge leveled against Protestants in general and Evangelicals in particular that subjective response becomes paramount. The Saviour's death was objective in the historical event of Jesus' death on the Cross (under Pontius Pilate). It remained objective in the continuing work of the Spirit. The elements "for me" and the experience of "the heart strangely warmed" were also essential; but these did not displace the necessity of Christ's objective work, as the Calvinists never tired of asserting. The life and faith of Jesse Mercer testify against the allegations made against all Protestants, and often against Baptists, that the Reformation meant individualism, subjectivism, and relativity. Community of churches and associations and the work of Baptists in the South and in the North and in Burma were urgent concerns of Mercer. Justification on the Cross and in the believer's heart were both necessary for salvation. Christ as living Lord was absolute for Mercer. For this man, as for the twentieth-century Karl Barth, Christocentrism and Christomonism could well be charged; yet both these men upheld a radical monotheism and affirmed the Trinity. Never could the Holy Spirit be manipulated by means of the whims of men, even saved men. Prayer was essential to get the spirits of men in line with what God was doing in history. Scripture had to be searched so that personal visions through prayer would not become wild and extravagant. Even reason could not be suspended nor dispensed with. Education and missions were to be fostered and encouraged even though the Holy Spirit was doing His own thing.

Contrary to the notions of many, immersion for Baptists weighs less heavily than another affirmation: faith must precede baptism, thus infants are not capable of being baptized. They must know and give consent to what is taking place. And the section on "Believers' Baptism" points less to the moral awareness and free decision of the baptized believer than to the example of Jesus at his baptism and the coming of the dove. To be Baptist, Evangelical, Calvinistic, Scriptural, and Christian was all of one piece, and none of this was seen in contradiction to reason and free will or to experience in life. To be sure, the sovereign grace of God stood over against the depravity of sinful people. Knowledge and love were both emphasized under the Lordship of Christ. The "contemporary" Christ, the Spirit acting in modern times, proved the accuracy of Biblical truths. Head and heart were not separated in the faith of Jesse Mercer.

Noteworthy in Mercer's organizational scheme is the section, "Christian Exercises" (the largest single section), which is broken down into nine subdivisions. That this Baptist minister wished his congregational members and others to practice daily the faith and to struggle in applying its goods to every part of their lives is clearly evident. It is altogether possible that the book's use in family and private devotions took precedence over its employment in Sunday congregational singing. While many of the hymns are revivalistic in nature, the remarkable fact is that the "hell-fire-and-damnation" entries come nowhere close in quantity to the joyous, enthusiastic, and triumphant hymns of grace and redemption which dominate the book. No sections appear for "Temperance" or "National Observances," though some of the hymnbooks prior to *The Cluster* contained them. The absence of "Christmas" and "Thanksgiving" sections meant that every day in the year was appropriate for such celebrations (the official designation of a national "Thanksgiving" was to come much later). Usage for prayer or singing kept alive and enthusiastic the daily faith of the Christian; and being a "parttime" or "lukewarm" Christian was to be actively challenged day by day. *The Cluster* was a simple, practical, and tangible instrument for the hard-working lay believer in paying homage to Christ the Lord during public, family, and private devotions and worship. Even slaves or those who could not read shared in the singing, for the song leader would "line out" the words and "hist the tune"; thus, praise and a didactic method were united in one action.

III

The question of the criteria for selecting certain hymns while omitting others, as utilized by Mercer, is complex and difficult to address. In his mind and heart were Baptist convictions, a high commitment to foreign and home missions, the Evangelical experience of the Lordship and sweetness of Christ, and a moderate Calvinistic theology. He nowhere speaks of a canon to be used in compiling the hymns in *The Cluster*. One standard, however, cannot be doubted—Scripture—and it was chief in importance, next to the living Christ. What C. D. Mallary has said about Mercer's knowledge and love of the Bible is beneficial for understanding the question of criteria:

> Mr. Mercer was not an extensive reader; nor was he *learned*, in the ordinary acceptation of that phrase. To an acquaintance with polite literature he made no pretensions. . . . The Bible with him was first and last. He generally kept lying by him on his desk a plain copy, without note or comment; this he *read*, and this he *studied*. . . . His principal canon . . . was to compare scripture with scripture. He always read slowly, and reflected profoundly upon what he read. His great intellectual strength, I conceive, was owing to this habit of reflection.[7]

The selection process was guided in large part by Mercer's understanding of Scripture, and it is well in our analysis to let *The Cluster* speak for itself.

The Bible is esteemed explicitly in a number of hymns: events in the life of Jesus as found in the Gospels are included, the Pauline theology about grace and works supplies the content of many hymns, the sacrificial system in Hebrews is stressed, and the New Jerusalem and end-time find representation. Old Testament persons and events are but types and shadows of things to come, the realities of the New Testament happenings. As Northrop Frye has recently reminded us: "The Old Testament conceals the New Testament; the New Testament reveals the Old Testament."[8]

In *The Cluster* are no less than four hymn texts paying tribute in a direct way to the Bible itself (118, 251, 306, 310), a strong identification of Mercer with the Protestant Reformation and especially with John Calvin. The Bible is a rule of faith and practice for the believer, a guide to eternal day, and food for hungry people. It is the Christian's shield and sword, medicine to cure both doubts and ills, and an antidote to "our drooping hearts." Yet it is the light of Christ, the risen Lord as Spirit, which is necessary for directing our understanding of Scripture. The contemporaneous, the present moment in history (the eighteenth and nineteenth centuries for Jesse Mercer), was the focal point where Scriptural truth was to be applied and exercised. "The Bible all books does outshine, But Jesus, his person and grace, affords it that lustre divine" (118). While Scripture is justly esteemed, it is nevertheless secondary to the power and grace of Jesus Christ.

Indexed sections, "The Glories of Christ" and "Christ Crucified," point to Jesus as Redeemer and Source of present-day strength. Biblical figures and metaphors abound: Christ as cornerstone, advocate, apple tree, builder, physician, bridegroom, and many others are taken directly from the Bible. While the division between "Jesus of history" and "Christ of faith" had not been made in Mercer's day, the Gospel accounts of the life of Jesus are abundantly reflected in numerous hymns.

Examples from his birth (106–111, 676) and baptism (252–256) are there, along with the miracles of Legion (5), Bartimaeus (352, 563), the man at Bethesda pool (241, 245), etc. The parables of the wheat and tares (660) and of Abraham and Lazarus (193) are numbered with others. The Great Commission found in Matthew 28 is included (265). Persons with whom Jesus came in contact are treated: Zaccheus (33), the Samaritan woman at the well (181), Mary Magdalene (12), and Lazarus, brother of Mary and Martha (405). As to balance, the Passion gets top consideration: the Last Supper (72–104), Gethsemane prayer (62, 71, 192), the trial and scourging (672), the dying penitent thief (29, 181), and finally the death (192). All of these events, recalled by the Evangelists, are bent towards the impact upon present-day believers; and it is not without significance that the use made of these in early America followed in part a similar use as made by New Testament authors of events previously recorded in the Old Testament. If Jesus could and did come to aid Mary, Zaccheus, the Samaritan woman, and the dying thief, how much more would he help present-day sinners in great need.

That Paul's faith and theology are almost as dominant as the theme of Christ's reign in the Gospels is apparent by the inclusion of the three main sections: "Christ Crucified" (1 Corinthians), "Imputed Righteousness" (Galatians and Romans), and "Perseverance in Grace" (Romans 8). The great theme of Paul and the Reformation, "justification by faith and not by works," is stressed throughout and especially in the section, "On Free Grace" (see also 7, 38, 45). Other themes from the Apostle appear: "seeing in a glass darkly" (21), the second Adam (176), baptism (260), justice (16, 224), "pray without ceasing" (397), "My grace is sufficient" (12), the tensions and contradictions described in Romans 7 (485), running the race (415), and the armor of the Christian soldier (565). It is estimated that well over half of the hymn selections express Pauline convictions about the sovereignty of God, the universality of sin, total depravity, justification by faith rather than by a works-righteousness, the fruits of the Spirit, the vindication of God's honor by Christ, and the love of God leading persons to a life of joy and gratitude and of service to the neighbor.

Though not emphasized today, Hebrews, with its elaborate sacrificial system, finds a great deal of notice in *The Cluster*. Jesus as both victim (Lamb) and sacrificer (priest) rely on Leviticus in the Old Testament for meaning (95). For Mercer "Jesus as priest" gets heavier stress than "Jesus as prophet"; but for him "Jesus as king" is unexcelled. The New Jerusalem and the coming judgment are treated with apocalyptical warning in the final sections of "Death" and "Judgment" (see also 128, 161, 166, 175).

The Old Testament was integrally related to the New, not divided in terms of any Marcionite split, and the method of "Christianizing" the events and persons of the Old Testament was not new for Mercer. Isaac Watts had sought to convert David into a Christian, and the Psalms had become Christian spirituals:

> Where he talks of sacrificing *Goats or Bullocks*, I rather chuse to mention the Sacrifice of *Christ, the Lamb of God*: Where he attends the *Ark with Shouting in Zion*, I sing the *Ascension of my Saviour* into Heaven, or his *Presence in his Church* on Earth.[9]

The term "saint" is used for David, but also for Noah, Moses, Joshua, Daniel, and other Old Testament heroes. "Zion" is synonymous with "church" or "the people of God"; and "the Body of Christ" in the eighteenth and nineteenth centuries was expressed by the terms "Israel" and "Zion." The Psalms and the great events of Sinai and exile had to be appropriated for a present-day meaning; there was a compulsion for relevance in the "now" of present history. So the hymn-writers found in Mercer's *Cluster* were not copycats of the Psalmists, the singers of Israel. They acted and composed as if original psalm-writers themselves. Christ's active workings as resurrected Lord were to be praised. The victories of Christ in the Gospels extended backward into the persons and events of Hebrew history and forward into the time of the hymn-writers of the eighteenth and nineteenth centuries, speaking a fresh language in a new world.

Some persons and events made the subjects of hymns in *The Cluster* may sound strange and obscure to those in a largely Bible-illiterate age: Jabez of 1 Chronicles 4:9 (452), the land called Meshech (301), Ebenezer of 1 Samuel 4 and 7 (371), and Bozrah of Genesis 36 (69). Yet Mercer knew the Old Testament as well as the New, and many of its small details. Psalm 23 gets full attention, but the scenes are applied to later times and situations (332, 333, 575–579, 614, and A-6). The brazen serpent (75), Sinai's terrors (191, 194), the death of Moses (638), as well as the scapegoats of Leviticus (58, 118), emerge. Abraham (567) and David (280) are heralded, and Adam (147, 148) and Noah (615, 582) are not left out. Specific citations include the following: Isaiah 41:10 (386), Micah 2:13 (194), Psalm 25 (382), Psalm 34 (509), Esther 4:16 (235), and Job 19:25 (126), to name but a few. The promises to Abraham that his people would be a blessing to all nations and Isaiah's vision of Israel's vocation to be "a light to the Gentiles" were known to the authors of hymns in Mercer's *Cluster*. Song of Songs, which symbolically played an important role in the Middle Ages, is allegorized in similar fashion (133, 138, 186). Significantly, Silas Mercer, father of Jesse, had written a treatise, *Tyranny Exposed and True Liberty Discovered*, arguing that predictions found in the apocalyptical Daniel were important signs for early America. More than once Daniel is recalled in *The Cluster* (see especially 568). If one compare the sermon texts taken from Scripture for Mercer's sermons, it would become apparent that he viewed the God of Abraham, Isaac, and Jacob as the Father of Jesus Christ, and that the same God was in control of judgment, governance, and redemption in eastern Georgia. "The types and figures were a glass In which they saw the Saviour's face" (58) when the "blood-besprinkled door" was related to Jesus as Lamb or Dove to be sacrificed. The scapegoat or scapebird "dipp'd in his fellow's blood" was a type prefiguring the death of our Saviour. Christ's action was seen whether the event dealt with Ezekiel (174), Joshua (275), or Samuel (375). To respond with reason and in freedom to God's great actions became the interpretive and organizing principle for selecting and arranging the hymns of *The Cluster*.

IV

An examination of five identifiable hymns composed by Jesse Mercer himself will extend these principles even further. To the literary sophisticate, the hymns he wrote may appear sentimental, speaking of the obvious with an uncouth meter-scheme, rough rhyming, and a simplistic Biblical proof-text methodology. To his contemporaries, however, Mercer's integrity and heartfelt poignancy, were convincing. For studying Mercer's own creations, hymns by Addison (576), Pope (627), and Cowper (91, 381, 477, 588, 596), three renowned and respected English poets, may provide the reader with an interesting backdrop. Their compositions are richer, more compact, and smoother in rhyme and metrical arrangement. While very real distinctions are to be made between the poet and the hymn-writer and even though a poem of excellence may find itself unfitting for transposition into a hymn, no case can be made to elevate Mercer to the high rank of poet. Yet as persons in love may find themselves under a compulsion to write and address poetry to the beloved, so a plain and poorly educated man felt himself constrained to sing in verse of his love and gratitude to Christ, with the hope that others too would be moved to the same love. Three of the five are found in the 1810 *Cluster* edition located at Duke University (Hymns 235, 468, and 471); and we have been able to date Hymn 364 as written in 1822. The hymn which relates Mercer's conversion experience in the first person probably was written earlier than 1810, even though it was not included in the 1810 edition.

Hymn 233, "In sin's howling waste, my poor soul was forlorn," describes the conversion experience of Jesse Mercer when he was seventeen. In a subheading he enters his initials, "The Experience of JM." One may find a similar account of his conversion in Mallary's biography of Mercer, pp. 23–25; and it is not without significance that Song 104, "Come all ye mourning Pilgrims, dear," in the 1810 edition of *The Cluster* (D-4) contains the phrase "howling waste" in the third stanza. Was this a phrase in general use or peculiarly Mercer's own? Does it allow the possibility of another hymn composition by the compiler of *The Cluster*?

In the summer of 1781 the light of Christ broke into his soul making his heart glad. This became decisive for him throughout the remainder of his life. As a personal testimony he retold the experience many times afterwards, always in the first person. Devoting the first two stanzas to introduction, he then related the issues of his life between the ages of six and fifteen. That he would have felt God's wrath when only six years of age may seem remarkable to some, or even morbid to others. But he had heard his father preach of God's anger and the judgment upon sin demanding a turnaround and conversion from the situation of original and actual sin. Looking back, the young Jesse understood that it had been God alone who had kept him from going under. He was inclined to sin, toward keeping bad companions, toward failing to control his passions, and he came early in life to fear his ultimate destiny at God's hands. He felt guilt but did not give concrete details. Was it for making resolves and then breaking them? Was it lack of sexual control during puberty? Did he feel alienated and left out? He tried reading the Bible, going to Meeting, and praying, yet to no avail. Was he not elected for salvation? He had heard time and again how salvation was possible through Christ's death on the cross; yet he began to believe he had been denied. He saw Christ's action in others, his comrades, but he himself felt no blessed assurance or joy in his heart. When hell stared him in the face, he counted himself among the damned. He would readily have exchanged places with a tree or a brute animal, for they had only to die and decay, while he would surely face God's awful judgment. Their destiny, he envied. Just at the right time, grace came to this boy of seventeen years and six months. Gladness filled his heart, and he knew that he had been saved by the gracious Christ.

As for Augustine, Luther, and John Wesley, Paul's understanding in faith led Jesse Mercer to know that where sin abounds, grace much more abounds (Romans 5 and 6). God's wrath and justice had to be faced realistically. Yet Christ's atoning death proved sufficient for God and for humanity, for satisfying God's anger, and for releasing sinful people from bondage to Satan, Law, sin, and death. The sacrifice of Jesus as Lamb was "Most just unto God, and sufficient to man, From sin, and from wrath to set free" (verse 10). Here joined the objective side of the atonement (God's side) and the subjective response of the believer (the human side). The Evangelical significance of the "for me," as personally and existentially appropriated, was a knowledge given to young Jesse in his conversion. Similar to Paul, he experienced an instantaneous conversion, though doubts and anxieties were to haunt him later on.

A second hymn, or rather, the second part of a hymn (235), is credited to Mercer's composition. Edmund Jones (1722–1765), an English Baptist from Exeter, had written a hymn, "Come humble sinner, in whose breast," based on Esther 4:16. A crisis of life and death led Queen Esther to King Ahasuerus to plead mercy for Mordecai and her Jewish kin. Jones "Christianized" the story, portraying a humble sinner resolved to trust solely in the mercy of King Jesus.

Mercer completed Jones' hymn by adding six stanzas, ending with a plea for all sinners to take courage and do the same. The resolve made, the sinner finds mercy and touches the scepter of the king. Seen are "Sweet majesty and awful grace" on the forehead of King Jesus, a significant switching of adjectives qualifying the nouns "majesty" and "grace." The smiles of the king bring forth tears to the humble, yet courageous, sinner who dares visit the king. With glad singing the forgiven sinner could now sing praise for Christ's "redeeming blood." All sinners can discover a similar mercy and power if only they resolve themselves and take the risk of begging the king for pardon. Furthermore, relating one's own experience could offer hope and courage to others. The last word in this hymn, "ME," is capitalized, indicating that others are not asked to base their courage on theoretical or idealistic grounds, but upon experience.

"I am a stranger here below" (468) continues to make use of the personal pronoun "I." Reminiscent of Paul's words in Romans 7, the contradictory elements of human nature are agonizingly felt and experienced. The phrase "so prone to sin" is twice used by Mercer. "What I desire I can't attain" expresses a universal human feeling and is linked with the assertion that the Law cannot be satisfied in its demands. Was he not one of those "born again"? His anxieties cause him to cry out: "Is there any one like me?" Is this the dilemma of every saint, every

Christian believer? It appears to have been Mercer's own experience, not unlike a severe crisis in the life of one of the Psalmists, not unlike Paul. Philosophical words are employed: experience, understanding, sense feeling; but "knowing oneself" waits upon the action of God. How could the redeemed Mercer say of himself: "I am lost, vile, prone to sin, fearful, doubting, contradictory, a stranger to himself"? The struggles of this believing Christian were real and tormenting. He knew personally and tragically what had been revealed to a Jeremiah: "The heart is deceitful above all things, and desperately wicked: who can know it?" (Jeremiah 17:9).

Hymn 471, "O how shall I myself assure," is the fourth composition by Mercer. In a day when the "blessed assurance" was seen to validate God's election, it may appear strange that this Baptist believer would reveal himself and his doubts so frankly. His consciousness of doubt is offered for comparison with that of other believers. Since the lack of assurance had brought despair, various efforts were made to extricate himself: reading the Bible, praying, and going to Meeting. None of these provided solace. The profusion of tears solved nothing. When he compares himself with the sense of acceptance and actual joy displayed by other Christians, the singer feels "cold and dead." While others triumph at the facing of death's spasms, he is terrified of death. "Is it so with you?" is the question poignantly asked others; and this becomes a demand to know if he is totally unique in his dark thoughts and feelings.

Emphasized in these four hymns is the necessity of God's sovereign grace for combatting human fears, sin, and bondage. No cheap or easy grace would answer Jesse Mercer's cries of anguish. Only the blood-atonement of a Savior-God, suffering on the cross, held out any hope of salvation. Why should not the death of Jesus, the one righteous and obedient man in history, cause all to despair? Instead, to our great surprise, faith and a gladsome heart enter our lives and lead us to a life of gratitude where the good of our neighbors supplants our selfishness. Under "Conviction and Conversion" hymns 233 and 235 are placed; while 468 and 471 are located within "Conflict" under the broader category, "Christian Exercises." It is easy to forget that Mercer begins his hymnbook with the joyous note, "On Free Grace," and places the section, "On the Glories of Christ," near the beginning. Hymns found in these opening sections are cheerful and positive in tone and substance and serve to surround the struggles of faith exhibited in these more somber compositions.

Undoubtedly, Hymn 364, "When faith presents the Saviour's death," is another of Mercer's own compositions. Only three stanzas with four lines each, it affirms that "Faith affords Comfort in every State" and is placed under the section title, "Christian Exercises—Faith and Prayer." The conclusive proof of Mercer's authorship is to be found written in his own hand in several pages of his 1822 "Accounts Book." At least five attempts were made to perfect the second stanza of this hymn, beginning with "Let outward things go as they will." Counting from the back, the fifteenth page contains the exact words appearing in the 1823 *Cluster* (page 289). The metrical form is the common meter or 8.6.8.6.; and "divine" is made to rhyme inexactly with "sublime." Transported back to the years, 1822–24, the modern reader may have the rare experience of observing this man in motion, in the act of composing, first trying out one word of rhyme pattern, then another, until satisfied with the result. Since the hymn is not in the selections of 1810, we may with reasonable assurance assume that the date of composition was around the year, 1822, when Father Mercer was fifty-three. (Cf. pp. 32, 44.)

The content of Hymn 364 is central to his faith: the personal trusting of the believer. It is "the Saviour's death," which he knew to be prior in time and in importance to the arrival of faith as the believing confidence made possible and actual to the believer. Appropriating that which is given in the Cross of Jesus, the Christian internalizes the experience of Christ and participates in it. But it would be too much to say that the Cross of Christ and the Christian's cross are merged together, for the death of God's Son is unique and irrepeatable.

It may be noticed that "Miss Hataway's Experience" (229) tells of another conversion experience, that of a woman. While different, it conveys the insight that the grace of Christ is efficacious for all, however varied or unique.

> I oftentimes to church did go,
> My beauty and fine clothes to show....
>
> At length I heard a *Baptist* preach,
> His words into my heart did reach....

Miss Hataway could ignore her uncle's offers of inheritance when the Pearl of Great Price was before her eyes.

Moreover, if we compare Mercer's authenticated hymns with Hymn 227 (see 484 as well), we may ask whether he did not compose this hymn:

> I thought the brute-creation
> Was better off than I....
>
> But now I find a warfare,
> Which often bends me low,
> The world, the flesh, and Satan,
> They do beset me so....

32   *The Cluster* Of Jesse Mercer

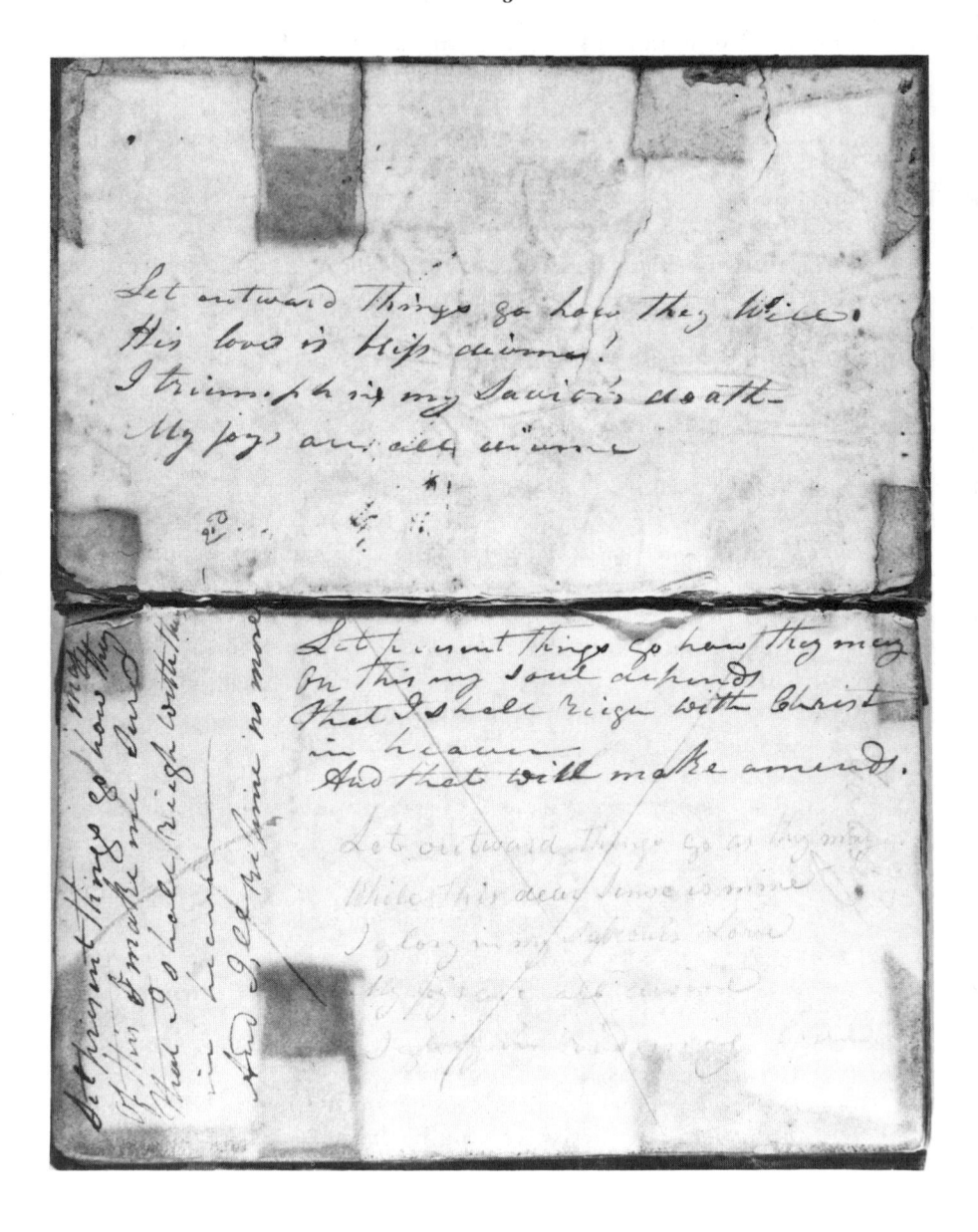

This photograph was taken of the inside cover and a page of Jesse Mercer's 1822 "Accounts book," showing his attempt to compose a hymn for *The Cluster* (Hymn 364, Stanza two).

> Can one who is a Christian
> Have such a heart as mine?

The similarities between this and other Mercer hymns are rather remarkable.

Nathaniel Hawthorne desired to create an American literary achievement equal to the accomplishments of "the scribbling sons of John Bull." Did not Mercer hope to collect and produce hymns of America that would match the hymn-writers of England? The need for one's own personal expression was paramount; to rely upon the experiences of others was insufficient praise to God. Hymn 164, "From realms where the day her first dawning extends," tells of the conflict between white Americans and red Indians. Updated is the vision of peace in Isaiah where the instruments of war become plowshares and pruninghooks, where the viper and the child play together in tranquility.

> The serpentile race shall seek venom in vain;
> The rattle-snake, harmless, shall bask on the plain;
> The infant shall play on the hole of the asp,
> And smile in the folds of the cockatrice' grasp.
>
> No more shall the sound of the war-whoop be heard,
> The ambush and slaughter no longer be fear'd;
> The tomahawk, buried, shall rest in the ground;
> And peace and good-will to the nations abound.

Could not Mercer have written this hymn for the benefit of missions? He championed education for the Indians and journeyed with Adiel Sherwood to the headwaters of the Chattahoochee for the purpose of evangelizing the Indians.

Hymn 288, "Good morning brother Pilgrim," exemplifies an early American spiritual folksong and is credited in later American hymnbooks to Mercer's *Cluster*. Happy throughout, the theme points to the "next life" rather than the earthly one now precariously lived. "No earthly joy shall charm us" carried warning in the midst of hope, and "The fiery chariot's rolling To bear me through the skies" directs us to ancient Elijah on the one hand and to the well-known Negro spiritual, "Swing Low, Sweet Chariot," on the other. Whether composed by Mercer or not, these hymns bear witness to the American experience. They caught his eye and were chosen for his hymnbook.

V

Churches have at times forsaken the glories of Christ and the counsel of the Cross for an interest in self-preservation and power politics. Not so for Jesse Mercer and the fast-growing Baptists of colonial America. Compiled, edited, and printed in the first third of the nineteenth-century, *The Cluster* bears ample testimony to the lordship of Christ as standing over against the forces of the secular society in which it circulated. Mercer and the Baptists sought to permeate the developing new nation with Christ's love rather than to accommodate themselves and their faith to economic or political forces. Established churches forced them and others into roles of protesting minorities and denied them the privilege of worshiping as their consciences directed. Anabaptists of the Continent, English Baptists of the early seventeenth century, and the Daniel Marshalls and Silas Mercers of eighteenth century America were persecuted for their faith, which only resulted in a more stubborn loyalty to their Lord. It is little wonder that Mercer could write in the opening words of his *History of the Georgia Association*:

> The Baptists, since the days of the Reformation, have striven, not so much to give tone to public sentiment upon religious subjects, as they have for a bare toleration. They have never been so ambitious to carry their points, as to subvert the religious liberties of those with whom they differed in opinion. Their course has been to adhere closely to the doctrines of the Bible, according to their understanding of those doctrines—to make a simple unvarnished exhibition of truth, and then leave the matter between God and the consciences of those whom they sought to instruct.

A people pursuing this noiseless, unostentatious course,

> could not be expected to figure so largely in ecclesiastical history, as those whose policy led them to court the favor of the great, and to blend their religious proceedings with the doings of civil governments. Owing to these causes the history of Baptists is exceedingly short, extending very little beyond a recital of their persecutions and sufferings.

Baptists in America initially were "a sect everywhere spoken against," and Mercer's vigorous language charged that plain preachers were looked down on with contempt: "To a titled, beneficed ecclesiastic, a poor Baptist preacher presented a spectacle as revolting as a Gentile 'dog' ever did to a self-righteous Pharisee."

Later thinkers such as Troeltsch, Weber, and Tawney went beyond a reductionist ideological approach and theological metaphysics in the consideration of the social factors influencing the life and thought of the churches. To subject *The Cluster* to these new methodologies is to do something Mercer did not have in mind, i.e., to give a sociological analysis which takes into account the social factors of nation, economic class, race, and the place of women. But it will help acquaint the reader with these hymns and serve to balance the Calvinistic, Evangelical, and Baptist illustrations given prominence elsewhere in our exposition.

Any attempt to speak of a national or American character of *The Cluster* must note much overlapping with other factors. This hymnbook was organized in America, printed and circulated in America, but can it rightfully be called an American hymnbook? We have already pointed out that half the hymns were written by authors in the British Isles; and the distances in spirit, if not travel, between the savannahs of Georgia and the mists of England were slight at first. Jonathan Edwards had seen the Americas as the "coastlands," the faraway places mentioned by Isaiah, to whom God's light and convenantal justice would come; and his own Protestant bias showed itself in his conviction that God in His wisdom had determined that the Reformation precede the settlement of the New World so that the church would have a fresh start, uncorrupted by the Roman Catholic aberations. However, many church divisions occurring in Europe were transported across the Atlantic: Dutch Reformed, Anglican, Roman Catholic, and to a degree, Methodists and Baptists.

There can be little doubt that Mercer felt a great sense of destiny about America, although his millennial hopes were not as strong as those of his father, Silas. Jesse Mercer's hope for building a kingdom on earth bowed to his concern for an eternal destiny in heaven. His missionary zeal did demonstrate his interests in this-world and included America along with the other continents. One hymn (273), "Our souls be love together knit," explicitly mentions the name, "America," in a rousing, militant, and triumphant testimony to God's irresistible grace and power, indicating, "'Tis heav'n on earth begun:"

> From east to west, from north to south,
>   O be thy name ador'd!
> Let *Europe* with its millions shout
>   *Hosannas* to *thee*, Lord;
> Let *Asia, Africa* resound
>   From shore to shore thy fame;
> And all *America* in songs
>   Redeeming love proclaim.   (Verse 4)

Jesse Mercer took this hymn from W. E. Miller's *Original and Select Hymns, 1802*. The fact that it was chorused reflects a new-found freedom and the onset of congregational participation in singing, characteristic in America for this date.

Hymn 141, "Did Christ o'er sinners weep?", was sung to the tune "America," but not the familiar tune we know as "My country 'tis of thee." It was written by the English Baptist, Benjamin Beddome. Tunes called "Columbus," "Jefferson," "Columbiana," and some with names of Georgia towns may or may not go back so far as Mercer's day, although they do express an American note.

The remarkable investigations of George Pullen Jackson into early American folksongs and spirituals reveal that he knew the importance of Mercer's *Cluster*, for he cites it many times. Almost one-third of ninety-eight folksongs chosen by Jackson are presented in *The Cluster*. Of fifty-one religious ballads, typically American, eighteen are found in *The Cluster*. Jackson's interests are more with the tunes; ours, with the texts. Associated with early America are two *Cluster* "hymns": *Wondrous Love* and *Come Ye Sinners, Poor and Wretched*. That *The Cluster* had great influence on later hymnbooks can be demonstrated easily by examining *The Sacred Harp, The Christian Harmony*, and *Lloyd's Hymnal* (Primitive Baptist).

One finds no patriotic, nationalistic hymns in *The Cluster*. As a matter of historical fact, several editions of Mercer's hymnbook had appeared before the composition of *The Star-Spangled Banner* in 1815, while *My Country 'Tis of Thee* (composed by an American Baptist) and *America the Beautiful* were to await a later day for their creation. Two songs did deal with the ravages of war and the call for a national fast day (Hymns 402 and 403); and there is one (164) which tells of rattlesnakes, tomahawks, and the war whoops of Indians, reflecting the American scene and probably arising from Georgia. Among Charles Wesley's more than six thousand hymns one finds numerous expressions of historical crises and events—panic over an earthquake, rumours of a French invasion, the defeat of Prince Charles Edward at Culloden, and even the Gordon rioting; but Mercer's selections center mainly on a generalized this-world experience and the longing for heaven rather than upon any recalled or anticipated American historical crisis. Silas Mercer, a soldier and chaplain in the Revolutionary War, had been rewarded for his valor and services with acreage of land in Georgia; and no doubt the imagery of soldier as drawn from this war, and also from Scripture, combined in the singers of *Cluster* hymns. (The term "soldier" or "Christian soldier" appears many times in hymns of *The Cluster*, almost used as frequently as the term "pilgrim.") But Mercer's collection—like those found in *Psalms* of the Bible—are difficult to relate to a definite and specific date in history.

Proper names and places are confined to "Sinai," "Jerusalem,""Ebenezer," "Golgotha," "Egypt," and "the land of Goshen," from Biblical sources mostly. Under "Missions," Hymns 161–180, it is possible to find mention of "Arabian darkness," "Ethiopia's scorching sand," "Greenland's icy mountains," "Africa's sunny fountains," "Java's isle," "India's plains," along with specific names of "Gentile, Turk and stubborn Jew," "Brahmans," "German and Dane," even a "panting sable Chief" from an African tribe. In each case these names are employed in the context of Christ's missionary work. These foreign peoples and nations are not seen as enemies to be conquered or subdued in any military or economic warfare.

Surely Mercer made a conscious selection of American authors for his hymnbook, for example, John Leland (231, 491, 533), Samuel Davies (8, 122, 161), and, above all, Samson Occom (223) a converted American Indian. The published hymnbooks of the Wesleys, who had their American experience, were known to Mercer (the signature of Silas Mercer is found in one of them given by his son, Jesse, to Mercer University archives). It is somewhat surprising that Jesse Mercer did not include Wesley's hymn, "Lo! on a narrow neck of land, 'Twixt two unbounded seas, I stand..." This hymn, written in Georgia while Wesley was secretary to General James Oglethorpe, did appear in Moravian hymnbooks and primitive Baptist collections (Cf. 655). Characteristically, Occom's hymn (223), "Awak'ed by Sinai's awful sound," demonstrates that Occom placed less emphasis on the modern historical character and more attention upon the relived terror of his own conversion experience when the Law gave way to a fresh new life under the Gospel. All in all Mercer was captivated more by the Kingdom of Christ and the coming of all nations to that Kingdom than in any pride that would permit his *Cluster* to serve societal, regional, and national interests (Cf. Hymns A-2 and A-3).

As for economic factors, did not Eli Whitney invent the cotton gin in 1793 when Mercer was only twenty-four years old? Economic and social historians would take note of that for sure, with its consequences for decades to come. Mercer was not averse to capitalistic enterprises, unlike Thomas Aquinas who as late as the thirteenth century condemned usury. Tawney and others have seen a parent-child relationship between Calvinism and the countries where capitalism had its developing successes. To work hard, to spend frugally, and to save, united the convincements of God's special blessings for justifying capitalistic endeavors. Mercer's time was too early for observing with the eyes of anthropologists and sociologists to conclude what happens when a mass of people undergo major occupational changes, e.g., from agricultural to technological and urban vocations.

Jesse Mercer was a propertied man, and a considerable amount of money and property passed through his hands. As his family Bible indicates, he owned slaves. His second marriage to the widow of a Jewish merchant, Captain Simons, brought him to affluence. The early days of this Baptist preacher were not so prosperous. He built by his own craftsmanship a log cabin (*c.* 1790) at the start of his first marriage. But Mercer knew the temptations of the world, the flesh and Satan. A number of hymns speak of the idolatries of the rich man (e.g., 53), those who put supreme confidence in their goods and possessions. Hymns 185, 189, 193, 275, and 305 depict the Biblical story of the rich man and poor Lazarus, while the experience of Miss Hataway (Hymn 229) does nothing less than pit her service to Christ over against the material enticements offered the young girl by her uncle. But for this Georgia Baptist minister it was stewardship, not a vow of poverty, that was the ideal. Mercer illustrated in his own life Wesley's remark: "Earn all you can, save all you can, give all you can." When the dilemma of choosing between Jesus and "silver and gold" arose, it was resolved by this minister of the Gospel by giving away most of the silver and gold. He did not fail to come to the aid of the poor, indigent young men who would study for the ministry, and to help penurious Indians and Blacks, whose needs were always close to his heart and pocketbook. His knowledge of the "riches of Christ" (cf. Hymn 305) led him to give priority to Matthew's rendering, "Blessed are the poor in spirit," rather than to the Lucan remembrance, "Blessed are you poor," i.e., the poor without material possessions. The "riches of Christ" applied to this-life and to the next. Neither he nor John Wesley were "social gospellers," in the sense that Gladden and Rauschenbusch were to be, offering plans to refurbish society and establish the Kingdom of God on earth. But there was an actual ambiguity about the goods of this-life and the heaven to come. The present world, when sin was faced, came to be perceived as a "thorny maze," "a howling waste," and a "barren desert." The hymns downplay any worldly delights as unworthy when compared to the gains of Christ upon reaching heaven. This life could be the beginning of heaven on earth; and it cannot be gainsaid that Mercer was a very active man for causes pertaining to the earthly existence, though the Calvinistic ideal of "intraworldly asceticism" does not seem quite fitting for this man. He wore a black coat with a yellow lining, drove a bright blue carriage, and his wife dressed out in stunningly colorful bonnets that caused notice. His economic class status did not enslave him; his accumulated wealth served his faith in Christ. *The Cluster* was not prepared for "the rich only," nor was the poor man to be helped only with the gift of material possessions. While Mercer worked hard all his life, thus reflecting what has come to be called "the Protestant work-ethic," the context was not for self-gain nor for results issuing from a narcissistic self-love permeated with greed. The Lord had set the example (the kenosis theology of Philippians 2) by emptying himself, by giving away and sacrificing his own life for the salvation of men, rather than to be grasping and greedy in his relationship to God on high.

A third social feature, race, is not easily separated from characteristics of nation or economic class. Was not Mercer typically a white, Anglo-Saxon, Protestant and a male chauvinist to boot? He did have dealings with Jews, Indians, and Blacks; and he once argued that women should be allowed to speak in the churches (praying and prophesying) but by no means should be allowed to vote in matters of church business. Like the author of the Fourth Gospel, Mercer saw "the Jews" as doing dreadful acts against Jesus; but does this fit under race prejudice? Reminiscent of an old Negro spiritual, "Were you there when they crucified my Lord?", this simple Baptist preacher looked instead to his own culpability and sin:

> "'Twas not the treach'rous Jews
>   That did my Lord betray:
> It was my heinous sins,
>   More treach'rous far than they."   (Hymn 63)

No one class of men, whether Jews, Blacks, or Indians, could obscure the reality he knew so well: all men are sinners. He recognized that "the Jews crucifi'd the God-man," but he himself was there, along with all mankind participating in that murder of God's Son. He was not one to locate the New Testament on a higher level than the Old Testament, following the style of a Marcion or any other Gnostic. Both were equally authoritative Scripture. For naming the church as Christ's body, Mercer used the terms, "Zion" and "Israel," even churches he himself served. It is noteworthy that Jesse Mercer counted a Jew, Captain Abram Simons, as trusted friend as early as 1813 and later married his widow, Nancy, in 1827. Monies and properties amassed by Simons eventually came to Mercer; and most of these he gave away, the bulk to the university bearing his name. In April, 1813, Jesse Mercer wrote a friend, introducing Simons as "a worldly man" but urging the man addressed to "treat him as myself."

Throughout the life of Mercer, Georgia had its problems with Indians. And, vice versa, the Indians had a specific name for colonial Georgians, which literally meant those who were "greedy for the lands of the Indians." Hymn 164 is a missionary hymn that transposes the messianic vision of Isaiah and Micah into the Georgia situation: rattlesnakes basking peacefully on the plains, little children playing by the snake's hole, and the burying of the tomahawk bringing an end to all "war-whoops." "Slight tinctures of skin" are seen as a small matter. (Would it have been different had there been more than "slight tinctures"?) While Elijah Clarke went forth killing Indians, Mercer and Sherwood went on evangelization tours in the region of the Chattahoochee's headwaters, preaching through an interpreter. Among the recipients of Mercer's benevolent monetary contributions, the Indians were included; he wished to educate them. He could refer to them as "heathens" and "savages," but they were fit for Christ's gospel and salvation; and the hymns of *The Cluster* were not reserved for "whites only."

The social issue instrumental in splitting Baptists into a North and South was brewing before Mercer's death (Cf. letters to Heman Lincoln and Lucius Bolles regarding abolition). Mercer owned slaves as his family Bible shows. He kept records of their names, births, marriages, and deaths; and he lamented especially the death of his fourteen year-old house maid, Mary, who in his judgment may not have been a Christian. In his churches he preached to slaves, although they sat in a special balcony section. Obviously the paternalism of his day prevailed, yet while Mercer took seriously Paul's admonitions for masters to be kind to their slaves (Ephesians), he maintained real community with all those of his household, including the slaves. This will not satisfy a later age any more than will the example of St. Paul, who cannot be made into a liberal social reformer attacking the institution of slavery. But, with the Apostle, he knew that in Christ there was neither slave nor free, and that the liberty made available through Christ was the paramount freedom which had been made possible to every man. Mercer did not include any section titled, "For Masters," as did Charles Wesley in one of the Wesleys' hymnbooks, containing a song for "inferiors":

> Inferiors, as a sacred trust,
> I from the Sovereign Lord receive
> That what is suitable and just,
> Impartial I to all may give.

In *The Cluster* Hymn 162 speaks of the "untaught savage" (Also cf. 115, S. 5), and Hymn 179 reads, "O send out preachers, gracious Lord, Among that dark, bewilder'd race," while Hymn 162 makes explicit mention of both Negro and Indian. And Hymn 167:

> "Go, tell th' unlettered wretched slave,
> Who groans beneath a tyrant's rod,
> You bring a freedom bought with blood,
> The blood of an incarnate God."

Slaves attending meeting most likely sang songs taken from *The Cluster*. They, for the most part, could not read; but the songleader lined out the verses and histed the tune so that the slaves could follow. Mercer was president of the Baptist's "American Foreign Mission Board" for many years; and he supported Luther Rice and the Judsons, gave the charge for John Mason Peck, and wrote Bro. Shuck in Macao in support of winning converts to Christ. We must conclude that Mercer did not move much beyond the thought of Paul; or, to say it differently, he went as far as Paul: "Here there cannot be Greek and Jew, circumcized and uncircumcized, barbarian, Scythian, slave, free man, but Christ is all, and in all," (Col. 3: 11); and added to this:

> There is neither Jew nor Greek, there is neither slave nor free, there is neither male nor female; for you are all one in Christ Jesus. And if you are Christ's, then you are Abraham's offspring, heirs according to promise. (Gal. 3:28.)

To inquire as to the place of women in Mercer's *Cluster* is to raise another difficult subject. Biblical stories of women appear among the selected hymns: the woman at the well with whom Jesus talked and also "Weeping Mary" (181); Esther's brave plea to save her people (235); the Mary with seven devils (563); confession of sin for the filthy "Mary, Manasseh, and I" (12, 19); "Mary's better part" in conversing with Jesus rather than to work in the kitchen, as did Martha (416) and "the foolish virgins" (652). Foretelling of Christ's advent is announced in "woman's promis'd seed" (108). One looks in vain to find the name, Eve, in *The Cluster*. Sin and bondage among all mankind are related to "our father Adam's blot" (147), and Adam is called "the first sinner man" (230). Mary, the mother of Jesus, gets very little attention, probably as a reaction to the cult of Mary as found in Catholic and Orthodox witnesses. At his birth it is the Christ-child who is in the limelight, not his mother.

Christian experiences of a contemporary nature appear: a widow's lament (647); a wife and daughters grieved by death (619); a husband grieved over the loss of his Sophronia (621); the fickleness of a woman's tender care of her own child (596); and numerous hymns addressing "Ye brethren and sisters" (e.g., 567). Miss Hataway's conversion experience is told for other young women to receive benefit (229). Hymns 645 and 646 offer the captions: (1) "The bereaved Mother's Condolence under the loss of an only Child"; and (2) "Mother bereaved because a daughter and her husband have died in quick succession." The reader may wonder whether Hymn 628 was written by a man or by a woman. Nowhere does Mercer, in his selections, seem to arise above the old convention of the place of women in roles confined to children, church, and kitchen. But it is significant that among Baptist authors contributing hymns to *The Cluster*, Anne Steele heads the list. Women did sing during the congregational worship meetings, and Mercer probably thought himself liberal in permitting them to speak in a limited way (when praying or prophesying). Yet by no means should they vote in matters of church authority and government. So far from his mind was the question of the ordination of women that the issue was never raised. Mercer was a child of his day in this respect as in others.

Other social factors could be applied to *The Cluster*—the young and the old; the rural versus the urban; the educated against the uneducated—but perhaps enough has been suggested to encourage a further examination by the interested reader. Language is basic to culture, and *The Cluster* can be justifiably criticized for its narrow scope as an English-speaking hymnbook. In *The Cluster* are a handful of translated hymns (mostly by John Wesley from the German-speaking Moravians) and at least one ode from the French. B. L. Manning in his book, *The Hymns of Wesley and Watts*, extols the use made by Isaac Watts of Anglo-Saxon words and of the greater, more adept use made by Charles Wesley in combining Latinisms with Anglo-Saxon phrases. Clearly Mercer did not have this sort of ability, either to compose or to select. In the *kairos* of the early nineteenth century, Mercer's Calvinism and Baptist convictions are to be evaluated in the context of the Evangelical revivals and the hard-working people of a growing New World, where opportunities and challenges came in seemingly unlimited fashion. *The Cluster* is not primarily an American hymnbook, is not for whites or the rich only; it is not selective when speaking about the sin and bondage of all men; and it finds an equality of men and women as they stand in their needs before the divine aggression. Yet strangely this early American hymnbook takes on a certain uniqueness in its own time, its own culture, and represents the particular action of God in that time.

Before concluding our present study of *The Cluster*, let us return to its title page and consider Mercer's understanding of the term "spiritual." The modesty of this Baptist preacher is evident as he blazed a trail by compiling a hymnbook that would lead his congregation and others to a closer walk with God. Surprisingly, *The Cluster* (1823 ed.) is without preface, dedication, or explanatory words, though Paul (Colossians 3:16) is quoted beneath the title, which reads, *The Cluster of Spiritual Songs, Divine Hymns, and Sacred Poems, Being Chiefly a Collection.* Under these words appears the compiler's simple identification, "Minister of the Gospel at Powelton, Georgia" (later editions would read, "at Washington, Georgia"). Over against "worldly" did the designation "spiritual" stand, pointing to the believer's ultimate destiny under God's own tutelage. The Evangelicals called attention to the intimate and personal lived-out relationship of the believer with his resurrected Lord. No split between "spiritual" and "material" was intended—rather, the distinction between Christ's Spirit and the life of the disciple. "Mercer's *Cluster*," as the book came to be called, contained a majority of hymns contrasting

An Introduction To Mercer's *Cluster*

the idolatries and vileness of sinners with the glories of him crucified and raised from the dead. As a handbook or manual for Christian believers the little book, weighing eight ounces and measuring 5.5 by 2.75 inches, came to serve many functions: congregational singing, family and private devotions, an aid to the Lord's Table, comfort at funerals, and use at the beginning and ending of sermons. That Mercer was supremely dedicated to the task of issuing a book of hymns is demonstrated by his own expenditure of thought, energy, and money for a quarter of a century. He was its primary distributor in addition to all this. The sale of a plain copy of *The Cluster* brought 75 cents, and the most expensive, with morocco binding, cost $2.25[10] There is no reason to think pecuniary gain was his motive; most of what he inherited or earned was given away. His largest gifts to education came after the decision had been made to honor a university with his name. May we speculate that in gratitude for *The Cluster* we find a prime influence which led the founders to call their institution Mercer University?

All has not been accomplished in this sketchy introduction to Mercer's *Cluster*. Many questions remain unanswered. To what music were the hymns sung? It is all but impossible to associate many of the hymn texts with tunes. Into what regions did the hymnbook go? Who were the people who bought and used *The Cluster*? Were they mainly Baptists? What influence did these songs of praises have upon later collections of hymns? Any serious evaluation would require a comparison of this collection with other hymnbooks of the times, e.g., those by the Wesleys. It is easy to criticize certain of Mercer's choices as overly sentimental, as too moralistic and didactic, as roughhewn in rhyme and meter, as monotonously "samey" in conveying their theological lessons. Great and lasting hymns that were available to him somehow were not included, e.g., "O God Our Help in Ages Past" and "When I Survey the Wondrous Cross." Yet, when all is said, *The Cluster* stands sturdy both for a pioneer and enduring faith and remains a not inconsiderable accomplishment as one of the significant early American collections of spiritual songs.

As Anglicans have shown their love and devotion for the realities about which their *Book of Common Prayer* speaks, so Baptists and others have found solace in *The Cluster*. When Jesse Mercer's first wife was dying, she requested the singing of two hymns, found in *The Cluster*, "Jerusalem, my happy home" (Hymn 284) and "How happy's every child of grace" (Hymn 300), and the reading of Samuel Pearce's "In the floods of tribulation (Hymn 474). Mercer consoled a friend in a letter written December 26, 1832, and recommended the reading of Newton's "'Tis a point I long to know" (Hymn 469) and his own hymn, "O how shall I myself assure?" (Hymn 471).

"Let outward things go how they will,
His love is bliss sublime!
I triumph in my Saviour's death—
My joys are all divine."

From Jesse Mercer's "Accounts book" of 1822, showing one stanza of a hymn (364) he had himself composed.

Addressing his purpose for publishing and editing *The Christian Index*, Mercer wrote "Sister Dolly" in 1836, "it is the most ardent desire of my heart to afford the readers of that paper some solid food to strengthen their faith, and improve their spiritual health." Doubtless the same purpose permeated all his efforts on behalf of *The Cluster*. For both he could say with self-assurance that it was "the Lord that spoke through me, as a *certain* sound is given by a skillful blower of a trumpet," but "to him be all the praise."

The last word is reserved for a contemporary friend of Mercer who characterized this rather awkward but devoted Christian collector and writer of hymns:

> There he is, a little child at the feet of the Saviour, tender, affectionate, humble, penitent, obedient, and adoring; glorying in Christ as his wisdom, righteousness, sanctification and redemption, and looking with a simple faith, and a calm, serene hope for the mercy of our Lord Jesus Christ unto eternal life."[11]

"Glorying in Christ" was the inspiration behind Mercer's *Cluster*.

CHAPTER THREE

HYMN TEXTS FROM *THE CLUSTER*

THE
CLUSTER

ON FREE GRACE

1. (C. M. DOUBLE.)
Grace, the Sweetest Sound.

1 NOW may the Lord reveal his face,
 And teach our stamm'ring tongues,
To make his glorious reign of grace,
 The subject of our songs.
No sweeter subject can invite
 A sinner's heart to sing,
Or more display the sov'reign right,
 Of our exalted King.

2 This subject fills the starry plains,
 With wonder, joy, and love,
And furnishes the noblest strains,
 For all the harps above:
While the redeem'd in praise combine,
 To grace upon the throne;
Angels in solemn chorus join,
 And make the theme their own.

3 Grace reigns to conquer rebel foes,
 By mild, and easy means,
And thus it manifestly shows,
 Of foes, it makes its friends;
O'ercome by love, they all delight
 To give to grace the praise,
And all their cheerful powers unite,
 The lofty theme to raise.

4 Grace reigns to pardon crimson sins,
 To melt the hardest hearts,
And from the work it once begins,
 It never more departs.
The world and Satan strive in vain,
 Against the chosen few,
Secure of grace's conqu'ring reign,
 They all shall conquer too.

5 Grace tills the soil, and sows the seeds,
 Provides the sun and rain,
'Till from the tender blade proceeds
 The ripen'd harvest grain.
'Twas grace that call'd our souls at first,
 By grace thus far we've come,
And grace will help us through the worst,
 And lead us safely home.

6 Lord, when this changing life is past,
 May we but see thy face,
How will we praise and love at last,
 And sing the reign of grace:
Yet, let us aim while here below,
 Thy glory to display,
And own at least the debt we owe,
 Although we cannot pay.

2. (11, 8.) 6S./4L.
Grace, Distinguishing and Free.

IN songs of sublime adoration and
 praise,

3. (8, 8, 6.) 5S./6L.
Grace, Inexpressible.

WERE oceans, rivers, floods, and lakes,

4. (P. M.)
Grace, Exhaustless and full of Glory.

1 TRANSPORTING news, the Saviour's come,
    To purchase our salvation;
Let every tongue now speak his praise,
    In strains of acclamation.
When hell's dark host, with wicked boast,
    Had 'complish'd man's subjection;
Christ's wond'rous grace, reliev'd our race,
    By mercy's sweet direction;
Th' eternal God's eternal Son,
The heir and partner of his throne,
    In pity stoop'd, was crucify'd,
    His blood and righteousness apply'd;
And thus our souls at freedom set,
By paying off the dreadful debt.
We, therefore, we, from sin set free,
Will joyfully adore him.

2 He comes the pris'ners to release,
    To cure poor souls all bleeding;
To give the troubled conscience peace,
    By 's death and interceding:
The cursed chain, he breaks in twain,
    With which our sins had bound us,
From Calvary, this pardon free,
    Has richly flow'd around us;
Our KING of kings, and LORD most high
Has ransom'd us to liberty;
And, in a garment dipp'd in blood,
Our foes beneath his feet has trod;
Rescu'd by grace, we now no more,
    Shall bonds or poverty deplore;
Fair Salem waits with pearly gates,
    Our ransom'd souls to welcome.

3 Then happy souls come sing his grace,
    Come sing exhaustless treasure,
'Till you behold him face to face,
    With most triumphant pleasure:
His grace and love with joy we prove,
    While with delight we ponder
On what in vain, tongue tries t'explain,
    To heaven and earth a wonder:
Thus while we sit beneath his cross,
All earthly things we count but loss,
And nothing think nor speak beside,
The blessed Jesus crucify'd;
In whom both love and vengeance join,
To make poor worms in glory shine;
O for this grace, let highest praise,
    Ascend with pleasing rapture!

4 Our glad hosannas Saviour God,
    Proclaim aloud thy praises,
While all the host, redeem'd by blood,
    In heav'n with transport gazes;
We too aspire with that bless'd choir,
    In humble, sweet prostration,
A glorious band with harp in hand,
    To sing complete salvation;
With them we'll drink immortal joys;
With them hear Jesus' glorious voice;
With them behold him face to face;
With them transported on him gaze;
With them in heavenly concert join;
With them in endless glory shine;
In loftiest voice, his praise rehearse,
    Adore his name forever.

5. (8, 7.)
Grace, All-conquering and charming.

1 LEGION was my name by nature,
    Satan rag'd within my breast;
Never misery was greater,
    Never sinner more possess'd:
Mischievous to all around me,
    To myself the greatest foe;
Thus I was, when Jesus found me,
    Fill'd with madness, sin, and woe.

2 Yet in this forlorn condition,
    When he came to set me free,
I reply'd to my Physician,
    "What have I to do with thee?"
But he would not be prevented,
    Rescued me against my will;
Had he staid till I'd consented,
    I had been a captive still.

3 "Satan, tho' thou fain would'st have it,
    Know this soul is none of thine;
I have shed my blood to save it,
    Now I challenge it for mine:
Though it long has thee resembled,
    Henceforth it shall me obey;"
Thus he spake while Satan trembled,
    Gnash'd his teeth and fled away.

4 Thus my frantic soul he healed,
    Bid my sins and sorrows cease;
"Take, said he, my pardon sealed,
    I have sav'd thee, go in peace:"
Rather take me, Lord, to heav'n,
    Now thy love and grace I know;
Since thou hast my sins forgiven,
    Why should I remain below!

5 "Love, said he, will sweeten labours,
    Thou hast something yet to do;
Go and tell your friends and neighbours
    What my love has done for you:
Live to manifest my glory,
    Wait for heaven a little space;
Sinners when they hear thy story,
    Will repent and seek my face."

6. (7, 6.) 5S./8L.
Grace, Healing and Transporting.

1 WHEN the wounded spirit hears

7. (11's.)
Grace, Free and Full.

1 THY mercy, my God, is the theme of my song,
The joy of my heart, and the boast of my tongue;   [last,
Thy free grace alone, from the first to the
Hath won my affections, and bound my soul fast.

2 Without thy sweet mercy I could not live here,
Sin soon would reduce me to utter despair;
But through thy free goodness my spirits revive,   [alive,
And he that first made me, still keeps me

3 Thy mercy is more than a match for my heart,   [depart;
Which wonders to feel its own hardness
Dissolv'd by thy sunshine, I fall to the ground,
And weep to the praise of the mercy I found.

4 The door of thy mercy stands open all day
To th' poor and the needy, who knock by the way;
No sinner shall ever be empty sent back,
Who comes seeking mercy for Jesus's sake.

5 Thy mercy in Jesus exempts me from hell!
Its glories I'll sing, and its wonders I'll tell:
'Twas Jesus, my friend, when he hung on the tree,
Who open'd the channel of mercy for me.

6 Great Father of mercies! thy goodness I own,
And the covenant love of thy crucify'd Son:
All praise to the Spirit, whose whisper divine
Seals mercy, and pardon, and righteousness mine!

8. (4 M. Chorus'd.)
Grace, Pardoning, Rich; and Free.

1 GREAT God of wonders! all thy ways,
Are matchless, Godlike, and divine;
But the fair glories of thy grace
    More Godlike and unrivall'd shine:
        Chorus.
Who is a pard'ning God like thee?
Or who has grace so rich and free?

2 Crimes of such horror to forgive,
Such guilty daring worms to spare,
This is thy grand prerogative
And none shall in the honour share.
Who is, &c.

3 Angels and men, resign your claim,
To pity, mercy, love and grace;
These glories crown Jehovah's name
With an incomparable blaze:
Who is, &c.

4 In wonder lost, with trembling joy,
We take the pardon of our God,
Pardon of crimes of deepest dye,
A pardon seal'd with JESUS' blood.
Who is, &c.

5 O may this strange, this matchless grace,
This Godlike miracle of love,
Fill the wide earth with grateful praise,
And all th' angelic choirs above!
Who is, &c.

9. (7's.)
Grace All-conquering.

1 O MY Lord, what must I do?
    Only thou the way can show:
Thou canst save me in this hour,
I have neither will nor power;
God if over all thou art,
Greater than a sinful heart,
Let it now on me be shown:
Take away the heart of stone.

2 Take away my darling sin,
Make me willing to be clean,
Make me willing to receive
What thy goodness waits to give;
Force me, Lord, with all to part,
Tear these idols from my heart:
All thy pow'r on me be shown:
Take away the heart of stone.

3 Jesus, mighty to renew.
Work in me to will and do;
Turn my nature's rapid tide,
Stem the torrent of my pride:
Stop the whirlwind of my will,
Speak, and bid the sun stand still,
Now thy love almighty shew:
Make e'en me a creature new.

4 Arm of God, thy strength put on,
Bow the heavens and come down;
All mine unbelief o'erthrow,
Lay th' aspiring mountain low,
Conquer thy worst foe in me,
Get thyself the victory,
Save the vilest of my race:
Force me to be sav'd by grace.

10. (8's.)
Grace, Constraining to Love.

1 THEE will I love, my strength, my tower,
   Thee will I love, my Joy, my crown,
   Thee will I love with all my power,
   In all my works, and thee alone;
   Thee will I love till the pure fire
   Fill my whole soul with chaste desire.

2 Ah! why did I so late thee know,
   Thee, lovelier than the sons of men?
   Ah! why did I no sooner go
   To thee, the only easc in pain?
   Asham'd I sigh, and inly mourn,
   That I so late to thee did turn.

3 In darkness willingly I stray'd
   I sought thee, yet from thee I rov'd:
   Far wide my wand'ring thoughts were spread,
   Thy creatures more than thee I lov'd:
   And now if more at length I see,
   'Tis thro' thy light, and comes from thee.

4 I thank thee uncreated Sun,
   That thy bright beams on me have shin'd
   I thank thee, who hast overthrown
   My foes, and heal'd my wounded mind:
   I thank thee, whose enliv'ning voice
   Bids my free heart in thee rejoice.

5 Uphold me in the doubtful race,
   Nor suffer me again to stray:
   Strengthen my feet with steady pace,
   Still to press forward in the way:
   My soul and flesh, O Lord of might,
   Fill, satiate with heavenly light.

6 Give to mine eyes refreshing tears,
   Give to my heart chaste hallow'd fires,
   Give to my soul with filial fears,
   The love that heaven's host inspires;
   That all my pow'rs, with all their might,
   In thy sole glory may unite.

7 Thee will I love, my joy, my crown,
   Thee will I love, my Lord, my God,
   Thee will I love, beneath thy frown
   Or smile, thy sceptre or thy rod:
   What though my flesh and heart decay,
   Thee shall I love in endless day.

11. (P. M.)
Grace Constrains to Grateful Acknowledgment.

1 LET the world their virtue boast,
   Their works of righteousness;
   I, a wretch undone and lost,
   Am freely sav'd by grace:
   Other title I disclaim,
   This, only this, is all my plea,
   I the chief of sinners am,
   But Jesus died for me.

2 Let the stronger sons of God
   Their liberty assert,
   Justly glory in the blood
   That made them pure in heart:
   I am full of guilt and shame,
   My heart as black as hell I see:
   I the chief of sinners am,
   But Jesus died for me.

3 Happy they whose joys abound,
   Like JORDAN's swelling stream,
   Who their heav'n in Christ have found
   And give their praise to him.
   Let them triumph in his name,
   Enjoy their full felicity:
   I the chief of sinners am,
   But Jesus died for me.

4 Blest are they, entirely blest,
   Who can in him rejoice,
   Lean on his beloved breast,
   And hear the bridegroom's voice:
   Meanest follower of the Lamb,
   His steps I at a distance see,
   I the chief of sinners am,
   But Jesus died for me.

12. (P. M.)
Grace, Rich, Full, and Free.

1 YE children of God,
   By faith in his Son,
   Redeem'd by his blood,
   And with him made one,
   This union with wonder
   And rapture be seen;
   Which nothing shall sunder,
   Without or within.

2 This Pardon, this Peace,
   Which none can destroy,
   This Treasure of Grace,
   This heavenly Joy,
   The worthless may crave it,
   It always come free;
   The vilest may have it,
   'Twas given to ME.

3 'Tis not for good deeds,
   Good tempers, nor frames;
   From grace it proceeds,
   And all is the Lamb's.
   No goodness, no fitness,
   Expects he from us:
   This I can well witness,
   For none could be worse.

Hymn Texts From *The Cluster*

4 Sick sinner, expect
   No balm, but Christ's blood:
   Thy own works reject,
     The bad, and the good.
   None ever miscarry
     That on him rely
   Though filthy as MARY,
     MANASSEH or I.

13. (8's.)
Grace, Exciting Eternal Praises.

1 I'LL praise my Maker while I've breath,
   And when my voice is lost in death,
  Praise shall employ my nobler pow'rs,
  My days of praise shall ne'er be past,
  While life, and thought, and being last,
   And immortality endures.

2 Happy the man whose hopes rely
  On Israel's God; he made the sky,
  And earth, and seas, with all their train;
   His truth forever stands secure!
  He saves th' opprest, he feeds the poor,
   And none shall find his promise vain.

3 The Lord pours eye-sight on the blind
  The Lord supports the fainting mind;
   He sends the lab'ring conscience peace;
  He helps the stranger in distress,
  The widows and the fatherless,
   And grants the pris'ner sweet release.

4 I'll praise him while he lends me breath,
  And when my voice is lost in death,
   Praise shall employ my nobler pow'rs:
  My days of praise shall ne'er be past,
  While life, and thought, and being last,
   Or immortality endures.

14. (L. M.) 6S./4L.
My Grace is sufficient for thee:

1 COME all ye chosen saints of God,

15. (8's.)
Free Grace a Sure Anchorage.

1 NOW I have found the ground wherein,
  My soul's sure anchor may remain,
  The wounds of Jesus for my sin,
   Before the world's foundations slain;
  Whose mercy shall unshaken stay,
  When heaven and earth are fled away.

2 Father, thine everlasting grace,
   Our scanty thoughts surpasses far,
  The heart still melts with tenderness;
   Thy arms of love still open are,
  Returning sinners to receive,
  That mercy they may taste, and live.

3 By faith I plunge me in this sea,
   Here is my hope, my joy and rest;
  'Tis here when hell assaults I flee,
   And look into my Saviour's breast:
  Away sad doubts and anxious fear,
  Mercy is all that's written there.

4 Tho' waves and storms go o'er my head;
   Tho' health and strength and friends be gone;
  Tho' joys be wither'd all, and dead—
   Tho' ev'ry comfort be withdrawn,
  On thee my stedfast soul relies;
  Father, thy mercy never dies.

5 Fix'd on this ground I will remain,
   Tho' heart should fail and flesh decay,
  This anchor shall my soul sustain,
   When earth's foundation melts away;
  Mercy's full pow'r I then shall prove,
  Lov'd with an everlasting love.

6 What in thy love possess I not?
   My star by night, my sun by day,
  My springs of life when parch'd with drought,
  My wine to cheer, my bread to stay,
  My shield, my strength, my safe abode,
  My palace, Saviour, and my God.

16. (8. 7.) 6S./4L.
Converting Grace constraining.

1 ON the brink of fi'ry ruin,

17. (6, 8.) Lenox. 6S./6L.
God's Thoughts Precious and Gracious.

1 INDULGENT God! how kind

18. (8. 8. 6.) 5S./6L.
Grace shining in the Covenant.

1 NOW for a hymn of praise to God

19. (8. 7. 4.)
Grace Super-abounding.

1 SOV'REIGN grace o'er sin abounding,

20. (8. 7.)
Grace, a Miracle!

1 HAIL! my ever blessed Jesus,
   Only thee I wish to sing;
  To my soul thy name is precious,
   Thou my prophet, priest, and king.
  O! what mercy flows from heaven,
   O, what joy and happiness!
  Love I much? I've much forgiven,
   I'm a miracle of grace.

[2 Once with Adam's race in ruin,
　　Unconcern'd in sin I lay;
　Swift destruction still pursuing,
　　Till my Saviour passed by.
　Witness, all ye hosts of heaven,
　　My Redeemer's tenderness;
　Love I much? I've much forgiven,
　　I'm a miracle of grace.]

3　Shout, ye bright angelic choir,
　　Praise the Lamb enthron'd above;
　Whilst astonish'd, I admire
　　God's free grace and boundless love.
　That blest moment I receiv'd him,
　　Fill'd my soul with joy and peace;
　Love I much? I've much forgiven,
　　I'm a miracle of grace.

21. (C. M.)
A Dark, though Gracious Providence.

1　THY way O God, is in the sea;
　　Thy paths I cannot trace:
　Nor comprehend the mystery
　　Of thy unbounded grace.

2　As thro' a glass, I dimly see
　　The wonders of thy love;
　How little do I know of thee,
　　Or of the joys above?

3　'Tis but in part I know thy will;
　　I bless thee for the sight;
　When will thy love the rest reveal,
　　In glory's clearer light?

4　With raptures shall I then survey
　　Thy providence and grace;
　And spend an everlasting day
　　In wonder, love, and praise.

22. (C. M.) 3S./4L.
Covenant Grace Secure.

1　MY God, the cov'nant of thy love

23. (C. M.)
Salvation by Mighty Grace.

1　AMAZING grace! how sweet the sound!
　　That sav'd a wretch like me!
　I once was lost, but now am found,
　　Was blind, but now I see.

2　'Twas grace that taught my heart to fear,
　　And grace my fears reliev'd;
　How precious did that grace appear
　　The hour I first believ'd!

3　Through many dangers, toils and snares,
　　I have already come;
　'Tis grace has brought me safe thus far,
　　And grace will lead me home.

　The Lord has promis'd good to me.
　　His word my hope secures;
　He will my shield and portion be,
　　As long as life endures.

3　Yea when this flesh and heart shall fail,
　　And mortal life shall cease;
　I shall possess within the veil,
　　A life of joy and peace.

6　The world shall soon to ruin go,
　　The sun forbear to shine;
　But God, who call'd me here below,
　　Shall be forever mine.

24. (C. M.) Majesty.
God Glorified in Grace.

1　THE Lord, descending from above,
　　Invites his children near;
　While pow'r, and truth, and boundless love,
　　Display their glories here.

2　Here in the Gospel's wond'rous frame,
　　Fresh wisdom we pursue;
　A thousand angels learn thy name,
　　Beyond whate'er they knew.

3　Thy name is writ in fairest lines,
　　Thy wonders here we trace;
　Wisdom through all the myst'ry shines,
　　And shines in Jesus' face.

4　The law is best obedience owes
　　To our incarnate God!
　And thy revenging justice shows
　　It's honours in his blood.

5　But still the lustre of thy grace
　　Our warmer thoughts employs,
　Gilds the whole scene with brighter rays,
　　And more exalts our joys.

25. (8, 8, 6.) 7S./6L.
Grace, Invincible and Constraining.

1　LORD, thou hast won, at length I yield;

26. (8, 7.) 7S./4L.
Covenant Grace.

1　FAR beyond all comprehension

27. (C. M.) 3S./4L.
The Grace of Christ Wonderous.

1　ALOUD we sing the wond'rous grace,

28. (7's.) 5S./4L.
Grace, or Love of Jesus.

1　LOVE divine, how sweet the sound

Hymn Texts From *The Cluster*

29. (7's.)
The Sovereignty of Grace.

1 SOV'REIGN grace has pow'r alone

30. (L. M.) 3S./4L.
Praise for Free Grace.

1 WHILE here on earth I'm call'd to stay,

31. (C. M.)
Grace, Converting and Free.

1 HAIL, mighty Jesus, how divine
    is thy victorious sword!
The stoutest rebel must resign
    At thy commanding word.

2 Still gird thy sword upon thy thigh,
    Ride with majestic sway;
Go forth, sweet prince, triumphantly,
    And make thy foes obey.

3 And when thy vict'ries are complete,
    And all the chosen race
Shall round the throne of glory meet
    To sing thy conqu'ring grace—

4 O may my humble soul be found
    Among that favour'd band!
And I, with them, thy praise will sound,
    Throughout Immanuel's land.

32. (C. M.) 4S./4L.
Grace displayed in the Conversion of the Jailor.

1 LORD we adore thy matchless ways

33. (C. M.) 4S./4L.
Grace in the Conversion of Zaccheus.

1 A SIGHT of Jesus with his eyes,

34. (C. M.) 5S./4L.
Grace inexhaustible.

1 JEHOVAH'S grace, how full, how free!

35. (C. M.)
Love is a Flower in Grace.

1 THE finest flow'r that ever blow'd,
    Open'd on Calv'ry's tree,
When Jesus' blood in rivers flow'd,
    For love of worthless me!

2 Its deepest hue, its richest smell,
    No mortal can declare
Nor can the tongue of angels tell
    How bright the colours are.

3 On Canaan's banks, supremely fair,
    This flow'r of glory blooms,
Transplanted to its native air,
    And all the shores perfumes.

4 And soon on yonder banks above,
    Shall ev'ry blossom here
Appear a full-blown flow'r of love,
    Like him, transplanted there.

36. (L. M.)
Free Grace, or the Loving-kindness of the Love.

1 AWAKE, my soul, in joyful lays,
    And sing thy great Redeemer's praise:
He justly claims a song from me,
His loving-kindness, O how free!

2 He saw me ruin'd in the fall,
Yet lov'd me notwithstanding all:
He sav'd me from my lost estate,
His loving-kindness, O how great!

3 Though num'rous hosts of mighty foes,
Though earth and hell my way oppose,
He safely leads my soul along,
His loving-kindness, O how strong!

4 When trouble, like a gloomy cloud,
Has gather'd thick, and thunder'd loud,
He near my soul has always stood,
His loving-kindness, O how good!

5 Often I feel my sinful heart
Prone from my Jesus to depart:
But though I have him oft forgot,
His loving-kindness changes not.

6 Soon shall I pass the gloomy vale,
Soon all my mortal pow'rs must fail:
O! may my last expiring breath
His loving-kindness sing in death.

7 Then let me mount and soar away
To the bright world of endless days;
And sing, with rapture and surprise,
His loving-kindness in the skies.

37. (C. M.)
Free Grace Displayed on the Cross.

1 AS on the cross the Saviour hung,
    And wept, and bled, and dy'd,
He pour'd salvation on a wretch,
    That languish'd at his side.

2 His crimes, with inward grief and shame,
    The penitent confess'd;
Then turn'd his dying eyes to Christ,
    And thus his pray'r address'd:

3 Jesus, thou Son and heir of heav'n!
    'Thou spotless Lamb of God!
'I see thee, bath'd in sweat and tears,
    'And welt'ring in thy blood.

4 'Yet quickly from these scenes of woe
    'In triumph thou shalt rise,

'Burst through the gloomy shades of death,
'And shine above the skies.
5 'Amid the glories of that world,
'Dear Saviour, think on me,
'And in the vict'ries of thy death
'Let me a sharer be.'
6 His pray'r the dying Jesus hears,
And instantly replies,
'To-day thy parting soul shall be
'With me in Paradise.'

38. (L. M.) 5S./4L.
Grace and Works Contrasted.

1 SELF-RIGHTEOUS souls on works rely,

39. (L. M.) 3S./4L.
Grace Displayed in Regeneration.

1 'TIS not the nat'ral birth of man,

40. (C. M.) 4S./4L.
Gracious Operations, Sovereign and Free.

1 THE blessed Spirit, like the wind,

41. (L. M.) 4S./4L.
The same.

1 ETERNAL Spirit! we confess

42. (L. M.) 5S./4L.
Grace, Justice, and Truth, Harmonized.

1 INFINITE grace! and can it be

43. (L. M.) 6S./4L.
Grace, Sovereign and Free.

1 DIFFUSE thy beams, and teach my heart,

44. (L. M.) 5S./4L.
Grace in Christ before the World began.

1 EXPAND my soul, arise and sing

45. (C. M.) 2S./4L.
Grace, Reigning in Election.

1 ELECTION! 'tis a joyful sound

46. (L. M.) 4S./4L.
Grace in Calling and Election.

1 THERE is a period known to God,

47. (C. M.) 4S./4L.
The same.

1 HOW vast the benefits divine!

48. (L. M.) 4S./4L.
Gospel-Grace, a Joyful Sound.

1 COME dearest Lord, who reigns above,

49. (S. M.)
Grace, a Charming Sound

1 GRACE! 'tis a charming sound!
Harmonious to the ear!
Heaven with the echo shall resound!
And all the earth shall hear.
2 Grace first contriv'd the way
To save rebellious man;
And all the steps *that* grace display
Which drew the wond'rous plan.
[3 Grace first inscrib'd my name
In God's eternal book:
'Twas grace that gave me to the Lamb,
Who all my sorrows took.]
4 Grace led my roving feet,
To tread the heav'nly road:
And new supplies each hour I meet,
While pressing on to God.
5 Grace all the work shall crown,
Thro' everlasting days;
It lays in heaven the topmost stone,
And well deserves the praise.

50. (C. M.) 4S./4L.
The Mysteries of Grace all explained in Heaven.

1 GREAT God of Providence! thy ways

51. (C. M.) 2S./4L.
All Means Vain without Free Grace.

1 IN vain Apollo's silver tongue,

52. (S. M.) 4S./4L.
Dependence on Grace.

1 TO keep the lamp alive,

53. (C. M.) 10S./4L.
Pharisaical Pride and the Humility of Gracious Men contrasted.

1 WHAT makes mistaken men afraid

54. (L. M.) 5S./4L.
Free Salvation.

1 LONG ere the sun began his days,

55. (C. M.) 6S./4L.
Truth and Grace.

1 WHEN first the God of boundless grace

Hymn Texts From *The Cluster*

56. (L. M.) 4S./4L.
Grace Excites to Prayer.

1 THE soul that's truly born of God

CHRIST CRUCIFIED.

---

57. (8, 8, 6.) 5S./6L.
A View of Christ on the Cross.

1 AS near to Calvary I pass,

58. (6's, 8's.) Lenox.
The Blood and Worth of Christ set forth in the Types.

1 ISRAEL in ancient days,
   Not only had a view
Of Sinai in a blaze,
   But learn'd the Gospel too:
The types and figures were a glass
In which they saw the Saviour's face.

2 The paschal sacrifice,
   And blood-besprinkled door,
Seen with enlighten'd eyes,
   And once apply'd with power,
Would teach the need of other blood,
To reconcile an angry God.

3 The Lamb, the Dove, set forth
   His perfect innocence.
Whose blood of matchless worth,
   Should be the soul's defence!
For he who can for sin atone,
Must have no failings of his own.

4 The scape-goat on his head,
   The people's trespass bore,
And to the desert led,
   Was to be seen no more:
In him our surety seem'd to say,
"Behold, I bear your sins away."

5 Dipp'd in his fellow's blood,
   The living bird went free;
The type, well understood,
   Express'd the sinner's plea;
Describ'd a guilty soul enlarg'd,
And by a Saviour's death discharg'd.

6 Jesus, I love to trace
   Throughout the sacred page,
The footsteps of thy grace,
   The same in ev'ry age.
O grant that I may faithful be
To clearer light vouchsaf'd to me!

59. (7, 6.) 4S./8L.
A sight of Christ on the Cross, breaks the Heart.

1 JESUS drinks the bitter cup,

60. (P. M.)
The Death of Christ entertains the darkest hours.

1 I'M tir'd of visits, modes and forms,
   And flatt'ry paid to fellow worms,
      Their conversation cloys;
   Their vain delights and empty stuff:
   But I can ne'er enjoy enough
      Of thy sweet company, my Lord,
      Thou life of all my joys.

2 When he begins to tell his love,
   Through every vein my passions move,
      The captives of his tongue;
   In midnight shades, on frosty ground,
   I could attend the pleasing sound,
   Nor should I feel December's cold,
      Nor think the darkness long.

3 There while I hear my Saviour God
   Count o'er the sins (a heavy load)
      He bore upon the tree,
   Inward I blush with secret shame,
   And weep, and love, and bless the name
   That knew not grief nor guilt his own,
      But bore it all for me.

4 Next he describes the thorns he wore,
   And talks his bloody passions o'er,
      Till I am drown'd in tears:
   Yet with a sympathetic smart,
   There's a strange joy beats round my heart
   The cursed tree has blessings in't,
      My sweetest balm it bears.

5 I hear the glorious sufferer tell,
   How on the cross he vanquish'd hell,
      And all the pow'rs beneath;
   Transported and inspir'd my tongue
   Attempts his triumph in a song:
   How hath the serpent lost his sting,
      And where's thy victory death?

6 But when he shows his hands, his heart,
   And those dear prints of dying smart,
      He sets my soul on fire;
   Not the beloved John could rest
   With more delight upon that breast,
   Nor Thomas pry into those wounds
      With more intense desire.

7 Kindly he opens me his ear,
   And bids me pour my sorrows there,
      And tell him all my pains;
   Thus while I ease my burthen'd heart,
   In ev'ry woe he bears a part:

His arms embrace me, and his hand
My drooping head sustains.

61. (8, 6.) 4S./6L.
Complete Atonement.

1 FROM whence this fear and unbelief?

62. (7's.) 6S./6L.
Gethsemane.

1 MANY woes had Christ endur'd,

63. (6's.) 5S./8L.
Look on Him, and Mourn.

1 MY Lord, my Saviour died,

64. (5's.) 6S./8L.
The Fountain of Cleansing.

1 THE Fountain of *Christ*,

65. (8, 7.)
It is finished.

1 HARK! the voice of love and mercy
  Sounds aloud from Calvary!
See! it rends the rocks asunder,
  Shakes the earth and veils the sky!
"It is finish'd!"
Hear the dying Saviour cry.

2 It is finish'd! O what pleasure
  Do these charming words afford!
Heav'nly blessings without measure,
  Flow to us from *Christ the Lord.*
It is finish'd!
Saints the dying words record.

3 Finish'd, all the types and shadows
  Of the ceremonial law!
Finish'd, all that *God* had promis'd:
  Death and hell no more shall awe.
It is finish'd!
Saints from hence your comfort draw.

[4 Happy souls approach the table,
  Taste the soul-reviving food;
Nothing half so sweet and pleasant
  As the Saviour's flesh and blood,
It is finish'd!
Christ has borne the heavy load.]

5 Tune your harps anew ye seraphs,
  Join to sing the pleasing theme;
All on earth and all in heaven,
  Join to praise Immanuel's name.
Hallelujah!
Glory to the bleeding Lamb!

66. (7, 6.) 5S./8L.
Christ Crucified the noblest theme.

1 VAIN, delusive world, adieu!

67. (P. M.) 7S./6L.
The Love of Christ inexplainable.

1 O GOD of all grace,

68. (P. M.) 6S./9L.
The Sufferings and Death of Christ.

1 THE Son of man they did betray,

69. (9, 8.)
The Sorrows of Christ recounted.

1 COME all ye skilful souls in weeping,
  Come join with me to weep and mourn,
To see the man of constant sorrows,
  Abus'd, forsaken, and forlorn:
The foxes they have holes prepared,
  And birds of air have pleasant nests;
But Christ the Son of man worse fared,
  He had nowhere to go to rest.

2 Behold him in cold mountains praying,
  He spent whole nights in prayer and praise;
He was with grief and tears acquainted,
  He went a mourner all his days:
Behold him in the garden lying,
  His soul in floods of sorrow drown'd,
And the large bloody sweat a running,
  In trickling drops down to the ground.

3 Behold him when the soldiers took him,
  And led him unto Pilate's bar,
His own disciples then forsook him,
  O Christians, come and drop a tear.
Behold him when he was condemned,
  In a *mock-robe* and thorny crown,
And see his tender temples pierced,
  Until the blood came trickling down.

4 Behold him when the soldiers scourg'd him,
  And put his soul to torturing pain,
See how with knotty whips they lash'd him,
  Until the naked bones were seen.
O who is this, that comes from Bozrah,
  With dyed garments all o'er red;
And whose apparel is all stained,
  Like those who in the wine-press tread?

5 He did not hide his face from spitting,
  Nor cheeks from those who pluck'd the hair,
Come all ye tender-hearted Christians,
  O come and help me drop a tear:
He gave his back unto the smiter,
  Who plough'd long furrows in the same,
And lo, his visage, was more marred,
  Than any of the sons of men.

6 Behold him on the cross a bleeding,
   His soul in keenest agony!
  The glittering sun forsook his shining,
   And blush'd this mournful sight to see;
  The flinty rocks were burst asunder,
   When Christ the Lamb gave up the ghost;
  And then the earth did quake and tremble,
   And many of the dead came forth.

7 They laid him in a new sepulchre,
   Where man was never laid before;
  He burst the bands of death, asunder,
   And brought salvation to the poor.
  Behold him pleading for poor sinners,
   Close at his heavenly Father's side,
  And when stern justice cries against them,
   Says *"Father, spare them, I have died."*

70. (8's.) 8S./8.L
The Sorrows of Christ a Lovely Story.

1 A STORY most lovely I'll tell,

71. (8, 7.)
The Sufferings of Christ in Gethsemane.

1 GREAT high priest, we view thee stooping,
   With our names upon thy breast;
  In the garden groaning, drooping,
   To the ground with sorrow prest.

2 Weeping Angels stood confounded,
   To behold their Maker thus;
  And can we remain unwounded,
   When we know 'twas all for us?

3 On the cross thy body broken
   Cancels ev'ry penal tie;
  Tempted souls, produce the token
   All demands to satisfy.

4 All is finish'd do not doubt it,
   But believe your dying Lord,
  Never reason more about it,
   Only take him at his word.

5 Lord, we fain would trust thee solely,
   'Twas for us thy blood was spilt;
  Praised bride-groom, take us wholly,
   Take and make us what thou wilt.

6 Thou has borne the bitter sentence
   Past on man's devoted race:—
  True belief and true repentance,
   Are thy gifts thou God of grace.

72. (8, 8, 6.)
Do this in Remembrance of Me.

1 THE table spread, my-soul there spies
   The victim bleed, the Saviour dies—
    In anguish on the tree!
  I hear his dying groans! I prove
  His bleeding heart, his dying love!
    He dy'd, my soul, for thee.

2 The table's spread—the royal food
  Is Jesus' sacred flesh and blood;
    A feast of love divine:
  His bleeding heart! his dying groans!
  His sacred blood for sin atones—
    Atones, my soul, for thine.

3 The feast is spread with bleeding hands,
  Bedew'd with blood, and lo, it stands
    To fill the hungry mind:
  'Tis free, and whosoever will,
  May feast his soul, and drink his fill,
    And grace and glory find.

4 Whilst at the table sits the King,
  Raptur'd with joy, my soul shall sing,
    With an immortal flame:
  My Saviour's grace I'll still adore,
  With joy I'll love him more and more,
    And bless his sacred name.

5 O sacred flesh! O solemn feast!
  When Christ my Lord, the royal guest,
    Is at his table found:
  This adds new glories to my joy—
  It bids me sing, and well I may,
    It makes my bliss abound.

6 'Tis thus my soul by faith is fed,
  On angels' food, with living bread,
    And manna from above:
  On sacred flesh, on dying blood
  I feast till I am full of God,
    And drink the wine of love.

7 It is an early antipast,
  Of heav'nly bliss it is a taste,
    A taste on earthly ground:
  If here so sweet, if here we prove
  Seraphic joy, celestial love,
    In heav'n what will be found?

73. (C. M.)
The Deity, Incarnation and Death of Christ.

1 EARTH has engross'd my love too long;
   'Tis time I lift mine eyes
  Upward, dear Father, to thy throne,
   And to my native skies.

2 There the blest man, my Saviour sits;
   The God how bright he shines?
  And scatters infinite delights
   On all the happy minds.

3 Seraphs with elevated strains,
   Circle the throne around;
  And move and charm the starry plains,
   With an immortal sound.

4 Jesus, the Lord, their harps employs;
    Jesus, my love, they sing:
    Jesus, the life of both our joys,
    Sounds sweet from every string.
[5 Hark, how beyond the narrow bounds
    Of time and space they run;
    And echo in majestic sounds
    The Godhead of the Son!
6 And now they sink the lofty tune,
    And gentler notes they play,
    And bring the Father's Equal down
    To dwell in humble clay.
7 O sacred beauties of the MAN!
    (The GOD resides within:)
    His flesh all pure without a stain;
    His soul without a sin.
8 But when to *Calvary* they turn,
    Silent their harps abide;
    Suspended songs, a moment mourn
    The God that lov'd and died.
9 Then all at once, to living strains
    They summon ev'ry chord;
    Tell how he triumph'd o'er his pains,
    And chant the rising Lord.]
10 Now let me mount and join their song,
    And be an angel too:
    My heart, my hand, my ear, my tongue,
    Here's joyful work for you.
11 I would begin the music here,
    And so my soul should rise,
    O for some heavenly notes to bear
    My passions to the skies!
12 There ye that love my Saviour sit;
    There I would fain have place,
    Among your thrones, or at your feet,
    So I might see his face.

74. (8, 7.) 4S./4L.
Gazing on the Cross.

1 SWEET the moments, rich in blessing,

75. (8. 7.)
The Brazen Serpent—Type of Christ.

1 WHEN the chosen tribes debated
    'Gainst their God, as hardly treated,
    And complain'd their hopes were spilt:
    God for murm'ring to requite them,
    Fiery serpents sent to bite them,
    Lively type of deadly guilt.
2 Stung by these they soon repented:
    And their God as soon relented.
    Moses pray'd; He answer gave:
    "Serpents are the beasts that strike them;
    "Make of brass a serpent like them:
    "That's the way I choose to save."

3 Vain was bandage, oil, or plaster:
    Rankling venom kill'd the faster;
    Till the serpent Moses took,
    Rear'd it high, that all might view it,
    Bid the bitten look up to it:
    Life attended ev'ry look.
4 Jesus thus, for sinners smitten,
    Wounded, bruised, serpent-bitten,
    To his cross directs their faith.
    Why should I then poison cherish?
    Why despair of cure, and perish?
    Look, my soul, tho' stung to death.
5 Thine's (alas!) a lost condition;
    Works cannot work thee remission,
    Nor thy goodness do thee good:
    Death's within thee, all about thee:
    But the remedy's without thee:
    See it in thy Saviour's blood.
6 See the Lord of glory dying!
    See him gasping! Hear him crying!
    See his burden'd bosom heave!
    Look, ye sinners, ye that hung him;
    Look, how deep your sins have stung him:
    Dying sinners, look and live.

76. (8, 8, 6.) 4S./6L.
Christ Crucified.

1 IS this my Jesus, this my God,

77. (C. M.) 4S./4L.
Christ's Death and Victory.

1 I SING my Saviour's wond'rous death;

78. (C. M.) 3S./4L.
Pardon brought to our senses.

1 LORD, how divine thy comforts are,

79. (C. M.)
Christ on the Cross, Dying.

1 BEHOLD the Saviour of mankind,
    Nail'd to the shameful tree!
    How vast that love, that him inclin'd
    To bleed and die for thee!
2 Hark, how he groans! while nature shakes,
    And earth's strong pillars bend;
    The temple-veil asunder breaks,
    The solid marbles rend.
3 'Tis done! the precious ransom's paid,
    "Receive my soul," he cries:
    See how he bows his sacred head—
    He bows his head and dies!
4 But soon he"ll break death's iron chain,
    And in full glory shine;
    O Lamb of God! was ever pain,
    Was ever love like thine?

Hymn Texts From *The Cluster*

80. (L. M.) 4S./4L.
Remembrance of Christ.

1 HIGH on a throne my Lord doth sit,

81. (S. M.) 4S./4L.
Desiring to Live before the Cross.

1 UP! haste to Calvary!

82. (L. M.) 3S./4L.
Gratitude for Christ's Sufferings.

1 TO Him who on the fatal tree

83. (C. M.) 4S./4L.
My Flesh and Blood is Meat indeed.

1 GREAT God, we now surround thy board,

84. (C. M.) 5S./4L.
Take, eat; this is my Body.

1 THE blest memorials of thy grief,

85. (L. M.)
The Lord's Supper Instituted.

1 'TWAS on that dark, that doleful night,
When pow'rs of earth and hell arose
Against the Son of God's delight,
And friends betray'd him to his foes.

2 Before the mournful scene began,
He took the bread, and blest, and brake:
What love through all his actions ran!
What wond'rous words of grace he spake!

3 "This is my body broke for sin;
Receive, and eat the living food:"
Then took the cup and blest the wine:
"Tis the new cov'nant in my blood."

86. (L. M.) 4S./4L.
Christ gave himself for us.

1 JESUS for us with nails was torn,

87. (C. M.)
The Dying Love of Jesus.

1 HOW condescending and how kind
Was God's eternal Son!
Our mis'ry reach'd his heav'nly mind,
And pity brought him down.

2 This was compassion like a God,
That when the Saviour knew
The price of pardon was his blood,
His pity ne'er withdrew.

3 Now, though he reigns exalted high,
His love is still as great:
Well he remembers Calvary,
Nor lets his saints forget.

4 Here let our hearts begin to melt,
While we his death record,
And, with our joy for pardon'd guilt,
Mourn that we pierc'd the Lord.

88. (C. M.) 5S./4L.
Divine Love makes the sweetest Feast.

1 HOW sweet and awful is the place,

89. (L. M.)
Glory in the Cross.

1 AT thy command, our dearest Lord,
Here we attend thy dying feast;
Thy blood, like wine, adorns thy board,
And thine own flesh, feeds every guest.

2 Our faith adores thy bleeding love,
And trusts for life in one that died:
We hope for heav'nly crowns above,
From a Redeemer crucifi'd.

3 Let the vain world pronounce it shame,
And fling their scandals in thy cause;
We come to boast our Saviour's name,
And make our triumphs in his cross.

4 With joy we tell the scoffing age,
He that was dead has left the tomb;
He lives above their utmost rage;
And we'are waiting till he come.

90. (C. M.) 4S./4L.
Grace and Glory, by the Death of Christ.

1 SITTING around our Father's board,

91. (C. M.)
Welcome to the Table.

1 THIS is the feast of heav'nly wine,
And God invites to sup;
The juices of the living vine,
Were press'd to fill the cup.

2 O, bless the Saviour, ye who eat,
With royal dainties fed:
Not heav'n affords a costlier treat,
For JESUS is the bread!

3 The vile, the lost—he calls to them;
"Ye trembling souls, appear!
"The righteous in their own esteem,
"Have no acceptance here.

4 "Approach, ye poor, nor dare refuse
"The banquet spread for you:"
Dear Saviour, this is welcome news,
Then I may venture too.

5 If guilt and sin afford a plea,
And may obtain a place;

Surely the Lord will welcome me,
And I shall see his face.

92. (C. M.) Repentance.
Repentance at the Cross.

1 OH, if my soul was form'd for woe,
How would I vent my sighs!
Repentance should like rivers flow
From both my streaming eyes.

2 'Twas for my sins, my dearest Lord
Hung on the cursed tree,
And groan'd away a dying life
For thee, my soul, for thee.

3 O, how I hate those lusts of mine
That crucify'd my God;
Those sins that pierc'd and nail'd his flesh
Fast to the fatal wood!

4 Yes, my Redeemer, they shall die;
My heart hath so decreed;
Nor will I spare the guilty things,
That made my Saviour bleed.

5 Whilst, with a melting broken heart,
My murder'd Lord I view,
I'll raise revenge against my sins,
And slay the murd'rers too.

93. (S. M.) Warren.
The Spirit witnesses to the Water and the Blood.

1 LET all our tongues be one,
To praise our God on high,
Who from his bosom sent his Son,
To fetch us, strangers, nigh.

2 Nor let our voices cease
To sing the Saviour's name;
Jesus, th' Ambassador of peace,
How cheerfully he came.

3 It cost him cries and tears
To bring us near to God;
Great was our debt, and he appears,
To make the payment good.

4 Look up, my soul, to him,
Whose death was thy desert,
And humbly view the living stream
Flow from his breaking heart.

5 Thus the Redeemer came,
By water and by blood;
And when the Spirit speaks the same,
We feel his witness good.

94. (C. M.) Lebanon.
The Love of Christ, in Death, to Sinners, typified in David.

1 BEHOLD the love, the gen'rous love,
That holy David shows:
Behold his kind compassion move
For his afflicted foes.

2 How did his flowing tears condole,
As for a brother dead!
And fasting mortified his soul,
While for their life he pray'd.

3 They groan'd, and curs'd him on their bed,
Yet still he pleads and mourns;
And double blessings on his head
The righteous God returns.

4 O glorious type of heav'nly grace!
Thus Christ the Lord appears;
While sinners curse, the Saviour prays,
And pities them with tears.

5 He, the true David, Israel's King,
Blest and belov'd of God,
To save us rebels, dead in sin,
Paid his own dearest blood.

95. (C. M.)
Christ Crucified, the burden of the Song.

1 THOU dear Redeemer, dying Lamb,
We love to hear of thee;
No musick's like thy charming name;
Nor half so sweet can be.

2 O let us ever hear thy voice,
In mercy to us speak,
And in our Priest we will rejoice,
Thou great Melchisedeck,

3 Our Jesus shall be still our theme,
While in this world we stay;
We'll sing our Jesus' lovely name,
When all things else decay.

4 When we appear in yonder cloud,
With all thy favour'd throng,
Then we will sing more sweet more loud,
And Christ shall be our song.

96. (C. M.) 9S./4L.
Ignatius going to the Stake, cry'd "My Love was Crucified."

1 WARM was his heart, his faith was strong,

97. (L. M.) 8S./4L.
Christ on the Cross in Dying Agonies.

1 SEE, on the mount of Calvary,

98. (L. M.) 4S./4L.
The Wonderous Effects of the Death of Christ.

1 BEHOLD, the blind their sight receive!

99. (L. M.) 2S./4L.
The Request of one Saved by Blood.

1 THOU, who for sinners once was slain,

100. (S. M.) 4S./4L.
Christ Crucified is the Bread of Life.

1 BEHOLD the gift of God!

101. (C. M.) 4S./4L.
At the Lord's Table there is room.

1 THE King of heaven his table spreads,

102. (C. M.)
The same.

1 YE wretched, hungry, starving poor,
Behold a royal feast!
Where mercy spreads her bounteous store,
For ev'ry humble guest.

2 See Jesus stands with open arms;
He calls, he bids you come!
Guilt holds you back, and fear alarms,
But see there yet is room!

3 O come, and with his children taste
The blessings of his love:
While hope attends the sweet repast
Of nobler joys above.

4 There, with united heart and voice,
Before th'eternal throne,
Ten thousand thousand souls rejoice,
In ecstacies unknown.

103. (C. M.) 4S./4L.
Christ the Sweetest Theme.

1 JESUS! in thy transporting name,

104. (C. M.)
Christ Crucified is Meat and Drink indeed.

1 LORD, at thy table I behold
The wonders of thy grace;
But most of all admire, that I
Should find a welcome place.

2 I that am all defil'd with sin,
A rebel to my God;
I that have crucify'd his Son,
And trampled on his blood.

3 What strange surprising grace is this,
That such a soul has room!
My Saviour takes me by the hand—
My Jesus bids me come.

4 Eat, O my friends, the Saviour cries,
The feast was made for you;
For you I groan'd, and bled, and dy'd,
And rose, and triumph'd too.

105. (P. M.) Crucifixion.
The Sufferings, Death, Ascension, and Mediation of Christ.

1 SAW ye my Saviour? saw ye my Saviour?
Saw ye my Saviour and God?
Oh! he dy'd on Calvary, to atone for you and me,
And to purchase our pardon with blood!

2 He was extended, he was extended—
Painfully nail'd to the cross!
'Till he bow'd his head and dy'd; Thus my Lord was crucify'd
To atone for my soul that was lost!

3 Jesus hung bleeding; Jesus hung bleeding—
Three dreadful hours in pain!
While the sun refus'd to shine, when the Majesty divine
Was derided, insulted and slain!

4 Darkness prevailed, darkness prevailed,
Darkness prevail'd o'er the land!
O the solid rocks were rent, thro' creation's vast extent,
When the Jews crucify'd the God-man!

5 When it was finish'd, when it was finish'd,
And the atonement was made,
He was taken by the great, and embalm'd in spices sweet,
With the rich in the grave softly laid.

6 Hail mighty Saviour! Hail mighty Saviour!
Prince and the author of Peace:

Bursting all the bars of Death, Triumph-
  ing o'er hell and earth,
Thou ascendest to mansions of bliss.
7 There interceding, there interceding,
  Pleading that sinners might live:
Saying Father, I have dy'd, (Oh! Behold
  my hands and side)
"To redeem them, I pray them forgive."
8 "I will forgive them, I will forgive them,"
  Says the kind Father to thee;
"Let them now return to thee, and be
  reconcil'd to me,
"And eternally sav'd they shall be."

THE GLORIES OF CHRIST.

106. (C. M.)
Mortals invited to unite with Angels in Song.

1 MORTALS awake, with angels join,
    And chant the solemn lay;
  Joy, love, and gratitude, combine
    'To hail th' auspicious day.
2 In heav'n the rapt'rous song began,
    And sweet seraphic fire
  Through all the shining legions ran,
    And strung and tun'd the lyre.
3 Swift through the vast expanse it flew,
    And loud the echo roll'd;
  The theme, the song, the joy was new
    'Twas more than heav'n could hold.
4 Down through the portals of the sky
    Th' impetuous torrent ran:
  And angels flew with eager joy,
    To bear the news to man.
[5 Wrapt in the silence of the night
    Lay all the eastern world,
  When bursting, glorious, heav'nly light
    The wond'rous scene unfurl'd.]
6 Hark! the cherubic armies shout,
    And glory leads the song;
  Good-will and peace are heard throughout
    Th' harmonious heav'nly throng.
[7 O for a glance of heav'nly love,
    Our hearts and songs to raise,
  Sweetly to bear our souls above,
    And mingle with their lays!]
8 With joy the chorus we'll repeat,
    "Glory to God on high!
  "Good-will and peace are now complete;
    "Jesus was born to die."

9 Hail, Prince of Life! for ever hail,
    Redeemer, brother, friend!
  Tho' earth, and time, and life should fail,
    Thy praise shall never end.

107. (6, 4.) Delight.
Angels Invoked to Join with Mortals in Song.

1 O YE immortal throng,
    Of Angels round the throne,
  Join with our feeble song
    To make the Saviour known;
      On earth ye knew
      His wond'rous grace,
      His beauteous face
      In heaven ye view.
2 Ye saw the heaven-born child
    In human flesh array'd;
  Benevolent and mild,
    While in the manger laid;
      And praise to God,
      And peace on earth,
      For such a birth,
      Proclaim aloud.
3 Ye in the wilderness
    Beheld the tempter spoil'd,
  Well known in every dress,
    In every combat foil'd;
      And joy'd to crown
      The victor's head,
      When Satan fled
      Before his frown.
4 Around the bloody tree
    Ye press'd with strong desire,
  That wond'rous sight to see,
    The Lord of life expire;
      And could your eyes
      Have known a tear
      Had dropp'd it there
      In sad surprise.
5 Around his sacred tomb
    A willing watch you keep:
  Till the blest moment come
    To rouse him from his sleep:
      Then roll'd the stone,
      And all ador'd
      Your rising Lord,
      With joy unknown.
6 When all array'd in light,
    The shining conqueror rode,
  Ye hail'd his rapturous flight
    Up to the throne of God;
      And wav'd around
      Your golden wings,
      And struck your strings,
      Of sweetest sound.

Hymn Texts From *The Cluster*

7 The warbling notes pursue,
    And louder anthems raise;
While mortals sing with you
    Their *own* Redeemer's praise;
    And thou my heart,
    With equal flame,
    And joy the same,
    Perform thy part.

108. (8, 7.) 7S./8L.
Christ's Birth Celebrated.

1 LET us all with grateful praises

109. (6, 8.) Lenox,
The Birth of Christ hailed.

1 AWAKE, awake, arise,
    And hail the glorious morn;
Hark! how the angels sing,
    "To you a Saviour's born:"
Now let our hearts in concert move,
And ev'ry tongue be tun'd to love.

2 He mortals came to save
    From sin's tyrannic pow'r:
Come, with the angels sing,
    At this auspicious hour:
Let ev'ry heart and tongue combine,
To praise the love, the grace divine.

3 The prophecies and types
    Are all this day fulfill'd;
With eastern sages join,
    To praise this wond'rous child:
God's only Son is come to bless
The earth with peace and righteousness.

4 Glory to God on high,
    For our Immanuel's birth!
To mortal men good will,
    And peace and joy on earth!
With angels now we will repeat
Their songs, still new and ever sweet.

110. (C. M.) Sherburn.
The Song of Angels at the Birth of Christ.

1 WHILE shepherds watch'd their flocks by night
    All seated on the ground,
The angel of the Lord came down,
    And glory shone around.

2 "Fear not," said he, (for mighty dread
    Had seiz'd their troubled mind,)
"Glad tidings of great joy I bring
    "To you and all mankind.

3 "To you in David's town, this day
    "Is born of David's line,
"The Saviour, who is Christ the Lord,
    "And this shall be the sign:

4 "The heavenly babe you there shall find
    "To human view display'd;
"All meanly wrapt in swathing bands
    "And in a manger laid."

5 Thus spake the seraph, and forthwith
    Appear'd a shining throng
Of angels, praising God, and thus
    Address'd their joyful song:

6 "All glory be to God on high!
    "And to the earth be peace!
"Good-will henceforth from heaven to men.
    "Begin and never cease!"

111. (C. M.) 8S./4L.
The Same.

1 SHEPHERDS! rejoice, lift up your eyes

112. (L. M.) 13S./4L.
The Glories of Immanuel.

1 HAIL! God the Father, eternal light,

113. (8, 7.)
Christ's Love, the noblest Passion.

1 LISTED into the cause of sin,
    Why should a good be evil?
Music, alas! too long has been
    Press'd to obey the devil:
Drunken, or lewd, or light the lay
    Flows to the soul's undoing,
Widens, and strews with flow'rs, the way
    Down to eternal ruin.

2 Who on the part of God will rise,
    Innocent mirth recover,
Fly on the prey, and take the prize,
    Plunder the carnal lover;
Strip him of every moving strain,
    Of ev'ry melting measure,
Music in virtue's cause regain,
    Revive the holy pleasure.

3 Come let us try if Jesus' love
    Will not as well inspire us:
This is the theme of those above,
    This upon earth should fire us,
Say are your hearts in tune to sing,
    Is there a subject greater?
Melody all her strains may bring,
    Jesus's name is sweeter.

4 Jesus the soul of music is,
    His is the noblest passion:
Jesus's name gives life and peace,
    Happiness and salvation.
Jesus's name the dead can raise,
    And shew our sins foregiven,

Fill us with all the life of grace,
  Carry us up to heaven.
5 Who has a right like us to sing,
  Us, whom his mercy raises:
Merry our hearts, for Christ is king;
  And merry all our voices:
Who of his love does once partake,
  He in his god rejoices;
Melody in our hearts we make,
  And melody with our voices.
6 He that a sprinkled conscience hath,
  He that in God is merry,
Let him sing psalms, the Spirit saith,
  Joyful and never weary;
Offer the sacrifice of praise,
  Hearty and never ceasing,
Spiritual songs and anthems raise,
  Worship and thanks, and blessing.
7 Come let us in his praises join,
  Triumph in his salvation;
Glory ascribe to love divine,
  Worship and adoration.
Heaven already is begun,
  Open'd in each believer:
Only believe, and then sing on,
  Heaven is ours forever.

114. (7, 6.)
Desiring to see Jesus.

1 O SIR, we would see Jesus,
  The blessed prince of love;
He only can relieve us,
  And all our griefs remove.
O tell us as a preacher,
  Where Jesus Christ doth dwell,
Describe his charming feature,
  His glowing beauties tell.
2 O Sir, we would see Jesus,
  The sinner's constant friend,
We know he won't deceive us,
  But love us to the end:
His blessed word assures us,
  His hidden ones shall stand,
His mighty arm secures us,
  From all the hostile band.
3 O Sir, we would see Jesus,
  The glorious King of grace,
A sight of him would ease us,
  And fill our souls with peace:
We would behold his beauty,
  And run into his arms,
And learn the christian's duty,
  Amidst those blessed charms.

4 O Sir, we would see Jesus,
  As Prophet, Priest, and King;
We hope he will receive us,
  Though we are poor and mean:
For in the holy scriptures,
  This sacred truth we find,
He saves such wretched creatures,
  Of meek and lowly mind.
5 O Sir, we would see Jesus,
  And at his feet adore,
His ways although mysterious,
  We humbly would explore.
O tell us how to find him,
  And how we may find him,
  And how we may him know,
Where does this *rose* of Sharon,
  This spotless *lilly* grow?
6 O Sir, we would see Jesus,
  And hearken to his voice,
O this would greatly please us,
  And make our hearts rejoice:
This sound is so inviting,
  It brings the dead to life;
This sound is so transporting,
  It ends the sinner's strife.
7 O Sir, we would see Jesus,
  Descending from above,
And making up his jewels,
  The objects of his love:
The sun and moon in mourning,
  The stars of heaven fall,
The awful trumpet sounding,
  The universal call.
8 O Sir, we would see Jesus,
  On that great burning day,
Collecting all his children,
  To carry them away,
Unto their seats in glory,
  Forever there to sing,
And tell the blessed story
  Of Jesus Christ their King.

115. (P. M.)
Christ All in All

1 CHRIST is the eternal *rock*,
  On which his church is built!
The *Shepherd* of his little flock;
  The *Lamb* that took our guilt;
Our *counsellor;* our *guide;*
  Our *brother;* and our *friend;*
The *bridegroom* of his chosen bride,
  Who loves her to the end.

Hymn Texts From *The Cluster*

2 He is the *Son* to free;
   The *Bishop* he to bless;
  The full *propitiation* he;
   The Lord our *righteousness;*
  His body's glorious *head;*
   Our *advocate* that pleads;
  Our *priest* that pray'd, aton'd, and bled,
   And ever intercedes.

3 Let all obedient souls
   Their grateful tribute bring;
  Submit to Jesus' righteous rules,
   And bow before their *King.*
  Our *prophet* Christ expounds
   His and our Father's will;
  This good *physician* cures our wounds
   With tenderness and skill.

4 When sin had sadly made
   'Twixt wrath and mercy strife;
  Our dear *Redeemer* dearly paid
   Our ransom with his life.
  Faith gives the full release;
   Our *surety* for us stood:
  The *Mediator* made the peace
   And sign'd it with his blood.

5 Soldiers, your *captain* own,
   Domestics, serve your *Lord,*
  Sinners the *Saviour's* love make known,
   Saints, hymn th' incarnate *Word;*
  The *witness* sure and true
   Of God's good will to men,
  The *Alpha* and th' *Omega* too,
   The first and last, *Amen.*

6 Poor Pilgrims shall not stray,
   Who frighten'd flee from wrath,
  A bleeding Jesus is the *way;*
   And blood tracks all the path.
  Christians in Christ obtain
   The *truth* that can't deceive;
  And never shall they die again,
   Who in the *life* believe.

116. (8's.) 5S./8L.
Christ; What think you of?

1 WHAT think you of Christ? is the test,

117. (8, 7.) 6S./6L.
Christ, the Best Friend.

1 ONE there is above all others,

118. (8's.)
Christ—the Glory of the Bible.

1 THE Bible is justly esteem'd
   The glory supreme of the land,
  Which shows how a sinner's redeem'd,
   And brought to Jehovah's right hand:
  With pleasure we freely confess,
   The Bible all books does outshine,
  But Jesus, his person and grace,
   Affords it that lustre divine.

2 In ev'ry *prophetical book*
   Where God his decrees hath unseal'd,
  With joy we behold as we look,
   The wonderful Saviour reveal'd;
  His glories project to the eye,
   And prove it was not his design,
  Those glories concealed should lie,
   But there in full majesty shine.

3 The *first gracious promise* to man,
   A blessed prediction appears;
  His work is the soul of the plan,
   And gives it the glory it wears.
  How cheering the truth must have been,
   That Jesus the promised seed,
  Should triumph o'er Satan and sin,
   And hell in captivity lead!

4 The *ancient, Levitical Law*
   Was prophesy after its kind,
  In types, there the faithful foresaw
   The Saviour that ransom'd mankind:
  The altar, the Lamb, and the priest,
   The blood that was sprinkled of old,
  Had life when the people could taste
   The blessings those shadows foretold.

5 Review each prophetical *song,*
   Which shines in perfection's rich train;
  The sweetest to Jesus belong,
   And point out his sufferings and reign:
  Sure David his harp never strung
   With more of true sacred delight,
  Than when of the Saviour he sung,
   And he was reveal'd to his sight.

6 May Jesus more precious become;
   His word be a lamp to our feet,
  While we in this wilderness roam,
   'Till brought in his presence to meet!
  Then, then will we gaze on thy face,
   Our prophet, our priest, and our king;
  Recount all thy wonders of grace,
   Thy praises eternally sing.

119. (6, 8.) Lenox.
Christ's Love above all Price.

1 COME ev'ry pious heart,
   That loves the Saviour's name,
  Your noblest powers exert
   To celebrate his fame:

Tell all above, and all below,
The debt of love to him you owe.

2 Such was his zeal for God,
    And such his love for you,
He nobly undertook
    What Gabriel could not do;
His every deed of love and grace
All worth exceeds, and thought surpass

3 He left his starry crown,
    And laid his robes aside;
On wings of love came down,
    And wept, and bled, and died;
What he endur'd, O who can tell,
To save our souls from death and hell.

4 From the dark grave he rose,
    The mansion of the dead;
And thence his mighty foes
    In glorious triumph led:
Up thro' the sky the conqueror rode,
And reigns on high, the Saviour God.

5 From thence he'll quickly come,
    His chariot will not stay,
And bear our spirits home
    To realms of endless day:
There shall we see his lovely face,
And ever be in his embrace.

6 Jesus we ne'er can pay
    The debt we owe thy love:
Yet, tell us how we may
    Our gratitude approve;
Our hearts, our all, to thee we give:
The gift, tho' small, thou wilt receive.

120. (6, 8.) Lenox.
Christ, the King of Saints.

1 REJOICE the Lord is King:
    Your God and King adore:
Mortals, give thanks and sing,
    And triumph evermore!
Lift up the heart, lift up the voice,
Rejoice aloud, ye saints rejoice.

2 Rejoice, the Saviour reigns,
    The God of truth and love;
When he had purg'd our stains,
    He took his seat above;
Lift up the heart, &c.

3 His kingdom cannot fail,
    He rules o'er earth and heaven,
The keys of death and hell
    Are to our Jesus given.
Lift up the heart, &c.

4 He all his foes shall quell,
    Shall all our sins destroy;
And every bosom swell
    With pure seraphic joy:
Lift up the heart, &c.

5 Rejoice in glorious hope,
    Jesus the Judge shall come,
And take his servants up
    To their eternal home:
We soon shall hear th' archangel's voice,
The trump of God shall sound rejoice.

121. (8's.) 5S./8L.
Christ the Chiefest among Ten Thousand.

1 HOW shall I my Saviour set forth?

122. (8's.)
Christ is Precious.

1 JESUS, how precious is thy name!
    The great Jehovah's darling thou!
O let me catch th' immortal flame,
    With which angelic bosoms glow!
Since angels love thee, I would love,
And imitate the blest above.

2 My Prophet thou, my heavenly guide;
    Thy sweet instructions I will hear;
The words that from thy lips proceed,
    O how divinely, sweet they are.
Thee my great Prophet, I would love,
And imitate the blest above.

3 My great High Priest, whose precious blood
    Did once atone upon the cross;
Who now doth intercede with God,
    And plead the friendless sinner's cause;
In thee I trust; thee I would love,
And imitate the blest above.

4 My King supreme, to thee I bow,
    A willing subject at thy feet;
All other lords I disavow,
    And to thy government submit.
My Saviour King, this heart would love,
And imitate the blest above.

123. (7's.)
Christ the Rock of Ages.

1 ROCK of ages, shelter me,
    Let me hide myself in thee!
Let the water and the blood,
From thy wounded side which flow'd,
Be of sin the double cure,
Cleanse me from its guilt and pow'r

2 Not the labour of my hands
    Can fulfil the law's demands:
Could my zeal no respite know,

Could my tears forever flow;
All for sin could not atone,
Thou must save, and thou alone.

3 Nothing in my hands I bring,
Simply to thy cross I cling;
Naked come to thee for dress,
Helpless look to thee for grace:
Black, I to the fountain fly,
Wash me, Saviour, or I die!

4 While I draw this fleeting breath,
When my eye-strings break in death,
When I soar to worlds unknown,
See thee on thy judgment throne,
Rock of ages shelter me,
Let me hide myself in thee.

124. (7, 6.)
Christ a matchless Physician.

1 HOW lost was my condition,
'Till Jesus made me whole!
There is but one Physician
Can cure a sin-sick soul.
Next door to death he found me,
And snatch'd me from the grave,
To tell to all around me
His won'drous pow'r to save.

2 The worst of all diseases,
Is light compar'd with sin:
On ev'ry part it seizes,
But rages most within;
'Tis palsy, plague, and fever,
And madness—all combin'd;
And none but a believer
The least relief can find.

3 From men, great skill professing,
I thought a cure to gain,
But this prov'd more distressing,
And added to my pain:
Some said that nothing ail'd me,
Some gave me up for lost;
Thus ev'ry refuge fail'd me,
And all my hopes were crost.

4 At length this great Physician—
How matchless is his grace!
Accepted my petition,
And undertook my case;
First gave me sight to view him—
For sin my eyes had seal'd—
Then bid me look unto him;
I look'd, and I was heal'd.

5 A dying, risen Jesus,
Seen by the eye of faith,
At once from danger frees us,
And saves the soul from death:
Come then to this Physician,
His help he'll freely give;
He makes no hard condition,
'Tis only—look and live.

125. (11's.) 9S./4L.
Christ the Rock that is higher than I.

1 CONVINC'D as a sinner, to Jesus I come,

126. (L. M.)
Christ ever lives our Intercessor.

1 "I KNOW that my Redeemer lives,"
What comfort this sweet sentence gives!
He lives, he lives, who once was dead,
He lives, my ever living HEAD!

2 He lives, to bless me with his love,
He lives, to plead my cause above,
He lives, my hungry soul to feed,
He lives, to help in time of need.

3 He lives, to give me full supplies
He lives, to bless me with his eyes,
He lives, to comfort me when faint,
He lives, to hear my soul's complaint.

4 He lives, to crush the fiends of hell,
He lives, and doth within me dwell,
He lives, to heal, and keep me whole.
He lives, to guide my feeble soul.

5 He lives, to banish all my fears,
He lives, to wipe away my tears,
He lives, to calm my troubled heart,
He lives, all blessings to impart.

6 He lives, my kind and gracious friend,
He lives, and loves me to the end:
He lives, and while he lives I'll sing,
He lives, my prophet, priest, and king.

7 He lives, all glory to his name,
He lives, my Jesus still the same:
O the sweet joy this sentence gives,
"I know that my Redeemer lives."

127. (L. M.)
Christ not to be ashamed of.

1 JESUS! and shall it ever be
A mortal man asham'd of thee?
Asham'd of thee, whom angels praise,
Whose glory shines through endless days?

2 Asham'd of Jesus! sooner far
Let evening blush to own a star;

He sheds the beams of light divine,
O'er this benighted soul of mine.
3 Asham'd of Jesus! just as soon
Let midnight be asham'd of noon;
'Tis midnight with my soul till he,
Bright morning-star! bid darkness flee.
4 Asham'd of Jesus! that dear friend
On whom my hopes of heaven depend:
No; when I blush—be this my shame
That I no more revere his name.
5 Asahm'd of Jesus! yes I may
When I've no guilt to wash away;
No tear to wipe, no good to crave,
No fear to quell, no soul to save.
6 'Till then—nor is my boasting vain;
'Till then I boast a Saviour slain!
And O may this my glory be,
That Christ is not asham'd of me!
[7 His institutions would I prize,
Take up my cross—the shame despise;
Dare to defend his noble cause,
And yield obedience to his laws.]

128. (L. M.) 4S./4L.
Christ the bright and morning Star.

1 YE worlds of light, that roll so near

129. (S. M.) 4S./4L.
Christ, the Alpha and Omega of the perfect man.

1 BEHOLD the perfect man,

130. (C. M.) 3S./4L.
Christ, the Head of the Church.

1 JESUS, I sing thy matchless grace,

131. (C. M.) 12S./4L.
Christ, the best Physician.

1 JESUS, since thou art still to-day

132. (S. M.) 4S./4L.
Christ, the Way, Truth, and Life.

1 I AM, saith Christ, *the Way:*—

133. (L. M.)
Christ, the Apple-Tree.

1 THE Tree of Life my soul hath seen,
  Laden with fruit, and always green
The trees of nature fruitless be
Compar'd with Christ the Apple-tree.
2 This beauty doth all things excel;
By faith I know, but ne'er can tell
The glory which I now can see
In Jesus Christ the Apple-tree.
3 For happiness I long have sought,
And pleasure dearly have I bought;
I miss'd of all, but now I see
'Tis found in Christ the Apple-tree.
4 I'm wearied with my former toil—
Here I will sit and rest awhile:
Under the shadow I will be
Of Jesus Christ the Apple-tree.
5 With great delight I'll make my stay,
There's none shall fright my soul away:
Among the sons of men I see
There's none like Christ the Apple-tree.
6 I'll sit, and eat this fruit divine;
It cheers my heart like precious wine:
Oh! how divinely sweet to me
Is Christ the lovely Apple-tree!
7 This fruit doth make my soul to thrive:
It keeps my dying faith alive;
Which makes my soul in haste to be
With Jesus Christ the Apple-tree.

134. (L. M.) 3S./4L.
Christ, the Corner Stone.

1 LAID by Jehovah's mighty hands,

135. (C. M.) 3S./4L.
Christ the Doer.

1 CHRIST is the way to heav'nly bliss,

136. (L. M.) 3S./4L.
Christ is Eternal Life.

1 'TIS life to know the dying Lamb;

137. (C. M.) 3S./4L.
Christ the Pearl of Great Price.

1 I'VE found the pearl of greatest price:

138. (S. M.) 2S./4L.
Christ the rose of Sharon.

1 IN Sharon's lovely Rose,

139. (L. M.)
Christ the High-way of Holiness.

1 JESUS, my all to heaven is gone,
  He whom I fix my hopes upon;
His track I see, and I'll pursue
The narrow way till him I view.
2 The way the holy prophets went,
The road that leads from banishment,
The king's highway of holiness
I'll go, for all his paths are peace.
3 This is the way I long have sought,
And mourn'd because I found it not;

My grief my burden long has been,
Because I could not cease from sin.
4 The more I strove against its pow'r,
I sinn'd and stumbled but the more;
Till late I heard my Saviour say,
"Come hither, soul, I am the way."
5 Lo! glad I come, and thou, blest Lamb,
Shalt take me to thee as I am;
My sinful self to thee I give—
Nothing but love I shall receive.
6 Then will I tell to sinners round,
What a dear Saviour I have found;
I'll point to thy redeeming blood,
And say, Behold the way to God.

140. (C. M.)
Christ the Captain of Salvation.

1 BEHOLD! the war-like trumpets blow,
    When foes in arms appear,
  To let the sons of freedom know
    The day of battle's near.

2 Christ's trumpet sounds, let saints be
      arm'd,
    The battle is begun;
  The hosts of Satan are alarm'd,
    The day will soon be won.

3 The glorious Captain, Jesus, sends
    The heralds of his might,
  To search and try who are his friends,
    And who will 'list to fight.

4 The Gospel calls for volunteers,
    Who come with sword in hand;
  Where is there one for Christ appears,
    Against the foe to stand.

5 Here's bounty-money shall be giv'n
    To all his soldiers here;
  And glorious crowns of joy in heav'n
    When Jesus shall appear.

6 Here's dress, and food, and drink, and
      arms,
    And pay, and vict'ry sure;
  This ev'ry christian solder charms,
    And makes him war endure.

7 The Captain never quits the field,
    But fights before his men;
  Until his foes are made to yield,
    Or fall among the slain.

8 His foes can neither stand nor fly,
    When he appears in sight;
  But none of those shall ever die,
    Who in his army fight.

9 Here, Lord, behold I set my name,
    A soldier I would be;
  Thy gracious promises I claim,
    And give myself to thee.

141. (S. M.) America.
Christ Glorious in Tears.

1 DID Christ o'er sinners weep,
    And shall our cheeks be dry?
  Let floods of penitential grief
    Burst forth from ev'ry eye.

2 The Son of God in tears,
    Angels with wonder see!
  Be thou astonish'd, O my soul—
    He shed those tears for thee.

3 He wept that we might weep:
    Each sin demands a tear;
  In heav'n alone no sin is found,
    And there's no weeping there.

142. (L. M.) 1S./8L.
Christ, the Sure Anchor of Hope.

1 IS Jesus mine! I'm now prepar'd
    To meet with what I thought most
      hard;
  Yes, let the winds of trouble blow,
  And comforts melt away like snow;
  No blasted trees of failing crops,
  Can hinder my eternal hopes;
  Tho' creatures change, the Lord's the
      same;
  Then let me triumph in his name.

143. (C. M.) 4S./4L.
Christ All in All.

1 CHRIST, as our great physician, heals

144. (L. M.)
The Breaker.—Mic. ii. 13.

1 SING the dear Saviour's glorious fame,
    Who bears the Breaker's wond'rous
      name:
  Sweet name! and it becomes him well,
  Who breaks down sin, guilt, death and
      hell.

2 A mighty Breaker sure is he;
  He broke my chains and set me free:
  A gracious Breaker to my soul;
  He breaks, and O, he makes me whole.

3 He breaks thro' ev'ry gloomy cloud,
  Which can my soul with darkness shroud;
  He breaks the bar of ev'ry snare,
  Which hellish foes for me prepare:

4 Great Breaker, O, thy love impart!
  Daily to break my stony heart;

O, break it Lord, and enter in,
And break, O, break the power of sin!

145. (C. M.) 4S./4L.
The Builder.

1 CHRIST plans the temple of the Lord,

146. (C. M.) 5S./4L.
Crown Him Lord of All.

1 INSPIRE our souls, thou heavenly Dove,

147. (7's.) 4S./4L.
Jesus, Immanuel.

1 GOD with us! O glorious name

148. (L. M.) 4S./4L.
Jesus Yesterday, To-day, and Forever, the Same.

1 HIGH on his Father's royal seat,

149. (L. M.)
Christ our Advocate.

1 HE lives, the great Redeemer lives:

150. (C. M.)
Christ is King of Saints.

1 COME, ye that love the Saviour's name,

151. (C. M.)
The Same.

1 WHEN in his earthly courts we view

152. (6, 4.)
King of Saints.

1 LET us awake our joys,
   Strike up with cheerful voice—
Each creature sing;
Angels—begin the song,
Mortals—the strain prolong,
In accents sweet and strong,
   "Jesus is King."

2 Proclaim abroad his name,
   Tell of his matchless fame—
What wonders done;
Shout thro' hell's dark profound,
Let the whole earth resound,
Till the high heavens rebound,
   "The vict'ry's won."

3 He vanquish'd sin and hell:
   And the last foe will quell;
Mourners rejoice!
His dying love adore,

Praise him now rais'd in pow'r.
And triumph evermore,
   With a glad voice.

4 All hail the glorious day,
When thro' the heavenly way
Lo, he shall come!
While they who pierc'd him wail,
His promise shall not fail,
Saints, see your King prevail;
   Come, dear Lord, come!

153. (L. M.) 5S./4L.
Christ the One Thing Needful.

1 JESUS, engrave it on my heart,

154. (L. M.) 5S./4L.
Christ a Divine Treasure.

1 JESUS is all I wish or want;

155. (C. M.) 4S./4L.
Jesus the true and living Vine.

1 JESUS, immutably the same,

156. (8, 8, 6.) 4S./6L.
The Excellency of Christ.

1 O COULD I speak the matchless worth,

157. (C. M.) 5S./4L.
Captain of Salvation.

1 HARK! 'tis our heav'nly leader's voice

158. (8's.)
King of Righteousness and Peace.

1 ALL glory to God in the sky,
   And peace upon earth be restor'd:
O Jesus exalted on high,
   Appear our omnipotent Lord!
Who meanly in Bethlehem born,
   Did stoop to redeem a lost race,
Once more to thy creatures return,
   And reign in thy kingdom of grace.

2 When thou in our flesh didst appear,
   All nature acknowledg'd thy birth:
Arose the acceptable year,
   And heav'n was open'd on earth:
Receiving its Lord from above,
   The world was united to bless
The Giver of concord and love,
   The Prince and the Author of Peace.

3 O wouldst thou again be made known,
   Again in the Spirit descend,

And set up in each of thine own
  A kingdom that never shall end.
Thou only art able to bless,
  And make the glad nations obey,
And bid the dire enmity cease,
  And bow the whole world to thy sway.

4 Come then to thy servants again,
    Who long thy appearance to know;
  Thy quiet and peaceable reign
    In mercy establish below!
  All sorrow before thee shall fly,
    And anger and hatred be o'er,
  And envy and malice shall die,
    And discord afflict us no more.

5 No horrid alarum of war
    Shall break our eternal repose;
  No sound of the trumpet is there,
    Where Jesus's Spirit o'erflows:
  Appeas'd by the charms of thy grace
    We all shall in amity join,
  And kindly each other embrace,
    And love with a passion like thine.

159. (P. M.)
The Lamb of God praised.

1 HAIL to the Lamb! that in triumph advances;
  Honour'd and bless'd be his ever dear name:
  Long may the church with his banner that glances   [fame:
  Flourish, and send forth the sound of his
  Heav'n send it happy dew,
  Grace lend it sap anew,
    Gaily to verge on, and broadly to grow,
      While ev'ry tongue and pen
      Send back the shout again,
    Glory to Jesus, glory is due!

2 Ours is no slim sapling, chance by the fountain,
  Blooming in spring, and in winter to fade;
  When winds ev'ry leaf have clean stript
      from the mountain,   [shade,
  The more shall we brethren, exult in our
    Moor'd in the tried Rock,
    Proof to the tempest's shock,
  The deeper to root, the ruder it blows;
      Angels and brethren then,
      Sound forth his praise again!
    Glory to Jesus, glory is due!

3 Rouse, Christians, rouse, and remember
    your station;   [Lord:
  Stretch to your oars for the cause of your
  O that the people composing this nation,
  Were like to rich olives surrounding his board:
    O that our seedling gem
    Worthy such noble stem,   [grow:
  Honour'd and bless'd in his shadow might
      Loud should his praises then
      Sound forth from babes and men,
    Glory to Jesus, glory is due!

4 Hail the bright prospect that rises to vision!
  Jesus the Lamb is gaining in conquest:
  Banners of love lead in every division,
  And nation on nation proclaims him the bless'd.
    May glory in the East,
    Soon fill the distant West,
  Then brightly to shine and eternally to reign:
      Churches in union then
      Shall shout the loud Amen,
    Glory to Jesus, glory is due!

160. (P. M.) Middletown.
Christ's Ascension and Intercession.

1 HAIL, the day that sees him rise,
    Ravish'd from our wishful eyes,
  Christ awhile to mortals giv'n
  Reascends his native heav'n:
  There the pompous triumph waits,
  Lift your heads ye 'ternal gates
  Wide unfold the radiant scene,
  Take the King of glory in.

2 Him, tho' highest heav'n receives,
  Still he loves the earth he leaves;
  Though returning to his throne,
  Still he calls mankind his own.
  Still for us he intercedes,
  Prevalent his death he pleads;
  Next himself prepares our place,
  Harbinger of human race.

3 Master (may we ever say,)
  Taken from our head to-day,
  See thy faithful servants, see,
  Ever gazing up to thee!
  Grant, tho' parted from our sight,
  High above yon azure height,
  Grant our hearts may thither rise,
  Foll'wing thee beyond the skies.

4 Ever upward let us move,
  Wafted on the wings of love;
  Looking when our Lord shall come;

Longing, gasping, after home:
There we shall with thee remain,
Partners of thine endless reign;
There thy face unclouded see,
Find our heav'n of heav'ns in thee.

MISSIONS

THE DAWNING OF THE LATTER-DAY GLORY.

161. (C. M.) Double.
The Universal Spread of the Gospel.

1 THAT glorious day is drawing nigh,
  When Zion's light shall come;
She shall arise and shine on high,
  Bright as the rising sun:
The north and south their sons resign,
  And earth's foundations bend,
When, like a bride, Jerusalem,
  All glorious shall descend.

2 The king who wears that glorious crown,
  The azure flaming bow,
The holy city shall bring down,
  To bless the church below:
When Zion's bleeding, conquering King,
  Shall sin and death destroy,
The morning stars will t'gether sing,
  And Zion shout for joy.

3 This holy, bright, musician band,
  Who hold the harps of God,
On Zion's holy mountain stand,
  In garments ting'd with blood;
Descending with most melting strains,
  Jehovah they'll adore;
Such, shouts thro' earth's extensive plains,
  Were never heard before.

4 Let Satan rage, and boast no more,
  Nor think his reign is long;
Though saints are feeble, weak and poor,
  Their great Redeemer's strong;
He is their shield and hiding place,
  A covert from the wind;
A stream of life, from Christ, *the rock*,
  Runs through this weary land.

5 This crystal stream runs down from heav'n,
  It issues from the throne;
The sons of strife away are driv'n,
  The church becomes but one;
This peaceful union she shall know,
  And live upon his love,
And sing, and shout his name below,
  As angels do above.

6 A thousand years shall roll around:
  The church shall be complete,
Call'd by the glorious trumpet's sound,
  Their Saviour they shall meet;
They'll rise with joy, and mount on high,
  They'll fly to Jesus' arms;
And gaze with wonder and delight,
  On their beloved's charms.

7 Like apples fair, his beauties are,
  To feed and cheer the mind;
No earthly fruit doth so recruit,
  Nor flagons fill'd with wine;
Their troubles o'er they'll grieve no more,
  But sing in strains of joy;
In raptures sweet, and bliss complete,
  They'll feast and never cloy.

162. (8, 7, 4.)
Desiring the Coming of the Kingdom of Christ.

1 O'ER the gloomy hills of darkness,
  Look, my soul, be still and gaze:
All the promises do travel
  With a glorious day of grace;
    Blessed Jubilee,
  Let thy glorious morning dawn!

2 Let the Indian, let the Negro,
  Let the rude barbarian see
That divine and glorious conquest,
  Once obtain'd on Calvary;
    Let the Gospel
  Loud resound from pole to pole.

3 Kingdoms wide that sit in darkness,
  Grant them, Lord, the glorious light,
And from eastern coast to western,
  May the morning chase the night,
    And redemption,
  Freely purchas'd, win the day.

[4 May the glorious day approaching.
  On the grossest darkness dawn,
And the everlasting Gospel
  Spread abroad thy holy name,
    All the borders
  Of the great IMMANUEL'S land.]

5 Fly abroad, thou mighty Gospel,
  Win and conquer, never cease;

May thy lasting wide dominions
  Multiply and still increase;
    Sway the sceptre,
Saviour, all the world around.

163. (11, 8.)
The Star in the East anew.

1 SEE! see in the east a new glory ascends,
    And pours its effulgence afar; [ends
  It glides on sublime, and earth's uttermost
    Acknowledge Immanuel's star.
2 O'er the 'Jew trodden down,' as the
      prophets foretold,
    It travels with lustre serene;
  While heathens transform'd as intent they
      behold,
    Are singing, 'The star we have seen.'
3 Hark! from yonder bold hills how the
      Syrians shout,
    While Comoron echoes the lay:
  The German and Dane spread the tidings
    And jubilees welcome the day. [about,
4 From the martyr'd Abdallah see Sabet
      retire,
    Arabian darkness he fears
  Love and zeal for a Saviour his bosom in-
      spire,
    And the Christian translator appears.
5 And still, see the day star its journey
      pursue,
    Even Brahmans pronounce it divine;
  Jehovah incarnate shall multitudes view,
    And scatter their gifts at his shrine.
6 Ye Herods, in vain do you menace and
      rage
    And vain is hell's horrible roar;
  Time, meeting with Prophecy, opens her
    And bids all the nations adore. [page,
7 Roll on, blessed Star, fill the world with thy
      light,
    The saints are expecting thy rays;
  Bid the latter-day morning ascend in its
      might,
    And shine on our incense of praise.

164. (11's.)
The Glorious Effects of the Gospel.

1 FROM realms where the day her first
      dawning extends,
  The Sun of the Gospel in glory ascends;
  Ye forests attend while your children
      combine,
  In accents unusual, in transports divine,
2 Involv'd in uncertainty, darkness and
      death,
  The clouds of destruction hung over our
      path.
  Till yon rising splendor illumin'd our way,
  And pointed our steps to the regions of
      day.
3 A council on high has been had to enquire,
    For the help of mankind—and peace
      kindled the fire;
  Provision was made for the nations
      distress'd,
  And with the rich treasure, all lands shall
      be bless'd.
4 The claim of salvation let down from
      above,
  Cemented by justice, and brighten'd by
      love,
  The safety of hope and the channel of
      grace
  Joins heaven and earth in its mighty
      embrace.
5 On high, see our Jesus, the penitent's
      friend,
  With banners of mercy compassionate
      bend;
  Entreating the wretched, rebellious and
      vile,
  From ruin to flee, and repose in his smile.
6 The Prince of Salvation is coming—pre-
      pare
  A way in the desert his blessings to share;
  He comes to release us from sin and from
      woes,
  And bids the rude wilderness bloom like
      the rose.
7 His reign shall extend from the east to the
      west,
  Composing the tumults of nature to rest;
  The day-spring of glory illumine the skies,
  And ages on ages of happiness rise.
8 The brute-hearted temper of man shall
      grow tame.   [lamb,
  The wolf and the lion lie down with the
  The bear with the kine shall contentedly
      feed,
  While children their young ones in har-
      mony lead.

9 The serpentile race shall seek venom in vain;
  The rattle-snake, harmless, shall bask on the plain;
  The infant shall play on the hole of the asp,
  And smile in the folds of the cockatrice grasp.

10 No more shall the sound of the war-whoop be heard,
   The ambush and slaughter no longer be fear'd;
   The tomahawk, buried, shail rest in the ground;
   And peace and good-will to the nations abound.

11 All spirit of war to the Gospel shall bow;
   The bow lie unstrung at the foot of the plough;
   To prune the young orchard the spear shall be bent,
   And love greet the world with a smile of content.

12 Slight tinctures of skin shall no longer engage,
   The fervour of jealousy, murder and rage;
   The white and the red shall in friendship be join'd,
   Wide spreading benevolence over mankind.

13 Hail! scene of felicity, transport and joy,
   When sin and vexation shall cease to annoy;
   Rich blessings of grace from above shall be given,
   And life only serve as a passage to heaven.

14 Roll forward, dear Saviour, roll forward the day,
   When all shall submit and rejoice in thy sway;
   When white men, and Indians, united in praise,
   One vast hallelujah, triumphant shall raise.

165. (P. M.) 16S./4L.
Praise for the success of the Gospel.

1 ALL thanks be to God,

166. (L. M.)
The Gospel Spreads and Babylon Falls.

1 PROUD Babylon yet waits her doom
  Nor can her *tott'ring* palace fall,
  Till some blest messenger arise,
  The spacious heathen world to call.

2 And see the glorious time approach!
  Behold the mighty Angel fly,
  The Gospel tidings to convey
  To ev'ry land beneath the sky!

3 O see, on both the Indies' coast,
  And Africa's unhappy shore,
  The untaught savage press to hear;
  And, hearing, wonder and adore.

4 The Islands, waiting for his law,
  With rapture greet the sacred sound;
  And, taught the Saviour's precious name,
  Cast all their idols to the ground.

5 Now, Babylon, thy hour is come,
  Thy curs'd foundation shall give way,
  And thine eternal overthrow
  The triumphs of the cross display.

167. (L. M.) 6S./4L.
And they went and Preached every where.

1 GO, Missionaries, and proclaim

168. (L. M.)
The Gospel as the Power of God desired.

1 SOV'REIGN of worlds display thy pow'r,
  Be this thy Zion's favour'd hour;
  Bid the bright morning star arise,
  And point the nations to the skies,

2 Set up thy throne where Satan reigns,
  On Afric's shore, on India's plains;
  On wilds and continents unknown,
  And claim the nations for thy own.

3 Speak, and the world shall hear thy voice:
  Speak, and the desert shall rejoice:
  Scatter the shades of moral night,
  And put vain idols all to flight.

169. (L. M.) 3S./4L.
The Kingdom Come.

1 ASCEND thy throne, Almighty King,

170. (L. M.) 2S./4L.
Universal Empire Desired.

1 TO distant lands thy Gospel send,

171. (8's.)
The Missionary's Farewell.

1 FAREWELL, my brethren in the Lord,
  The Gospel sounds a Jubilee;
  My stamm'ring tongue shall sound aloud,
  From land to land, from sea to sea:
  And as I preach from place to place,
  I'll trust alone in God's free grace.

Hymn Texts From *The Cluster*

2 Farewell, in bonds and union dear,
    Like strings you twine about my heart,
I humbly beg your earnest pray'r,
    Till we shall meet no more to part:
Till we shall meet in worlds above,
Encircled in eternal love.

3 Farewell, my earthly friends below,
    Though all so kind and dear to me;
My Jesus calls, and I must go
    To sound the Gospel-jubilee:
To sound the joys, and bear the news,
To Gentile worlds, and royal Jews.

4 Farewell young people, one and all—
    While God shall grant me breath to breathe,
I'll pray to the eternal All
    That your dear souls in Christ may live:
That your dear souls prepar'd may be
To reign in bliss eternally.

5 Farewell, ye ancients of this place,
    Your race in life is almost run;
But if your souls are void of grace,
    Your sorrows are but just begun:
Your grey hairs, without grace to save,
Will come with sorrow to the grave.

6 Farewell to all below the sun
    And as I pass in tears below
The path is straight, my feet shall run,
    And God shall keep me as I go
And God will keep me in his hand,
And bring me to the promis'd land.

7 Farewell, farewell, I look above;
    Jesus, my friend, to thee I call—
My joy, my crown, my only love,
    My safeguard and my heav'nly all:
My song to sing, my preaching theme.
My only hope till death—amen.

    172. (6, 5.) 5S./8L.
    The Same.

1 O NOW, my dear brethren,

    173. (6, 8.) Lenox.
A Minister subject to the greatest anxiety or joy.

1 WHAT contradictions meet
    In ministers' employ!
It is a bitter sweet,
    A sorrow full of joy.
No other post affords a place
For equal honour or disgrace.

2 Who can describe the pain
    Which faithful preachers feel,
Constrain'd to speak in vain,
    To hearts as hard as steel?
Or who can tell the pleasures felt,
When stubborn hearts begin to melt.

3 The Saviour's dying love,
    The soul's amazing worth,
Their utmost efforts move,
    And draw their bowels forth;
They pray and strive, their rest departs,
Till Christ be form'd in sinners' hearts.

4 If some small hope appear,
    They still are not content;
But, with a jealous fear,
    They watch'd for the event:
Too oft they find their hopes deceiv'd,
Then how their inmost souls are griev'd!

5 But when their pains succeed,
    And from the tender blade
The rip'ning ears proceed,
    Their toils are overpaid:
No harvest joy can equal theirs,
To find the fruit of all their cares.

6 On what has now been sown,
    Thy blessing, Lord, bestow;
The pow'r is thine alone,
    To make it spring and grow:
Do thou the gracious harvest raise,
And thou alone shalt have the praise.

    174. (C. M.) 6S./4L.
    A Minister loving his People.

1 WHEN Paul was parted from his friends,

    175. (C. M.) 5S./4L.
    The Latter Day Glory.

1 REJOICE, ye nations of the world,

    176. (L. M.) 4S./4L.
    Universal Empire expected.

1 EXERT thy pow'r, thy rights maintain,

    177. (L. M.) 4S./4L.
    For the Concert Prayer-Meeting.

1 THY people, Lord, who trust thy word,

    178. (L. M.) 4S./4L.
    The Prospect of Missionary Success.

1 BEHOLD th' expected time draws near,

    179. (L. M.) 4S./4L.
    More Labourers Wanted.

1 LORD, when we cast our eyes abroad,

180. (C. M.) 4S./4L.
A Prayer for Missionaries.

1 LORD, send thy word, and let it fly,

WARNING AND INVITATION.

181. (P. M.)
Thirsty Souls invited to the Waters of Life.

1 SEE the fountain open'd wide,
  That from pollution frees us,
  Flowering from the precious side
  Of our Immanuel Jesus.
      Chorus.
  Ho every one that thirsteth,
    Come ye to the waters,
  Freely drink and quench your thirst.
    With Zion's sons and daughters.
2 Sinners, hear your Saviour's call,
    Consider what you're doing,
  Jesus Christ can cleanse you all,
    Will you not come unto him?
3 Dying sinners come and try—
    These waters will relieve you:
  Without money come and buy,
    For Christ will freely give you.
4 He who drinks shall never die;
    These waters fail him never:
  Sinners come and now apply,
    And drink and live for ever!
5 Weeping Mary full of grief
    Applied for these waters:
  Jesus gave her full relief
    With Zion's sons and daughters.
6 See the woman at the well
    Disputing with the Saviour;
  Soon she found that he could tell
    Her all her past behaviour.
7 When she ask'd and when she got
    A drink, her heart was flaming:
  She forgot her water-pot,
    And ran to town proclaiming.
8 The Thief had only time to think,
    And tell his doleful story;
  Jesus gave him leave to drink—
    He drank, and fled to glory!
9 Christians, you can fully tell
    The virtues of these waters:
  You were once the heirs of hell,
    But now you're sons and daughters!

182. (10's.) 5S./4L.
I AM hath sent me to you.

1 COME sinners attend, and make no delay,

183. (9, 8.) 5S./8L.
Conversions of Sinners supernatural.

1 MY soul forever stand and wonder,

184. (11's.) 9S./4L.
The Fountain opened for Sin.

1 IN th' house of King David, a fountain did spring,

185. (11's.)
Sinners warned from the Rich Man's fate.

1 COME all ye poor sinners who from Adam came,
  Ye poor and ye blind, and ye halt and ye lame,
  Close in with the gospel upon its own terms,
  Or you'll burn for ever, like poor mortal worms.
2 You've heard of a rich man, a beggar likewise,
  The beggar he dy'd, and he rests in the skies;
  The rich man dy'd also, and to his surprise,
  Awaked in hell, and he lift up his eyes!
3 Seeing Abra'm far off, in the mansions above,
  And Laz'rus in his bosom in raptures of love:
  He cry'd, "Father Abra'm, O send me relief!
  For I am tormented in pain and in grief."
4 He said, "Son, remember when you liv'd so bold,
  Dress'd in your fine linen, your purple and gold,
  While Lazarus lay at your gate full of sores,
  You had no compassion nor pitied his woes.
5 "Besides, there's a great gulf betwixt us you see.
  That those who would pass from hence can't come to thee,
  But there you must lie and lament your sad state,
  For now you are sending your cries up too late."

Hymn Texts From *The Cluster*

6 He cried, "Father Abra'm, I pray then provide,   [beside,
    Send one from the dead, I've five brethren
    They hearing of me, and of my wretched state,
    Perhaps will repent now before its too late."

7 "They have a just warning, that spreads far and wide:
    They've Moses to teach them, the prophets beside:
    If these can't persuade them to turn and repent,
    They will not believe though one from the dead went."

8 Come, poor Zion mourners, O don't you despair,
    But look, unto Jesus, he still answers pray'r;
    He'll hear your complaints and he'll heal all your grief,
    He'll pardon your sins, and will give you relief.

9 And when these vile bodies you come to lay down,
    You'll fly to the regions where you'll wear a crown:
    The smiles which will come from sweet Jesus's face,
    Will make you adore and admire his free grace.

186. (P.M.)
Redemption complete in Christ.

1 COME friends and relations, let's join heart in hand,
    The voice of the turtle is heard in our land;
    Let's all walk together, and follow the sound,
    And march to the place where redemption is found.

2 The place it is hidden by reason of sin;
    You cannot discover the state you are in:
    You're blinded, polluted, in prison and pain:
    O how shall such rebels redemption obtain?

3 The place is obscured from wisest of men,
    Nor can mortals know it until 'tis made plain:
    The place is in Jesus, to him let us go,
    We'll there find redemption from sorrow and woe.

4 And if you feel wounded and bruis'd by the fall,

Then rise and rejoice, for such he doth call;
    Or if you are tempted to doubt or despair,
    Still wait at Christ's feet, for redemption is there.

5 And you my dear brethren, the called of God.
    Who witness free pardon by faith in his blood;
    Let patience attend you wherever you go,
    From Jesus your Saviour redemption doth flow.

6 We read of commotions, and signs in the skies—
    That the sun and the moon shall be cloth'd in disguise;
    And when you shall see all these tokens appear,
    Then hold up your head, your redemption is near.

7 O then the arch-angel the trumpet shall sound,
    And 'waken the dead that sleep under the ground   [arise,
    The sound of the trumpet shall bid you
    To meet your redemption, with love and surprise.

8 And then loving Jesus our souls will receive,
    From bonds of corruption our bodies relieve;
    Then we shall be all uncorrupted and free,
    And sing of redemption wherever we be,

9 Redeemed from sin, and redeemed from death!
    Redeem'd from corruption, redeem'd from the earth!
    Redeem'd from damnation, redeem'd from all woe!
    We'll sing of redemption wherever we go.

10 Redeemed from pain, and redeem'd from distress!
    The fruits of redemption no tongue can express;
    Redemption was brought us by Jesus's love:
    We'll sing of redemption in heaven above.

187. (C. M.) Double.
Solemn Addresses to Young People.

1 YOUNG people all attention give,
    And hear what I shall say:
    I wish your souls with Christ to live,
    In everlasting day.

Remember you are hast'ning on
   To death's dark, gloomy shade;
Your joys on earth will soon be gone,
   Your flesh in dust be laid.
2 Death's iron gate you must pass through,
   Ere long, my dear young friends;
With whom then do you think to go,
   With saints or fiery fiends?
Pray meditate before too late,
   While in a gospel land;
Behold, King Jesus at the gate
   Most lovingly doth stand.
3 Young men, how can you turn your face
   From such a glorious friend;
Will you pursue your dang'rous ways?
   O don't you fear the end?
Will you pursue that dang'rous road,
   Which leads to death and hell?
Will you refuse all peace with God,
   With devils for to dwell?
4 Young women too, what will you do,
   If out of Christ you die?
From all God's people you must go,
   To weep, lament, and cry:
Where you the least relief can't find,
   To mitigate your pain;
Your good things all be left behind;
   Your souls in death remain.
5 Young people all I pray then view,
   The fountain open'd wide;
The spring of life open'd for sin,
   Which flow'd from Jesus' side:
There you may drink in endless joy,
   And reign with Christ your King,
In his glad notes your souls employ,
   And Hallelujahs sing.

188. (P. M.)
Sinners earnestly Warned and Intreated.

1 STOP poor sinner stop and think,
   Before you farther go;
Can you sport upon the brink
   Of everlasting woe?
Hell beneath is gaping wide,
   Vengeance waits the dread command,
Soon to stop your sport and pride,
   And sink you with the damn'd.

Chorus.
Then be entreated now to stop—
   For unless you warning take,
Ere you are aware you'll drop
   Into the burning lake.

2 Say, have you an arm like God,
   That you his will oppose?
Fear you not that iron rod,
   With which he breaks his foes?
Can you stand in that great day,
   When *he* judgment shall proclaim;
When the earth shall melt away,
   Like wax before the flame?
Then be, &c.

3 Ghastly death will quickly come,
   And drag you to the bar;
There, to hear your final doom,
   Will fill you with despair:
All your sins will round you crowd,
   Sins of a blood-crimson die,
Each for vengeance crying loud,
   And what will you reply?
Then be, &c.

4 Though your hearts be made of steel,
   Your foreheads lin'd with brass,
God at length will make you feel.
   He will not let you pass.
Sinners then in vain will call,
   Though they now despise his grace,
"Rocks and mountains on us fall,
   And hide us from his face."
Then be, &c.

5 But as yet there is a hope,
   You may his mercy know;
Though his arm be lifted up,
   He still forbears the blow;
It was for sinners Jesus dy'd:
   Sinners he invites to come;
None who comes shall be deny'd;
   He says there still is room.
Then be, &c.

189. (P. M.)
A Warning to Presumptuous Sinners.

1 I NOW consider, O my God,
   How rich men roll in pleasure,
Upon this frail, transient abode,
   Heaping up wealth and treasure;
Not much they make, their souls to stake,
   T' uphold their pride in station:
If one them tell of heaven and hell,
   Or th' wicked in damnation;
They laugh and jeer, they ridicule,
   And call such person, *but a fool*,
To tell to them such things as these,
   When they will do but what they please.
Say they, "we cannot now incline,
   To meditate on things divine,
For in our prime it is our time,
   To take our recreation."

2 O how their conscience they do bribe,
   Under such vain pretences!

Hymn Texts From *The Cluster*

To gratify their carnal pride,
  Committing gross offences.
They acquiesce there's a place of bliss,
  Where righteous men do enter;
They likewise tell there is a hell,
  Where wicked men must centre;
But say they, "while we're on earth,
  We'll spend our days in jovial mirth,
And when our sinful pleasure's past,
  We'll then turn unto God at last;
Few weeks repentance will secure,
  Make our effectual calling sure,
And save us from eternal doom,
  Of wrath and indignation."

3 But, O sinners, where'er you are,
    Possess'd of such a notion,
  The awful day will soon appear
    When all things shall have notion,
  The heav'ns shall roll up like a scroll,
    And vanish with a great noise;
  And the earth sweat with fervent heat,
    And melt at the great God's voice.
  When the archangel shall be sent,
    To call the world unto judgment,
  At God's tribunal to appear,
    To answer at his awful bar.
  For all the deeds done here on earth,
    And sentence shall be pronounc'd forth,
  And you must go to bliss or woe,
    Eternal and forever!

4 For if you slight this glorious light,
    You're under condemnation;
  Since there remains nothing but wrath,
    For slighters of salvation:
  Then let our contemplation rise
    To heavenly things above the skies—
  To that celestial abode,
    Where Christ co-equal is with God;
  Believe in him the Scripture saith,
    Embrace him with a lively faith,
  Then shall our glitt'ring souls possess
    His everlasting righteousness;
  And Christ our King shall be our friend,
    And sin and sorrow have an end,
  And he'll us bring where we shall reign,
    Along with him in glory.

190. (8, 6.) 4S./6L.
The Chief of Sinners invited.

1 YE scarlet-colour'd sinners, come;

191. (8, 7.) 8S./8L.
A Call to Sinners in Security.

1 COME sinners all, attend the call,

192. (P. M.)
The worst of Sinners may be Saved.

1 COME ye sinners, poor and wretched,
    Weak and wounded, sick and sore!
  Jesus ready stands to save you,
    Full of pity join'd with power;
      He is able,
  He is willing: doubt no more!

2 Come, ye thirsty, come and welcome;
    God's free bounty glorify:
  True belief, and true repentance,
    Ev'ry grace that brings you nigh—
      Without money
  Come to Jesus Christ, and buy.

3 Let not conscience make you linger,
    Nor of fitness fondly dream;
  All the fitness he requireth,
    Is to feel your need of him;
      This he gives you;
  'Tis his Spirit's rising beam.

4 Come ye weary, heavy laden,
    Lost and ruin'd by the fall;
  If you tarry till you're better,
    You will never come at all:
      Not the righteous,
  Sinners Jesus came to call.

5 View him prostrate in the garden;
    On the ground your Maker lies!
  On the bloody tree behold him;
    Hear him cry before he dies,
      "It is finish'd;"
  Sinner will not this suffice?

6 Lo, th' incarnate God ascended,
    Pleads the merit of his blood:
  Venture on him, venture wholly,
    Let no other trust intrude;
      None but Jesus
  Can do helpless sinners good.

7 Saints and angels, join'd in concert
    Sing the praises of the Lamb:
  While the blissful seats of heaven
    Sweetly echo with his name.
      Hallelujah!
  Sinners, here may sing the same.

193. (6, 8.) Lenox.
The Rich Man and Lazarus.

1 A WORLDLING spent each day
    In luxury and state;
  While a believer lay
    A beggar at his gate:
  Think not the Lord's appointment strange,
  Death made a great and lasting change.

2 Death brought the saint release
   From want, disease and scorn;
   And to the land of peace,
   His soul by angels borne,
   In Abra'm's bosom safely plac'd,
   Enjoys an everlasting feast.
3 The rich man also dy'd,
   And in a moment fell,
   From all his pomp and pride,
   Into the flames of hell:
   The beggar's bliss from far beheld,
   His soul with double anguish fill'd.
4 "O Abra'm send, he cries,
   (But his request was vain)
   The beggar from the skies,
   To mitigate my pain!
   One drop of water I entreat,
   To soothe my tongue's tormenting heat."
5 Let all who worldly pelf,
   And worldly spirits have,
   Observe, each for himself,
   The answer Abra'm gave:
   "Remember thou wast fill'd with good,
   While the poor beggar pin'd for food.
6 Neglected at thy door,
   With tears he begg'd his bread;
   But now he weeps no more,
   His griefs and pains are fled:
   His joys eternally will flow,
   While thine expire in endless woe."
7 Lord make us truly wise,
   To choose thy people's lot,
   And earthly joys despise,
   Which soon will be forgot:
   The greatest evil we can fear,
   Is to possess our portion here!

194. (L. M.) Double. 5S./8L.
Law and Grace contrasted.

1 IN thunder once Jehovah spoke,

195. (P. M.) 10S./5L.
The Sinner's Warning.

1 WHILE angels strike their tunefull strings,

196. (9, 7.) 9S./4L.
The plan of Redemption, ground of expostulation.

1 THE glorious plan of man's Redemption,

197. (6, 8.) Lenox.
The Jubilee.

1 BLOW ye the trumpet, blow
   The gladly solemn sound!
   Let all the nations know,
   To earth's remotest bound!
   The year of Jubilee is come,
   Return, ye ransom'd sinners, home.
2 Exalt the Lamb of God,
   The sin atoning Lamb;
   Redemption by his blood
   Thro' all the lands proclaim:
   The year, &c.
3 Ye, who have sold for nought
   The heritage above,
   Shall have it back unbought,
   The gift of Jesus' love:
   The year, &c.
4 Ye slaves of sin and hell,
   Your liberty receive;
   And safe in Jesus dwell,
   And blest in Jesus live:
   The year, &c.
5 Ye hapless debtors, know
   The sov'reign grace of heav'n;
   Though sums immense ye owe,
   A free discharge is giv'n:
   The year, &c.
6 The gospel-trumpet hear,
   The news of pard'ning grace;
   Ye happy souls draw near,
   Behold your Saviour's face:
   The year, &c.
7 Jesus our great High-Priest,
   Has full atonement made;
   Ye weary spirits, rest:
   Ye mournful souls, be glad!
   The year, &c.

198. (8, 7, 4.) 4S./6L.
The Gospel message, "Be ye reconciled."

1 SINNERS, you are now addressed

199. (8, 7, 4.)
Address to Sinners after Sermon.

1 SINNERS, will you scorn the message,
   Sent in mercy from above?
   Ev'ry sentence, O how tender!
   Ev'ry line is full of love.
      Listen to it,
   Ev'ry line is full of love,

2 Hear the heralds of the gospel,
   News from Zion's King proclaim,
   To each rebel-sinner—"Pardon,
   "Free forgiveness in his name;"
      How important!
   Free forgiveness in his name!
3 Tempted souls, they bring you succour—
   Fearful hearts, they quell your fears,
   And with news of consolation,
   Chase away the falling tears:
      Pleasant tidings,
   Chase away the falling tears.
4 False professors, grov'ling worldings,
   Callous hearers of the word!
   While the messengers address you,
   Take the warning they afford;
      We entreat you,
   Take the warning they afford.
5 Who hath our report believ'd!
   Who receiv'd the joyful word?
   Who embrac'd the news of pardon.
   Given to you by the Lord;
      Can you slight it,
   Given to you by the Lord?
6 O ye angels, hov'ring round us,
   Waiting spirits, speed your way.
   Hasten to the court of heaven,
   Tidings bear without delay:
      Rebel sinners
   Glad the message will obey.

200. (7's.) 8S./4L.
Sinners invited to the Well of living Water.

1 JESUS' precious name excels

201. (5's.)
The Prisoners of Hope.

1 YE pris'ners of hope
   O'erwhelmed with grief,
   To Jesus look up
      For certain relief.
   There's no cond'mnation
      In Jesus the Lord,
   But strong cons'lation
      His grace doth afford.
2 Should justice appear
      A merciless foe,
   Yet be of good cheer,
      And soon shall ye know
   That sinners confessing
      Their wickedness past,
   A plentiful blessing
      Of pardon shall taste,
3 Then dry up your tears,
      Ye children of grief,
   For Jesus appears
      To give you relief;
   If you are returning
      To Jesus your friend,
   Your sighing and mourning
      In singing shall end.
4 "None will I cast out
      Who comes," saith the Lord;
   Why then do you doubt?
      Lay hold of his word:
   Ye mourners of Sion,
      Be bold to believe,
   For ever rely on
      Your Saviour, and live.

202. (L. M.) 4S./4L.
The sin-sick Sinner excited to look up to Christ the Physician.

1 SIN, like a raging fever, reigns

203. (6, 8.) 6S./6L.
Come, and let us reason together.

1 YE sin-sick souls draw near,

204. (L. M.)
To-day if ye will hear his voice, harden not your hearts.

1 TO-day, if you will hear his voice,
   Now is the time to make your choice:
   Say will you to mount Zion go?
   Say will you have this Christ or no?
2 Say, will you be for ever blest,
   And with this glorious Jesus rest?
   Will you be sav'd from guilt and pain?
   Will you with Christ for ever reign?
3 Make now your choice, and halt no more,
   For now he's waiting for the poor;
   Say now, poor souls, what will you do?
   Say will you have this Christ or no?
4 Ye dear young men for ruin bound,
   Amidst the Gospel's joyful sound,
   Come go with us, and seek to prove
   The joys of Christ's redeeming love.
5 Your sports and all your glitt'ring toys,
   Compar'd with our celestial joys,
   Like momentary dreams appear:
   Come go with us,—your souls are dear.

6 Or must we leave you bound to hell!
  Resolv'd with devils there to dwell!
  Still we will weep, lament, and cry,
  That God may change you ere you die.
7 Young women, now we look to you:
  Are you resolv'd to perish too?
  To rush in carnal pleasures on,
  And sink in flaming ruin down?
8 Then, dear young friends, a long farewell!
  We're bound to heav'n, but you to hell:
  Still God may hear us while we pray,
  And change you ere the burning day.
9 Once more I ask you in his name:
  I know his love remains the same;
  Say will you to mount Zion go?
  Say will you have this Christ or no?

205. (C. M.) 7S./4L.
Sinners warned of impending Ruin.

1 WHEN pity prompts me to look round,

206. (S. M.) 4S./4L.
O that they would consider their latter end.

1 SINNERS, awake to know

207. (C. M.) 5S./4L.
Whoever will, let him come.

1 O WHAT amazing words of grace

208. (C.M.) 2S./4L.
The Guilty invited to Christ.

1 COME guilty souls, and flee away

209. (L. M.) 2S./4L.
The trembling Sinner Encouraged.

1 WHO is the trembling sinner, who

210. (L. M.)
Christ the only Plea before God.

1 HOW shall the sons of men appear,
  Great God, before thine awful bar!
  How may the guilty hope to find
  Acceptance with th' eternal Mind?
2 Not vows, nor groans, nor broken cries,
  Not the most costly sacrifice,
  Not infant blood, profusely spilt,
  Will expiate the sinner's guilt.
3 Thy blood, dear Jesus, thine, alone,
  Hath sov'reign virtue to atone;
  Here we will rest our only plea,
  When we approach, great God, to thee.

211. (L. M.) 4S./4L.
Ask for the good old Way.

1 INQUIRING souls who long to find

212. (C. M.) 5S./4L.
Ye must be born again!

1 SINNERS, this solemn truth regard!

213. (C. M.) 3S./4L.
Cast your burden on the Lord.

1 YE burden'd souls to Jesus come,

214. (L. M.)
Christ at the Door.

1 BEHOLD the Saviour at thy door,
  He gently knocks, has knock'd before;
  Has waited long, is waiting still:
  You treat no other friend so ill.
2 Admit him; for the human breast
  Ne'er entertain'd so kind a guest;
  Admit him, or the hour's at hand,
  When at his door deny'd you'll stand.
3 Open my heart, Lord, enter in,
  Slay ev'ry foe, and conquer sin:
  I now to thee my all resign,
  My body, soul, shall all be thine.

215. (L. M.) 5S./4L.
The coming Sinner encouraged.

1 HARK! 'tis the Saviour's voice I hear,

216. (S. M.) 4S./4L.
Behold, now is the accepted Time.

1 NOW is th' accepted time,

217. (7's.) 4S./4L.
Compel them to come in.

1 LORD, how large thy bounties are,

218. (7's.) 4S./4L.
The weary invited to Christ for rest.

1 COME, ye weary souls opprest,

219. (L. M.) 3S./4L.
A Solemn Warning.

1 SINNER, O why so thoughtless grown?

220. (L. M.) Windham.
Warning against Hypocrisy.

1 BROAD is the road that leads to death,
  And thousands walk together there:

But wisdom shows a narrower path,
  With here and there a traveller.
2 "Deny thyself, and take thy cross,"
  Is the Redeemer's great command;
  Nature must count her gold but dross,
  If she would gain this heav'nly land.
3 The fearful soul, that tires and faints,
  And walks the ways of God no more,
  Is but esteem'd almost a saint,
  And makes his own destruction sure.
4 Lord, let not all my hopes be vain;
  Create my heart entirely new;
  Which hypocrites could ne'er attain;
  Which false apostates never knew.

221. (L. M.) Greenwich.
The Prosperity of the Wicked cursed.

1 LORD what a thoughtless wretch was I,
    To mourn, and murmur, and repine,
  To see the wicked plac'd on high,
    In pride and robes of honour shine!
2 But oh, their end, their dreadful end!
    Thy sanctuary taught me so:
  On slipp'ry rocks I see them stand,
    And fiery billows roll below.
3 Their fancy'd joys, how fast they flee!
    Like dreams as fleeting and as vain;
  Their songs of softest harmony
    Are but a prelude to their pain.
4 Now I esteem their mirth and wine
    Too dear to purchase with my blood:
  Lord, 'tis enough that thou art mine,
    My life, my portion, and my God.

222. (L. M.) Exhortation. 4S./4L.
Advice to Youth.

1 NOW, the heat of youthful blood,

CONVICTION AND CONVERSION.

223. (8, 8, 6.)
The Sinner "must be born again."

1 AWAK'D by Sinai's awful sound,
    My soul in guilt and thrall I found,
  And knew not what to do:
  O'erwhelm'd with guilt, and with anguish slain,
  I saw 'I must be born again,'
    Or sink in endless woe.
2 Amaz'd I stood, but could not tell,
  Which way to shun a *moving* hell,
    (For death and hell drew near:)
  I strove indeed, but strove in vain,
  'The sinner must be born again,'
    Still sounded in my ear.
3 When to the law I trembling fled,
  It curs'd me, and pronounc'd me dead;
    I fell beneath its weight:
  This perfect truth renew'd my pain,
  'The sinner must be born again,'
    My woe I can't relate!
4 Again did Sinai's thunders roll,
  And guilt lay heavy on my soul;
    A vast and pond'rous load;
  I read, and saw this truth most plain,
  'The sinner must be born again,'
    Or drink the wrath of God.
5 Oft as I heard the preachers tell,
  How Jesus conquer'd death and hell,
    And broke the fowlers' snare;
  So oft I found this truth remain,
  'The sinner must be born again,'
    Or sink in deep despair.
6 But while I thus in anguish lay,
  Jesus of Naz'reth pass'd that way
    On me his pity mov'd:
  Although I might be justly slain,
  He spake, and I was born again,
    By grace redeem'd and lov'd.
7 To heav'n the joyful tidings flew;
  The angels tun'd their harps anew,
    And loftier notes did raise:
  All hail! the *Lamb*, on Calv'ry slain,
  For all who shall be born again;
    We'll shout thine endless praise.

224. (P. M.) 10S./7L.
The Chief of Sinners saved.

1 COME all who fear the Lord, and see

225. (8, 7.)
Despair brightened by Hope.

1 POOR mourning soul! in deep distress,
    Just waken'd from a slumber,
  Who wanders in sun's wilderness;
    One of the condemn'd number:

The thunder roars from Sinai's mount,
 Fills him with awful terror,
And he like nought in God's account,
 All drown'd with grief and sorrow.
2 Oh! woe is me that I was born,
 Or after death have being;
Fain would I be some earthly worm,
 Which has no future being:
Or had I dy'd when I was young;
 O what would I have given!
Then might *with babes,* my little tongue,
 Been praising God in heaven.
3 But now may I lament my case,
 Just worn away by trouble,
From day to day I look for peace,
 But find my sorrows double:
Cries Satan, "desp'rate is your state,
 Time's been you might repented,
But now you see it is too late.
 So make yourself contented."
4 How can I live! how can I rest!
 Under this sore temptation:
Fearing the day of grace is past;
 Lord hear my lamentation!
For I am weary of my life,
 My groans and bitter crying,
My wants are great, my mind's in strife,
 My spirit's almost dying.
5 Without relief I soon shall die,
 No hope of getting better,
Show pity, Lord, and hear the cry,
 Of a distressed sinner;
For I'm resolved here to trust,
 At thy foot-stool for favour,
Pleading for life, *tho' death be just,*
 Make haste Lord to deliver!
6 "Come hungry, weary, naked soul,
 For such I ne'er rejected;
My righteousness sufficient is,
 Tho' you have long neglected;
Come weary souls, *for right you have,*
 I am such soul's protector,
My honor is engag'd to save
 All under this character."
7 "I come to seek, I come to save,
 I come to make atonement,
I liv'd, I dy'd, laid in the grave,
 To save you from the judgment,"
By faith my glorious Lord I see,
 O how it doth amaze me!
To see him bleeding on the tree,
 From hell and death to raise me.
8 O! who is this that looketh forth,
 Brith as the blooming morning,

Fair as the moon, clear as the sun?
 Jesus is so adorning:
Jesus hath cloth'd my naked soul,
 O he for me has died!
And now I may with pleasure sing,
 My wants are all supplied
9 Lord give me grace to spend my days,
 In living to thy honour,
And not be found in sinners' ways,
 Acting to thy dishonour;
But let my life devoted be
 To Jesus Christ, my Saviour,
And Glory to the sacred Three,
 All glory now and ever!

226. (5's.)
The Humble Beggar.

1 DEAR Jesus here comes,
 And knocks at thy door,
A beggar for *crumbs,*
 Distressed and poor,
Blind, lame, and forsaken,
 And roll'd in his blood,
At length overtaken,
 When running from God.
2 To ask children's bread,
 I durst not presume,
Yet Lord, to be fed
 With fragments I've come,
Some crumbs from thy table,
 O let me obtain;
For lo! thou art able
 My wants to sustain.
3 I own I deserve,
 No favour to see,
So long did I swerve,
 And wander from thee,
'Till brought by affliction
 My follies to mourn,
Now under conviction,
 To thee I return.
4 Great God, my desert
 Is nothing but death!
And hence to depart,
 Forever in wrath;
Yet still to the city
 Of refuge I fly,
O let thine eye pity!
 Since Jesus did die!
5 And since thou hast said
 "Thou wilt cast out none,"
Who fly to thy aid,
 As sinners undone,
Here Lord, I am come
 Condemned to die,

But on *this* sweet crumb
I humbly rely.
6 I cannot depart,
Dear Jesus, nor yield,
'Till feels my poor heart,
This promise fulfill'd,
That I may forever
A monument be,
To praise the sweet Saviour
Of sinners like me.

227. (7, 6.)
Christian Experience.

1 COME all ye weary Pilgrims,
Who feel your need of Christ,
Surrounded by temptations,
And by the world despis'd;
Attend to what I'll tell you,
My exercise I'll shew,
And then you may inform me
If it be so with you.

2 Long time I liv'd in darkness,
Nor saw my dang'rous state,
And when I was awaken'd
I thought it was too late:
A lost and helpless sinner,
Myself I plainly saw.
Expos'd to God's displeasure,
Condemn'd by his law.

3 I thought the brute-creation
Was better off than I,
I spent my days in anguish,
In pain and misery:
Thro' deep distress and sorrow,
My Saviour led me on,
Reveal'd to me his kindness,
When all my hopes were gone.

4 When first I was deliver'd,
I hardly could believe
That I so vile a sinner,
Such favours should receive;
Altho' his solemn praises
Were flowing from my tongue,
Yet fears were oft suggested,
That yet I might be wrong.

5 But soon these fears were banish'd
And tears began to flow,
That I so vile a sinner,
Should be beloved so:
I thought my trials over,
And all my troubles gone,
And joy, and peace, and pleasure,
Should be my lot alone.

6 But now I find a warfare,
Which often bends me low,
The world, the flesh, and Satan,
They do beset me so;
Can one who is a Christian
Have such a heart as mine?
I fear I never witness'd
Th' effects of love divine.

7 I find I'm often backward,
To do my Master's will,
Or else I want the glory
Of what I do fulfil.
In duties I feel weakness,
And oftentimes I find
A hard deceitful spirit,
And wretched wandering mind,

8 Sure others do not feel
What's often felt by me,
Such trials and temptations,
Perhaps they never see:
For I'm the chief of sinners,
I freely own with Paul;
Or if I am a Christian,
I am the least of all.

9 And now I have related
What trials I have seen,
Perhaps my brethren know what
Such sore temptations mean;
I've told you of my conflicts,
Believe my friends 'tis true,
And now you may inform me,
If it be so with you.

228. (L. M.)
The Hiding-Place.

1 HAIL sov'reign *love* which first began
The scheme to rescue fallen man:
Hail matchless, free, eternal *grace*,
Which gave my soul a hiding-place.

2 Against the God who rules the sky,
I fought with hands uplifted high,
Despis'd the mention of his grace;
Too proud to seek a hiding-place.

3 Enwrapt in sin's Egyptian night,
Fonder of darkness than of light,
Madly I ran the sinful race,
Secure without a hiding-place.

4 But thus eternal counsels ran,
"Almighty love arrest the man;"
I felt the arrows of disgrace,
And found I had no hiding-place.

5 Vindictive Justice stood in view,
To Sinai's fi'ry mount I flew;

But justice cry'd, with frowning face,
"This mountain is no hiding-place."
6 At length a heavenly voice I heard,
And mercy for my soul appear'd,
Which led me on with smiling face,
To Jesus Christ *my* hiding-place.
7 Should storms of sev'nfold thunder roll,
And shake the globe from pole to pole,
No storm can change my happy case,
Since Jesus is *my* hiding-place.
8 On him Almighty vengeance fell,
Which might have crush'd a world to hell;
He bore it for his chosen race;
And so became their hiding-place.
9 A few more rolling scenes, at most,
Will land my soul on Canaan's coast,
Where I shall sing a song of grace,
Safe in my glorious hiding-place.

229. (L. M.) Double.
Miss Hataway's Experience.

1 YOUNG women all I pray draw near,
Listen awhile and you shall hear,
How sin and Satan both did try,
To land my soul in misery.
I, like the rest of human kind,
Was born in sin, both deaf and blind,
And as my days advanc'd I grew
The more debas'd and form'd for woe!
2 No greater crimes did I commit,
Than thousands do delight in yet;
That heinous sin call'd civil mirth,
God threatens with his dreadful wrath.
I oftentimes to church did go
My beauty and fine clothes to show;
About my soul I took no thought,
Christ and his grace to me were nought.
3 Full eighteen years around did roll,
Before I thought of my poor soul;
Which makes me shudder when I think,
How near I stood upon the brink!
At length I heard a *Baptist* preach,
His words into my heart did reach;
He said, "I must be born again,
If ever heav'n I would obtain."
4 To keep the law I then was bent,
But found I fail'd in every point;
The law appear'd so just and true,
Not one good duty could I do,
In silent watches of the night,

I went in secret, where I might
Upon my knees pour out my grief,
And pray to God for some relief.
5 My *uncle* said, "don't look so dull,
Come go with me to yonder ball;
I'll dress you up in silk most fine,
And make you *heir* of all that's mine."
Dear *uncle* that will never do,
It only will augment my woe;
Nor can I think true bliss to win,
If I shall still add sin to sin.
6 "Well if you are resolv'd to turn,
And after silly babblers run,
None of my portion you shall have,
I will *it* to some other leave."
I am resolv'd to seek the Lord,
Perhaps, he may his help afford,
O help me mourn my wretched case,
For I am host without *free grace!*
7 Just in this great extremity!
As almost helpless I did lie,
I thought I heard a small still voice
Cry out "Rise up in me rejoice."
Then to my mind one did appear,
Wounded by whip, and nail, and spear.
Bearing my sin, a mighty load,
That I might be a child of God.
8 Immediately my soul did rise
On wings of faith above the skies;
I count all earthly things but loss,
And glory in my Saviour's cross:
I see none but the Lord himself,
Can save a soul from sin and death:
And since he was by *John* baptiz'd,
I'll follow him tho' I'm despis'd.
9 I am dispos'd to serve the Lord,
It is to me a full reward;
I value not man's scoffing frown;
I hope to wear a starry crown.
Come all who know his works and ways.
Let's join to sing his lasting praise;
But I must strive to praise him best,
I've run so deep in debt to grace.

230. (11's.) 11S./4L.
The Sinner's Pedigree.

1 YE people who wonder at me and my ways,

231. (8, 8, 6.)
The proud Complainer humbled.

1 I SET myself against the Lord,
　Despis'd his Spirit and his word,
　　And wish'd to take his place:
　It vex'd me so that I must die,
　And perish too eternally,
　　Or else be sav'd by grace.

2 Of ev'ry preacher I'd complain:
　One spoke through pride, and one for gain,
　　Another's learning small.
　One spoke too fast, and one too slow,
　One pray'd too loud, and one too low;
　　Another had no call.

3 Some walk too straight to make a show,
　While others far too crooked go;
　　And both of these I scorn:
　Some odd, fantastic motions make,
　Some stoop too low, some stand too straight,
　　No one is faultless born.

4 With no professor could I join,
　Some dress'd too mean, and some too fine,
　　And some would talk too long:
　Some had a tone, some had no gift,
　Some talk'd too slow, and some too swift,
　　And all of them were wrong.

5 I thought they'd better keep at home,
　Than to exhort where'er they come,
　　And tell us of their joys:
　They'd better keep their garden free
　From weeds, than to examine me,
　　And vex me with their noise.

6 Kindreds and neighbours too are bad,
　And no true friend is to be had:
　　My rulers too are vile.
　But I at length was brought to see,
　The faults did mostly lie on me,
　　And had done all the while.

7 The horrid load of guilt and shame,
　Being conscious too I was to blame,
　　Did wound my frighted soul;
　I've sinn'd so much against my God,
　I've crouch'd so low beneath his rod,
　　How can I be made whole?

8 O! Christ's free love, a boundless sea!
　What! to expire for wretched me?
　　Yes! 'tis a truth divine.
　My heart did melt, my soul o'er-run
　With love, to see what God had done
　　For souls so vile as mine.

9 Now I can hear a child proclaim
　The joyful news, and praise the name
　　Of Jesus Christ my King:
　I know no sect—Christians are one;
　With my complaints I now have done,
　　And God's free grace I sing.

232. (8, 8, 6.) 4S./6L.
The Love of Christ recounted.

1 UNCLEAN! unclean! and full of sin

233. (11, 8.)
The Experience of J. M.

1 IN sin's howling waste, my poor soul was forlorn,
　And loved the distance full well,
　When grace, on the wings of the dove to me borne,
　Did snatch me, the fire-brand of hell.

2 O how shall I praise,—shall I glorify him,
　Who bore with my manners long time,
　And waited with patience to save me from sin,
　And made his long-suffering shine!

3 Six years had completed their round, when I saw,
　My soul was in danger of wrath;
　He then with the cords of his goodness did draw,
　And kept me, and held me from death.

4 I sought him by pray'r, and desir'd to know,
　His favour to Christians most free;
　But still I inclined to sin as I grew,
　And wish'd him comforted to me.

5 Entic'd by my comrades I oft went astray,
　And grieved and vexed my soul;
　I then would resolve, and go often to pray,
　But could not my passions controul.

6 So making and breaking resolves I went on,
　And sinning and praying by times,
　Till fifteen full years had their numbers sent on,
　Nor mourned but *actual* crime.

7 Alarmed more fully, I call'd on the Lord,
　And wonder'd I could not attain:

I pray'd, and I heard, and I searched his word,
But found all my efforts in vain.

8 The evil of sin I was then brought to view;
The fountain of nature broke forth:
I thought that I quickly with hell's trembling crew,
Should sink into oceans of wrath.

9 I wished to change with the beasts of the field,
My state with the trees of the wood;
My soul lay in sin, and with anguish was fill'd,
Because it was unlike to God.

10 The way of salvation I saw through the Lamb,
Who yielded his life on the tree;
Most just unto God, and sufficient to man,
From sin, and from wrath to set free.

11 For others, I saw this salvation by grace,
And envy'd their happier state;
But fear'd that this plan would not answer my case,
Although 'twas stupendously great.

12 When seventeen years and six months had gone round,
And sundry goods promises had,
Where sin did abound, grace did much more abound,
And I was in Jesus made *glad*.

13 I calmly sojourned, and praised his name,
Who precious to me did appear;
Believing, I ventur'd his kingdom to claim,
And serv'd him with trembling and fear.

14 Believing, I hop'd, and I lov'd, and I liv'd,
Have halted along to this day:
And surely the goodness which I have receiv'd,
Will help to the *end* of the way.

234. (L. M.) 12S.4L.
The Experience of the Philosopher.

1 I WALK'D abroad one morning fair,

235. (C. M.)
The successful Resolve.

1 COME humble sinner, in whose breast
A thousand thoughts revolve;
Come, with your guilt and fear opprest,
And make this last resolve.—

2 "I'll go to *Jesus*, though my sin
"Hath like a mountain rose;
"I know his counts, I'll enter in,
"Whatever may oppose."

3 "Prostrate I'll lie before his throne,
"And there my guilt confess;
"I'll tell him I'm a wretch undone,
"Without his sov'reign grace.

4 "I'll to the gracious King approach,
"Whose sceptre pardon gives;
"Perhaps he may command my touch,
"And then the suppliant lives.

5 "Perhaps he will admit my plea,
"Perhaps will hear my pray'r;
"But if I perish I will pray,
"And perish only there.

6 "I can but perish if I go—
"I am resolv'd to try;
"For if I stay away, I know
"I must for ever die."

SECOND PART.—*Responsive.*

1 RESOLVING thus, I entered in,
Though trembling and depress'd;
I bow'd before the gracious King,
And all my sins confess'd.

2 Sweet majesty and awful grace,
Sat smiling on his brow;
He turn'd to me his glorious face,
And made my eyes o'erflow.

3 He held the sceptre out to me,
And bade me touch and live;
I touch'd, and (O what mercy free!)
He did my sins forgive.

4 I touch'd, and liv'd, and learn'd to love,
And triumph'd in my God;
I sat my heart on things above,
And sang redeeming blood.

5 Come sinners griev'd, with sins distress'd,
And ready to despair,
Take courage, though with guilt oppress'd,
Jesus still answers pray'r.

6 Come enter in with cheerful haste;
You may his glory see,
You may his richest mercy taste—
He has forgiven ME.

236. (L. M.) 8S./4L.
Humble Pleadings.

1 O GIVE me, Lord, my sins to mourn;

237. (L. M.) 3S./4L.
The Penitent venturing.

1 PITY a helpless sinner, Lord,

238. (S. M.) Norwich.
Confession and Forgiveness.

1 MY sorrows like a flood,
    Impatient of restraint,
Into thy bosom, O my God!
    Pour out a long complaint.

2 This impious heart of mine
    Could once defy the Lord,
Could rush with vi'lence on to sin,
    In presence of thy sword.

3 How often have I stood
    A rebel to the skies,
And yet, and yet, O matchless grace!
    Thy thunder silent lies.

4 O, shall I never feel
    The meltings of thy love?
Am I of such hell-harden'd steel,
    That mercy cannot move?

5 O'ercome by dying love,
    Here at thy cross I lie,
And throw my flesh, my soul, my all,
    And weep, and love, and die.

6 "Rise," says the Saviour, "rise!
    "Behold my wounded veins!
"Here flows a sacred crimson flood,
    "To wash away thy stains."

7 See, God is reconcil'd!
    Behold his smiling face!
Let joyful cherubs clap their wings,
    And sound aloud his grace.

239. (L. M.) 3S./4L.
Humble pleadings under conviction.

1 LORD! with a griev'd and aching heart,

240. (L. M.) 3S./4L.
The same.

1 BEHOLD a sinner, dearest Lord,

241. (S. M.)
The Pool of Bethesda.

1 BESIDE the gospel pool,
    Appointed for the poor,
From time to time my helpless soul
    Has waited for a cure.

2 How often have I seen
    The healing waters move;
And others round me stepping in,
    Their efficacy prove?

3 But my complaints remain:
    I feel the very same:
And full of guilt, and fear, and pain,
    As when at first I came.

4 O, would the Lord appear
    My malady to heal;
He knows how long I've languish'd here,
    And what distress I feel.

[5 How often have I thought,
    Why should I longer lie?
Surely the mercy I have sought
    Is not for such as I?

6 But whither can I go?
    There is no other pool
Where streams of sov'reign virtue flow
    To make a sinner whole.]

7 Here, then, from day to day,
    I'll wait, and hope, and try;
Can Jesus hear a sinner pray,
    Yet suffer him to die?

8 No—he is full of grace;
    He never will permit
A soul that fain would see his face,
    To perish at his feet.

242. (C. M.) 3S./4L.
Faith fulfilling the Law.

1 WHEN from the precepts to the cross

243. (S. M.) Double.
Mispent Mercies lamented.

1 QUITE weary, near to faint,
    I my hard lot deplore—
I would myself with God acquaint,
    But 'tis not in my pow'r;
I know my dang'rous state,
    'Tis carnal, sold to sin;
Corrupt, impure, degenerate,
    Have all my doings been.

2 How many precious days,
    Have I mispent and lost,
Lov'd to frequent unholy ways,
    And made of sin my boast?
Alas! those days are gone,
    Those golden days are o'er;

    The gospel here, that lately shone,
      Perhaps may shine no more.
3 O! whither shall I fly,
    If God hath me forsook?
    To whom, or where for mercy cry,
      Or where for refuge look?
    How shall I meet the Lord,
      Or how his anger bear,
    When I shall see his flaming sword,
      And banner in the air?
4 When by the trumpet's sound,
    The dead to life shall come,
    And all the nations under ground,
      Shall rise to know their doom?—
    When time shall have an end,
      When Jesus on a cloud,
    Shall with his angel host descend,
      And with the trump of God?
5 O Lord my crimes forgive,
    If I may be forgiven,
    And with thy chosen me receive,
      When thou shalt come from heav'n:
    Spare me, in mercy spare,
      O! wash and make me clean,
    And fit me for the day when here,
      I shall no more be seen.
6 And when I'm dead and gone,
    May I in glory be,
    To sing in strains till then unknown—
      Thy lovely face to see;
    O may I bear some part,
      With the redeemed race,
    And play upon a golden harp
      Thy well-deserved praise.

      244. (6, 8.) Lenox. 2S./6L.
Bartimeus, or a convicted Sinner begging.

1 SINFUL, and blind, and poor,

      245. (L. M.) 4S./4L.
      The Pool of Bethesda.

1 HOW long, thou faithful God, shall I,

      246. (C. M.) 3S./4L.
The Worth of the Soul contrasted with the world.

1 LORD, shall we part with gold for dress,

      247. (C. M.) 5S./4L.
The Omniscience of God, and Meditation of Christ.

1 GREAT God, though from myself conceal'd,

      248. (C. M.) 4S./4L.
    The Penitent imploring Mercy.

1 LORD at thy feet in dust I lie,

      249. (L. M.) 4S./4L.
    Blessed are they that mourn.

1 WHY, mourning soul, why flow these tears?

      250. (L. M.) Williamstown.
    A Penitent pleading for Pardon.

1 SHEW pity, Lord; O Lord forgive;
    Let a repenting sinner live:
    Are not thy mercies large and free?
    May not a sinner trust in thee?
2 My crimes are great, but can't surpass
    The pow'r and glory of thy grace:
    Great God, thy nature hath no bound,
    So let thy pard'ning love be found.
3 O wash my soul from ev'ry sin,
    And make my guilty conscience clean:
    Here on my heart the burden lies,
    And past offences pain mine eyes.
4 My lips with shame my sins confess,
    Against thy law, against thy grace;
    Lord should thy judgments grow severe,
    I am condemn'd, but thou art clear.
5 Yet save a trembling sinner, Lord,
    Whose hope, still hov'ring round thy word,
    Would light on some sweet promise there,
    Some sure support against despair.

BELIEVERS' BAPTISM.

      251. (10, 11.)
  The Word, a Rule of Faith and Practice.

1 YOU captives restor'd, and saints of the Lord,   [word,
    Who follow the Lamb, and are led by his
    Let's read it and see, if we can agree,
    And pray for his Spirit our leader to be,
2 We'll read it aright, and pray for a sight,
    Of each gospel duty, and in it delight;
    And is it your case, through rich and free grace,
    That you are secure in a Saviour's embrace?
3 And do you enquire, with earnest desire,
    To know what the Lord of his servants require?
    His Spirit and word directions afford;
    Let's search for our duty and follow the Lord.

4 We'll follow him down to Jordan's fair
      stream,   [blaspheme;
  And tread in his footsteps, though sinners
  From Galilee, he did travel we see,
  To Jordan, and on its banks bended his
      knee.
5 Thus cheerfully bent, with the herald's
      consent,   [went:
  And straightway down into the water he
  See here what a brave example we have,
  Behold him immers'd in a watery grave.
6 And herein we see, bless'd Saviour that he
  Came out of the water in miracles three:
  The heavens were rent, the Spirit was sent,
  The voice of the Father proclaimed consent.
7 This stoop of our Lord, we have on record,
  Then pray let us always take heed to his
      word:
  Although Zion's foes will dare to oppose,
  We'll follow the Lamb wherever he goes.
8 Although Zion cries, ere long she'll arise,
  Above the blue curtains in the higher skies,
  Where angels do stand, and wait the
      command,
  To meet us and guide us to Jesus' right
      hand.

252. (8's.)
Christ's Baptism by John our Example.

1 IN Jordan's tide the Baptist stands,
     Immersing the repenting Jews;
  The Son of God the rite demands,
     Nor dares the holy man refuse:
  Jesus descends beneath the wave,
  The emblem of his future grave.
2 Wonder, ye heav'ns! your Maker lies
     In deeps conceal'd from human view,
  Ye saints behold him sink and rise,
     A fit example this for you:
  This sacred record, while you read,
  Calls you to imitate the deed.
3 But, lo! from yonder opening skies,
     What beams of dazzling glory spread!
  Dove-like th' eternal Spirit flies,
     And lights on the Redeemer's head;
  Amaz'd they see the pow'r divine,
  Around the Saviour's temples shine.
4 But hark, my soul, hark and adore!
     What sounds are those that roll along,
  Not like loud Sinai's awful roar.
     But soft and sweet as Gabriel's song!
  "This is my well-beloved Son,
  "I see well pleas'd what he hath done."

5 Thus the eternal Father spoke,
     Who shakes creation with a nod:
  Through parting skies the accents broke,
     And bid us hear the Son of God:
  O hear the awful word to-day,
  Hear, all ye nations, and obey!

253. (8, 7.)
The Humble invited to imitate Christ.

1 HUMBLE souls who seek salvation
     Thro' the Lamb's redeeming blood,
  Hear the voice of Revelation,
     Tread the path that Jesus trod.
  Flee to him your only Saviour,
     In his mighty name confide;
  In the whole of your behaviour,
     Own him as your Sov'reign guide.
2 Hear the bless'd Redeemer call you,
     Listen to his gracious voice:
  Dread no ills that can befall you,
     While you make his ways your choice;
  Jesus says, "Let each believer
     "Be baptized in my name:"
  He himself in Jordan's river,
     Was immers'd beneath the stream.
3 Plainly here his footsteps tracing,
     Follow him without delay;
  Gladly his command embracing,
     Lo! your captain leads the way:
  View the rite with understanding;
     Jesus' grave before you lies;
  Be interr'd at his commanding,
     After his example rise.

254. (8, 8, 6.) 4S./6L.
Thus it becometh us, &c.

1 THUS it became the Prince of grace,

255. (P. M.) 4S./12L.
Christ the Christian's Exemplar.

1 HAIL sacred Saviour! Prince of Light,

256. (6, 8.) Lenox. 4S./6L.
The descent of the Dove in Baptism.

1 DESCEND, celestial Dove,

257. (6, 8.) Lenox. 5S./6L.
Encouragement to be Baptized.

1 "WHY tarriest thou, arise

258. (C. M.) 4S./4L.
Love to Christ constrains to Obedience.

1 DEAR Lord, and will thy pard'ning love

259. (C. M.) 3S./4L.
Christ's Example worthy of Imitation.

1 THUS was the great Redeemer plung'd

260. (L. M.) 4S./4L.
Baptism representing the Death and Resurrection of Christ.

1 LORD, to this fountain we repair,

261. (C. M.) 5S./4L.
Baptism urged from the command of Christ.

1 DESPISE me not, my carnal friends,

262. (C. M.)
"Hinder me not."

1 IN all my Lord's appointed ways,
  My journey I'll pursue;
  Hinder me not, ye much-lov'd saints,
  For I must go with you.

2 Through floods and flames, If Jesus lead,
  I'll follow where he goes;
  Hinder me not, shall be my cry,
  Though earth and hell oppose.

3 Through duty, and through trials too,
  I'll go at his command;
  Hinder me not, for I am bound
  To my IMMANUEL's land.

4 And when my Saviour calls me home,
  Still this my cry shall be,
  Hinder me not, come welcome death,
  I'll gladly go with thee.

263. (S. M.) 4S./4L.
The Duty in Baptism urged.

1 "ARISE and be baptiz'd,

264. (C. M.) 2S./4L.
A Prayer for Baptized persons

1 ETERNAL God, now smile on those,

265. (L. M.) 4S./4L.
The Commission.

1 'TWAS the commission of our Lord;

266. (L. M.) 3S./4L.
Believers buried in Baptism.

1 DO we not know that solemn word,

CHRISTIAN EXERCISES.

267. (P. M.)
Rejoicing in Divine Union.

1 COME saints and sinners hear me tell
  The wonders of Immanuel,
  Who snatch'd me from a burning hell,
  And brought my soul with him to dwell
    To dwell in sweetest union.

2 When Jesus from his throne on high,
  Beheld my soul in ruin lie,
  He look'd on me with pitying eye,
  And said to me, as he pass'd by,
    "With God you have no union."

3 This information made me cry,
  I strove salvation hard to buy,
  And with my tears to satisfy;
  I look'd this way and that to fly,
    For still I lack'd this union.

4 But when depress'd and lost in sin,
  My dear Redeemer took me in,
  And with his blood he wash'd me clean,
  And O what seasons I have seen,
    Since first I felt this union.

5 I prais'd the Lord both night and day,
  And went from house to house to pray,
  And if I met one in the way,
  Something I always found to say
    About this heavenly union.

6 O come ye lukewarm, come away,
  And learn to do as well as say,
  And hear your cross from day to day,
  And mind to walk the narrow way,
    And then you'll feel this union.

7 I wonder that the saints don't sing,
  And make the hills and vallies ring,
  With loud hosannas to their King,
  Who sav'd their souls from hell and sin,
    And brought about this union.

8 We soon shall leave these climes below,
  And ev'ry scene of pain and woe!
  We all shall then to glory go!
  And there we'll see, and hear, and know,
    And join in perfect union.

9 Come heav'n and earth unite your lays,
   And give Jehovah-Jesus praise:
   And thou my soul look up and gaze,
   He bleeds, he dies, thy debt he pays!
   To give thee heav'nly union.
10 O were I like an angel found,
   Salvation through the earth I'd sound,
   The devil's kingdom to confound,
   I'd triumph on Immanuel's ground,
   And spread this glorious union.

268. (L. M.)
Rejoicing in Hope of Glory.

1 O MAY I worthy prove to see
   The saints in full prosperity,
   To see the bride, the glittering bride,
   Close seated by her Saviour's side.

The Chorus.
And I'll sing Glory, Glory,
And glory be to God on high.

2 O may I find some humble seat,
   Beneath my dear Redeemer's feet;
   A servant, as before he's been,
   I'll sing salvation to my King.

3 I'm glad that I am born to die,
   From grief and woe my soul shall fly!
   Bright angels shall convey me home,
   Away to th' new Jerusalem.

4 I'll praise him while he gives me breath,
   I hope to praise him after death,
   I hope to praise him when I die,
   And shout salvation as I fly!

5 Farewell vain world, I'm going home,
   My Jesus smiles, and bids me come,
   Sweet angels beckon me away,
   To sing God's praise in endless day.

6 I soon shall pass the vale of death,
   And in his arms resign my breath:
   O then my happy soul shall tell
   "My Jesus has done all things well."

7 I soon shall hear the awful sound,
   "Awake ye nations under ground;
   Arise and drop your dying shrouds,
   And meet King Jesus in the clouds."

8 When to the blessed world I rise,
   And join the anthems round the skies,
   Of all the notes there, this shall swell,
   "My Jesus has done all things well."

9 Then shall I see my blessed God,
   And praise him in his bright abode,
   My theme to all eternity,
   Shall *Glory, Glory, Glory,* be.

269. (8, 7.)
Extatic Praises.

1 BRIGHT scenes of glory strike my sense,
      And all my passions capture,
   Eternal beauty round me shines,
      Infusing warmest rapture;
   I dive in pleasures deep, and full,
      In swelling waves of glory,
   And feel my Saviour in my soul,
      And groan to tell my story.

2 I feast on honey, milk, and wine,
      And drink perpetual sweetness,
   Mount Zion's odours through me roll
      While Christ unfolds his greatness:
   No mortal tongue can speak my joys,
      Nor can an angel tell them,
   Ten thousand times surpassing all
      Terrestial worlds of emblem.

3 My captivated spirits fly
      Through shining worlds of beauty,
   Dissolv'd in blushes then I cry,
      In praises loud and mighty;
   Here will I sit, and swell the theme
      Of harmony, delighted!
   And with the millions learn the notes
      Of saints, in Christ united.

4 The bliss that rolls through those above,
      Through those in glory seated,
   Which causes them loud songs to sing,
      Ten thousand times repeated,
   Darts through my soul with radiant beams,
      Constraining loudest praises,
   O'erwhelming all my pow'rs with joy,
      While all within me blazes.

5 When earth and seas shall be no more,
      And all their glory perish,
   When sun and moon shall cease to shine.
      And stars at midnight languish;
   My joys refin'd shall brighter shine,
      Mount heaven's radiant glory,

And tell through one eternal day,
   Love's *all immortal* story.

270. (C. M.) Double.
The Love of Christ is better than Wine.

1 MY soul doth magnify the Lord,
   My spirit doth rejoice
In God my Saviour, and my God,
   I hear his joyful voice:
I need not go abroad for joys,
   I have a feast at home,
My sighs are turned into songs,
   The Comforter is come.

2 Down from above, the blessed Dove,
   Is come into my breast,
Witness of God's eternal love,
   This makes me *abba* father cry,
With confidence of soul;
This makes me cry, my Lord, my God,
   And that without control.

3 There is a stream which issues forth
   From God's eternal throne;
And from the Lamb a living stream,
   Clear as a crystal stone;
This stream doth water Paradise,
   It makes the angels sing,
One cordial drop revives my heart,
   Thence all my joys do spring.

4 Such joys as these unspeakable,
   And full of glory too!
Such hidden manna, hidden pearls!
   As worldings do not know;
Eye hath not seen, nor ear hath heard,
   From fancy 'tis conceal'd,
What thou, Lord, hast laid up for thine,
   And hast to me reveal'd

5 I see thy face, I hear thy voice,
   I taste thy sweetest love,
My soul doth leap, but O for wings!
   The wings of Noah's dove:
Then would I fly far hence away,
   And leave this world of sin,
Then would my Lord put forth his hand,
   And kindly take me in.

6 Then would my soul with angels feast,
   On joys that ever last;
Refined, full and always sweet,
   Delighting to the taste,
Bless'd be my God, the God of joys,
   Who gives me here a crumb,
And fills my soul with earnest hope
   'Till I arrive at home.

271. (L. M.)
Troubles ending in Glory.

1 O BRETHREN, we are going on,
   To join the holy, hymning throng,
Of angels bright, and saints that shine,
   Enrob'd in righteousness divine.

Chorus.
And we'll sing glory, glory,
And shout the Lamb who came to die,
And gave to us the victory—
And glory be to God on high.

2 We're now oppress'd with various doubt,
We've fears within, and foes without;
Through hosts of devils now we fight,
But then we'll join the saints in light.

3 Our suff'ring time will soon be o'er,
We'll sin, and grieve, and doubt no more,
But on that ever peaceful shore,
We'll shout our trials all are o'er.

4 Our praying time will soon be o'er,
We'll join with them who're gone before,
To love, and bless, and praise the name,
Of Jesus Christ, the bleeding Lamb.

5 Our parting time will soon be past,
Our joys will then for ever last;
In union sweet we'll join to tell,
The love of dear Immanuel.

6 Our preaching time will soon be done,
We'll see the *travail* of the *Son*,
Unite and gather all in one,
And march in splendor to the throne.

7 The gulf of death will soon be cross'd,
We'll fear no more that we'll be lost;
But on that happy, happy shore,
We'll sing and triumph evermore.

8 Oh! this shall be our theme above,
When we're solac'd in unknown love;
We'll bow around the golden throne,
And sing the boundless great *Three-One.*

9 When we've been there ten thousand days,
We've no less time to sing God's praise;
Eternity is but begun—
Our praising time will ever run.

10 Our raptur'd souls are all on fire,
To join the everlasting choir;
To bear a part in that bless'd lay,
Where none shall ever *Amen* say.

272. (L. M.)
The glorious Mystery.

1 'TIS a glorious mystery,
   That I should ever saved be!

No heart can think or fully tell,
Why God has sav'd my soul from hell.
2 Great mystery! I can't tell why,
That Christ for sinners e'er should die;
But greater still the mystery,
That he should ever die for me.
3 No creature can a reason give,
Why I wa'nt left in sin to live;
To spend my days in guilt and fear,
And die at last in deep despair.
4 No mortal can a reason find—
'Tis grace most free and mercy kind;
O 'tis a glorious mystery!
And will be to eternity.
5 O brethren we'll soon see the Lord,
And sit around his sacred board,
To drink in full mysterious love,
Which flows in Paradise above.
6 There we shall see our Father's face,
And sing of his redeeming grace,
With rapture join th' angelic throng,
And Christ the burden of the song.
7 With them the jasper walls we'll see,
With them in glory we shall be;
Through pearly gates we'll enter in,
And God's eternal praises sing.
8 There, there with joy we all shall meet.
In Jesus' glories be complete;
Eternity shall roll around,
And Jesus in the midst be found.

273. (C. M. Chorus 8's.)
Christian Love expanding its Desires.

1 OUR souls by love together knit,
　　Cemented, mix'd in one;
　　One hope, one heart, one mind, one voice,
　　'Tis heav'n on earth begun:
　　Our hearts have burn'd while Jesus spake,
　　And glow'd with sacred fire;
　　He stopp'd, and talk'd, and fed, and bless'd
　　And fill'd th' enlarg'd desire.

Chorus.

A Saviour! let creation sing,
A Saviour! let all heaven ring;
He's God with us, we feel him ours,
His fulness in our souls he pours;
Tis almost done, 'tis almost o'er,
We're joining them who're gone before,
We soon shall meet to part no more.

2 We're soldiers fighting for our God,
　　Let trembling cowards fly;
　　We stand unshaken, firm and fix'd,
　　With Christ to live and die:

Let devils rage and hell assail,
　　We'll cut our passage through:
Though foes unite, and friends all fail,
　　We'll seize the crown we view.
　　　　　　　　A Saviour, &c.

3 The little cloud increases fast,
　　The heav'ns are big with rain;
We haste to catch the teeming show'rs,
　　And all the moisture drain:
A rill, a stream, a torrent flows,
　　Yea pours a mighty flood;
O sweep the nations, shake the earth,
　　We'll all proclaim thee God.
　　　　　　　　A Saviour, &c.

4 From east to west, from north to south,
　　O be thy name ador'd!
Let *Europe* with her millions shout
　　Hosannas to *thee*, Lord:
Let *Asia, Africa* resound
　　From shore to shore thy fame;
And all *America* in songs
　　Redeeming love proclaim.
　　　　　　　　A Saviour, &c.

5 And when thou mak'st thy jewels up,
　　And set'st thy starry crown;
When all thy sparkling gems shall shine,
　　Proclaim'd *by thee* thy own;
May we, a little band of love,
　　Be sinners sav'd by grace;
From glory into glory chang'd,
　　Behold thee face to face.
　　　　　　　　A Saviour, &c.

274. (11's.)
The Children of Zion invited to unite in Praise.

1 YE children of Zion, who're bound for
　　　the kingdom,
　　Attune all your voices and help me to
　　　sing
Sweet anthems of praises to my blessed
　　Jesus,
　　For he is my Prophet, my Priest, and my
　　　King.
When Jesus first found me, to hell I was
　　going,
　　His love did surround me, and sav'd me
　　　from ruin;
He kindly receiv'd me, and from sin re-
　　liev'd me,　　　　　　　　　　[sing.
　　And taught me aloud his sweet praises to

2 Why should you go mourning from such a
　　physician,　　　　　　　　　　[cure;
　　Who is able and willing your sickness to

Come to him believing—though bad your condition, [sure,
His Father has promis'd your case to en-
My soul he has healed, my heart it rejoices,
He's brought me to Zion to join the glad voices;
I'll serve him, and praise him, and always adore him, [o'er.
Till we meet in glory where sickness is

3 My heart's now in heaven, to Jesus ascended,
I'm bound to set forward, to th' mark for the prize;
And when my temptations and trials are ended, [shall rise.
On the wings of bright seraphs my soul it
O, Christians! I'm happy in this contemplation.
My soul it drinks in the sweet streams of salvation—
I long to be flying, that I may be vying,
With th' tallest archangel that shouts in the skies.

4 Cheer up, ye dear pilgrims, fair Canaan's before you,
We'll scale the high mountain, still shouting free grace:
On Jerusalem's bright tower we'll sing hallelujah.
And sit in the smiles of sweet Jesus's face.
No sorrow, no sighing, no weeping, no mourning,
To those who there enter there is no returning,
But feasting, and resting, and for ever singing [grace;
And glory to Jesus, who bought us free

5 My soul, full of glory, can't stay here much longer,
The angels of heaven now call me away;
The Spirit of Jesus draws stronger and stronger— [day.
My soul now exults to behold the glad
O Christians! O Christians! O had you not rather, [ther,
Be shouting in glory with your blessed Fa-
Where clouds and temptations, sins, pains, and vexations,
Are all lost together in endless bright day?

6 This moment the angels are hov'ring around us, [sweet King.
And joining with mortals to praise their
And waiting for Jesus to call us and crown us,
To make all the arches of heaven to ring,
There, with our dear Father, we'll meet one another, [brother;—
The wife and the husband, the sister and
In the fathomless ocean of love's sweet emotion,
Salvation to Jesus, for ever we'll sing.

275. (8, 8, 6.) 7S./6L.
Rejoicing in warmest Hope.

1 O GLORIOUS hope of perfect love!

276. (8, 8, 6.)
The same.

1 HOW happy is the Pilgrim's lot,
How free from anxious care and tho't,
From worldly hope and fear!
Confin'd to neither court nor cell,
His soul disdains on earth to dwell,
He only sojourns here.

2 His happiness in part is mine,
Already sav'd from self-design,
From ev'ry creature-love:
Bless'd with the scorn of finite good,
My soul is lighten'd of its load,
And seeks the things above.

3 The things eternal I pursue,
And happiness, beyond the view
Of those, who basely pant
For things, by nature felt and seen:
Their honours, wealth, and pleasures mean.
I neither have, nor want.

4 Nothing on earth I call my own—
A stranger to the world, unknown,
I all their goods despise:
I trample on their whole delight,
And seek a country out of sight,
A country in the skies.

5 There is my house and portion fair.
My treasure and my heart are there,
And my abiding home:
For me my elder brethren stay,
And angels beckon me away,
And Jesus bids me come,

6 I come! thy servant, Lord, replies,
I come to meet thee in the skies,
And claim my heav'nly rest!
Now let the pilgrim's journey end,
Now, O my Saviour, brother, friend,
Receive me to thy breast!

277. (11's.) 7S./4L.
The Joys of a Revival long sought.

1 O HOW I have long'd for the coming of God,

278. (11's.)
Christian Harmony.

1 SWEET singers of Israel, begin your sweet strains,
We'll join you in walking through these flowery plains:
Your theme is applauded, and jovial the lay,
Let's walk in sweet concert to eternal day.

2 We came out of darkness to dwell in the light, [sight:
The brightness so sparkles, it dazzles our
So bright is the morning, the clouds flees away,
The sun is now dawning its eternal day.

3 We'll 'scend up the stairs, though most winding they be,
Till we gain the heaven of highest degree:
We'll stand in sweet wonder to view the bright ray,
Which 'lumines the mountain of eternal day.

4 Religion and friendship unite heart and hand,
Like two loving brothers together we'll stand,
Like well order'd armies that move by due sway,
We'll march in due order for eternal day.

5 Built on the foundation of Christ, *the sure Rock,* [the work:
With line, rule, and compass, made fit for
Like gold, silver, stones, wholly precious entire, [on fire.
We'll stand in that day when the world is

279. (8, 7, 7.) 5S./6L.
Thanksgiving for Redemption.

1 RANSOM'D sinners, sing the praises,

280. (6.8.) Lenox.
The All-sufficience of Christ celebrated.

1 BY whom was David taught,
To aim the dreadful blow,
When he Goliah fought,
And laid the Gittite low?
No sword nor spear the strippling took,
But chose a pebble from the brook.

2 'Twas Israel's God and King,
Who sent him to the fight;
Who gave him strength to sling,
And skill to aim aright.
Ye feeble saints, your strength endures,
Because young David's God is yours.

3 Who order'd Gideon forth,
To storm th' invaders camp,
With arms of little worth,
A pitcher and a lamp?
The trumpets made his coming known,
And all the host was overthrown.

4 Oh! I have seen the day,
When with a single word,
God helping me to say,
My trust is in the Lord;
My soul has quell'd a thousand foes,
Fearless of all that could oppose.

5 But unbelief, self-will,
Self-righteousness and pride,
How often do they steal,
My weapon from my side:
But David's Lord, and Gideon's friend,
Will help his servant to the end.

281. (11, 8.)
The Praises of Christ.

1 O THOU, in whose presence my soul takes delight,
On whom in affliction I call,
My comfort by day, and my song in the night,
My hope, my salvation, my all.

2 Where dost thou at noon-tide resort with thy sheep.
To feed on the pastures of love,
For why, in the valley of death, should I weep?
Or, alone in the wilderness rove?

3 O why should I wander an alien from thee,
And cry in the desert for bread?
Thy foes will rejoice when my sorrows they see,
And smile at the tears I have shed.

4 Ye daughters of Zion, declare if ye've seen
The *Star* that on Israel shone;
Say if in your tents my Beloved has been,
And where with his flocks he has gone.

5 Thou fairest of women, O what's thy Belov'd,
Above those around whom we see?
Why charge us so straitly to know where he's rov'd?
Declare what his beauties may be.

6 If he is possess'd of more dignify'd charms
    Than any about whom we know,
  We'll turn, with disdain, from their beauties and arms,
    And seek him intensely with you.

7 *This is my Beloved*—his form is divine,
    His vestments shed odours around,
  The locks on his head are as grapes on the vine,
    When autumn with plenty is crown'd.

8 The roses of Saron, the lillies that grow
    In the vales on the banks of the streams,
  On his cheeks in the beauty of excellence blow,
    And his eyes are as quivers of beams.

9 His voice as the sound of a dulcimer sweet,
    Is heard through the shadows of death;
  The cedars of Lebanon bow at his feet,
    The air is perfum'd with his breath.

10 His lips as the fountain of righteousness flow,
    And water the garden of grace,
  From which their salvation the Gentiles shall know,
    And bask in the smiles of his face.

11 Love sits on his eye-lids and scatters delight,
    Through all the bright mansions on high;
  Their faces the cherubims veil in his sight,
    And tremble with fulness of joy.

12 He looks—and ten thousand of angels rejoice,
    And myriads wait for his word;
  He speaks—and eternity filled with his voice,
    Re-echoes the praise of her Lord.

13 His vestment of righteousness, who shall describe?
    Its purity words would defile,
  The heav'ns from his presence fresh beauties imbibe,
    And earth is enrich'd by his smile.

14 Such is my Beloved in excellence bright,
    When pleas'd he looks down from above,
  Like the morn when he breathes from the chambers of light,
    And comforts his people with love.

282. (12, 11.)
The same.

1 HOSANNA to Jesus! my soul's fill'd with praises,
  Come, O my dear brethren, and help me to sing,
  No theme is so charming, no love is so warming, [within.
  It gives life and comfort, and gladness

2 Hosanna is ringing—O how I love singing!
  There's nothing so sweet as the sound of his name:
  The angels in glory repeat the glad story
  Of love, which in Jesus is made known to man.

3 Hosanna to Jesus! who died to save us;
  I'll love him, and serve him wherever I go;
  He's now gone to heav'n, but the Spirit is giv'n, [low.
  To quicken and comfort his children be-

4 Hosanna forever! His grace like a river,
  Is rising and spreading all over its banks;
  His love is unbounded, and hell is confounded, [thanks.
  And sinners are drinking and giving of

5 Hosanna to Jesus! my soul how it pleases,
  To see sinners crying, and turning to God;
  To see them uniting, is truly delighting,
  And praising for pardon through Jesus's blood.

6 Hosanna is ringing, O how I love singing
  The praising of Jesus, and tasting his love!
  The sound goes to heav'n, the Spirit is given:
  It rolls through my soul from the ocean above.

7 Hosanna to Jesus! my soul feels him precious
  In streams of salvation which come from above:
  My heart is now glowing, I feel his love flowing [love.
  And filling my soul from the fountain of

8 Hosanna is ringing—the saints now are singing, [bands:
  And marching to glory, in bright royal
  Come on my dear brethren, let's all go to heaven, [hands.
  For Jesus invites us with out-stretched

9 Hosanna to Jesus! my soul sweetly rises—
  We soon will attain a far happier clime,
  Where we will see Jesus, and dwell on his praises,
  And with him in glory eternally shine.

10 Hosanna dear *Jesus* how then it will please us,
   To bow and adore the great *Father* divine;

Hymn Texts From *The Cluster*

    The *Spirit* well bless it, and humbly con-
fess it,
That not unto us, but all glory be thine.

283. (8, 7, 4.) 9S./4L.
Joining in Praise with Angels.

1 MIGHTY God! while angels bless thee,

284. (C. M.) Chorused.
The New Jerusalem described and desired.

1 JERUSALEM, my happy home,
    O how I long for thee,
When will my sorrows have an end,
    Thy joys when shall I see.

Chorus.

O the place, the happy place,
    The place where Jesus is,
The place where Christians all shall meet
    In everlasting bliss!

2 Thy walls are all of precious stone,
    Most glorious to behold!
Thy gates are richly set with pearls,
    Thy streets are pav'd with gold.

3 Thy gardens and thy pleasant greens,
    My study long have been;
Such sparkling light, by human sight,
    Hath never yet been seen.

4 If heaven be thus glorious Lord,
    Why should I stay from thence?
What folly 'tis that makes me dread,
    To die and go from hence.

5 Reach down, reach down thy arm of grace,
    And cause me to ascend,
Where congregations ne'er break up,
    And Sabbaths never end.

6 Jesus my love to glory's gone,
    Him will I go and see;
And all my brethren here below,
    Will soon come after me.

7 My friends, I bid you all adieu
    I leave you in God's care;
And if no more I here see you,
    Go on, I'll meet you there.

8 And if our happiness below
    In Jesus be so sweet,
What heights of rapture shall we know,
    When round his throne we meet.

9 There we shall meet and no more part.
    And heav'n shall ring with praise,
While Jesus' love in every heart,
    Shall tune the song *free grace.*

10 Millions of years around shall run—
    Our song shall still go on,
To praise the *Father* and the *Son*,
    And *Spirit, three* in *One.*

285. (C. M.) Double 8S./8L.
Desiring to be present with the Lord.

1 SWEET rivers of redeeming love

286. (10's.)
Worldly Treasures lost in the Joyful Hope of the True.

1 O TELL me no more of this world's vain store!
The time for such trifles with me is now o'er:
A country I've found where true joys abound,
And to dwell I'm determin'd on that happy ground.

2 No mortal doth know, what Christ will bestow,
What life, strength, and comfort! go after him go.
Lo onward I move, to see Christ above,
None guesses how wond'rous my journey will prove.

3 Great spoils I shall win, from death, hell and sin;
'Midst outward affliction shall feel Christ within;
And still, which is best, I in his dear breast,
As at the beginning, find pardon and rest.

4 When I am to die, receive me, I'll cry,
For Jesus has lov'd me, I cannot tell why;
But this I do find, we *two* are so join'd,
He'll not live in glory and leave me behind.

5 This blessing is mine, thro' favour divine,
And, *O my dear Jesus*, the praise shall be thine;
In heav'n we'll meet, in harmony sweet,
And glory to Jesus! we'll then be complete.

287. (8, 7.)
Zion is Defended and Supplied.

1 GLORIOUS things of thee are spoken,
    Zion, city of our God!
He whose word cannot be broken,
    Form'd thee for his own abode;
On the rock of ages founded,
    What can shake thy sure respose?
With salvation's wall surrounded,
    Thou may'st smile at all thy foes.

2 See! the streams of living waters,
    Springing from eternal love,
Well supply thy sons and daughters,
    And all fear of want remove;
Who can faint while such a river
    Ever flows their thirst t' assuage?

Grace, which like the Lord, the giver,
  Never fails from age to age.
3 Round each habitation hov'ring,
   See the cloud and fire appear!
  For a glory and a cov'ring,
   Showing that the Lord is near:
  Thus deriving from their banner
   Light by night, and shade by day;
  Safe they feed upon the manna
   Which he gives them when they pray.
4 Blest inhabitants of Zion,
   Wash'd in the Redeemer's blood!
  Jesus, whom their souls rely on,
   Makes them kings and priests to God,
  'Tis his love his people raises
   Over self to reign as kings,
  And as priests—his solemn praises
   Each for a thank-off'ring brings.
5 Saviour, if of Zion's city,
   I through grace a member am,
  Let the world decide or pity,
   I will glory in thy name:
  Fading is the worlding's pleasure,
   All his boasted pomp and show;
  Solid joys and lasting treasure,
   None but Zion's children know.

288. (7, 6.)
The Joyful Pilgrim bound to Canaan.

1 GOOD morning, brother Pilgrim,
   What! bound for Salem's coasts?
  Let's march for new-Jerusalem,
   To join the heav'nly hosts:
  Pray wherefore are you smiling,
   While tears run down your face?
  We soon shall cease from toiling,
   And reach that happy place.
2 To Canaan's coast we'll hasten,
   To join the heav'nly throng,
  Hark! from the bank of Jordan,
   How sweet the pilgrim-song!
  Their Jesus they are viewing,
   By faith we see him too,
  We smile, and weep, and praise him,
   And on our way pursue.
3 Though sinners do despise us,
   And treat us with disdain,
  Our former comrades slight us,
   Esteem us low and mean:
  No earthly joy shall charm us,
   While marching on our way,
  Our Jesus will defend us,
   In the distressing day.
4 The frowns of old companions,
   We're willing to sustain,
  And in divine compassions
   To pray for them again:
  For Christ our loving Saviour,
   Our Comforter and Friend,
  Will bless us with his favour,
   And guide us to the end.
5 With streams of consolation,
   We're fill'd as with new wine,
  We die to transient pleasures,
   And live to things divine:
  We sink in holy raptures,
   While viewing things above,
  Why glory to my Saviour!
   My soul is full of love.
6 Beyond the streams of Jordan,
   Behold the shining throng,
  Salvation to their Jesus,
   Is flowing from their tongue:
  The sparkling gates are open,
   The golden streets I view,
  My happy soul would join 'em,
   And praise my Jesus too.
7 The gales of grace are blowing,
   My soul is on the wing,
  Salvation's current flowing,
   And well may Christians sing:
  The fiery chariot's rolling,
   To bear me through the skies,
  Hail, lovely precious Jesus,
   To thee my spirit flies!

289. (C. M.)
Love the Sweetest Passion.

1 DO not I love thee, O my Lord?
   Behold my heart, and see;
  And turn each cursed idol out,
   That dares to rival thee.
2 Do not I love thee from my soul?
   Then let me nothing love:
  Dead be my heart to ev'ry joy,
   Which thou dost not approve.
3 Is not thy name melodious still
   To mine attentive ear?
  Doth not each pulse with pleasure beat
   My Saviour's voice to hear?
4 Thou know'st I love thee, dearest Lord,
   But O, I long to soar
  Far from the sphere of mortal joys,
   That I may love thee more.

290. (C. M.) 4S./4L.
The Same.

1 THOU lovely source of true delight,

291. (L. M.) 4S./4L.
The Joys of Christian Fellowship.

1 KINDRED in Christ, for his dear sake,

Hymn Texts From *The Cluster*

292. (L. M.) 6S./4L.
Young Converts in their First Love.

1 WHEN converts first begin to sing,

293. (C. M.) 10S./4L.
The Love of Christ Constraining.

1 A HEAVENLY flame creates my song,

294. (C. M.) New Jordan.
A Transporting View of the Heavenly Canaan.

1 ON Jordan's stormy banks I stand,
  And cast a wishful eye
To Canaan's fair and happy land,
  Where my possessions lie.

2 O the transporting, rapt'rous scene,
  That rises to my sight!
Sweet fields array'd in living green,
  And rivers of delight!

3 There gen'rous fruits that never fail,
  On trees immortal grow;   [vales,
There rocks, and hills, and brooks, and
  With milk and honey flow.

[4 All o'er these wide extended plains,
  Shines one eternal day;
There God the Son for ever reigns,
  And scatters night away.

5 No chilling winds, nor pois'nous breath
  Can reach that healthful shore;
Sickness and sorrow, pain and death,
  Are felt and fear'd no more.]

6 When shall I reach that happy place,
  And be forever blest?
When shall I see my Father's face,
  And in his bosom rest?

7 Fill'd with delight my raptur'd soul
  Would here no longer stay;
Though Jordan's waves around me roll,
  Fearless I'd launch away.

295. (C. M.) 4S./4L.
The Condescension of Christ.

1 SAVIOUR of men, and Lord of love,

296. (C. M.) 4S./4L.
The Advent of Christ Joyful News.

1 HARK, the glad sound, the Saviour comes,

297. (L. M.) 2S./4L.
A Glimpse of Christ is Joyful.

1 JESUS, what shall I do to show,

298. (L. M.) 3S./4L.
The Pleasing Welcome.

1 WELCOME, thou well belov'd of God,

299. (C. M.) 4S./4L.
Rejoicing in the Mercies of God.

1 FAIN would my soul with wonder trace

300. (C. M.) Double.
The happy Child of Grace.

1 HOW happy's every child of grace
  Who feels his sins forgiv'n!
This world, he cries, is not my place,
  I seek a place in heav'n.
A country far from mortal sight,
  Yet O! by faith I see
The land of rest, the saints' delight,
  A heav'n prepar'd for me.

2 A stranger in this world below,
  I only sojourn here:
Nor can its happiness or woe,
  Provoke my hope or fear.
Its evils in a moment end,
  Its joys as soon are past:
But O! the bliss to which I tend,
  Eternally shall last.

3 To that Jerusalem above,
  With singing I'll repair;
While in the flesh by hope and love,
  My heart and soul are there;
There my exalted Saviour stands,
  My merciful high-priest,
And still extends his wounded hands,
  To take me to his breast.

4 What is there here to court my stay,
  And keep me back from home,
When angels beckon me away,
  And Jesus bids me come?
Shall I regret my parted friends,
  Here in this vale confin'd?
Nay, but whene'er my soul ascends,
  They will not stay behind.

5 The race we all are running now,
  And if I first attain,
They too their willing heads shall bow,
  They too the prize shall gain:
Now on the brink of death I stand,
  And if I pass before,
They too shall all escape to land,
  And hail me on that shore.

6 Then let me suddenly remove
  That hidden life to share;
I shall not lose my friends above,
  But more enjoy them there:
There we in Jesus praise shall join,
  His boundless love proclaim,
And solemnize in songs divine,
  The marriage of the Lamb.

7 O what a blessed hope is ours!
    While here on earth we stay;
We more than taste the heav'nly pow'rs,
    And antedate that day:
We feel the resurrection near,
    Our life in Christ conceal'd,
And with his glorious presence here,
    Our earthen vessels fill'd.

8 O! would he more of heav'n bestow,
    And let this vessel break,
And let my ransom'd spirit go,
    To grasp the God I seek:
In rapturous awe on him to gaze,
    Who fought the fight for me,
And shout and wonder at his grace,
    Through all eternity.

301. (8's.)
Desiring to leave this evil World.

1 MY gracious Redeemer I love,
    His praises aloud I'll proclaim,
And join with the armies above,
    To shout his adorable name.
To gaze on his glories divine,
    Shall be my eternal employ,
And feel them incessantly shine,
    My boundless ineffable joy.

2 He freely redeem'd with his blood
    My soul from the confines of hell,
To live on the smiles of my God,
    And in his sweet presence to dwell;
To shine with angels of light,
    With saints and with seraphs to sing,
To view with eternal delight,
    My Jesus, my Saviour, my King.

3 In *Meshech*, as yet I reside,
    A darksome and restless abode!
Molested with foes on each side,
    And longing to dwell with my God,
O! when shall my spirit exchange
    This cell of corruptible clay,
For mansions celestial, and range
    Through realms of ineffable day!

4 My glorious Redeemer! I long
    To see thee descend on the cloud,
Amidst the bright numberless throng,
    And mix with the triumphing crowd;
O! when wilt thou bid me ascend,
    To join in thy praises above,
To gaze on thee world without end,
    And feast on thy ravishing love?

5 Nor sorrow, nor sickness, nor pain,
    Nor sin, nor temptation, nor fear,
Shall ever molest me again.
    Perfection of glory reigns there;
This soul and this body shall shine
    In robes of salvation and praise,
And banquet on pleasures divine,
    Where God his full beauty displays.

6 Ye palaces, sceptres, and crowns,
    Your pride with disdain I survey:
Your pomps are but shadows and sounds,
    And pass in a moment away:
The crown that my Saviour bestows,
    Yon permanent sun shall outshine;
My joy everlasting flows;
    My God, my Redeemer, is mine.

302. (P. M.) 5S./12L.
The happiness of a Soul safe in Jesus.

1 HOW bless'd is ev'ry child of grace—

303. (7, 7, 7, 6.) 5S./8L.
The Love of Jesus Wonderous.

1 THE wond'rous love of Jesus,

304. (7, 7, 7, 6.) 6S./8L.
The same.

1 O THE sweet love of Jesus,

305. (11's.)
Happy Poverty.

1 MY heart and my tongue shall unite in the praise
Of Jesus, my Saviour, for mercy and grace;
My pardon is sealed through his precious blood;
By him I inherit the peace of my God.

2 My lot may be low, and my parentage mean,
Yet born of my God, I have glories unseen,
Surpassing all joys 'mongst sinners on earth,
Prepared for souls of an heavenly birth.

3 Secur'd from a thousand allurements to sin,
I find in my cottage a heaven begin;
And soon I shall lay all my poverty by,
And mansions of glory for ever enjoy.

4 By the sweat of my brow I labour for bread,
Yet guarded by Jesus, no evil I dread;
And Lord, while possess'd of all riches in thee,
My poverty comes with a blessing to me.

5 My labouring dress I shall soon lay aside,
   For robes rich and splendid, a dress for a bride;
   The bride that is married to Jesus the Lamb,
   And clad in a garment that's ever the same.
6 Though fare be but scant while I travel below,
   A feast that's eternal will Jesus bestow;
   No sorrow nor sighing shall ever annoy
   The heavenly banquet I there shall enjoy.
7 Then what though the body goes weary to rest,
   Yet, sav'd by the merits of Jesus, I'm blest;
   Fresh strength for my labour on earth he bestows,
   And soon I shall bask in eternal repose.

306. (8, 7.) 2S./6L.
The Bible—O what a Treasure.

1 PRECIOUS Bible! what a treasure

307. (7's.)
Rejoice evermore.

1 CHILDREN of the heav'nly King,
   As ye journey sweetly sing;
   Sing your Saviour's worthy praise,
   Glorious in his works and ways.
2 Ye are trav'ling home to God,
   In the way the fathers trod;
   They are happy now, and ye
   Soon their happiness shall see.
3 O ye banish'd seed, be glad!
   Christ our advocate is made;
   Us to save our flesh assumes,
   Brother to our souls becomes.
4 Shout ye little flock and blest,
   You on Jesus' throne shall rest;
   There your seat is now prepar'd,
   There's your kingdom and reward.
5 Fear not, brethren—joyful stand
   On the borders of your land;
   Jesus Christ your Father's Son,
   Bids you undismay'd go on.
6 Lord, submissive make us go,
   Gladly leaving all below;
   Only thou our leader be,
   And we still will follow thee!

308. (L. M.) 9S./5L.
Divine Communion.

1 A UNION rare divinely shines—

309. (L. M.) 3S./4L.
Christ the End of the Law, &c.

1 WHEN Jesus for his people died,

310. (C. M.)
Precious Bible.

1 HOW precious is the book divine,
   By inspiration giv'n!
   Bright as a lamp its doctrines shine,
   To guide our souls to heav'n.
2 It sweetly cheers our drooping hearts
   In this dark vale of tears;
   Life, light, and joy, it still imparts,
   And quells our rising fears.
3 This lamp through all the tedious night
   Of life shall guide our way;
   Till we behold the clearer light
   Of an eternal day.

311. (L. M.) 3S./4L.
Joying in Christ as a Friend indeed.

1 POOR, weak, and worthless tho' I am,

312. (L. M.) 3S./4L.
The Time of Love.

1 LORD, 'twas a time of wond'rous love

313. (C. M.) 4S./4L.
Complete Salvation.

1 SALVATION, through our dying God,

314. (C. M.) 5S./4L.
Love and Gratitude.

1 AND have I, Christ, no love for thee,

315. (7's.) 2S./4L.
The Pleasures of Religion.

1 'TIS religion that can give,

316. (C. M.) 4S./4L.
Not unto us, but to thy Name give glory.

1 NOT unto us, but thee alone,

317. (C. M.) 3S./4L.
Glorying in God only.

1 YE saints of ev'ry rank, with joy,

318. (C. M.)
Fortitude and Holy Boldness.

1 AM I a soldier of the cross,
   A follower of the Lamb?

And shall I fear to own his cause,
  Or blush to speak his name?
2 Must I be carried to the skies,
  On flowery beds of ease;
  While others fought to win the prize,
  And sail'd through bloody seas?
3 Are there no foes for me to face?
  Must I not stem the flood?
  Is this vile world a friend to grace,
  To help me on to God?
4 Sure I must fight, if I would reign;
  Increase my courage, Lord!
  I'll bear the toil, endure the pain,
  Supported by thy word.
5 Thy saints, in all this glorious war,
  Shall conquer though they die;
  They see the triumph from afar,
  And seize it with their eye.
6 When that illustrious day shall rise,
  And all thy armies shine
  In robes of victory through the skies,
  The glory shall be thine.

319. (L. M.) 2S./4L.
Israel's Glory and Defence.

1 WITH Israel's God who can compare

320. (C. M.) 2S./4L.
Through much tribulation we go to Heaven.

1 WE seek a rest beyond the skies,

321. (S. M.) 5S./4L.
Rejoicing in the Ways of God.

1 NOW let our voices join

322. (C. M.) 4S./4L.
The Dominion of God celebrated.

1 THE Lord, the God of glory reigns,

323. (C. M.)
The Goodness of God adored.

1 THY goodness, Lord, our souls confess,
    Thy goodness we adore;
  A spring whose blessings never fail—
  A sea without a shore!
2 Sun, moon, and stars, thy love attest
  In ev'ry golden ray,
  Love draws the curtains of the night,
  And love brings back the day.
3 Thy bounty ev'ry season crowns,
  With all the bliss it yields;
  With joyful clusters loads the vines,
  With strength'ning grain the fields.

4 But chiefly thy compassion, Lord,
  Is in the gospel seen;
  There, like a sun thy mercy shines,
  Without a cloud between.
5 Pardon, acceptance, peace, and joy,
  Through Jesus' name are giv'n;
  He on the cross was lifted high,
  That we might reign in heaven.

324. (C. M.) 4S./4L.
God's Love, John iii. 16

1 'TWAS not to make Jehovah's love

325. (C. M.) 6S./4L.
Omniscience and Omnipresence of God celebrated.

1 WHERE from thy Spirit shall I stretch

326. (C. M.) 5S./4L.
Christ the Desire of all the Saints.

1 COME, thou desire of all thy saints,

327. (C. M.) 4S./4L.
Christ the Door.

1 THUS saith the Shepherd of the sheep,

328. (C. M.) 4S./4L.
The Praises of Christ.

1 INFINITE excellence is thine,

329. (C. M.) 2S./4L.
Christ's Love unchangeable.

1 COME let our hearts and voices join,

330. (C. M.)
Jesus Precious.

1 BLEST Jesus, when my soaring
    thoughts
  O'er all thy graces rove,
  How is my soul in transport lost—
  In wonder, joy, and love!
2 Not softest strains can charm mine ears,
  Like thy beloved name;
  Nor aught beneath the skies inspire
  My heart with equal flame.
3 No, thou art precious to my heart,
  My portion and my joy;
  Forever let thy boundless grace
  My sweetest thoughts employ.
4 When nature faints, around my bed
  Let thy bright glories shine;
  And death shall all his terrors lose,
  In raptures so divine.

Hymn Texts From *The Cluster*

331. (C. M.) 6S./4L.
Praise to the Redeemer.

1 TO our Redeemer's glorious name

332. (C. M.) 6S./4L.
To Christ the Good Shepherd.

1 TO thee, my Shepherd and my Lord,

333. (C. M.) 4S./4L.
The Same.

1 IN one harmonious, cheerful song,

334. (L. M.) 5S./4L.
Eternal Life.

1 ETERNAL life! how sweet the sound

335. (C. M.) 4S./4L.
Joy over dead Sinners coming to Life.

1 HOW much the hearts of those revive

336. (L. M.) 3S./4L.
The Fulness of Christ.

1 IN Christ alone all fulness dwells:

337. (C. M.) 4S./4L.
Gratitude to God for his Gifts.

1 MY Father God! and may these lips

338. (C. M.) 4S./4L.
A Young Person Devoting himself to God.

1 SHALL mortals aim at themes so great,

339. (L. M.) 3S./4L.
Praise for Divine Fulness.

1 THE food on which thy children live,

340. (C. M.) Rochester.
Jesus Worthy of all Praise.

1 COME, let us join our cheerful songs
  With angels round the throne:
Ten thousand thousand are their tongues;
  But all their joys are one.
2 "Worthy the Lamb that died," they cry
  "To be exalted thus:
"Worthy the Lamb," our lips reply,
  For he was slain for us.
3 Jesus is worthy to receive
  Honour and pow'r divine;
And blessings, more than we can give,
  Be, Lord, forever thine.
4 Let all that dwell above the sky,
  And air, and earth, and seas,
Conspire to lift thy glories high,
  And speak thine endless praise.
5 The whole creation join in one,
  To bless the sacred name
Of him that sits upon the throne,
  And to adore the Lamb.

341. (C. M.) Ocean.
Mariners Constrained to Praise.

1 THY works of glory, mighty Lord,
  That rule the boist'rous sea,
The sons of courage shall record,
  Who 'tempt that dang'rous way.
2 At thy commands the winds arise,
  And swell the tow'ring waves;
The men astonish'd, mount the skies,
  And sink in gaping graves.
3 Then to the Lord they raise their cries,
  He hears their loud request,
And orders silence through the skies,
  And lays the floods to rest.
4 Sailors rejoice to lose their fears,
  And see the storm allay'd:
Now to their eyes the port appears;
  There let their vows be paid.
5 Oh that the sons of men would praise
  The goodness of the Lord!
And those that see thy wond'rous ways,
  Thy wond'rous love record.

342. (S. M.) L. Marlboro.
Joy in the Lord's Day.

1 WELCOME, sweet day of rest,
  That saw the Lord arise;
Welcome to this reviving breast,
  And these rejoicing eyes!
2 The king himself comes near,
  And feasts his saints to-day;
Here we may sit and see him here,
  And love, and praise, and pray.
3 One day amidst the place
  Where my dear God hath been,
Is sweeter than ten thousand days
  Of pleasurable sin.
4 My willing soul would stay
  In such a frame as this.
And sit and sing herself away
  To everlasting bliss.

343. (S. M.) Newburg.
Universal Praise.

1 LET ev'ry creature join
  To praise th' eternal God;

Ye heav'nly hosts, the song begin,
  And sound his name abroad.
2 Thou sun with golden beams,
    And moon with paler rays,
  Ye starry lights, ye twinkling flames,
    Shine to your Maker's praise.
3 He built those worlds above,
    And fix'd their wond'rous frame:
  By his command they stand or move,
    And ever speak his name.
4 By all his works above
    His honours be exprest;
  But saints that taste his saving love,
    Should sing his praises best.

344. (C. M.) New Jerusalem.
The New Jerusalem.

1 LO, what a glorious sight appears
    To our believing eyes!
  The earth and seas are pass'd away,
    And the old rolling skies.
2 From the third heav'n, where God resides,
    That holy, happy place,
  The new Jerusalem comes down,
    Adorn'd with shining grace.
3 Attending angels shout for joy,
    And the bright armies sing,
  "Mortals, behold the sacred seat
    "Of your descending King!
4 "The God of glory down to men
    "Removes his blest abode!
  "Men, the dear objects of his grace,
    "And he the loving God.
5 "His own soft hand shall wipe the tears
    "From ev'ry weeping eye;   [fears,
  "And pains, and groans, and griefs, and
    "And death itself, shall die."
6 How long, dear Saviour, O how long!
    Shall this bright hour delay?
  Fly swiftly round, ye wheels of time,
    And bring the welcome day.

345. (8, 8, 6.)
A Revival began, increases Desire.

1 THE Lord into his garden's come,
  The spices yield a rich perfume,
    The lilies grow and thrive;
  Refreshing streams of grace divine,
  From Jesus flow to ev'ry vine,
    And make the dead alive.
2 O that this dry and barren ground
  With springs of water may abound,
    A fruitful soil become—
  The spring in youthful bloom appear,
  And zephyrs blow each plant to cheer,
    And bring the harvest on!
3 Come, brethren dear, who love the Lord,
  Who taste the sweets of Jesus' word,
    In Jesus' ways go on;
  Our poverty and trials here
  Will only make us richer there,
    When we arrive at home.
4 We feel that heav'n is now begun—
  Grace issues from the heav'nly throne,
    As never heretofore;
  It comes in floods we can't contain,
  We drink, and drink, and drink again,
    And still we long for more.
5 But when to that bless'd world we come,
  And we surround the glorious throne,
    We'll drink a full supply;
  Jesus will lead his ransom'd forth,
  To living streams of richer worth,
    That never will run dry.
6 Then we shall smile, and sweetly sing,
  And make the heav'nly arches ring,
    When all his saints get home.
  Come on! come on! my brethren dear—
  We soon shall meet together there—
    For Jesus bids us come.
7 Amen! amen! my soul replies;
  I long to meet you in the skies,
    Where sin and death are o'er:
  Now here's my heart, and here's my hand
  To meet you in that heavenly land,
    Where parting is no more.
8 Then shall we join in sweet accord,
  To chant the loving, bleeding Lord,
    And enter to his rest;
  We then in high, immortal strains,
  Will move and charm the starry plains,
    And be forever bless'd.

346. (L. M.) Double 5S./8L.
Longing for abounding Grace.

1 MY God, my heart with love inflame,

347. (8's.)
The Presence of Christ makes all well.

1 HOW tedious and tasteless the hours,
    When Jesus no longer I see,
  Sweet prospects, sweet birds, and sweet flow'rs,
    Have lost all their sweetness with me:
  The mid-summer sun shines but dim,
    The fields strive in vain to look gay;
  But when I am happy in him.
    December's as pleasant as May.

2 His name yields the richest perfume,
   And sweeter than music his voice;
His presence disperses my gloom,
   And makes all within me rejoice:
I should, were he always thus nigh,
   Have nothing to wish or to fear;
No mortal so happy as I,
   My summer would last all the year.

3 Content with beholding his face,
   My all to his pleasure resign'd;
No changes of seasons or place,
   Would make any change in my mind:
While bless'd with a sense of his love,
   A palace a toy would appear;
And prisons would palaces prove,
   If Jesus would dwell with me there.

4 Dear Lord, if indeed I am thine,
   If thou art my sun and my song;
Say, why do I languish and pine,
   And why are my winters so long?
O drive these dark clouds from my sky,
   Thy soul-cheering presence restore;
Or take me unto thee on high,
   Where winter and clouds are no more.

348. (C. M.) Double.
The Christian's best and only Wish.

1 IF dust and ashes might presume
   Great God, to talk to thee;
If in thy presence can be room
   For crawling worms like me;
I humbly would my *wish* present;
   For *wishes* I have none;
All my desires are now content
   To be compris'd in one.

2 I would not sue for length of days;
   For honour, or for wealth;
Nor, that which far surpasseth these,
   Uninterrupted health.
I would not ask, a monarch heir,
   Or counsellor to be;
A better wisdom I would share,
   A nobler pedigree.

3 Not joy, nor strength would I request;
   Though neither I contemn;
But would petition to be blest
   With what transcendeth them.
'Tis not that angels might convey
   My soul this night to heav'n:
Thy time with patience I can stay,
   Since all my sin's forgiv'n.

4 Nor would I crave in highest state,
   At thy right hand to sit.
(The suit of *Zeb'dee's* sons;) for *that*
   I know myself unfit,
Nor in thy church on earth would strive
   A pompous post to fill;
For fear I might not well perceive,
   Or fail to do thy will.

5 The single boon I would entreat
   Is to be led by thee,
To gaze upon the bloody sweat
   In sad *Gethsemane.*
To view (as I could bear at least)
   Thy tender broken heart,
Like a rich olive, bruis'd and prest
   With agonizing smart.

6 To see thee bow'd beneath my guilt,
   Intolerable load!
To see thy blood for sinners spilt,
   My groaning, gasping God!
With sympathizing grief to mourn
   The sorrows of thy soul;
The pangs and tortures by thee borne,
   In some degree condole.

7 There musing on thy mighty love,
   I always would remain;
Or but to *Golgotha* remove,
   And thence return again.
In each dear place the same rich scene
   Should ever be renew'd;
No object else could intervene,
   But all be love and blood.

8 For this one favour oft I've sought:
   And if this one be giv'n,
I seek on earth no happier lot;
   And hope the like in heav'n.
Lord, pardon what I ask amiss,
   For knowledge I have none;
I do but humbly speak my wish;
   And may thy will be done.

349. (8, 7.)
For Mercies acknowledged, and Future ones sought.

1 COME thou fount of ev'ry blessing,
   Tune my heart to sing thy grace!
Streams of mercy, never ceasing,
   Call for songs of loudest praise:
Teach me some melodious sonnet,
   Sung by flaming tongues above;
Praise the mount—I'm fix'd upon it,
   Mount of thy redeeming love.

2 Here I raise my Ebenezer,
   Hither by thy grace I've come;
And I trust by thy good pleasure
   Safely to arrive at home:
Jesus sought me when a stranger
   Wand'ring from the fold of God,
He, to rescue me from danger,
   Interpos'd with precious blood.

3 O to grace, how great a debtor,
    Daily I'm constrain'd to be!
  Let thy goodness, like a fetter,
    Bind my wand'ring soul to thee:
  Prone to wander, Lord I feel it,
    Prone to leave the God I love;
  Here's my heart—O take and seal it!
    Seal it for thy courts above.
4 O that day when freed from sinning,
    I shall see thy lovely face!
  Richly cloth'd in blood-wash'd linen,
    How I'll sing thy sov'reign grace!
  Come, dear Lord, no longer tarry,
    Take my raptur'd soul away;
  Send thy angels down to carry
    Me to realms of endless day.
5 I thou ever didst discover,
    To my faith the promis'd land;
  Bid me now the stream pass over,
    On the heav'nly border stand:
  Now surmount whate'er opposes,
    Into thy embrace I fly;
  Speak the word thou spak'st to Moses,
    Bid me "get me up and die."

350. (8, 7.)
Breathing after the Indwelling of the Spirit.

1 LOVE divine, all loves excelling,
    Joy of heav'n to earth come down;
  Fix in us thy humble dwelling.
    All thy faithful mercies crown.
  Jesus, thou art all compassion,
    Pure unbounded love thou art;
  Visit us with thy salvation,
    Enter ev'ry trembling heart.
2 Breathe, O breathe thy loving Spirit
    Into ev'ry troubled breast;
  Let us all in thee inherit,
    Let us find that second rest.
  Take away our pow'r of sinning,
    Alpha and Omega be;
  End of faith as its beginning,
    Set our hearts at liberty.
3 Come, Almighty to deliver,
    Let us all thy life receive,
  Suddenly return, and never,
    Never more thy temples leave:
  Thee we would be always blessing,
    Serve thee as thy hosts above,
  Pray, and praise thee without ceasing,
    Glory in thy perfect love.
4 Finish then thy new creation,
    Pure and spotless let us be:
  Let us see thy great salvation,
    Perfectly restor'd in thee.
  Chang'd from glory into glory,
    'Till in heaven we take our place,
  'Till we cast our crowns before thee,
    Lost in wonder, love, and praise.

351. (7's.)
Christ's in Covert from the Tempest.

1 JESUS, lover of my soul,
    Let me to thy bosom fly,
  While the raging billows roll,
    While the tempest still is high!
  Hide me, O my Saviour, hide,
    Till the storm of life is past:
  Safe into the haven guide;
    O receive my soul at last.
2 Other refuge have I none,
    Hangs my helpless soul on thee;
  Leave, ah! leave me not alone,
    Still support and comfort me:
  All my trust on thee is staid,
    All my help from thee I bring;
  Cover my defenceless head
    With the shadow of thy wing.
3 Thou, O Christ, art all I want;
    All in all in thee I find:
  Raise the fallen, cheer the faint,
    Heal the sick, and lead the blind;
  Just and holy is thy name,
    I am all unrighteousness;
  Vile and full of sin I am,
    Thou art full of truth and grace.
3 Plenteous grace with thee is found,
    Grace to pardon all my sin;
  Let the healing streams abound;
    Make and keep me pure within:
  Thou of life the fountain art,
    Freely let me take of thee;
  Spring thou up within my heart,
    Rise to all eternity.

352. (8, 7.)
Blind Bartimeus Healed and Praising.

1 "MERCY, O thou Son of David,"
    Thus blind Bartimeus cry'd;
  "Others by thy grace are sav'd,
    O vouch save to me thine aid,"
  For his crying many chid him,
    But he cry'd the louder still;
  'Till his gracious Saviour bid him,
    "Come and ask me what you will."
2 Money was not what he wanted,
    Though by begging us'd to live:
  Yet he ask'd, and Jesus granted
    Alms, that none but he could give:

"Lord, remove this grievous blindness,
   Let mine eyes behold the day;"
Straight he saw, and won by kindness,
   Follow'd Jesus in the way.

3 Now methinks I hear him praising,
      Publishing to all around;
   "Friends is not my case amazing,
      What a Saviour I have found!
   O that all the blind but knew him,
      Or could be advis'd by me;
   Sure if they were brought unto him,
      He would cause them all to see."

4 "Now I freely leave my garments,
      Follow Jesus in the way,
   He'll direct me by his counsel,
      Bring me to eternal day:
   There shall I behold my Saviour,
      Spotless, innocent and pure;
   I shall reign with him for ever,
      For his promises are sure."

5 Don't you see my Jesus coming,
      See him now in yonder cloud,
   With ten thousand angels round him;
      O behold the glorious crowd!
   I will rise and go and meet him,
      And embrace him in my arms;
   In the arms of my dear Jesus,
      O! he hath ten thousand charms.

353. (6, 5.) 8S./8L.
To be Sung at the close of Worship.

1 WITH gladness, dear brethren,

354. (L. M.) Portugal. 4S./4L.
The Blessedness of Public Worship.

1 HOW lovely, how divinely sweet,

355. (C. M.)
Christ more Precious than Rubies.

1 JESUS, to multitudes unknown,—

356. (C. M.) 4S./4L.
The Saviour Praised.

1 THE Saviour! O what endless charms

357. (7's.) 3S./4L.
Christ King of Righteousness and Peace.

1 KING of Salem, bless my soul!

358. (L. M.) 5S./4L.
The Power of God encouraging Prayer.

1 JEHOVAH is a God of might,

359. (L. M.) 4S./4L.
Praises for the Wisdom and Love of God.

1 AWAKE, my tongue, thy tribute bring

360. (L. M.) 3S./4L.
Christ the Advocate.

1 LOOK up my soul, with cheerful eye,

361. (L. M.) 4S./4L.
Christ the best Gift of God.

1 JESUS, my Lord, my soul's delight,

362. (C. M.) 4S./4L.
Not ashamed of Christ.

1 DEAR Saviour, will thy pard'ning love

363. (L. M.)
Growth in Grace—Praise for.

1 PRAISE to thy name eternal God,
   For all the grace thou shed'st abroad;
  For all thy influence from above,
  To warm our souls with sacred love.

2 Blest be thy hand, which from the skies
  Brought down this plant of Paradise,
  And gave its heavenly glories birth,
  To deck the wilderness of earth.

2 Unchanging sun, thy beams display,
  To drive the frosts and storms away;
  Make all thy potent virtues known,
  To cheer a plant so much thine own.

4 And thou, blest Spirit, deign to blow,
  Fresh gales of heaven on shrubs below;
  So shall they grow and breathe abroad,
  A fragrance grateful to our God.

364. (C. M.)
Faith affords Comfort in every State.

1 WHEN faith presents the Saviour's death,
      And whispers, "this is mine:"
   Sweetly my rising hours advance,
      And peacefully decline.

2 Let outward things go how they will,
      His love is bliss divine;
   I triumph in my Saviour's death—
      My joys are all sublime!

3 Faith in thy love shall sweeten death,
      And smooth the rugged way;
   Smile on me, dearest Lord, and then
      I shall not wish to stay.

365. (C. M.) 3S./4L.
Confidence.

1 FIRMLY I stand on Zion's hill,

366. (C. M.) 3S./4L.
Faith and Resignation.

1 THROUGH all the downward tracts of time,

367. (C. M.) 4S./4L.
Bring your Burden to the Lord.

1 THE cause that is for me too hard,

368. (L. M.) 4S./4L.
Cast down, but not in Despair.

1 WHY, O my soul, these anxious cares?

369. (C. M.) 4S./4L.
Cast down, but not Destroyed.

1 NOW in thy praise, eternal King,

370. (C. M.) 5S./4L.
Devil's believe and tremble.

1 TO God who lives and reigns on high,

371. (L. M.) 4S./4L.
Ebenezer.

1 ETERNAL God, I bless thy name—

372. (L. M.) 4S./4L.
Reflections on Life and Eternity.

1 ETERNITY is just at hand;

373. (L. M.) 4S./4L.
The Same.

1 O THOU eternal glorious Lord,

374. (C. M.) 4S./4L.
Faith Conquering.

1 RISE, O my soul, pursue the path,

375. (C. M.) 4S./4L.
To Obey is better than Sacrifice.

1 WHY should the dread of sinful man

376. (L. M.) 4S./4L.
The Ways of God mysterious, yet sure.

1 THY ways, O God, with wise design,

377. (C. M.)
Self-denial, or taking up the Cross.

1 DIDST thou, dear Jesus, suffer shame,
   And bear the cross for me?
And shall I fear to own thy name,
   Or thy disciple be?

2 Inspire my soul with life divine,
   And make me truly bold;
Let knowledge, faith, and meekness shine,
   Nor love, nor zeal grow cold.

3 'Let mockers scoff, let men defame,
   And treat me with disdain;
Still may I glorify thy name,
   And count their slender gain.'

4 To thee I cheerfully submit,
   And all my pow'rs resign;
Let wisdom point out what is fit,
   And I'll no more repine.

378. (C. M.)
Submission to the Divine Will.

1 SUBMISSIVE to thy will, my God,
   I all to thee resign;
And bow before thy chast'ning rod—
   I mourn, but not repine.

2 Why should my foolish heart, complain,
   When wisdom, truth, and love,
Direct the stroke, inflict the pain,
   And point to joys above?

3 How short are all my suff'rings here,
   How needful ev'ry cross;
Away, my unbelieving fear,
   Nor call my gain my loss.

4 Then give, dear Lord, or take away,
   I'll bless thy sacred name;
My Jesus, yesterday, to-day,
   Forever is the same!

379. (C. M.) 6S./4L.
Another.

1 DEAR Lord my best desires fulfil,

380. (C. M.) 3S./4L.
Submission, or Divine Direction sought.

1 LORD, hast thou call'd me by thy grace,

381. (C. M.)
Desiring a closer Walk with God.

1 O FOR a closer walk with God,
   A calm and heav'nly frame;
A light to shine upon the road,
   That leads me to the Lamb.

2 Where is the blessedness I knew
   When first I saw the Lord?
Where is the soul-refreshing view,
   Of Jesus, and his word?

3 What peaceful hours I then enjoy'd!
   How sweet their mem'ry still!
But they have left an aching void,
   The world can never fill.

4 Return, O holy dove, return,
   Sweet messenger of rest;

I hate the sins that made thee mourn,
And drove thee from my breast.

5 The dearest idol I have known,
Whate'er that idol be;
Help me to tear it from thy throne,
And worship only thee.

6 So shall my walk be close with God,
Calm and serene my frame;
So purer light shall mark the road,
That leads me to the Lamb.

382. (S. M.) Ps. xxv. 4S./4L.
Waiting for Pardon and Direction.

1 I LIFT my soul to God,

383. (6, 8.) Lenox, Delight.
The Christian's life perilous.

1 JESUS, at thy command,
I launch into the deep;
And leave my native land,
Where sin lulls all asleep:
For thee I would the world resign,
And sail to heav'n with thee and thine.

2 Thou art my pilot wise:
My compass is thy word:
My soul each storm defies,
While I have such a Lord.
I trust thy faithfulness and pow'r,
To save me in the trying hour.

3 Though rocks and quicksands deep
Through all my passage lie;
Yet Christ will safely keep,
And guide me with his eye.
My anchor hope shall firm abide,
And I each boist'rous storm outride.

4 By faith I see the land,
The port of endless rest:
My soul, thy sails expand,
And fly to Jesus' breast!
O! may I reach the heavenly shore,
Where winds and waves distress no more.

5 Whene'er becalm'd I lie,
And storms forbear to toss;
Be thou, dear Lord, still nigh,
Lest I should suffer loss:
For more the treach'rous calm I dread,
Than tempests bursting o'er my head.

6 Come, Holy Ghost, and blow
A prosp'rous gale of grace,
Waft me from all below,
To heav'n my destin'd place!
Then, in full sail, my port I'll find,
And leave the world and sin behind.

384. (C. M.)
The Effort.

1 APPROACH, my soul, the mercy-seat
Where Jesus, answers pray'r;
There humbly fall before his feet,
For none can perish there.

2 Thy promise is my only plea,
With this I venture nigh;
Thou callest burden'd souls to thee,
And such, O Lord, am I.

3 Bow'd down beneath a load of sin,
By Satan sorely prest;
By war without and fears within,
I come to thee for rest.

4 Be thou my shield and hiding-place!
That, shelter'd near thy side,
I may my fierce accuser face,
And tell him, "thou hast dy'd."

5 Oh wond'rous love! to bleed and die,
To bear the cross and shame;
That guilty sinners, such as I,
Might plead thy gracious name.

6 "Poor temptest tossed soul be still,
"My promis'd grace receive;"
'Tis Jesus speaks—I must—I will,
I can, I do believe.

385. (8's.) 5S./6L.
Self-abhorrence and humble Prayer.

1 FATHER of light, from whom proceeds

386. (C. M.) 4S./4L.
Fear not, I am with you. Is. xli. 10.

1 AND art thou with us, gracious Lord,

387. (7's.)
A Prayer for Humility.

1 LORD, if thou thy grace impart,—
Poor in spirit, meek in heart,
I shall, as my Master be
Rooted in humility.

2 Simple, teachable, and mild,
Chang'd into a little child:
Pleas'd with all the Lord provides;
Wean'd from all the world besides.

3 Father, fix my soul on thee;
Ev'ry evil let me flee:
Nothing want, beneath, above,—
Happy in thy precious love.

4 O that all may seek and find
Ev'ry good in Jesus join'd!
Him let Isr'el still adore,
Trust him, praise him, evermore.

388. (L. M.) 3S./4L.
Patience and Submission.

1 DEAR Lord! though bitter is the cup

389. (L. M.) 3S./4L.
Trusting in God in darkness.

1 LORD, we adore thy vast designs,

390. (L.M.) 3S./4L.
All things work for good to them that love God.

1 TEMPTATIONS, trials, doubts, and fears,

391. (L. M.) 3S./4L.
Faith and Unbelief struggling.

1 JESUS, our soul's delightful choice,

392. (S. M.)
Submission and Prayer.

1 DOST thou my profit seek,
   And chasten as a friend?
 O God, I'll kiss the smarting rod,
   There's honey at the end.

2 Dost thou through death's dark vale
   Conduct to heav'n at last?
 The future good will make amends
   For all the evil past.

3 Lord, I would not repine
   At strokes in mercy sent;
 If the chastisement comes in love,
   My soul shall be content.

393. (C. M.) 2S./4L.
A Blessing sought in the Beginning of Worship.

1 THY promise, Lord, and thy command,

394. (L. M.)
The same.

1 HUNGRY, and faint, and poor,
   Behold us, Lord, again
 Assembled at thy mercy's door,
   Thy bounty to obtain.

2 Thy word invites us nigh,
   Or we must starve indeed;
 For we no money have to buy,
   No righteousness to plead.

3 The food our spirits want
   Thy hand alone can give;
 Oh, hear the prayer of faith, and grant
   That we may eat, and live.

395. (8, 7, 4.)
Christ the Pilgrim's Guide.

1 GUIDE me, O thou great Jehovah,
   Pilgrim through this barren land;
 I am weak, but thou art mighty—
   Hold me in thy pow'rful hand:
 Bread of heaven,
 Feed me till I want no more.

2 Open now the chrystal fountain,
   Whence the heating streams do flow:
 Let the fiery, cloudy pillar,
   Lead me all my journey thro':
 Strong deliv'rer!
 Be thou still my strength and shield.

3 Feed me with the heavenly manna,
   In this barren wilderness:
 By my sword, my shield, and banner—
   Be my robe of righteousness:
 Fight and conquer
 All my foes by sov'reign grace

4 When I tread the verge of Jordan,
   Bid my anxious fears subside;
 Foe to death, and hell's destruction,
   Land me safe on Canaan's side:
 Songs of praises
 I will ever give to thee.

396. (L. M.) 4S./4L.
An Exhortation to Prayer.

1 PRAY'R makes the darken'd cloud withdraw;

397. (L. M.) 4S./4L.
Pray without Ceasing.

1 PRAY'R was appointed to convey

398. (L. M.) 4S./4L.
The Spirit's Influences Desired.

1 BLESS'D Jesus! source of grace divine,

399. (S. M.)
The same.

1 COME, Holy Spirit, come,
   With energy divine:
 And on this poor, benighted soul,
   And beams of mercy shine.

2 From the celestial hills
   Life, light, and joy, dispense!
 And may I daily, hourly feel
   Thy quick'ning influence.

Hymn Texts From *The Cluster*   113

3 Melt, melt this frozen heart;
   This stubborn will subdue;
   Each evil passion overcome,
   And form me all anew.
4 Mine will the profit be,
   But thine shall be the praise;
   And unto thee I will devote
   The remnant of my days.

400. (L. M.)
A Prosperous Gale longed for.

1 AT anchor laid, remote from home,
    Toiling I cry, "Sweet Spirit, come!
  "Celestial breeze, no longer stay,
  "But swell my sails, and speed my way!
2 "Fain would I mount, fain would I glow,
  "And loose my cable from below;
  "But I can only spread my sail;   [gale!"
  "Thou, thou must breathe th' auspicious

401. (C. M.) 4S./4L.
The Spirit's Return Entreated.

1 MY grace so weak, my sin so strong;

402. (L. M.)
A Prayer for Peace.

1 O LORD, thy mourning people bow,
   And raise to thee their pensive cry;
  By sore affliction pressed now,
   To thee they breathe their plaintive sigh,
2 Behold their foes, with mighty hosts,
   In hostile rage, without a cause
  Rush on our undefended coasts,
   Regardless of thy holy laws.
3 Wilt thou not judge them, O our God!
   The heathen they employ to kill
  Our men, and wives, and helpless brood,
   And so our land with horrors fill.
4 Be thou our refuge, mighty God!
   Till these calamities shall cease;
  Say to our foes, as to the flood,
   Thus far—and send us speedy peace.

403. (C. M.)
For a National Fast.

1 O LORD, behold thy people bow,
   And send their cries to thee;
  A nation in affliction now
   Bends in humility.
2 The terrors of thy chast'ning sword,
   In awful triumphs spread;

  We haste to seek thy face, O Lord!
   As by thy promise led.
3 All things are in thy potent hand—
   O bid this war now cease!
  O hear thy people through the land,
   And grant their pray'r for peace.

404. (L. M.) 3S./4L.
The Spirit's Aid Implored.

1 GIVE me thy Spirit, O my God!

405. (L. M.)
Faith Conquering.

1 O SAVE me, save me! O my God,
   For sorrows break into my soul;
  And like a risen angry flood,
   The mighty billows o'er me roll.
2 Each rising surge proclaims my death,
   I sink in black and quaggy mire;
  My lungs heave with such strangling breath,
   Which brings my dissolution higher.
3 From such a state, Lord, canst thou save;
   For I am quite o'erwhelm'd and sunk?
  Yes; thou didst Lazarus from the grave
   Save, when his friends said that he stunk.
4 Well, then my soul shall courage take,
   Although I sink, and drown, and die!
  For thou the bonds of death canst break,
   And set my soul at liberty.

406. (L. M.) 9S./4L.
An Evil Heart Lamented.

1 LORD what a barren heart is mine,

407. (L. M.) 3S./4L.
Pleading the Covenant.

1 O LORD, my God! whose sovereign love

408. (C. M.)
My Peace I give unto you.—St. John, xiv. 27.

1 MY SAVIOUR, let me hear thy voice
   Pronounce the words of peace!
  And all my warmest pow'rs shall join
   To celebrate thy grace.
2 With gentle smiles call me thy child,
   And speak my sins forgiv'n;
  The accents mild shall charm mine ear,
   And like the harps of heav'n.

3 Cheerful, where'er thy hand shall lead,
   The darkest path I'll tread;
   Cheerful, I'll quit these mortal shores,
   And mingle with the dead.
4 When dreadful guilt is done away,
   No other fears we'll know;
   That hand which scatters pardons down
   Shall crowns of life bestow.

409. (L. M.) 3S./4L.
Desiring Communion with God.

1 MY rising soul with strong desires,

410. (C. M.) 3S./4L.
Why Weepest Thou?

1 WHY, O my soul! why weepest thou?

411. (C. M.) 4S./4L.
Self-denial and Prayer.

1 AND must I part with all I have,

412. (S. M.) 3S./4L.
Sincerity Desired.

1 IF secret fraud should dwell

413. (C. M.) 4S./4L.
Spiritual Mindedness.

1 OH, may my heart, by grace renew'd,

414. (C. M.) 3S./4L.
Holy Zeal and Diligence Desired.

1 WHILE carnal men with all their might,

415. (C. M.) 3S./4L.
Desiring to Run the Christian Race.

1 OH! let me run the christian race

416. (L. M.)
Choosing the better part.

1 BESET with snares on every hand,
   In life's uncertain path I stand:
   Saviour divine! diffuse thy light
   To guide my doubtful footsteps right.
2 Engage this roving treach'rous heart
   To fix on Mary's better part;
   To scorn the trifles of a day,
   For joys that none can take away.
3 Then let the wildest storms arise;
   Let tempests mingle earth and skies;
   No fatal shipwreck shall I fear,
   But all my treasures with me bear.

4 If thou, my Jesus! still be nigh:
   Cheerful I live, and joyful die;
   Secure when mortal comforts flee,
   To find ten thousand worlds in thee.

417. (S.M.) 3S./4L.
Offering a Living Sacrifice.

1 AND will th' eternal King

418. (C.M.) 4S./4L.
A Glimpse of Christ better than the World.

1 LORD! let me see thy beauteous face;

419. (C.M.)
The Request.

1 FATHER, what'er of earthly bliss
   Thy sov'reign will denies,
   Accepted at thy throne of grace,
   Let this petition rise.
2 "Give me a calm, a thankful heart,
   "From every murmur free;
   "The blessings of thy grace impart,
   "And make me live to thee.
3 "Let the sweet hope, that thou art mine,
   "My life and death attend;
   "Thy presence through my journey shine
   "And crown my journey's end."

420. (C. M.) 4S./4L.
Secret Prayer.

1 FATHER divine, thy piercing eye

421. (L. M.) 3S./4L.
The Noble Resolution.

1 AH, wretched souls, who strive in vain,

422. (S. M.) 3S./4L.
A broken Heart, and a bleeding Saviour.

1 UNTO thine altar, Lord,

423. (L. M.) 3S./4L.
Social Prayer.

1 "WHERE two or three with sweet accord,

424. (L. M.) 3S./4L.
A Revival sought.

1 LOOK from on high, great God; and see

425. (7's.)
A Blessing humbly requested.

1 LORD, we come before thee now,
   At thy feet we humbly bow;

Hymn Texts From *The Cluster* 115

O! do not our suit disdain;
Shall we seek thee, Lord, in vain?
2 In thy own appointed way,
Now we seek thee, here we stay;
Lord, from hence we would not go,
Till a blessing thou bestow.
3 Send some message from thy word,
That may joy and peace afford;
Let thy Spirit now impart
Full salvation to each heart.
4 Grant that all may seek and find
Thee a God supremely kind;
Heal the sick, the captive free;
Let us all rejoice in thee.

426. (L. M.) 3S./4L.
Hope in God alone.

1 NOW, while the gospel net is cast,

427. (C. M.) 3S./4L.
A Blessing prayed for on the Word.

1 NOW, Lord, the heav'nly seed is sown,

428. (C. M.) 4S./4L.
Earnest desires to be taught and led in the Way.

1 LORD God, omnipotent to bless,

429. (C. M.) 4S./4L.
Perfection desired.

1 NOW may the God of peace and love,

430. (L. M.) 2S./4L.
A Blessing implored on all present.

1 THE peace which God alone reveals,

431. (L. M.) 4S./4L.
Thirsting for quickening Grace.

1 I THIRST, but not as once I did,

432. (L. M.) 4S./4L.
Hope in Darkness longing for Light.

1 O GOD, my Sun, thy blissful rays

433. (L. M.) 3S./4L.
Let brotherly Love continue.

1 GREAT Spirit of immortal love,

434. (8's.) 2S./6L.
Sloth deprecated.

1 THE Saviour meets his flock to-day,

435. (L. M.) 3S./4L.
A Prayer for persevering Grace, on giving ourselves to the Church of Christ.

1 RENEW'D by grace, we love the word,

436. (C. M.) 3S./4L.
The Pleasure of receiving new Converts into the Church, and a Prayer for them.

1 O WITH what pleasure we behold

437. (S. M.) 4S./4L.
Desiring to be found ready.

1 PREPARE me, gracious God,

438. (C. M.)
Humble Pleadings—Remember me.

1 JESUS, thou art the sinner's friend,
And such I look to thee;
Now in the bowels of thy love,
O Lord, remember me.
2 Remember thy pure word of grace,
Remember Calvary;
Remember all thy dying groans,
And then remember me.
3 Thou wond'rous advocate with God,
I yield myself to thee,
While thou art sitting on thy throne,
Dear Lord, remember me.
4 I own I'm guilty, own I'm vile,
Yet thy salvation's is free;
Then in thy all abounding grace,
Dear Lord, remember me.
5 Howe'er forsaken or distrest,
Howe'er oppress'd I be,
Howe'er afflicted here on earth,
Do thou remember me.
6 And when I close my eyes in death,
And creature-helps all flee,
Then, O my dear Redeemer, God,
I pray remember me.

439. (L.M.) 4S./3L.
The absence of God insupportable.

1 I CANNOT bear thine absence, Lord;

440. (L. M.) 2S./4L.
A Prayer for hardened Sinners.

1 SIN, in ten thousand treach'rous ways,

441. (7's.) 4S./4L.
A Prayer on parting.

1 FOR a season call'd to part,

442. (L. M.) 4S./4L.
A universal Blessing sought.

1 THY presence, everlasting God,

443. (C. M.) 5S./4L.
Refuge in God the Saints' Privilege.

1 DEAR refuge of my weary soul,

444. (L. M.) 4S./4L.
The Request.

1 LORD, dost thou say, "ask what thou wilt?"

445. (C. M.) 4S./4L.
My God will hear me.

1 THO' I am poor and needy too,

446. (S. M.) 4S./4L.
Importunate Prayer prevalent.

1 THE Lord, who truly knows,

447. (L. M.) 4S./4L.
Prayer before Sermon.

1 O THOU, at whose almighty word,

448. (C. M.) 3S./4L.
Public Worship.

1 LORD, in thy courts we now appear,

449. (C. M.)
A Prayer for Divine Influence.

1 IN thy great name, O Lord, we come;
  To worship at thy feet;
O pour thy Holy Spirit down
  On all that now shall meet.

2 Teach us to pray, and praise, and hear,
  And understand thy word,
To feel thy blissful presence near,
  And trust our living Lord.

3 Here let thy pow'r and grace be felt;
  Thy love and mercy known;
Our icy hearts, dear Jesus, melt,
  And break this flinty stone.

4 Let sinners, Lord, thy goodness prove,
  And saints rejoice in thee;
Let rebels be subdu'd by love,
  And to the Saviour flee.

450. (7's.) 3S./4L.
A Prayer before Sermon.

1 GRACIOUS Father, gracious Lord,

451. (S. M.)
Religion vain without Sincerity.

1 RELIGION'S form is vain,
  While we deny its pow'r!
What will the hypocrite obtain,
  In death's tremendous hour?

2 Now he may credit gain,
  And in affluence roll;
But all his profit will be pain,
  When God shall take his soul.

3 Then, O what dread surprise,
  What horror and dismay,
When death shall open wide his eyes,
  And tear his mask way!

4 Lord, search and know my heart,
  And make my soul sincere;
And bid hypocrisy depart,
  And keep my conscience clear.

452. (S. M.)
Jobez's Prayer imitated.

1 THOU God of Jabez, hear,
  While we intreat thy grace,
And borrow that expressive pray'r,
  With which he sought thy face.

2 "O that the Lord indeed
  "Would me his servant bless,
"From every evil shield my head,
  "And crown my paths with peace!

3 "Be his almighty hand,
  "My helper and my guide,
"Till, with his saints in Cannan's land,
  "My portion he divide."

4 Thus pious Jabez pray'd,
  While God inclin'd his ear;
And all by whom this suit is made,
  Shall find the blessing near.

453. (L. M.) 4S./4L.
Pity and Prayer for thoughtless Men.

1 O WERE my heart but form'd for wo,

454. (C. M.) 4S./4L.
O, that it was with me as in days past.

1 AGAIN, indulgent Lord, return
  With thy sweet quick'ning grace,
To animate my sluggish soul,
  And speed me in my race.

2 O may I feel as once I felt.
  When pain'd and griev'd at heart;

Thy kind, forgiving, melting look,
  Reliev'd my ev'ry smart.
3 Let graces then in exercise,
  But exercis'd again:
  And, nurtur'd by celestial pow'r,
  In exercise remain.
4 Awake, my love, my faith, my hope,
  My fortitude and joy;
  Vain world, be gone, let things above
  My happy thoughts employ.

455. (C. M.) 5S./4L.
Remember me.

1 O THOU, from whom all goodness flows,

456. (C. M.) 6S./4L.
The Sorrow of Parting mitigated.

1 LORD, when together here we meet,

457. (L. M.) 2S./4L.
The Sun of Righteousness Invoked.

1 GREAT Sun of Righteousness arise,

458. (S. M.)
A Prayer for the Spirit.

1 COME, Holy Spirit, come,
  Let thy bright beams arise;
  Dispel the sorrow from our minds,
  The darkness from our eyes.
2 Convince us of our sin;
  Then lead to Jesus' blood;
  And to our wond'ring view reveal
  The secret love of God.
3 Revive our drooping faith;
  Our doubts and fears remove,
  And kindle in our breasts the flame
  Of never-dying love.
4 'Tis thine to cleanse the heart,
  To sanctify the soul,
  To pour fresh life in ev'ry part,
  And new create the whole.
5 Dwell, therefore, in our hearts;
  Our minds from bondage free;
  Then shall we know, and praise and love
  The Father, Son, and Thee.

459. (L. M.)
The Stony Heart Lamented.

1 O FOR a glance of heav'nly day,
  To melt this stubborn stone away;
  And thaw, with beams of love divine,
  This heart, this frozen heart of mine.
2 The rocks can rend, the earth can quake,
  The seas can roar, the mountains shake,
  Of feelings all things show some sign
  But this unfeeling heart of mine.
3 To hear the sorrows thou hast felt,
  What but an adamant would melt?
  But I can read each moving line,
  And nothing moves this heart of mine.
4 Eternal Spirit, mighty God,
  Apply within the Saviour's blood;
  'Tis his rich blood, and his alone,
  Can move and melt this heart of stone.

460. (L. M.) 5S./4L.
The same.

1 LORD, hear a burden'd sinner mourn,

THE FOLLOWING SHORT HYMNS
SUNG AT THE CLOSE OF MEETING.

461. (8, 7, 4.) 2S/6L.

1 LORD, before we leave thy temple,

462. (6, 8.) Delight. 1S./6L.

1 TO thee our wants are known,

463. (8, 7.)

1 MAY the grace of Christ, our Saviour,
  And the Father's boundless love,
  With the holy Spirit's favour,
  Rest upon us from above.
2 Thus may we abide in union,
  With each other and the Lord;
  And possess, in sweet communion,
  Joys which earth cannot afford.

464. (L. M.)
Praise to the Trinity.

1 HAIL, Father! hail, eternal Son!
  Hail, sacred Spirit, Three in One!
  Blessing and thanks, and pow'r divine,
  Thrice holy Lord, be ever thine!

465. (8, 7.) 2S./4L., Chorus.

1 LORD, dismiss us with thy blessing,

466. (8, 7, 4.) 3S./6L.

1 LORD vouchsafe to us thy blessing,

467. (S. M.) Double.
Serious Inquiries as to a Future State.

1 AND am I born to die,
    To lay this body down?
And must this trembling spirit fly
    Into a world unknown?
A world of darkest shade,
    Unpierc'd by human thought,
The dreary regions of the dead,
    Where all things are forgot?

2 Soon as from earth I go,
    What will become of me?
Eternal happiness or woe
    Must then my portion be.
Wak'd by the trumpet's sound,
    I from my grave shall rise,
To see the Judge in glory crown'd,
    And view the flaming skies,

3 How shall I leave the tomb?
    With triumph or regret?
A fearful or a joyful doom,
    A curse or blessing meet?
Shall angel-bands convey
    Their brother to the bar?
Or devils drag my soul away,
    To meet its sentence there?

4 O thou who wouldst not have
    One mourning sinner die,
Who died thyself that soul to save
    From endless misery!
Shew me some way to shun
    Thy dreadful wrath severe—
That when thou comest on thy throne,
    I may with joy appear.

5 Thou art thyself the way,
    Thyself in me reveal;
So shall I spend my life's short day
    Obedient to thy will;
So shall I love my God,
    Because he first lov'd me,
And praise him in his bright abode,
    To all eternity.

468. (L. M.)
Self-abhorrence, Fear, and Hope.

1 I AM a stranger here below,
And what I am 'tis hard to know;
I am so vile, so prone to sin,
I fear that I'm not born again.

2 When I experience call to mind,
My understanding is so blind—
All feeling sense seems to be gone,
Which makes me think that I am wrong.

3 I find myself out of the way,
My thoughts are often gone astray;
Like one alone I seem to be—
O! is there any one like me?

4 'Tis seldom I can ever see
Myself as I would wish to be:
What I desire I can't attain,
And what I hate I can't refrain.

5 So far from God I seem to lie—
Which makes me often weep and cry;
I fear at last that I shall fall:
For if a saint, the least of all.

6 I seldom find a heart to pray,
So many things step in my way;
Thus fill'd with doubts I ask to know,
Come, tell me, is it thus with you.

7 So by experience I do know,
There's nothing good that I can do;
I cannot satisfy the law,
Nor hope, nor comfort from it draw.

8 My nature is so prone to sin,
Which makes my duty so unclean,
That when I count up all the cost,
If not free grace, then I am lost.

469. (7's.)
The important Point

1 'TIS a point I long to know,
    Oft it causes anxious thought;
Do I love the Lord, or no?
    Am I his, or am I not?

2 If I love, why am I thus?
    Why this dull and lifeless frame?
Hardly, sure, can they be worse,
    Who have never heard his name?

3 Could my heart so hard remain,
    Pray'r a task and burden prove,
Ev'ry trifle give me pain,
    If I knew a Saviour's love?

4 When I turn my eyes within
    All is dark, and vain, and wild:
Fill'd with unbelief and sin,
    Can I deem myself a child?

5 If I pray, or hear, or read,
    Sin is mix'd with all I do;
You that love the Lord indeed,
    Tell me, is it thus with you?

6 Yet I mourn my stubborn will,
    Find my sin a grief and thrall;
Should I grieve for what I feel,
    If I did not love at all?

7 Could I joy his saints to meet,
    Choose the ways I once abhorr'd,
Find, at times, the promise sweet,
    If I did not love the Lord?

8 Lord, decide the doubtful case!
    Thou who art thy people's sun,
Shine upon thy work of grace,
    If it be indeed begun.

9 Let me love thee more and more,
    If I love at all, I pray;
If I have not lov'd before,
    Help me to begin to-day.

470. (8's.) 6S./6L.
Remaining Sin, and Reigning Grace.

1 STRANGE and mysterious is my life,

471. (L. M.)
Assurance Sought under great Misgivings.

1 O HOW shall I myself assure,
    That I am safe in Christ secure,
Or that I do in him believe,
And from him grace for grace receive?

2 When I with christians do compare
My daily exercise and prayer,
I seem to fall so far behind,
That gloomy fears o'erwhelm my mind.

3 I read the precious word of God,
Which Jesus ratify'd with blood;
But while I read my fears arise,
And hide the promise from my eyes.

4 I go to meeting as the rest,
To hear and learn, and to be bless'd;
But while they're comforted in bliss,
My heart's just like a rock of ice.

5 Or if I'm ever made to weep,
And weeping, rank with Jesus' sheep;
Those comforts are but transient guests,
My blessings make but partial feasts.

6 Sometimes I seek some lonely place,
To muse, and pray for greater grace,
But there can only groan and sigh:
O what a wretched soul am I!

7 Others I hear say they have found
The Saviour precious all around;
But I am mostly cold and dead,
Which often makes me sore afraid.

8 Some christians when they come to die,
Seem full of joy and long to fly;
But I have oft a tortur'd mind,
Lest I shall then be left behind.

9 Come christians dear, of ev'ry tongue,
Whose hearts and lips agree in one,
Unfold the truth and let me know
If it indeed be so with you.

10 Are these the trials which you know?
Is this the gloomy way you go?
Come tell me quick for Jesus' sake,
Or my poor heart must surely break.

472. (8's.)
Faith Triumphing over Unbelief.

1 AWAY, my unbelieving fear,
    Fear shall in me no more have place,
My Saviour does not yet appear,
    He hides the brightness of his face:
But shall I therefore let him go,
    And basely to the tempter yield!
No—in the strength of Jesus, no,
    I never will give up my shield.

2 Although the vine its fruit deny,
    Although the olive yield no oil,
The with'ring fig-tree droop and die,
    The fields elude the tiller's toil,
The empty stall no herd afford,
    And perish all the bleeting race,
Yet will I triumph in the Lord,
    The God of my salvation praise.

3 Barren although my soul remain,
    And not one bud of grace appear:
No fruit of all my toil or pain,
    But sin, and only sin is here;
Although my gifts and comforts lost,
    My blooming hopes cut off I see.
Yet will I in my Saviour trust,
    And glory that he dy'd for me.

4 In hope believing against hope,
    Jesus, my Lord, my God I claim,
Jesus, my strength, shall lift me up,
    Salvation is in Jesus' name:
To me he soon shall bring it nigh,
    My soul shall then outstrip the wind:
On wongs of love mount up on high,
    And leave the world and sin behind.

473. (8's, 11.) 6S./4L.
In Distress Longing for Deliverance.

1 WHILE sorrows encompass me round,

474. (8, 7, 4.)
Sanctified Afflictions are Sweet.

1 IN the floods of tribulation,
    While the billows o'er me roll,
Jesus whispers consolation,
    And supports my fainting soul.

Hallelujah, Hallelujah,
Hallelujah, praise the Lord.

2 Thus, the lion yields me honey,
    From the eater food is given,
Strengthen'd thus I still press forward,
    Singing as I wade to heaven—
Sweet affliction, sweet affliction,
    And my sins are all forgiv'n.

3 'Mid the gloom the vivid light'nings
    With increasing brightness play,
'Mid the thorn-brake beauteous flowrets
    Look more beautiful ang gay:
Hallelujah, &c.

4 So, in darkest dispensations,
    Doth my faithful Lord appear
With his richest consolations,
    To reanimate and cheer;
Sweet affliction, sweet affliction.
Thus to bring my Saviour near.

5 Floods of tribulation heighten,
    Billows still around me roar,
Those that know not Christ—ye frighten;
    But *my soul* defies your power.
Hallelujah, &c.

6 In the sacred page recorded
    Thus the word securely stands,
"Fear not, I'm in trouble near thee,
    "Nought shall pluck you from my hands
Sweet affliction, sweet affliction,
Every word my love demands.

7 All I meet I find assists me
    In my path to heavenly joy,
Where, though trials now attend me.
    Trials never more annoy;
Hallelujah, &c.

8 Wearing there a weight of glory
    Still the path I'll ne'er forget;
But, exulting, cry, it led me
    "To my blessed Saviour's seat—
Sweet affliction, sweet affliction,
Which has brought to Jesus' feet.

475. (8's.)
Faith Cast Down, but not Destroyed.

1 ENCOMPASS'D with clouds of distress,
    Just ready all hope to resign,
I pant for the light of thy face,
    And fear it will never be mine:
Dishearten'd with waiting so long,
    I sink at thy feet with my load,
All plaintive I pour out my song,
    And stretch forth my hands unto God.

2 Shine, Lord, and my terror shall cease,
    The blood of atonement apply;
And lead me to Jesus for peace,
    The Rock that is higher than I;
Speak, Saviour, for sweet is thy voice;
    Thy presence is fair to behold;
Attend to my sorrows and cries,
    My gronning that cannot be told.

3 If sometimes I strive as I mourn,
    My hold of thy promise to keep,
The billows more fiercely return,
    And plunge me again in the deep:
While harass'd and cast from thy sight
    The tempter suggests with a roar,
"The Lord has forsaken thee quite;
    Thy God will be gracious no more."

4 Yet, Lord, if thy love hath design'd
    No covenant blessing for me,
Ah, tell me, how it is I find
    Some pleasure in waiting for thee?
Almighty to rescue thou art;
    Thy grace is my shield and my tow'r;
Come succour and gladden my heart,
    Let this be the day of thy power.

476. (8, 7, 4.) 5S./6L.
Sad, yet Hoping.

1 O MY soul, what means this sadness?

477. (7's.)
Welcoming the Cross.

1 'TIS my happiness below
    Not to live without the cross,
But the Saviour's pow'r to know.
    Sanctifying ev'ry loss:
Trials must and will befal;
    But—with humble faith to see
Love inscrib'd upon them all—
    This is happiness to me.

2 God, in Israel, sows the seeds
    Of affliction, pain, and toil;
These spring up and choke the weeds
    Which would else o'erspread the soil:
Trials make the promise sweet;
    Trials give new life to pray'r;
Trials bring me to his feet,—
    Lay me low, and keep me there.

3 Did I meet no trials here—
    No chastlsement by the way—
Might I not, with reason, fear
    I should prove a cast away?

Bastards may escape the rod,
  Sunk in earthly vain delight;
But the true-born child of God
  Must not—would not, if he might.

478. (L.M.)
Christ a Presence Banishes Fear.

1 IN darkest hours and greatest grief,
    A view of Christ gives joy and light;
  Among ten thousand he's the chief,
  He turns to day the darkest night.

2 When past offences me assail,
  And Sinai's thunders loudest roar,
  Then Jesus shows himself my bail,
  And justice says, "I ask no more."

3 When sins again to mountains rise,
  And fears like raging billows swell;
  Then Christ appears my sacrifice,
  And sweetly whispers "all is well."

4 Then let me trust, nor yield to fear,
  Though I in thickest darkness dwell;
  Since he, my Lord, is ever near,
  The pow'rs of hell and sin to quell.

479. (L. M.)
The Days of Trouble are long and many.

1 HOW long and tedious are the days,
    In which my Jesus does not show,
  His smiling face, his cheering rays,
  Nor give my soul his love to know.

2 In vain do all things here below,
  Without my God attempt to give
  That happiness I long to know;
  Without my God I cannot live.

3 Each day's a year, each year's an age,
  When my Redeemer is withdrawn;
  Then darkness and temptations rage,
  And happiness! a guest unknown.

4 But while my soul thus mourning lies,
  And longs to see her Saviour's face;
  He speaks; and at his voice I rise,
  And in his strength pursue my race.

480. (S. M.)
The Evils of the Heart Lamented.

1 ASTONISH'D and distress'd
    I turn mine eyes within;
  My heart with loads of guilt opprest,
  The seat of ev'ry sin.

2 What crowds of evil thoughts,
    What vile affections there!
  Distrust, presumption, artful guile,
  Pride, envy, slavish fear.

3 Almighty King of saints,
    These tyrant lusts subdue;
  Expel the darkness of my mind,
  And all my pow'rs renew.

4 This done, my cheerful voice
    Shall loud hosannas raise;
  My soul shall glow with gratitude,
  My lips proclaim thy praise.

481. (C. M.) 4S./4L.
The Path to Heaven lies through a Maze.

1 LORD! what a wretched land is this,

482. (C. M.) 7S./4L.
Who are these? and whence are they?

1 WHAT poor despised company

483. (C. M.) 4S./4L.
A Christian's Changes.

1 STRANGE that so much of heaven and hell

484. (7, 6.) 9S./8L.
The same.

1 MIXTURES of joy and sorrow

485. (L. M.) 4S./4L.
Flesh and spirit in Struggle.

1 HOW sad and awful is my state!

486. (C. M.) 5S./4L.
A Struggle between Sin and Holiness.

1 WHEN heaven does grant at certain times,

487. (L. M.) 3S./4L.
Inconstancy Lamented.

1 DEAR Jesus, when, when shall it be

488. (S. M.) 8S./4L.
I would, if I could.

1 I WOULD, but cannot sing,

489. (C. M.) 6S./4L.
The Exercises of Saints various.

1 HOW hard and rugged is the way

490. (L. M.) Russia.
No Trust in Creatures.

1 MY spirit looks to God alone;
   My rock and refuge is his throne;
In all my fears, in all my straits,
My soul on his salvation waits.

2 Trust him, ye saints, in all your ways,
Pour out your hearts before his face;
When helpers fail, and foes invade,
God is our all sufficient aid.

3 False are the men of high degree,
The baser sort are vanity;
Laid in the balance both appear
Light as a puff of empty air.

4 Make not increasing gold your trust,
Nor set your hearts on glitt'ring dust;
Why will you grasp the fleeting smoke,
And not believe what God has spoke?

5 Once has his awful voice declar'd,
Once and again my ears have heard,
"All pow'r is his eternal due;
"He must be fear'd, and trusted too."

6 For sov'reign pow'r reigns not alone,
Grace is a partner of the throne;
Thy grace and justice, Mighty Lord,
Shall well divide our last reward.

491. (7, 6.)
Longing for, and encouraging others in the Way to Heaven.

1 O WHEN shall I see Jesus,
   And reign with him above,
And drink the flowing fountain
   Of everlasting love?
When shall I be deliver'd
   From this vain world of sin,
And with my blessed Jesus,
   Drink endless pleasures in.

2 But now I am a soldier,
   My captain's gone before,
Has given me my orders,
   And tells me not to fear;
For since he's gain'd the vict'ry,
   It to his own he'll give,
And all his valiant soldiers
   Eternally shall live.

3 Thro' grace I feel determin'd
   To conquer tho' I die,
And then away to Jesus
   On wings of love I'll fly;
Farewell to sin and sorrow,
   I bid them both adieu,
And you my friends prove faithful,
   And on your way pursue.

4 O do not be discourag'd,
   For Jesus is your friend,
And if you lack for knowledge,
   He'll guide you to the end:
Neither will he upbraid you,
   Tho' often you request,
But give you grace to conquer,
   And take you home to rest,

5 And if you meet with trials
   And troubles by the way,
Then cast your care on Jesus,
   And don't forget to pray;
Gird on the blessed armour,
   Of faith, and truth, and love,
And when your race is ended,
   He'll take you home above.

6 O then press on with courage,
   To meet your dearest Lord,
He has a place prepared,
   He tells us in his word,
For all who live uprightly,
   And obedient to his will;
Bright angels shall convey them
   To the New Jerusalem.

7 And when my race is ended,
   I'll go away to God,
And there I'll see my Jesus,
   Who bought me with his blood:
I'll sit, and sing, and praise him,
   For a crown he gives to me,
And sing the song of free-grace,
   To all eternity.

492. (6, 8.) Lenox. 8S./6L.
The Beggar's Plea made before the Lord.

1 ENCOURAG'D by thy word

493. (8's.)
Christian Fortitude and Resignation.

1 LONG have I view'd, long have I tho't,
   And trembling held this bitter draught,
When only to my lips applied,
Nature shrank in, my courage died;
But now resolv'd, and firm I'll be,
Since, Lord, 'tis mixt and giv'n by thee.

2 I'll trust my great physician's skill,
What he prescribes can ne'er be ill;
For each disease he knows what's fit,
He's wise and good, and I submit:
No longer will I grieve or pine;
Thy pleasure 'tis, it shall be mine.

3 Thy medicine puts me to great smart,
Thou wound'st me in the tend'rest part,
But 'tis with a design to cure,

I must and will thy touch endure;
All that I priz'd below is gone,
Yet Father, still thy will be done.
4 Since 'tis thy sentence I should part,
With what was nearest to my heart,
I freely that and more resign,
Behold, my heart itself is thine:
My little all I give to thee,
Thou hast bestow'd thy Son on me.
5 He left true bliss and joy above,
Empty'd himself of all but love;
For me he freely did forsake
More than from me he e'er can take:
A mortal life for a divine,
He took, and did e'en that resign.
6 Take all, great GOD, I will not grieve,
But still wish I had more to give;
I hear thy voice, thou bid'st me quit
My paradise, and I submit;
I will not murmur at thy word,
Nor beg thee to sheath up thy sword.

494. (C.M.) Double. 5S./8L.
Courage taken from the Approach of Death.

1 MY span of life will soon be done,

495. (7, 6.)
The Lord is our Refuge and Strength.

1 THE Lord is my protector,
To him I fly for aid;
My Refuge and Director;
Why is my heart afraid?
Though amid threat'ning danger,
Oppress'd by many a care,
My heart, be thou a stranger
To unbelieving fear.
2 Thy God with love unceasing,
His people will secure;
Their fainting strength increasing,
He proves his promise sure.
Oft at this baneful hour,
That teems with ev'ry ill,
Faith manifests his power,
And bids the heart be still.
3 Though like a roaring lion
The prince of darkness roam,
The souls that dwell in Sion
Have there a peaceful home.
In vain the force of legions.
All impotent their might;
Peace from the heavenly regions,
Breaks through the gloom of night.
4 Some guardian spirit near me,
Whose office is of love,

Methinks is sent to cheer me
With comfort from above:
Or what's this blest sensation,
This gleam of cordial hope?
Kind tokens of salvation,
That bear my spirits up?
5 Yes—from their heav'nly places
Commission'd angels fly,
To cheer the Christian's graces,
And raise his courage high.
Oh pleasure past expressing!
What rapture must be theirs,
Who bring the cup of blessing
That God himself prepares!

496. (7's.) Double.
Mutual Encouragement.

1 BRETHREN, while we sojourn here,
Fight we must, but should not fear;
Foes we have, but we've a Friend,
One that loves us to the end.
Forward then with courage go,
Long we shall not dwell below;
Soon the joyful news will come,
"Child, your Father calls—come home."
2 In the way a thousand snares
Lie, to take us unawares;
Satan with malicious art,
Watches each unguarded part;
But from Satan's malice free,
Saints shall soon victorious be;
Soon the joyful news will come,
"Child, your Father calls—come home."
3 But, of all the foes we meet,
None so oft mislead our feet;
None betray us into sin,
Like the foes that dwell within.
Yet, let nothing spoil your peace,
Christ will also conquer these;
Then the joyful news will come,
"Child, your Father calls—come home."

497. (7, 6.) 10S./8L.
The Christian and his Soul.

1 COME, my soul, and let us try,

498. (C.M.) 4S./4L.
Sanctified afflictions our best Mercies.

1 THY people, Lord, have ever found

499. (C.M.) 4S./4L.
Ye believe in God, believe also in Me.

1 LET not your hearts within you grieve,

500. (L. M.)
Despair prevented by Faith.

1 LORD, didst thou die, but not for me?
   Am I forbid to trust thy blood?
   Is not thy mercy rich and free,
   Seal'd in the kind atoning flood?

2 Who then shall drive my trembling soul
   From thee, to regions of despair?
   Who has survey'd the sacred roll,
   And found my name not written there?

3 Presumptuous thought! to fix the bound—
   To limit mercy's sov'reign reign:
   What other happy souls have found,
   I'll seek; nor shall I seek in vain.

4 Lord at thy feet I'll cast me down,
   To thee reveal my guilt and fear;
   And if thou spurn me from thy throne
   I'll be the first who perish'd there.

501. (P. M.)
The final Farewell.

1 FAREWELL, dear Friends, I must be gone,
   I have no home nor stay with you,
   I'll take my staff and travel on,
   Till I a better world can view;
   Farewell, farewell, farewell,
   My loving friends, farewell.

2 Farewell, my friends, time rolls along,
   Nor waits for mortal's care or bliss;
   I leave you here and travel on,
   Till I arrive where Jesus is:
                        Farewell, &c.

3 Farewell, my brethren in the Lord,
   To you I'm bound in cords of love;
   Yet we believe his gracious word,
   That soon we all shall meet above:
                        Farewell, &c.

4 Farewell, old soldiers of the cross,
   You've struggled long and hard for heav'n;
   You've counted all things here but dross—
   Fight on, the crown shall soon be giv'n!
   Fight on, fight on, fight on,
   The crown shall soon be giv'n.

5 Farewell, ye younger saints of God,
   Sore conflicts yet may wait for you;
   Yet dauntless keep the heav'nly road,
   Till Canaan's happy land you view:
                        Farewell, &c.

6 Farewell, poor careless sinners, too,
   It grieves my heart to leave you here;
   Eternal vengeance waits for you—
   O turn and seek salvation here;
   O turn, O turn, O turn,
   And seek salvation here.

502. (L. M.) 4S./4L.
Faith in Darkness gives Consolation.

1 AMID the dark, the dismal scene,

503. (C. M.) 4S./4L.
Hope encourages.

1 A THOUSAND promises are wrote

504. (C. M.)
Good Hope through Grace.

1 COME humble souls, ye mourners, come,
   And wipe away your tears:
   Adieu to all your sad complaints,
   Your sorrows and your fears.

2 Come shout aloud the Father's grace,
   And sing the Saviour's love:
   Soon shall you join the glorious theme
   In loftier strains above.

3 God th' eternal, mighty God,
   To dearer names descends:
   Calls you his treasure and his joy,
   His children and his friends.

505. (6, 8.) Lenox. 5S./6L.
Who can tell?

1 GREAT God! to thee I make

506. (L. M.) 4S./4L.
Resolving to look again.

1 SEE a poor sinner, dearest Lord,

507. (6, 4.) Delight. Bethesda.
God, our Guardian, never sleeps.

1 UPWARD I lift mine eyes,
   From God is all my aid;
   The God that built the skies,
   And earth and nature made.
   God is the tow'r
   To which I fly;
   His grace is nigh
   In ev'ry hour.

2 My feet shall never slide,
   Nor fall in fatal snares,

Hymn Texts From *The Cluster*

 Since God, my guard and guide,
  Defends me from my fears.
   Those wakeful eyes
   That never sleep,
  Shall Isr'el keep,
   When dangers rise.
3 No burning heat by day,
  Nor blasts of ev'ning air,
 Shall take my health away,
  If God be with me there.
   Thou art my sun,
   And thou my shade,
  To guard my head
   By night or noon.
4 Hast thou not giv'n thy word
  To save my soul from death?
 And I can trust my Lord
  To keep my mortal breath.
   I'll go and come,
   Nor fear to die,
  'Till from on high
   Thou call me home.

  508. (8's.) Greenfield.
God is our Refuge in Trouble.

1 GOD is our refuge in distress,
 A present help when dangers press;
In him undaunted we'll confide:
Though earth were from her centre tost,
And mountains in the ocean lost,
Torn piece-meal by the roaring tide.

2 A gentler stream with gladness still
The city of our Lord shall fill,
 The royal seat of God most high:
God dwells in Sion, whose fair tow'rs
Shall mock th' assaults of earthly pow'rs,
 While his Almighty aid is nigh.

3 In tumults when the heathen rag'd,
And kingdom's war against us wag'd,
 He thunder'd and dispers'd their pow'rs!
The Lord of hosts conducts our arms,
Our tow'r of refuge in alarms,
 Our Father's Guardian-God and ours.

4 Come see the wonders he hath wrought,
On earth what desolation brought,
 How he has calm'd the jarring world:
He broke the warlike spear and bow;
With them the thundering chariots too
 Into devouring flames were hurl'd.

5 Submit to God's Almighty sway;
 For him the heathen shall obey,
  And earth her sov'reign Lord confess:

The God of hosts conducts our arms,
Our tow'r of refuge in alarms,
  As to our fathers in distress.

  509. (C. M.) Ps. 34.
Trust in God at all times.

1 THRO' all the changing scenes of life,
 In trouble and in joy;
The praises of my God shall still
 My heart and tongue employ.

2 Of his deliverance I will boast,
 Till all, who are distrest,
From my example comfort take,
 And charm their griefs to rest.

3 The hosts of God encamp around
 The dwellings of the just:
Protection he affords to all
 Who make his name their trust.

4 Oh, make but trial of his love!—
 Experience will decide,
How blest are they, and only they,
 Who in his truth confide.

5 Fear him, ye saints! and you will then
 Have nothing else to fear;
Make you his service your delight.—
 Your wants shall be his care.

6 While hungry lions lack their prey,
 The Lord will food provide
For such as put their trust in him,
 And see their needs supply'd.

  510. (L. M.) 3S./4L.
Past Mercies acknowledged, and future ones sought.

1 THIS morning let my praise arise,

  511. (S. M.) 2S./4L.
The Sun in its Course a Christian Monitor.

1 SEE how the mounting sun

  512. (L. M.) 4S./4L.
The same.

1 GOD of the morning, at whose voice

  513. (S. M.)
Desiring to emulate Nature in Praise.

1 ALMIGHTY Maker, God!
 How wondrous is thy name!
Thy glories how diffus'd abroad
 Through the creation's frame.

2 Nature in ev'ry dress
 Her humble homage pays,

And finds a thousand ways t' express
  Thy undissembled praise.
3 My soul would rise and sing
  To her Creator too,
  Fain would my tongue adore my King,
  And pay the worship due.
4 Let joy and worship spend
  The remnant of my days,
  And to my God, my soul ascend
  In sweet perfumes of praise.

514. (L. M.) 3S./4L.
Morning Praise.

1 BEGIN, my soul, thy morning song,

515. (C. M.) 4S./4L.
It is good to praise God early in the Morning.

1 GOD of my life, my morning song

516. (L. M.)
The Being of God bespoke every Morning.

1 THERE is a God, all nature speaks,
  Through earth, and air, and seas,
    and skies;
  See from the clouds his glory breaks,
  When the first beams of morning rise.
2 The rising sun, serenely bright,
  O'er the wide world's extended frame.
  Inscribes in characters of light,
  His mighty Maker's glorious name,
3 The flow'ry tribes all blooming rise,
  Above the weak attempts of art;
  The smallest worms, the meanest flies,
  Speak sweet convictions to the heart.
4 Ye curious minds, who roam abroad,
  And trace creation's wonders o'er,
  Confess the footsteps of the God—
  Bow down, before him and adore.

517. (L. M.) 3S./4L.
The Sabbath Morning.

1 COME, dearest Lord, and bless this day,

518. (C. M.)
Another.

1 COME, let us join in sweet accord
    In hymns around the throne;
  This is the day our rising Lord
  Hath made and call'd his own.
2 This is the day which God hath blest,
  The brightest of the sev'n;
  Type of that everlasting rest,
  The saints enjoy in heaven.

519. (C. M.) 4S./4L.
Another.

1 THE Lord of Sabbaths let us praise,

520. (C. M.) Montgomery.
Another.

1 EARLY, my God without delay,
    I haste to seek thy face;
  My thirsty spirit faints away,
    Without thy cheering grace.
2 So pilgrims on the scorching sand,
    Beneath the burning sky,
  Long for a cooling stream at hand,
    And they must drink, or die.
3 I've seen thy glory and thy pow'r,
    Through all thy temple shine;
  My God, repeat that heav'nly hour.
    That vision so divine.
4 Not all the blessings of a feast,
    Can please my soul so well,
  As when thy richer grace I taste,
    And in thy presence dwell.

521. (L. M.) Bridgewater.
Another.

1 SWEET is the work, my God, my King,
    To praise thy name, give thanks
      and sing,
  To show thy love by morning light,
  And talk of all thy truth at night.
2 Sweet is the day of sacred rest,
  No mortal care shall seize my breast;
  O may my heart in tune be found,
  Like David's harp of solemn sound.
3 My heart shall triumph in my Lord,
  And bless his works, and bless his word;
  Thy works of grace how bright they shine!
  How deep thy counsels! how divine!
4 There shall I see, and hear, and know,
  And I desir'd or wish'd below;
  And ev'ry pow'r find sweet employ
  In that eternal world of joy.

522. (C. M.) Walsall.
Morning Prayer.

1 LORD, in the morning thou shalt hear,
    My voice ascending high;
  To thee will I direct my pray'r,
    To thee lift up mine eye.
2 Up to the hills where Christ is gone
    To plead for all his saints,
  Presenting at his Father's throne
    Our songs and our complaints.

Hymn Texts From *The Cluster*

3 O may thy Spirit guide my feet
    In ways of righteousness!
Make ev'ry path of duty straight,
    And plain before my face.

523 (C. M.) 4S./4L.
Morning and Evening Prayer and Praise.

1 ONCE more, my soul, the rising day

524. (L. M.) 4S./4L.
Another.

1 MY God, accept my early vows,

525. (L. M.) 3S./4L.
Another.

1 MY God, how endless is thy love!

526. (S. M.) Florida.
Another.

1 LET sinners take their course,
    And choose the road to death;
But in the worship of my God
    I'll spend my daily breath.

2 My thoughts address his throne,
    When morning brings the light,
I seek his blessings ev'ry noon,
    And pay my vows at night.

3 Thou wilt regard my cries,
    O my eternal God,
While sinners perish in surprise
    Beneath thine angry rod,

4 Because they dwell at ease,
    And no sad changes feel,
They neither fear nor trust thy name,
    Nor learn to do thy will.

527. (7's.) 4S./4L.
Mercies incessant.

1 THRO' the wisdom of the skies,

528. (C. M.) 2S./4L.
Morning praise.

1 WITH morning light let us rejoice,

529. (7's.) 3S./4L.
Morning Prayer.

1 IN the morning let us pray,

530. (7's.) 3S./4L.
Hourly dependence.

1 IN the morning of the day,

531. (C. M.) 4S./4L.
Praise God in the morning.

1 COME let us lift our voices high

532. (P. M.)
The Christian's Nightly Song.

1 I'LL sing my Saviour's grace,
    And his sweet name I'll praise,
While in this land of sorrow I remain
    My sorrow soon shall end,
    And then my soul ascend,
Where freed from trouble, sorrow,
    sin, and pain.

2 A pilgrim here below,
    While in this vale of woe,
An exile banish'd, wandering I rove:
    My days in sorrow roll,
    And then my weary soul,
In earnest longings pants to mount above.

3 Though few my days have been,
    Much sorrow I have seen,
And deep afflictions I have waded thro':
    But thorny is the way
    Unto eternal day—
Then forward will I press and onward go.

4 Another day is gone,
    And yon declining sun
Hath veil'd its radiant beams in sable
    shades.
    And gloomy darkness reigns,
    O'er the extensive plains,
And silence, awful silence, clothes the
    main.

5 Thus swiftly flies away
    Ev'ry succeeding day,
And life's declining light draws to a close;
    And long life's setting sun,
    Will soon in death go down,
And lay my weary dust in calm repose.

6 Then happy, sweet surprise—
    And what new wonders rise,
When freed from this dull, crazy,
    cumbrous clay:
    On eagles' wings of love,
    I then shall mount above,
And find a passage to eternal day.

7 Then, O the glorious sight!
    What sweet, supreme delight,
Will strike my ravish'd soul when I behold!
    When Salem's gates I see,
    Wide open fly to me,   [gold!
With streets of glitt'ring, pure, transparent

8 But O! and shall I then,
    Behold the friend of men,
   The man who suffer'd, groan'd, and died
     for me?
   Who bore my load of sin,
   Of sorrow, grief and pain,
   To make me happy and to set me free.

9 To living fountains then,
    And to rich pastures green,
   And trees of Paradise he'll lead his lambs:
   While millions fall around,
   Prostrated on the ground,
   And at his footstool cast their starry
     crowns.

10 Ye heav'nly arches ring,
     Sing, hallelujah sing!
   Hail holy, holy, holy, bleeding Lamb!
   Once we were dead in sin,
   But now we live again—
   Sing glory, glory, glory to the Lamb.

533. (S. M.)
The Night an Emblem of Death.

1 THE day is past and gone;
     The evening shades appear;
   Oh! may we all remember well
   The night of death is near.

2 We lay our garments by,
     Upon our beds to rest,
   So death will soon disrobe us all
   Of what we here possest.

3 Lord keep us safe this night,
     Secure from all our fears,
   Beneath the pinions of thy love,
   Till morning light appears.

4 And when we early rise,
     And view th' unclouded sun,
   May we set out to win the prize,
   And after glory run.

5 And when our days are past,
     And we from time remove,
   O! may we in thy bosom rest—
   The bosom of thy love.

534. (L. M.) 3S./4L.
Mercies are new every Evening.

1 THUS far the Lord hath led me on,

535. (L. M.) 3S./4L.
An Evening Song.

1 GREAT God, to thee my ev'ning song

536. (L. M.) 3S./4L.
Another.

1 GLORY to thee, my God, this night,

537. (C. M.) 4S./4L.
Evening Prayer and Praise.

1 DREAD Sov'reign, let my ev'ning song

538. (C. M.)
An Evening Psalm.

1 LORD, thou wilt hear me when I pray;
     I am forever thine;
   I fear before thee all the day;
   Nor would I dare to sin.

2 And while I rest my weary head,
     From cares and bus'ness free,
   'Tis sweet conversing on my bed
   With my own heart and thee.

3 I pay this ev'ning sacrifice;
     And when my work is done,
   Great God, my faith and hope relies
   Upon thy grace alone.

4 Thus, with my thoughts compos'd to peace,
     I'll give mine eyes to sleep;
   Thy hand in safety keeps my days,
   And will my slumbers keep.

539. (C. M.) 3S./4L.
Another.

1 LORD, when I count thy mercies o'er,

540. (L. M.) 4S./4L.
Evening of the Lord's Day.

1 LORD, how delightful 'tis to see

541. (C. M.)
Another.

1 FREQUENT the day of God returns
     To shed its quick'ning beams;
   And yet how slow devotion burns—
   How languid are its flames.

2 Accept my faint attempts to love,
     My frailties, Lord forgive;
   I would be like thy saints above,
   And praise thee while I live.

3 Increase, O Lord, my faith and hope,
     And fit me to ascend,
   Where the assembly ne'er breaks up,
   And Sabbaths never end.

542. (7's.) 4S./4L.
The Planets Praise God by Night.

1 NIGHTLY to the list'ning ear,

543. (7's.) 3S./4L.
Another.

1 NOW the gloomy night comes on,

Hymn Texts From *The Cluster*

544. (C. M.) Double.
Perplexed, but not in Despair.

1 OH! once I had a glorious view
    Of my redeeming Lord!
He said, "I'll be a God to you"—
    And I believ'd his word:
But now I have a deeper stroke,
    Than all my groanings are:
My God has me of late forsook—
    He's gone, I know not where.

Chorus.
O that I knew the sacred place,
    Where I might find my God!
I'd bow before his gracious face,
    And pour my woes abroad.

2 O what immortal joys I felt,
    On that celestial day,
When my hard heart began to melt,
    By love dissolv'd away!
But my complaint is bitter now,
    For all my joys are gone;
I've stray'd!—I'm left!—I know not how!
    The light's from me withdrawn.

3 Once I could joy the saints to meet,
    To me they were most dear;
I then could stoop to wash their feet,
    And shed a joyful tear:
But now I meet them as the rest,
    And with them joyless stay;
My conversation's spiritless,
    Or else I've nought to say.

4 I once could mourn o'er dying men,
    And long'd their souls to win;
I travail'd for their poor children,
    And warn'd them of their sin:
But now my heart's so careless grown,
    Although they're drown'd in vice,
My bowels o'er them cease to yearn—
    The tears have left mine eyes.

5 I forward go in duty's way,
    But can't perceive him there;
Then backward on the road I stray,
    But cannot find him there:
On the left hand, where he doth work,
    Among the wicked crew,
And on the right, I find him not,
    Among the favour'd few.

6 What shall I do?—shall I lie down,
    And sink in deep despair?
Will he forever wear a frown,
    Nor hear my feeble pray'r?
No: he will put his strength in me,
    He knows the way I've stroll'd;
And when I'm tried sufficiently,
    I shall come forth as gold.

545. (8, 7.) 10S./4L.
Decline Lamented, and a Revival Sought.
    & Chorus

1 SAVIOUR, visit thy plantation;

546. (9, 8.) 5S./8L.
The Backslider Humbled.

1 MY soul with Zion claims salvation,

547. (L. M.)
The Penitential Cries of a Backslider.

1 O GREAT Jehovah, God of love!
    Look down, in pity, from above,
On me whose heart is careless grown,
Who walks in darkness all forlorn;
    Show pity, Lord, and draw me home,
    Without thy grace I cannot come.

2 O that thy quick'ning grace may raise
My falt'ring tongue to sing thy praise!
O that thy smiles once more may cheer
My fainting soul, just in despair!
    Show pity, &c.

3 Oh! once my God was my delight,
I sang his praises day and night:
But now, O now, this is my grief,
My soul is full of unbelief.
    Show pity, &c.

4 Oh! once I thought I had a view
Of Jesus, and his suff'rings too,
Applied to pardon all my sin,
And make my guilty conscience clean.
    Show pity, &c.

5 But now my soul is in the dark—
Of light I scarcely have a spark—
Which makes me fear I'm void of grace,
And to condole my helpless case.
    Show pity, &c.

6 The earnest of thy Spirit give;
Lord, make me in thy precepts live:
Among thy saints I'd spend my days,
And to thy name give lasting praise.
    Show pity, Lord, and make me blest;
    Without thy grace I cannot rest.

548. (P. M.) 6S./6L. & Chorus
The Backslider's Prayer.

1 JESUS, let thy pitying eye

549. (11's.) 9S./4L.
An Apostate Minister's Lamentation.

1 MY thoughts are inditing of some solemn theme,

550. (L. M.)
Imploring the Return of God's Spirit.

1 FOR ever shall my fainting soul,
  O God, thy just displeasure mourn;
  Thy grieved Spirit, long withdrawn,
  Will he no more to me return?

2 Once I enjoy'd, O happy time!
  The heart-felt visits of his grace;
  Nor can a thousand varying scenes
  The sweet remembrance quite efface!

3 Important Guest! thrice happy soul.
  While honour'd with his blest abode;
  But, ah! my sins, accursed things,
  Ye griev'd, ye chas'd away my God.

4 Great Source of light and peace, return,
  Nor let me mourn and sigh in vain;
  Come, repossess this longing heart,
  With all the graces of thy train.

5 This temple, hallow'd by thine hand,
  Once more be with thy presence blest;
  Here be thy grace anew display'd,
  And this thy everlasting rest.

551. (L. M.) 4S./4L.
A Barren State Lamented.

1 LORD, must thy gospel fly away?

552. (L. M.) 4S./4L.
Inconstancy Lamented.

1 AH! wretched, vile, ungrateful heart,

553. (C. M.) 4S./4L.
Humbled Backsliders Addressed.

1 BACKSLIDERS, who your mis'ry feel,

554. (C. M.) Mere.
The Church Mourning and Pleading under Desertion.

1 WILL God forever cast us off?
  His wrath forever smoke
  Against the people of his love,
  His little chosen flock?

2 Think of the tribes so dearly bought
  With the Redeemer's blood;
  Nor let thy Zion be forgot,
  Where once thy glory stood.

3 Where once thy churches pray'd and sang,
  Thy foes profanely rage;
  Amid thy gates their ensigns hang,
  And there their hosts engage.

4 And, still to heighten our distress,
  Thy presence is withdrawn;
  Thy wonted signs of pow'r and grace,
  Thy pow'r and grace are gone.

5 No prophets speak to calm our grief,
  But all in silence mourn;
  Nor know the times of our relief,
  The hour of thy return.

CHRISTIANS ENCOURAGED.

555. (11's.)
Zion Comforted in Affliction.

1 O ZION afflicted with wave upon wave,
  Whom no man can comfort, whom no man can save;   [may'd,
  With darkness surrounded, by terror dis-
  In toiling and rowing thy strength is decay'd.

2 Loud roaring the billows now nigh overwhelm,
  But skilful's the pilot who sits at the helm;
  His wisdom conducts thee, his pow'r thee defends,
  In safety and quiet thy warfare he ends.

3 "O fearful! O faithless!" in mercy he cries,
  "My promise, my truth, are the light in thine eyes: [stand;
  Still, still, I am with thee, my promise shall
  Through tempest and tossing I'll bring thee to land.

4 Forget thee I will not, I cannot thy name,
  Engrav'd on my heart doth for ever remain;
  The palms of my hands whilst I look on, I see   [thee.
  The wounds I received when suff'ring for

5 I feel at my heart all thy sighs and thy groans,
  For thou art most near me, my flesh and my bones.
  In all thy distresses my head feels the pain,
  Yet all are most needful, not one is in vain.

6 Then trust me, and fear not; thy life is secure;
  My wisdom is perfect, supreme is my pow'r;
  In love I correct thee, thy soul to refine,
  To make thee at length in my likeness to shine.

7 The foolish, the fearful, the weak are my
                    care,   [pray'r;
  The helpless, the hopeless, I hear their sad
  From all their afflictions my glory shall
                    spring,   [they'll sing."
  And the deeper their sorrows, the louder.

556. (P. M.)
Stand fast in the Liberty, &c.

1 COME Christians, be wise,
    Learn your liberty to prize,
  Each moment in virtue excel:
    Since God has made you free,
    Stand for your liberty,
  And in Jesus you ever shall dwell.

2 Like strangers you rove,
    While you seek a world above—
  O let love to each other abound!
    While surrounded with foes,
    Who your liberty oppose,
  Your succour in Jesus is found.

3 If faith you have possess'd,
    You have enter'd into rest,
  But perfection you have not obtain'd:
    Salvation's before,
    And the Lord hath made it sure,
  So your labour shall not be in vain.

4 For God is your friend,
    And his love shall never end,
  To protect you although you are few;
    So you need not despair,
    And your breaches he'll repair,
  And fresh vigour and strength he'll renew.

5 He's bless'd you with peace,
    And his love shall never cease,
  He's bless'd you with his smiling charms;
    So look home and rejoice,
    Wait for that inviting voice,
  And ere long you shall be in his arms.

6 'Twill be a happy day,
    When he calls us all away,
  And advances us into his throne;
    Where in pleasure we'll reign,
    And our freedom shall remain,
  When our Jesus and we are both one.

7 Our souls will be pleas'd,
    With those rivers and seas,
  While we bathe in this fountain of love;
    No affliction comes there,
    No, nor grief shall interfere,
  And none can our freedom remove.

557. (11's.)
Awake thou that sleepest, &c.

1 YE soldiers of Jesus, awake from your
      sleep!
  Ye trav'llers to Zion, how slowly you creep!
  The wicked out-run you in their sinful
      way,
  Who serve the worst master, and hell is
      their pay.

2 Our Jesus invites us with mercy's sweet
      voice;   [joice,
  So charming the music, we all should re-
  To leave all behind us, and fly to his
      arms;—   [farms.
  Let sinners reject him for stores and for

3 Remember you'r passing from life unto
      death—   [breath;
  A few scenes remaining will finish your
  Your friends will desert you in your dusty
      bed,   [dread.
  And pass by your dwelling with a solemn

4 How happy the spirits whom angels
      convey
  To regions of glory, where always 'tis day,
  To dwell with sweet Jesus, bright angels,
      and saints,   [plaints.
  Where all are so happy they have no com-

5 With gladness we'll leave all these trifles
      below,   [know;
  For heav'nly glory, which then we shall
  Our bodies they'll moulder, and crumble
      to dust,
  Till the resurrection of just and unjust.

6 And when the dread trumpet the wicked
      alarms,
  And calls all the righteous to Jesus's arms,
  With shouts all triumphant our bodies
      shall rise,   [skies,
  And fly to meet Jesus the Lord, in the

558. (8's.)
Take heed lest ye be deceived.

1 NO prophet, no dreamer of dreams,
    No master of plausible speech,
  Who looks like an angel, or seems
    Like to an apostle to preach:
  No tempter, without or within,
    No spirit, though ever so bright,
  Who comes crying out against sin,
    And looks like an angel of light—

2 Though reason, though scripture he urge,
    And plead with the words of a friend,

    And wonderful arguments forge,
    And deep revelations pretend,
    Should meet with a moment's regard,
    But rather be boldly withstood,
    If any thing, easy or hard,
    He preach, save the Lamb and his blood.
3 Remember, O Christians, indeed,
    When sunk under sentence of death,
    When you from your bondage were freed—
    Say, was it by works or by faith?
    On Christ your affections were fix'd,
    Through faith in his conjugal vow;
    Was there any thing then with him mix'd?
    And what will you mix with him now?
4 If close to your Lord you would live,
    Depend on his promise alone:
    His righteousness would you receive,
    Then learn to renounce all your own;
    The faith of a Christian indeed,
    Is more than a notion or whim:
    United to Jesus his head,
    He draws life and comfort from him.
5 Deceiv'd by the father of lies,
    Blind guides cry, lo here!, and lo there!
    By these the Redeemer was try'd,
    And bids us of such to beware;
    Poor comfort to mourners they give,
    But set them to labour in vain,
    And strive with a *Do this and live*,
    To drive them to Egypt again.
6 But what says the Shepherd divine?
    For his blessed words we must keep—
    "The flock which the Father's made mine;
    "I lay down my life for the sheep;
    "'Tis life everlasting I give,
    "My blood is the price which it cost;
    "Not one, who in me doth believe,
    "Shall ever be finally lost."
7 This God is the God we adore,.
    Our faithful unchangeable friend;
    His love is as great as his pow'r,
    And neither knows measure nor end;
    Tis Jesus the first and the last—
    His Spirit shall guide us safe home;
    We'll praise him for all that is past,
    And trust him for all that's to come.

559. (L. M.)
Christians animated to Courage.

1 COME ye who know the Lord indeed,
    Who are from sin and bondage freed,
    Submit to all the ways of God,
    And walk the narrow, happy road.

2 Great tribulation you shall meet,
    But soon shall walk the golden street;
    Though hell may rage and vent her spite,
    Yet Christ will save his heart's delight.
3 That awful day will soon appear,
    When Gabriel's trumpet you shall hear
    Sound through the earth, yea down to hell,
    To call the nations great and small.
4 To see the earth in burning flames,
    The trumpet louder here proclaims,
    "The world shall hear and know her doom,
    "The separation now is come."
5 Behold the righteous marching home,
    And all the angels bid them come;
    While Christ, the judge, with joy proclaims,
    "Here come my saints, I'll own their names.
6 "Ye everlasting doors fly wide,
    "Make ready to receive my bride;
    "Ye trumps of heav'n proclaim abroad,
    "Here comes the purchase of my blood."
7 In grandeur see the royal line
    In glitt'ring robes the sun outshine;
    See saints and angels join in one
    And march in splendour to the throne.
8 They stand and wonder, and look on—
    They join in one eternal song,
    Their great Redeemer to admire,
    While raptures set their souls on fire.

560. (7, 6.)
An Exhortation to Bravery.

1 COME all ye Christian soldiers,
    Who follow love and peace,
    Who walk the way of Zion,
    Though foes and fears increase:
    Our Captain stood the fiery test,
    And gain'd the vict'ry too,
    Then let us boldly follow him—
    He'll safely bring us through.
2 The sin which doth beset us,
    O let us lay aside,
    That cursed sin of unbelief,
    And spiritual pride:
    The race that's set before us,
    With patience let us run,
    And stand fast in the liberty
    Of God's eternal Son.
3 Gird on the heav'nly armour,
    And keep it clean and bright,
    The buckler, shield, and helmet,
    And venture on the fight:

Still on the Captain calling,
    And keep the prize in view—
We shall be conqu'rors all ere long,
    And more than conqu'rors too.

4 For when the last loud trumpet
    Shall rend the earth and sky—
Shall summon all the quick and dead,
    And bid the world draw nigh:
With shouting all victorious,
    Our bodies then shall rise,
Put on a form most glorious,
    And fly above the skies.

5 Adieu world, flesh, and devil,
    And sin forever cease:
Your rage you'll no more level
    Against the sons of peace;
Our Saviour now doth call us,
    Most lovingly to come—
Adieu to you for evermore,
    For we are going home.—

6 Where saints, with admiration,
    Their Saviour will behold;
They'll drink in full salvation,
    And shine in robes of gold;
They'll join the heav'nly choirs above,
    Their Saviour's praise to sing,
Redeeming grace, and dying love,
    For evermore to ring.

561. (10's.)

Jehovah-Jiram, or, the Lord will help.

1 THOUGH troubles assail, and dangers affright, [unite—
Though friends should all fail, and foes all
Yet one thing secures us, whatever betide,
The scripture assures us, the LORD will provide.

2 The birds without barn or storehouse, are fed: [bread:
From them let us learn to trust for our
His saints, what are fitting shall ne'er be denied. [vide.
So long as 'tis written, the LORD will pro-

3 We may, like the ships, by tempests be toss'd
On perilous deeps, but cannot be lost:
Though Satan enrages the wind and the tide, [vide.
The promise engages the LORD will pro-

4 His call we obey, like Abra'm of old,
Not knowing our way, but faith makes us bold: [good guide,
For though we are strangers, we have a
And trust, in all dangers the LORD will provide.

5 When Satan appears, to stop up our path,
And fill us with fears, we triumph by faith;
He cannot take from us, though oft he has tried, [provide,
This heart-cheering promise is in the LORD will

6 He tells us we're weak, our hope is in vain:
The good that we seek we ne'er shall obtain; [plied,
But when such suggestions our spirits have
This answers all questions, the LORD will provide.

7 No strength of our own, or goodness we claim; [great name,
Yet since we have known the Saviour's
In this our strong tow'r for safety we hide:
The Lord is our pow'r, the LORD will provide.

8 When life sinks apace, and death is in view,
This word of his grace shall comfort us through: [our side,
No fearing or doubting, with CHRIST on
We hope to die shouting the LORD will provide.

562. (8, 7.) 5S./8L.

Exhortations to rejoice in Christ, and have no Confidence in the Flesh.

1 COME, ye Christians, sing the praises

563. (8, 7.) 6S./8L.

Christians encouraged against their Weaknesses.

1 WAND'RING pilgrims, mourning Christians,

564. (P. M.)

The Gospel animates to Hope.

1 HARK how the gospel-trumpet sounds!
    Thro' all the world the echo bounds;
And Jesus, by redeeming blood,
Is bringing sinners home to God,
And guides them safely by his word,
    To endless day.

2 Hail! all-victorious, conqu'ring Lord!
By all the heav'nly host ador'd,
Who undertook for fallen man,
And brought salvation through thy name,
That we with thee might live and reign
    In endless day.

3 Fight on, ye conquering saints, fight on,
And when the conquest you have won,
Then palms of vict'ry you shall bear,
And in his kingdom have a share,
And crowns of glory you shall wear,
    In endless day.

4 Thy blood, dear Jesus, once was spilt,
  To save our souls from sin and guilt;
  And sinners now may come to God,
  And find salvation through thy blood,
  And sail by faith upon that flood,
    To endless day.

5 Thro' storms and calms by faith we steer,
  By feeble hope and gloomy fear,
  Till we arrive at Canaan's shore,
  Where sin and sorrow are no more;
  We'll shout, Our trials all are o'er
    To endless day.

6 There we shall in sweet chorus join,
  With saints and angels all combine,
  To sing of his redeeming love,
  When rolling years shall cease to move;
  And this shall be our theme above,
    In endless day.

7 Here we are kept by sov'reign grace,
  Till we have run the heav'nly race;
  But soon we shall in glory dwell,
  To praise our dear Immanuel,
  And bid our troubles then farewell,
    To endless day.

8 We are but pilgrims here below,
  And all our lives are full of woe;
  Lord, give us courage on our way,
  That we may never go astray,
  But live thy glory to display
    In endless day.

565. (8, 7.) 5S./8L.
The Christian Soldier encouraged.

1 GIRD thy loins up, Christian soldier,

566. (6, 5.)
Exceeding great and precious Promises.

1 HOW firm a foundation,
    Ye saints of the Lord,
  Is laid for your faith
    In his excellent word!
  What more can he say
    Than to you he hath said?
  You, who unto JESUS
    For refuge have fled.

2 In every condition,
    In sickness, in health,
  In poverty's vale,
    Or abounding in wealth;
  At home and abroad,
    On the land, on the sea,
  "As thy days may demand,
    "Shall thy strength ever be,

3 "Fear not, I am with thee,
    "O be not dismay'd,
  "I, I am thy God,
    "And will still give thee aid;
  "I'll strengthen thee, help thee,
    "And cause thee to stand,
  "Upheld by my righteous
    "Omnipotent hand.

4 "When through the deep waters
    "I call thee to go,
  "The rivers of woe
    "Shall not thee o'erflow;
  "For I will be with thee,
    "Thy troubles to bless,
  "And sanctify to thee,
    "Thy deepest distress.

5 "When through fiery trials
    "Thy pathway shall lie,
  "My grace all-sufficient
    "Shall be thy supply;
  "The flame shall not hurt thee,
    "I only design
  "Thy dross to consume,
    "And thy gold to refine.

6 "Ev'n down to old age,
    "All my people shall prove
  "My sovereign, eternal,
    "Unchangeable love;
  "And when hoary hairs
    "Shall their temples adorn,
  "Like lambs they shall still
    "In my bosom be borne.

7 "The soul that on JESUS
    "Hath lean'd for repose,
  "<i>I will not, I will not</i>
    "Desert to his foes;
  "That soul, though all hell
    "Should endeavour to shake,
  "<i>I'll never, no never,</i>
    "No, <i>never forsake.</i>"

567. (6, 5.) 10S./8L.
Victory Sure, and the War not long.

1 YE brethren and sisters,

568. (6, 8.) Lenox. 6S./6L.
This is the Victory, even our Faith.

1 SUPPORTED by thy word,

569. (7's.) 6S./8L.
Young Christians encouraged against sudden and
unexpected changes.

1 THOUGH the morn may be serene,

Hymn Texts From *The Cluster*

570. (8, 7.) 5S./8L.
Examine yourselves whether ye be in the Faith.

1 LET us ask th' important question,

571. (S. M.) Double 4S./8L.
They that trust in the Lord shall not be confounded.

1 COMMIT thou all thy griefs

572. (S. M.) Double.
The same.

1 GIVE to the wind thy fears,
   Hope, and be undismay'd:
God hears thy sighs, and counts thy tears,
   God shall lift up thy head;
Through waves, and clouds, and storms,
   He gently clears the way;
Wait thou his time, so shall this night
   Soon end in joyous day.

2 Still heavy is thy heart,
   Still sink thy spirits down:
Cast off the weight, let fear depart,
   And ev'ey care be gone:
What though thou rulest not,
   Yet heaven, and earth, and hell
Proclaim, God sitteth on the throne,
   And ruleth all things well.

3 Leave to his sov'reign sway
   To choose and to command,
So shalt thou, wond'ring, own his way—
   How wise, how strong his hand!
Far, far above thy thought
   His counsel shall appear,
When fully he the work hath wrought,
   That caus'd thy needless fear.

4 Thou seest our weakness, Lord,
   Our hearts are known to thee:
O lift thou up the sinking hand,
   Confirm the feeble knee;
Let us in life, in death,
   Thy stedfast truth declare,
And publish, with our latest breath,
   Thy love and guardian care.

573. (S. M.) 14S./4L.
Pride the worst of sins.

1 INNUMERABLE foes

574. (10's.) 5S./4L.
'Tis all for the best.

1 MY soul now arise, my passions take wing:

575. (6, 5.)
The Lord is my Shepherd.

1 THE Lord is my shepherd,
   My guard and my guide,
Whatsoever I want
   He will kindly provide;
E'er since I was born,
   It is he who has crown'd
The life which he gave me,
   With blessings all round.

2 While yet on the breast,
   A poor infant I hung,
E'er time had unloosed
   The strings of my tongue;
He gave me the help,
   Which I then could not ask,
Now therefore to praise him,
   Shall be my tongue's task.

3 Through my tenderest years,
   With as tender a care,
My soul, like a lamb,
   In his bosom he bare;
To the brook he would lead me
   Whene'er I had need,
And point out the pastures,
   Where best I might feed.

4 No harm could approach me
   For he was my shield,
From the fowls of the air,
   And the beasts of the field;
The wolf to devour me
   Did oftentimes prowl,
But the Lord was my Shepherd
   And guarded my soul.

5 How oft in my youth,
   Have I wander'd astray;
But still he has brought me
   Back to the right way;
When lost in dark errors
   No path I could meet,
His word like a lantern
   Still guided my feet.

6 What wond'rous escapes
   To his kindness I owe,
When rash and unguarded,
   I sought my own woe!
My soul long e'er now,
   Would have been in the deep,
If the Lord had not watched
   When I was asleep.

7 Whene'er at a distance,
   He sees me afraid,
He skips o'er the mountains,
   And comes to my aid;

Then leads me back gently,
　　　　And bids me abide,
　　　In the midst of his flock,
　　　　And keep close to his side.
 8 How safe in his keeping,
　　　How happy and free,
　　　Could I always abide
　　　　Where he bids me to be!
　　　Yea, bless'd are the people,
　　　　And happy thrice told,
　　　Who hear the Lord's voice,
　　　　And abide in his fold.
 9 The fountain is full,
　　　　And the pasture is green,
　　　All is friendship and love,
　　　　And no poison therein;
　　　The Lord dwells among them,
　　　　Upon his own hill,
　　　And the flock all around him,
　　　　A waiting his will;
10 Himself in the midst
　　　With a provident eye,
　　　Regarding their wants,
　　　　And providing supply;
　　　Abundance springs up
　　　　Of most nourishing food,
　　　And the flocks are all fill'd
　　　　With *the fulness of God.*
11 At his voice, or example,
　　　They move or they stay,
　　　For the Lord is himself
　　　　Both their leader and way;
　　　What e'er the condition,
　　　　He places them in.
　　　They're assur'd 'tis the best,
　　　　And they're happy therein.
12 If they hunger or thirst,
　　　And are ready to faint,
　　　A relief in due season
　　　　Prevents the complaint;
　　　The rain of his word
　　　　Brings them food from the sky,
　　　And the rocks become rivers
　　　　When they are a dry.
13 From the fruitfulest hills
　　　To the barrenest rock,
　　　The Lord has made all
　　　　For the good of his flock;
　　　And the flock in return,
　　　　The Lord doth confess,
　　　In plenty their joy,
　　　　And their hope in distress.
14 He beholds in their welfare
　　　His glory display'd,
　　　And they find their bliss,
　　　　In obedience repay'd,

　　　With a cheerful regard,
　　　　They attend to his ways,
　　　Their attention is pray'r,
　　　　And their cheerfulness praise.
15 The Lord is my Shepherd;
　　　What then shall I fear;
　　　No danger shall fright me
　　　　While he is so near;
　　　For I know that his judgments
　　　　When me they have try'd
　　　Will bring me and seat me
　　　　Down close by his side.
16 The Lord he is good,
　　　　And his mercy is sure,
　　　He only afflicts me,
　　　　In order to cure.
　　　The Lord will I praise,
　　　　As long as I've breath,
　　　Be content all my days,
　　　　And resign at my death.

　　　　　576. (8's.)
　　　　　The same.

 1 THE Lord my pasture shall prepare,
　　　And feed me with a shepherd's care;
　　His presence shall my wants supply,
　　And guard me with a watchful eye;
　　My noon-day walks he shall attend,
　　And all my midnight hours defend.

 2 When in the sultry glebe I faint,
　　Or on the thirsty mountain pant,
　　To fertile vales and dewy meads,
　　My weary wand'ring steps he leads;
　　Where peaceful rivers, soft and slow,
　　Amid the verdant landscape flow.

 3 Though in the paths of death I tread,
　　With gloomy horrors overspread,
　　My stedfast heart shall fear no ill,
　　For thou, O Lord, art with me still;
　　Thy friendly crook shall give me aid,
　　And guide me through the dreadful
　　　　shade.

 4 Though in a bare and rugged way,
　　Through devious lonely wilds I stray,
　　Thy bounty shall my pains beguile;
　　The barren wilderness shall smile,
　　With sudden greens and herbage crown'd,
　　And streams shall murmur all around.

　　　　　577. (8's.)
　　　　　The same.

 1 THOU Shepherd of Israel, and mine,
　　　The joy and desire of my heart,
　　For closer communion I pine,
　　　I long to reside where thou art;

Hymn Texts From *The Cluster*

The pasture I languish to find,
   Where all who their Shepherd obey,
   Are fed on thy bosom reclin'd,
   Are screen'd from the heat of the day.
2 Ah! show me that happiest place,
   The place of thy people's abode,
   Where saints in an ecstacy gaze,
   And hang on a crucify'd God:
   Thy love for a sinner declare,
   Thy passion and death on the tree:
   My spirit to Calvary bear,
   To suffer and triumph with thee.
3 'Tis there with the lambs of thy flock,
   There only I covet to rest,
   To lie at the foot of the rock,
   Or rise to be hid in thy breast;
   'Tis there I would always abide,
   And never a moment depart;
   Conceal'd in the cleft of thy side,
   Eternally held in thy heart.

578. (8's.) 5S./8L.
The same.

1 WHEN my Saviour, my Shepherd,
   near,

579. (L. M.) 7S./4L.
Feed my Lambs.

1 WHEN Christ the Lord was here below

580. (C. M.)
The Danger of worldly Attachments.

1 SCARCE in this cold declining day,
   Can one for God be found;
   Christians have lost their zeal to pray,
   And yielded up the ground.
2 Scarce can the sons of God be known,
   From Satan's captives led;
   They've David's sling, but not his stone,
   That slew Goliath dead.
3 Lull'd in Delilah's sofa arms,
   Her courtship proves a snare,
   Deluded by her flattering charms,
   They've lost their Samson-hair.
4 But shall the Lord his cause forsake,
   And leave his sons forlorn,
   Shall Dagon down his purpose break,
   And set upon his throne?
5 Their Samson-hair again shall grow,
   Their strength again renew,
   Down they shall Dagon's temple throw,
   With all the mocking crew.
6 Help us this once we humbly pray,
   Jehovah-Jirah, Lord,
   To plant our footsteps in the way,
   That leads to thee our God.
7 Again from thee no more to stray,
   No more to leave thy fold,
   But in thy presence ever stay,
   Thy glories to behold.
8 "O may thy beauties ever be
   Our souls' eternal food,
   And grace command our souls away
   From all created good."

581. (L. M.) 4S./4L.
Christ is our Peace.

1 PEACE, by his cross, hath Jesus made,

582. (L. M.) 4S./4L.
The Rainbow, sign of Peace.

1 WHEN in the cloud, with colours fair,

583. (C. M.) 3S./4L.
Duties and Privileges.

1 WHILE sinners, who presume to bear

584. (S. M.)
Weak Believers encouraged.

1 YOUR harps, ye trembling saints,
   Down from the willows take,
   Loud to the praise of love divine,
   Bid ev'ry string awake.
2 Though in a foreign land,
   We are not far from home;
   And nearer to our house above,
   We ev'ry moment come.
3 His grace shall to the end
   Stronger and brighter shine;
   Nor present things, nor things to come,
   Shall quench the spark divine.
4 Wait till the shadows flee;
   Wait the appointed hour;
   Wait till the Bridegroom of thy soul
   Reveals his love with pow'r.
5 The time of love will come,
   When we shall clearly see,
   Not only that he shed his blood,
   But each shall say, "for me."

585. (C. M.) 4S./4L.
Let Brotherly Love continue.

1 HOW sweet, how heav'nly is the sight,

586. (C. M.)
The Love of Christ is constant.

1 THE intercession of our Lord

587. (L. M.)
Trust and not be afraid.

1 IS anything too hard for God?

588. (C. M.)
Trust in dark Providences.

1 GOD moves in a mysterious way,
   His wonders to perform;
   He plants his footsteps in the sea,
   And rides upon the storm.

2 Deep in unfathomable mines
   Of never-failing skill,
   He treasures up his bright designs,
   And works his sov'reign will.

3 Ye fearful saints, fresh courage take;
   The clouds ye so much dread
   Are big with mercy, and shall break
   In blessings on your head.

4 Judge not the Lord by feeble sense,
   But trust him for his grace;
   Behind a frowning providence
   He hides a smiling face.

IMPUTED RIGHTEOUSNESS.

589. (C. M.)
The Gospel Uniform.

1 DRESS'D uniform the soldiers are,
   When duty calls abroad;
   Not purchas'd by their cost or care,
   But by their prince bestow'd.

2 Christ's soldiers too, *if Christ-like bred*,
   Have a regimental dress:
   'Tis lining white, and fac'd with red,
   'Tis Christ's own righteousness.

3 A rich and costly robe it is,
   And to the soldier dear:
   No rose can learn to blush like this,
   No lilly look so fair.

4 'Tis wrought by Jesus' skilful hand,
   And ting'd in his own blood,
   It makes the christian gazing stand,
   To view this robe of God.

5 No art of men can weave this robe,
   'Tis of such texture fine;
   Nor could the wealth of all this globe,
   By purchase make it mine.

6 'Tis of one piece, and wove throughout,
   So curious wove that none
   Can dress up in this seamless coat,
   Till Jesus puts it on.

7 This vesture never waxes old,
   No spot thereon can fall,
   It makes the Christian brisk and bold,
   And dutiful withal.

8 This robe put on me, Lord, each day,
   And it shall hide my shame,
   Shall make me fight, and sing, and pray,
   And bless my captain's name.

590. (L. M.) 6S./4L.
Christ's Righteousness the Believer's only Plea.

1 JESUS, thy blood and righteousness

591. (8's.)
The same.

1 A DEBTOR to mercy alone,
   Of covenant mercy I sing:
   Nor fear with thy righteousness on,
   My person and off'rings to bring.

2 The terrors of law and of God
   With me can have nothing to do;
   My Saviour's obedience and blood
   Hide all my transgressions from view.

3 The work which his goodness began
   The arm of his strength will complete:
   His promise is yea and amen,
   And never was forfeited yet.

4 Things future, nor things that are now,
   Not all things below nor above,
   Can make him his purpose forego,
   Or sever my soul from his love.

5 My name from the palms of his hands
   Eternity will not erase;
   Imprest on his heart it remains,
   In marks of indelible grace.

6 Yes I to the end shall endure,
   As sure as the earnest is giv'n;
   More happy, but not more secure,
   The glorify'd spirits in heaven.

592. (L. M.) 6S./4L.
Come and see Free Grace and Righteousness in Christ.

1 JESUS, dear name, how sweet it sounds!

593. (L. M.) 4S./4L.
Justification by Faith.

1 SINNERS, away from Sinai fly;

594. (C. M.) Bray.
The Role of Righteousness.

1 AWAKE my heart, arise my tongue,
   Prepare a tuneful voice:
   In God, the life of all my joys,
   Aloud will I rejoice.

2 'Tis he adorn'd my naked soul,
　　And made salvation mine:
　Upon a poor polluted worm
　　He makes his graces shine.
3 And lest the shadow of a spot
　　Should on my soul be found,
　He took the robe the Saviour wrought,
　　And cast it all around.
4 How far the heav'nly robe exceeds
　　What earthly princes wear!
　These ornaments, how bright they shine!
　　How white these garments are!
5 The Spirit wrought my faith and love,
　　And hope, and ev'ry grace;
　But Jesus spent his life to work
　　The robe of righteousness.
6 Strangely, my soul, art thou array'd
　　By the great sacred Three!
　In sweetest harmony of praise
　　Let all thy pow'rs agree.

PERSEVERANCE IN GRACE.

595. (8's.) 7S./6L.
Salvation certain to the Redeemed.

1 THE Saviour comes to set you free,

596. (7's.)
"Lovest thou me."

1 HARK, my soul! It is the Lord
　　'Tis thy Saviour, hear his word,
　Jesus speaks, and speaks to thee;
　"Say, poor sinner, lov'st thou me?"
2 I deliver'd thee when bound,
　And, when wounded, heal'd thy wound;
　Sought thee wand'ring, set thee right,
　Turn'd thy darkness into light.
3 Can a woman's tender care
　Cease towards the child she bare?
　Yes, she may forgetful be,
　Yet will I remember thee.
4 Mine is an unchanging love,
　Higher than the heights above;
　Deeper than the depths beneath,
　Free and faithful, strong as death.
5 Thou shalt see my glory soon,
　When the work of grace is done:

　Partner of my throne shalt be,
　"Say, poor sinner, lov'st thou me?"
6 Lord, it is my chief complaint,
　That my love is weak and faint;
　Yet I love thee and adore,
　Oh for grace to love thee more!

597. (7, 6.) 5S./8L.
The Fears of finally falling unreasonable.

1 IF to Jesus for relief

598. (10's.)
Unbelief Conquered.

1 BEGONE, unbelief my Saviour is near,
　　And for my relief will surely appear;
　By prayer let me wrestle, and he will per-
　　　form;　　　　　　　　　　　[storm.
　With Christ in the vessel, I smile at the
2 Though dark be my way, since he is my
　　　guide,
　'Tis mine to obey, 'tis his to provide;
　Though cisterns be broken, and creatures
　　　all fail,　　　　　　　　　　[vail.
　The word he has spoken shall surely pre-
3 His love in time past, forbids me to think
　He'll leave me at last in trouble to sink;
　Each sweet Ebenezer I have in review,
　Confirms his good pleasure to help me
　　　quite through.
4 Determin'd to save, he watch'd o'er my
　　　path,　　　　　　　　　　　[death;
　When Satan's blind slave, I sported with
　And can he have taught me to trust in his
　　　name,　　　　　　　　　　　[shame?
　And thus far have brought me to put me to
5 Why should I complain of want or distress,
　Temptation or pain? he told me no less:
　The heirs of salvation, I know from his
　　　word,
　Thro' much tribulation, must follow their
　　　Lord.
6 How bitter that cup, no heart can conceive,
　Which he drank quite up, that sinners
　　　might live!　　　　　　[than mine;
　His way was much rougher, and darker
　Did Christ, my Lord, suffer, and shall I
　　　repine?
7 Since all that I meet shall work for my
　　　good,
　The bitter is sweet, the med'cine is food;
　Though painful at present, 'twill cease be-
　　　fore long,　　　　　　　　　[song!
　And then O how pleasant the conqueror's

599. (8's.)
If final apostacy was probable, it would be inevitable.

1 IF ever it could come to pass,
    That sheep of Christ might fall away;
My fickle feeble soul, alas!
    Would fall a thousand times a day.
Were not thy love as firm as free,
    Thou soon would'st take it, Lord, from me.

2 I on thy promises depend,
    (At least, I to depend desire)
That thou wilt love me to the end;
    Be with me in temptation's fire;
τ 2
Wilt *for* me work, and *in* me too;
    And guide me right and bring me through.

2 No other stay have I beside;
    If these can alter, I must fall:
I look to thee to be supply'd
    With life, with will, with pow'r, with all.
Rich souls may glory in their store;
    But Jesus will relieve the poor.

600. (8's.) 5S./8L.
The Believer safe, while Christ stands.

1 THE sinner that truly believes,

601. (6, 8.) Lenox. 4S./6L.
Distrust overcome by Faith.

1 O MY distrustful heart,

602. (8, 7.) 7S./6L.
Election the source of perseverance.

1 SONS we are, through God's election,

603. (8's.)
Heirs of God and joint Heirs with Christ.

1 LET others boast their ancient line
    In long succession great:
In the proud list let heroes shine,
    And monarchs swell the state:
Descended from the King of kings,
Each saint a nobler title sings.

2 Pronounce me gracious God, thy son,
    Own me an heir divine:
I'll pity princes on the throne,
    When I can call thee mine;
Sceptres and crowns unenvied rise,
And lose their lustre in mine eyes.

3 Content, obscure I pass my days,
    To all I meet unknown,
And wait till thou thy child shalt rise,
    And seat me near thy throne;
No name, no honours here I crave,
Well pleas'd with those beyond the grave.

4 Jesus, my elder brother lives,
    With him I too shall reign:
Nor sin, nor death, while he survives,
    Shall make the promise vain:
In him my title stands secure,
And shall, while endless years endure.

5 When he, in robes divinely bright,
    Shall once again appear,
Thou too my soul, shalt shine in light,
    And his full image bear:
Enough! I wait th' appointed day,
Bless'd Saviour, haste, and come away.

604. (7's.) 7S./4L. & Chorus.
The Blessedness of the Sons of God.

1 BLESSED are the sons of God,

605. (8, 7.)
Salvation complete in Christ.

1 JESUS is our great salvation,
    Worthy of our best esteem;
He has sav'd his fav'rite nation;
    Join to sing aloud to him:
He has sav'd us,
Christ alone could us redeem.

2 When involv'd in sin and ruin,
    And no helper there was found,
Jesus our distress was viewing,
    Grace did more than sin abound:
He has call'd us,
With salvation in the sound.

3 Save us from a mere profession,
    Save us from hypocrisy;
Give us, *Lord*, the sweet possession
    Of thy righteousness and thee:
Best of favours,
None compar'd with this can be.

4 Let us never, Lord, forget thee,
    Make us walk as pilgrims here;
We will give thee all the glory
    Of the love that brought us near:
Bid us praise thee,
And rejoice with holy fear.

5 Free election, known by calling,
    Is a privilege divine;
Saints are kept from final falling:
    All the glory, *Lord*, be thine:
All the glory,
All the glory, *Lord*, is thine.

606. (10's.)
The Fulness of Grace.

1. A FULNESS resides in *Jesus* our head,
   And ever abides to answer our need:
   The Father's good pleasure has laid up in store,
   A plentiful treasure to give to the poor.

2. What'er be our wants we need not to fear:
   Our num'rous complaints his mercy will hear.
   His fulness shall yield us abundant supplies,
   His power shall shield us when dangers arise.

3. The fountain o'erflows, our woes to redress;
   Still more he bestows, and grace upon grace;
   His gifts in abundance we daily receive—
   He has a redundance for all that believe.

4. Whatever distress awaits us below,
   Such plentiful grace will *Jesus* bestow;
   And still shall support us, and silence our fear:
   For nothing can hurt us while *Jesus* is near.

5. When troubles attend, or danger or strife,
   His love will defend, and guard us through life:
   And when we are fainting, and ready to die,
   Whatever is wanting his hand will supply.

607. (L. M.)
The Reason of Perseverance.

1. THE reason Christians persevere,
   Is not because they are sincere,
   Disposed well in ev'ry thing,
   Nor with deceit read, pray, or sing.

2. 'Tis not that they themselves have join'd,
   With some religious band combin'd,
   To walk in piety and love,
   And seek for blessings from above.

3. 'Tis not because they faithful prove,
   And in obedience freely move,
   Nor that by suff'rings here they're tried,
   Or that in heav'nly joys they glide.

4. 'Tis not that they are justified,
   Nor yet because they're sanctified,
   And in Christ's glorious righteousness
   Feel humble joy and constant peace.

5. 'Tis not their zeal, nor courage rare,
   Their holy fortitude and fear,
   Their resolution's highest flame,
   That can insure immortal fame.

6. But 'tis, that to the light of grace
   They oft receive increasing rays.
   That in temptation's darkest hour
   Of grace they feel the saving pow'r.

7. Jehovah Jesus is their friend,
   And loves and saves them to the end;
   To justify righteousness
   He adds renewed sense of peace.

8. It is that God has given them
   In the remission of their sin,
   Himself to be their God; in whom
   They do enjoy eternal noon.

9. These are the reasons that they rise
   To mansions in the higher skies;
   If these should fail, in vain we prove
   The virtues of all other love.

608. (11, 8.) 7S./4L.
Rejoicing in Hope.

1. HOW bright is the prospect the saint has in view,

609. (C. M.)
Perseverance Desired.

1. LORD, thou hast made me know thy [ways!

610. (L. M.)
The Righteousness shall not be utterly cast down.

1. ALTHO' the righteous man may fail,

611. (L. M.)
As thy days, thy strength shall be.

1. AFFLICTED saint, to Christ draw near,

612. (C. M.)
My God, &c.

1. MY God!—how cheerful is the sound!

613. (C. M.)
Hope in Christ secures enjoyment.

1. IF, Lord, in thy fair book of life

614. (C. M.)
Fear not, the Kingdom is yours.

1. YE little flock, whom Jesus feeds,

615. (C. M.)
The Ark of Safety, or, Sure Salvation in Christ.

1 WHEN Noah, with his favour'd few,
    Was order'd to embark,
Eight human souls, a little crew,
    Enter'd on board his ark.

2 Though ev'ry part he might secure,
    With bar, or bolt, or pin:
To make the preservation sure,
    Jehovah shut him in.

3 The waters then might swell their tides,
    The billows rage and roar;
They could not stave th' assaulted sides,
    Nor burst the batter'd door.

4 So souls, that into Christ believe,
    Quicken'd by vital faith,
Eternal life at once receive,
    And never shall see death.

5 In Christ their ark they safely ride,
    Nor wreck'd by death or sin:—
How is it they so safe abide?
    The Lord has shut them in.

DEATH.

616. (8's.)
Death Awful yet Delightful.

1 AH! lovely appearance of death,
    What sight upon earth is so fair?
Not all the gay pageants that breathe,
    Can with a dead body compare:
With solemn delight I survey
    The corpse when the spirit is fled,
In love with the beautiful clay,
    And longing to lie in its stead.

2 How blest is our brother, bereft
    Of all that could burden his mind;
How easy the soul that has left
    This wearisome body behind!
Of evil incapable thou,
    Whose relics with envy I see,
No longer in misery now,
    No longer a sinner like me.

3 This earth is affected no more
    With sickness, or shaken with pain:
The war in the members is o'er,
    And never shall vex him again:
No anger henceforward, or shame,
    Shall redden this innocent clay;
Extinct is the animal flame,
    And passion is vanish'd away.

4 This languishing head is at rest,
    Its thinking and aching are o'er;
This quiet immovable breast
    Is heav'd by affliction no more:
This heart is no longer the seat
    Of trouble and torturing pain;
It ceases to flutter and beat,
    It never shall flutter again.

5 The lids he so seldom could close,
    By sorrow forbidden to sleep,
Seal'd up in eternal repose,
    Have strangely forgotten to weep:
The fountains can yield no supplies;
    These hollows from water are free;
The tears are all wip'd from these eyes,
    And evil they never shall see.

6 To mourn and to suffer is mine,
    While bound in a prison I breathe,
And still for deliverance pine,
    And press to the issues of death:
What now with my tears I bedew,
    O might I this moment become!
My spirit created anew,
    My flesh be consign'd to the tomb!

617. (10's.)
On the Death of a Christian.

1 'TIS finish'd! 'tis done! the spirit is fled,

618. (11, 8.)
The dying Christian.

1 YE objects of sense, and enjoyments of time,
    Which oft have delighted my heart,
I soon shall exchange you for views more sublime,
    For joys that shall never depart.

2 Thou Lord of the day, and thou Queen of the night,
    To me ye no longer are known,
I soon shall behold, with increasing delight,
    A sun that shall never go down.

3 Ye wonderful orbs that astonish my eyes,
    Your glories recede from my sight,
I soon shall contemplate more beautiful skies,
    And stars more resplendently bright.

4 Ye mountains and vallies, groves, rivers and plains,
    Thou earth and thou ocean adieu,

Hymn Texts From *The Cluster*

More permanent regions where righteousness reigns.
Present their bright hills to my view.

5 My lov'd habitation and gardens adieu,
No longer my footsteps ye greet,
A mansion celestial stands full in my view,
And paradise welcomes my feet.

6 My weeping, relations, my brethren, and friends
Whose souls are entwin'd with my own,
Adieu for the present, my spirit ascends
Where pleasure immortal is known.

7 My cares and my labours, my sickness and pain,
And sorrow are now at an end;
The summit of bliss I shall speedily gain,
The height of perfection ascend.

8 Thou vale of affliction my footsteps have trod [tears,
With trembling, with grief, and with
I joyfully quit for the mansion of God,
There, there, its bright summit appears.

9 No lurking temptation, defilement or fear,
Again shall disquiet my breast,
In Jesus's fair image I soon shall appear,
Forever ineffably bless'd.

10 My sabbaths below, that have been my delight,
And thou the bless'd volume divine,
Ye guided my footsteps like stars during night:
Adieu my conductors benign.

11 The sun, that illumines the regions of light,
Now shines on my eyes from above,
But O how transcendently glorious the sight,
My soul is all wonder and love!

12 Thou tottering seat of disease and of pain,
Adieu my dissolving abode;
But I shall behold and possess thee again,
A beautiful building of God.

13 Come death with cold hands and my eyelids now close,
And lay my cold corpse in the tomb;
My soul shall enjoy an eternal repose,
Above in my heavenly home.

14 But O what a life! what a rest! what a joy!
Shall I know when I've mounted above,
Praise! praise! shall my pow'rs triumphant employ:
My God I shall dwell in thy love!

15 Come, come my Redeemer, this moment release
The soul thou hast bought with thy blood,
And bid me ascend the bright regions of peace,
To feast on the smiles of my God.

619. (P. M.)
The Approaches of Death in Sickness.

1 WHAT solemn signal's that which daunts my courage,
And chills my spirits with a freezing power?
Presage of ruin! and commands attention
From the reluctant.

2 'Tis the approach of death in wild career,
Gigantic, striding, and with hell attended,
Comes on the pale horse, to the bar commanding
Guilty immortals.

3 The feeble spirit trembles at the monster!
Who, in full triumph, passes and repasses,
Through the adjacents, 'till at length, he, foaming
Leaps o'er the palings.

4 He, thus position'd furious, and ghastly,
Spreads wild confusion through the lonely mansion.
Passing he smites one of the stately pillars,
Threat'ning destruction.

5 The smitten fabric trembles to the centre,
And from the basis to the summit totters:
While death spreads trophies, through the ruin'd dwelling
Doleful to mention.

6 Hope's blooming prospect now reclines its head, and [glory,
To disappointment yields its pride and
While joy's fading, like untimely flowers,
Nipp'd by the black frost.

7 The wife or daughters, now indulge their weakness, [order;
And like their nature, shriek in wild dis-
While the more manly sobs of son or father,
Give air to mourning.

8 Like to proud Jordan, swelling o'er its banks, so
Swells grief the passions, and drowns all the spirits:
Terrifick visions haunt the timid soul in
Fearful succession.

9 Have we no refuge where we may retreat, and [horrors?

Secure from death, live in this vale of
Or, is there no one mighty to deliver.
                  Bearing salvation?
10 There's Juda's lion travelling in strength, who
Met the pale monster, in his rage and fury,
Wounding his head, he from his tail did wrench sin,
                  Sad cause of death-woes.
11 Here, dying mortals may, secure from ruin,
High in salvation ride, and triumph ever:
While deathless pleasures, and bright scenes of glory,
                  Endear duration.

620. (Bunker's Hill.)
Submission to Death in any Shape.

1 WHY should vain mortals tremble at the sight of

621. (10, 8.) 7S./4L.
The Death of Sophronia.

1 FORBEAR, my friends, forbear, and ask no more

622. (L. M.) 4S./4L.
There the Wicked cease from troubling.

1 DEATH and the grave are doleful themes

623. (L. M.)
The Same.

1 JESUS, the mighty Saviour, lives,

624. (C. M.)
The Death of a Child rather joyous.

1 AND is thy lovely shadow fled?

625. (C. M.)
The safe and happy Exit.

1 LORD, must I die? O let me die
   Trusting in thee alone!
My *living* testimony giv'n,
   Then leave my *dying* one!

2 If I must die—O let me die
   In peace with all mankind;
And change these fleeting joys below
   For pleasures all refin'd.

3 If I must die—as die I must—
   Let some kind seraph come,
And bear me on his friendly wing
   To my celestial home!

4 Of Canaan's land, from Pisgah's top,
   May I but have a view!
Though Jordan should o'erflow its banks,
   I'll boldly venture through.

626. (C. M.)
The time is short—"Be sober."

1 THE time is short! the season near,

627. (P. M.)
The dying Saint's Address to his Soul.

1 VITAL spark of heav'nly flame,
   Quit, O quit this mortal flame!
Trembling, hoping, ling'ring, flying,
O the pain, the bliss of dying!
Cease, fond nature, cease the strife,
And let me languish into life.

2 Hark! they whisper—angels say
   "Sister spirit, come away;"
What is this absorbs me quite?
Steals my senses, shuts my sight?
Drowns my spirit, draws my breath?
Tell me, my soul, can this be death?

3 The world recedes, it disappears!
Heav'n opens on my eyes—my ears
With sounds seraphic ring!
Lend, lend your wings—I mount! I fly!
O grave, where is thy victory?
O death, where is thy sting?

628. (C. M.) 5S./4L.
Resignation in the Death of a child.

1 GOD hath bereav'd me of my child;

629. (C. M.)
Death approaching fast.

1 COME, O my soul, look up and see

630. (C. M.)
The prospect of Death joyful.

1 YE fleeting charms of earth farewell!
   Your springs of joy are dry;
My soul now seeks another home—
   A brighter world on high.

2 Farewell, ye friends, whose tender care
   Has long engag'd my love;
Your fond embrace I now exchange
   For better friends above.

3 Cheerful I leave this vale of tears,
   Where pains and sorrows grow;
Welcome the day that ends my toil,
   And ev'ry scene of woe.

Hymn Texts From *The Cluster*

4 No more shall sin disturb my breast—
  My God shall frown no more;
  The streams of love divine shall yield
  Transports unknown before.

631. (C. M.)
The Happiness of departed Saints.

1 HOW happy are the souls above,

632. (C. M.)
Victory over Death by Faith.

1 WHEN death appears before my sight,

633. (C. M.)
Lord Jesus receive my Spirit.

1 LORD I commit my soul to thee—

634. (S. M.)
Support in Death.

1 BEHOLD the gloomy vale,

635. (L. M.)
The Death of a Christian.

1 THE busy scene of life is clos'd

636. (C. M.)
Victory over Death.

1 O FOR an overcoming faith,

637. (C. M.)
The Dead in the Lord are blessed.

1 HEAR what the voice from heav'n proclaims

638. (C. M.)
Death of Moses.

1 DEATH cannot make our souls afraid,
  If God be with us there;
  We may walk through its darkest shade,
  And never yield to fear.

2 I could renounce my all below,
  If my Creator bid;
  And run, if I were call'd to go,
  And die as Moses did.

3 Might I but climb to Pisgah's top,
  And view the promis'd land,
  My flesh itself would long to drop,
  And pray for the command.

4 Clasp'd in my heav'nly Father's arms,
  I would forget my breath,
  And lose my life among the charms
  Of so divine a death.

639. (L. M.)
Christ's Presence makes Death easy.

1 WHY should we start, and fear to die?
  What tim'rous worms we mortals are!
  Death is the gate of endless joy,
  And yet we dread to enter there.

2 The pains, the groans, and dying strife,
  Fright our approaching souls away;
  Still we shrink back again to life,
  Fond of our prison and our clay.

3 Oh! if my Lord would come and meet,
  My soul should stretch her wings in haste,
  Fly fearless through death's iron gate,
  Nor feel the terrors as she pass'd.

4 Jesus can make a dying bed
  Feel soft as downy pillows are,
  While on his breast I lean my head,
  And breathe my life out sweetly there.

640. (C. M.)
The Burial of a Saint.

1 WHY do we mourn departing friends?
  Or shake at death's alarms?
  'Tis but the voice that Jesus sends,
  To call them to his arms.

2 Why should we tremble to convey
  Their bodies to the tomb?
  There the dear flesh of Jesus lay,
  And left a long perfume.

3 The graves of all his saints he blest,
  And soften'd ev'ry bed:
  Where should the dying members rest,
  But with their dying head?

4 Thence he arose, ascending high,
  And show'd our feet the way:
  Up to the Lord our flesh shall fly,
  At the great rising day.

641. (L. M.)
Mortality and Hope.

1 REMEMBER, Lord, our mortal state,

642. (C. M.) Martyrs.
The fast approach of Death.

1 THEE we adore eternal name!
  And humbly own to thee,
  How feeble is our mortal frame;
  What dying worms are we!

2 The year rolls round, and steals away
  The breath that first it gave;
  Whate'er we do, where'er we be,
  We're trav'lling to the grave.

3 Good God! on what a slender thread
   Hang everlasting things!
   Th' eternal states of all the dead
   Upon life's feeble strings.
4 Infinite joy or endlesss woe
   Attends on ev'ry breath;
   And yet how unconcern'd we go
   Upon the brink of death!
5 Waken, O Lord, our drowsy sense,
   To walk this dang'rous road;
   And if our souls are hurried hence,
   May they be found with God.

643. (C. M.) New Durham.
A Funeral Thought.

1 HARK! from the tombs a doleful sound,
   My ears attend the cry;
   "Ye living men, come view the ground,
   "Where you must shortly lie.
2 "Princes, this clay must be your bed,
   "In spite of all your tow'rs:
   "The tall, the wise, the rev'rend head,
   "Must lie as low as ours."
3 Great God! is this our certain doom?
   And are we still secure?
   Still walking downward to the tomb,
   And yet prepare no more!
4 Grant us the pow'r of quick'ning grace,
   To fit our souls to fly;
   Then, when we drop this dying flesh,
   We'll rise above the sky.

644. (C. M.) Mortality.
Death and Eternity.

1 STOOP down my thoughts, that us'd to rise,
   Converse awhile with death:
   Think how a gasping mortal lies,
   And pants away his breath.
2 His quiv'ring lip hangs feebly down,
   His pulse is faint and few;
   Then speechless, with a doleful groan,
   He bids the world adieu.
3 But, O, the soul that never dies!
   At once it leaves the clay!
   Ye thoughts pursue it where it flies,
   And track its wond'rous way.
4 Up to the courts where Angels dwell,
   It mounts, triumphing, there
   Or angels plunge it down to hell,
   In infinite despair.

5 And must my body faint and die?
   And must this soul remove?
   Oh, for some guardian angel nigh,
   To bear it safe above!
6 Jesus, to thy dear faithful hand
   My naked soul I trust;
   And my flesh waits for thy command,
   To drop into my dust.

645. (C. M.)
The bereaved Mother's Condolence under the loss of an only Child.

1 MY brethen, and my sisters dear,

646. (C. M.)
A Mother, bereaved of a lovely Daughter and dear Husband in quick succession, venting her sorrows to her Sisters in Christ.

1 MY sisters, hear, and I'll relate

647. (C. M.)
The Widows' Complaint and consolation.

1 COME Christians dear, of every name,

648. (C. M.)
Death lovely, in the Prospect of Heaven.

1 AND let this feeble body fail,
   And let it faint or die
   My soul shall quit the mournful vale,
   And soar to worlds on high:
   Shall join the disembodied saints,
   And find its long-sought rest:
   That only bliss for which it pants
   In the Redeemer's breast.
2 In hope of that immortal crown,
   I now the cross sustain;
   And gladly wander up and down,
   And smile at toil and pain:
   I suffer on my threescore years
   Till my Deliv'rer come;
   And wipe away his servant's tears,
   And take his exile home.
3 O what hath Jesus bought for me!
   Before my ravish'd eyes,
   Rivers of life divine I see,
   And trees of paradise!
   I see a world of spirits bright,
   Who taste the pleasure there!
   They all are rob'd in spotless white,
   And conqu'ring palms they bear.
4 O what are all my suff'rings here,
   If, Lord, thou count me meet,
   With that enraptur'd host t' appear,
   And worship at thy feet!

Hymn Texts From *The Cluster*

Give joy or grief, give ease or pain,
   Take life or friends away:
But let me find them all again
   In that eternal day.

JUDGMENT.

649. (9, 8.)
The Day of Judgment tremendous.

1 THE great tremendous day's approaching.

650. (11's.)
The Judgment Dream.

1 YE Pilgrims who often look up for the train,

651. (C. M.) 5S./8L.
Then shall the Righteous shine out of obscurity.

1 ARISE, and shine, O Zion fair,

652. (7, 6.)
The Midnight Cry.

1 WHEN, descending from the sky,

653. (P. M.)
The day of Judgment, to the Unprepared, a day of horrors.

1 DAY of Judgment, day of wonders,
   Hark! the trumpet's awful sound,
Louder than a thousand thunders,
   Shakes the vast creation round!
How the summons will the sinner's heart confound.

2 See the Judge our nature wearing,
   Cloth'd in majesty divine!
You who long for his appearing,
   Then shall say, this God is mine!
Gracious Saviour, own me in that day for thine!

3 At his call the dead awaken,
   Rise to life from earth and sea;
All the powers of nature shaken,
   By his looks prepare to flee;
Careless sinner, what will then become of thee?

4 Horrors past imagination
   Will suprise your trembling heart
When you hear your condemnation,
   "Hence, accursed wretch, depart!
Thou with Satan and his angels have thy part!"

5 Satan, who now tries to please you,
   Lest you timely warning take,
When that word is past, will seize you,
   Plunge you in the burning lake:
Think, poor sinner, thy eternal all's at stake.

6 But to those who have confessed,
   Lov'd and serv'd the Lord below,
He will say, "Come near, ye blessed,
   "See the kingdom I bestow:
"You for ever shall my love and glory know."

7 Under sorrows and reproaches,
   May this thought your courage raise!
Swiftly God's great day approaches,
   Sighs shall then be chang'd to praise:
We shall triumph when the world is in a blaze.

654. (P. M.)
The Last Judgment.

1 LO! he comes with clouds descending,
   Once for favour'd sinners slain!
Thousand thousand saints attending,
   Swell the triumph of his train;
   Hallelujah,
Jesus now shall ever reign.

2 Every eye shall now behold him
   Rob'd in dreadful majesty:
Those who set at nought, and sold him,
   Pierc'd and nail'd him to the tree,
   Deeply wailing,
Shall the great Messiah see.

3 Every island, sea, and mountain,
   Heaven and earth shall flee away:
All who hate him, must, confounded,
   Hear the trump proclaim the day;
   Come to judgment!
Come to judgment! come away!

4 Now redemption, long expected,
   See in solemn pomp appear!
All his saints, by man rejected,
   Now shall meet him in the air!
   Hallelujah,
See the day of God appear!

5 Answer thine own bride and spirit,
   Hasten, Lord, the general doom!
The new heaven and earth t' inherit,
   Take thy pining exiles home;
   All creation
Travails, groans, and bids thee come!

6 Yea, Amen! let all adore thee,
High on thy exalted throne!
Saviour, take thy power and glory:
Claim the kingdoms for thine own!
O come quickly.
Hallelujah! Come, Lord, come!

655. (8, 8, 6.)
A Prayer to be deeply affected in view of the last judgment.

1 THOU God of glorious majesty!
To thee, against myself to thee,
A sinful worm, I cry:
An half-awaken'd child of man,
An heir of endless bliss or pain,
A sinner born to die.

2 Lo! on a narrow neck of land,
'Twixt two unbounded seas I stand,
Yet how insensible
A point of time, a moment's space,
Removes me to yon heavenly place,
Or—shuts me up in hell.

3 O God, my inmost soul convert,
And deeply on my thoughtful heart
Eternal things impress;
Give me to feel their solemn weight,
And save me ere it be too late,
Wake me to righteousness.

4 Before me place in bright array,
The pomp of that tremendous day,
When thou with clouds shalt come
To judge the nations at thy bar;
And tell me, Lord, shall I be there
To meet a joyful doom?

5 Be this my one great business here,
With holy trembling, holy fear,
To make my calling sure
Thine utmost council to fulfil,
And suffer all thy righteous will,
And to the end endure?

6 Then Saviour, then my soul receive,
Transported from this vale, to live
And reign with thee above;
Where faith is sweetly lost in sight,
And hope, in full supreme delight
And everlasting love.

656. (8, 8, 6)
Desiring to be found in peace, at the coming of Christ.

1 WHEN Thou my righteous Judge shalt come,
To fetch thy ransom'd people home,
Shall I among them stand?
Shall such a worthless worm as I,
Who sometimes am afraid to die,
Be found at thy right hand?

2 I love to meet among them now,
Before thy gracious feet to bow,
Though vilest of them all;
But can I bear the piercing thought!
What if my name should be left out,
When thou for them shalt call?

3 Prevent, prevent it by thy grace;
Be thou, dear Lord, my hiding place,
In this th' accepted day;
Thy pardoning voice, O let me hear,
To still my unbelieving fear;
Nor let me fall, I pray.

4 Let me among thy saints be found,
Whene'er th' archangel's trump shall sound,
To see thy smiling face:
Then loudest of the crowd I'll sing,
While heaven's resounding mansions ring,
With shouts of sovereign grace.

657. (L. M.) 10S./4L.
Judgment: (A dream of the Rev. Peter Poyner.)

1 COME in this cold declining day,

658. (Lenox.)
The Midnight Cry.

1 YE virgin souls arise!

659. (P. M.) or Bunker's Hill.
A Storm at Sea, the Resemblance of the Judgment.

1 WHEN the fierce north-wind, with his airy forces,
Rears up the Baltic to a foaming fury,
And the red lightning, with a storm of hail, comes
Rushing amain down—

2 How the poor sailors stand amaz'd and tremble; [trumpet,
While the hoarse thunder, like a bloody
Roars a loud onset to the gaping waters
Quick to devour them.

3 Such shall the noise be, and the wild disorder,
(If things eternal may be like these earthly)
Such the dire terror when the great archangel
Shakes the creation;

4 Tears the strong pillars of the vault of heaven, [ces;
Breaks up old marble, the repose of prin-

Hymn Texts From *The Cluster*

See the graves open, and the bones arising,
    Flames all around 'em!
5 Hark, the shrill outcries of the guilty wretches!
Lively bright horror, and amazing anguish
Stare through their eye-lids, while the living worm lies
    Gnawing within them.
6 Thoughts, like old vultures, prey upon their heart-strings,
And the smart twinges when the eye beholds the   [geance
Lofty Judge frowning, and a flood of ven-
    Rolling before him.
7 Hopeless immortals! how they scream and shiver,
While devils push them to the pit, wide yawning,
Hideous and gloomy, to receive them headlong
    Down to the centre.
8 Stop here, my fancy: (all away ye horrid
Doleful ideas;) come arise to JESUS;
How he sits God-like! and the saints around him
    Thron'd, yet adoring.
9 O may I sit there when he comes triumphant,
Dooming the nations! then ascend to glory,
While our hosannas all along the passage
    Shout the Redeemer.

660. (L. M.) Chorused.
The near Approach of the Judgment, or Separation of the Wheat and Tares.

1 THIS is the field, the world below,
In which the sowers came to sow,
Jesus the wheat, Satan the tares,
For so the word of truth declares.

Chorus.

And soon the reaping time will come,
And angels shout the harvest home.
2 Most awful truth! and is it so?
Must all mankind the harvest know?
Is every one a wheat or tare?
Me for the harvest, Lord prepare!
    For soon the reaping, &c.
3 We seem alike when thus we meet,
Strangers might think we all are wheat,
But to the Lord's all-seeing eyes,
Each heart appears without disguise;
    And soon the reaping, &c.

4 The tares are spar'd for various ends,
Some for the sake of praying friends:
But though they grow so tall and strong
His plan will not require them long;
    For soon the reaping, &c.
5 Will it relieve their horrors there
To recollect their stations here,
How much they pray'd, how much they knew,
How long among the wheat they grew?
    For soon the reaping, &c.
6 To love my sins, a saint t' appear,
To grow with wheat and be a tare,
May serve me whilst on earth below,
Where tares and wheat together grow;
    But soon the reaping, &c.
7 Then all who truly righteous be,
Shall soon their Father's kingdom see;
But tares in bundles shall be bound,
And cast in hell—O dreadful sound!
    For then the reaping, &c.

661. (L. M.)
The general Wreck.

1 HOW great, how terrible that God,
Who shakes creation with his nod!
He frowns, and earth's foundations shake,
And all the wheels of nature break.
2 Where now, O where shall sinners seek
For shelter in the gen'ral wreck?
Shall falling rocks be o'er them thrown?
See rocks, like snow, dissolving down!
3 In vain for mercy now they cry;
In lakes of liquid fire they lie;
There on the flaming billows tost,
Forever, O, forever lost!
4 Jesus, the helpless sinner's friend,
To thee my all I dare commend;
Thou canst preserve my feeble soul,
When lightnings blaze from pole to pole,

662. (L. M.)
The Books opened.

1 METHINKS the last great day is come,

663. (8, 7, 4.)
The awful Judgment.

1 LO, he comes, array'd in vengeance,

664. (P. M.)
The final Destination.

1 THE day of the Lord—the day of salvation!

MISCELLANEOUS POEMS.

665. (8's.)
Happy Solitude.

1 I HAVE no leisure to bestow
   Where nought but sin and folly grow,
The world's society unknown,
My choicest hours are pass'd alone:
Alone indeed I cannot be,
If God vouchsafe to dwell with me.

  Think not, my friend, I censure those
Whom providence hath wisely chose
To shine in more conspicuous light,
As stars that gild the darksome night:
Such, whose high worth their deeds proclaim,
And fix them in the ranks of fame:
Those to the world are blessings given,
The bounty of all-bounteous heaven.
But I—whom no distinctions charm,
Whose breast no public praise can warm;
Who, from life's gay scenes retir'd,
Taste pleasures more to be desir'd
Than wealth, or power, or honours give;
Must live unknown, or cease to live.
Oh! happy hours that once I knew,
Ere yet I bade thy shade adieu,
My native haunt!—yet here I find
Content, that sunshine of the mind;
Her influence my bosom fills,
Soother of life's ten thousand ills.

  Come then, retirement, peaceful guest;
And love, true harbinger of rest!
That "love divine all loves excelling;"
Illuminate my humble dwelling.
Every choicest blessing bring
From Piety's exhaustless spring;
For some delightful theme explore
All contemplation's richest store.
Let wisdom's heavenly force impart
Divine instruction to my heart;
The salutary use explain
Of trials, cares, affliction, pain;
How needful each to erring man,
Too ignorant himself to scan,
Too blind his interest to discern,
Too proud the ways of heav'n to learn;
In self-conceit supremely wise,
He scorns the wisdom of the skies,
Doats on the toys of time and sense,
Nor looks beyond what those dispense.

  Tremble, my soul, for men at ease,
Whose painted bark no ruffling breeze
Impedes; but rapidly they glide,
Unthinking, down the silver tide
Of gay prosperity; nor know
Of other heav'n than that below.

666. (10's.)
An Ode on the Judgment, translated from the French.

1 THE toiling ocean groans, the stars
   grow pale,

667. (5, 3.)
God manifested in his Works.

1 THROUGH all the world below,
   God we see all around;
Search hills and valleys through,
  There he's found.
The growing of the corn,
The lily and the thorn,
The pleasant and forlorn—
All declare God is there:
On meadows dress'd in green,
  There he's seen.

2 See springs of water rise,
Fountains flow, rivers run;
The mist below the skies
  Hides the sun;
Then down the rain doth pour,
The ocean it doth roar.
And dash against the shore,
All to praise, in their lays,
That God that ne'er declines
  His designs.

3 The sun, to my surprise,
Speaks of God as he flies;
The comets in their blaze
  Give him praise;
The shining of the stars,
The moon as it appears,
His sacred name declares;
See them shine all divine!
The shades in silence prove
  God's above.

4 Then let my station be
Here on earth, as I see
The sacred One in Three
  All agree;
Through all the world is made,
The forest and the glade;
Nor let me be afraid,
Though I dwell on the hill,
Since nature's works declare
  God is there.

Hymn Texts From *The Cluster*

668. (10's.)
The Believer's To-day and To-morrow.

1 TO-DAY the saint with time-things has to do

669. (10's.)
The Sinner's To-day and To-morrow.

1 TO-DAY the sinner's state is much admir'd,

670. (8's.)
The Kite; or Pride must have a Fall.

My waking dreams are best conceal'd,
Much folly little good they yield;
But now and then I gain, when sleeping,
A friendly hint that's worth the keeping:
Lately I dreamt of one who cry'd,
"Beware of self, beware of pride;
When you are prone to build a Babel,
Recall to mind this little fable."

1 ONCE on a time a paper kite
Was mounted to a wond'rous height,
Where giddy with its elevation,
It thus express'd self-admiration:
"See how yon crowds of gazing people
Admire my flight above the steeple;
How would they wonder if they knew
All that a kite like me can do?
Were I but free, I'd take a flight,
And pierce the clouds beyond their sight,
But, ah! like a poor pris'ner bound,
My string confines me near the ground:
I'd brave the eagle's tow'ring wing,
Might I but fly without a string."

It tugg'd and pull'd while thus it spoke,
To break the string—at last it broke
Depriv'd at once of all its stay,
In vain it try'd to soar away;
Unable its own weight to bear,
It flutter'd downward thro' the air;
Unable its own course to guide,
The winds soon plung'd it in the tide.
Ah! foolish kite, thou had'st no wing,
How could'st thou fly without a string!

My heart reply'd, "O Lord I see
How much this kite resembles me!
Forgetful that by thee I stand,
Impatient of thy ruling hand;
How oft I've wish'd to break the lines
Thy wisdom for my lot assigns?
How oft indulg'd a vain desire
For something more or something higher?

And, but for grace and love divine,
A fall thus dreadful had been mine."

671. (8's.)
The Spider and Toad.

1 SOME author (no great matter who,

672. (11, 9.)
The Love of Christ Constraining.

1 FATIGU'D in spirit, and void of merit,

673. (P. M.)
The wonderous Love of God.

1 WHAT wondrous love is this,
O my soul, O my soul,
What wondrous love is this,
O my soul:
What wondrous love is this,
That caus'd the Lord of bliss,
To bear the dreadful curse,
For my soul, for my soul,
To bear the dreadful curse,
For my soul.

2 When I was sinking down,
Sinking down, sinking down;
When I was sinking down,
Sinking down.
When I was sinking down,
Beneath God's righteous frown,
Christ laid aside his crown,
For my soul, for my soul;
Christ laid aside his crown,
For my soul.

3 Ye winged seraphs fly,
Bear the news, bear the news,
Ye winged seraphs fly,
Bear the news,
Ye winged seraphs fly,
Like comets thro' the sky,
Fill vast eternity,
With the news, with the news,
Fill vast eternity,
With the news.

4 To God, and to the Lamb,
I will sing, I will sing.
To God, and to the Lamb,
I will sing,
To God, and the Lamb,
And the great I AM,
While millions join the theme,
I will sing, I will sing,
While millions join the theme,
I will sing.

5 Come friends of Zion's King,
　　Join the praise, join the praise,
　Come friends of Zion's King,
　　Join the praise:
　Come friends of Zion's King,
　　With hearts, and voices sing,
　And strike each tuneful string,
　　In his praise, in his praise;
　And strike each tuneful string,
　　In his praise.
6 Thus while from death we're free,
　　We'll sing on, we'll sing on,
　Thus while from death we're free,
　　We'll sing on;
　Thus while from death we're free,
　　We'll sing and joyful be,
　And thro' eternity,
　　We'll sing on, we'll sing on;
　And thro' eternity,
　　We'll sing on.
7 And when to that bright world,
　　We arise, we arise,
　And when to that bright world,
　　We arise;
　When to that world we go,
　　Free from all pain and woe,
　We'll join the happy throng,
　　And sing on, and sing on,
　We'll join the happy throng,
　　And sing on.

674. (8, 7.)
The Autumnal Gloom.

1 HAIL, ye sighing sons of sorrow,
　　View with me th' autumnal gloom;
　Learn from thence your fate to-morrow—
　　Dead! perhaps laid in the tomb.
　See all nature, fading, dying,
　　Silent; all things seem to mourn;
　Life from vegetation flying,
　　Brings to mind my mould'ring urn.
2 Oft the autumn's tempest rising
　　Makes the lofty forest nod:
　Scenes of nature, how surprising
　　Read in nature nature's God.
　See our Sovereign, sole Creator
　　Lives eternal in the sky,
　While we mortals yield to nature—
　　Bloom awhile, then fade and die!
3 Nations dying, O how solemn!
　　Thro' enrag'd tyrannic kings;
　Not like plants, which fade in autumn,
　　Fall to rise in future springs.
　Mournful scenes when vegetation
　　Dies, by frosts or worms devour'd:
　Doubly mournful when a nation
　　Falls, by neighb'ring kings o'erpower'd:
4 Death and war my mind depresses—
　　Autumn shows me my decay—
　Calls to mind my past distresses—
　　Warns me of my dying day!
　Autumn gives me melancholy—
　　Strikes dejection thro' my soul!
　While I mourn my former folly,
　　Waves of sorrow o'er me roll!
5 Lo! I hear the air resounding,
　　With expiring insects' cries;
　Ah! their moans, to me how wounding!
　　Emblem of my aged sighs,
　Hollow winds about me roaring—
　　Noisy waters round me rise;
　While I sit my fate deploring—
　　Tears fast streaming from my eyes!
6 What to me are autumn's treasures,
　　Since I know no real joy?
　Long I've lost all youthful pleasures—
　　Time must youth and health destroy!
　Pleasures, once I fondly courted,
　　Shar'd each bliss, that youth bestows;
　But to see where then I sported,
　　Now embitters all my woes!
7 Age and sorrow since have blasted
　　Ev'ry youthful pleasing dream;
　Quiv'ring age with youth contrasted—
　　O how short their glories seem!
　As the annual frosts are cropping
　　Leaves and tendrils from the trees,
　So my friends are yearly dropping
　　Thro' old age and dire disease!
8 Former friends, O how I've sought 'em!
　　Just to cheer my drooping mind;
　But they're gone like leaves of autumn—
　　Driven before the dreary wind!
　When a few more years are wasted—
　　When a few more springs are o'er—
　When a few more griefs I've tasted—
　　I shall fall to bloom no more!
9 Fast my sun of life's declining—
　　Soon 'twill set in dismal night!
　But my hopes, pure and refining,
　　Rest in future life and light.
　Cease then trembling, fearing, sighing,
　　Death will break the sullen gloom;
　Soon my spirit flutt'ring, flying
　　Shall be borne beyond the tomb!

675. (C. M.) 20S./4L.
God's conduct towards Israel the encouragement of Faith.

1 GIVE thanks to God, invoke his name,

676. (L. M.)
The Star of Bethlehem.

1 WHEN marshall'd on the nightly plain,
   The glittering host bestud the sky;
One star alone, of all the train,
   Can fix the sinner's wandering eye.

2 Hark! hark! to God the chorus breaks,
   From ev'ry host, from ev'ry gem;
But one alone, the Saviour speaks,
   It is the star of Bethlehem.

3 Once on the raging seas I rode. [dark,
   The storm was loud,—the night was
The ocean yawn'd—and rudely blow'd
   The wind that toss'd my found'ring bark.

4 Deep horror then my vitals froze,
   Death-struck I ceas'd the tide to stem;
When suddenly a star arose,
   It was the star of Bethlehem.

5 It was my guide, my light, my all,
   It bade my dark forebodings cease;
And through the storm and danger's thrall,
   It led me to the part of peace.

6 Now safely moor'd—my perils o'er,
   I'll sing, first in night's diadem,
For ever and for evermore,
   The star!—The star of Bethlehem!

677. (10's.)
The Character, Death, &c. of the Rev. SILAS MERCER, who Departed this Life, August 1st, 1796, in the 52nd year of his Age.—By his Friend Benjamin Moseley, V.D.M.

1 WHILE poets, in exalted strains of verse,
The mighty acts of heroes, do rehearse,
And stretch imagination, high to fame
A *Caesar's* or an *Alexander's* name:
While they attention give to former times,
To unknown countries and to distant climes,
And strive to act the lofty poet's part,
To move the passions and to mend the heart;
A MERCER'S name demands a work of love,
Should we neglect, would not the stones reprove?
Behold him standing in the great concourse,
The cross he urges with a mighty force;
In order human wisdom to confound.
He pours the name of Christ on all around;
He seems determin'd nought to know beside,
The blessed Jesus, and him crudify'd:
Scripture and reason, each must have its place, [grace.
To shew 'tis clear, that men are sav'd by
This MERCER preaches with unweary'd zeal,
For this he make to heav'n his great appeal;
From this no pow'r of darkness can him move,
He stands supported while his theme is love:
Yet hear his views most finely he extends,
And shews the means connected with the ends.
His testimony makes it very plain,
That we are sav'd, and sav'd, and sav'd again,
First, sav'd by *price* from condemnation's weight,
Next, sav'd by *pow'r* so that our sins we hate,
And lastly, sav'd from this *imperfect* state.
To show that empty names are of no worth,
The marks of this salvation he sets forth.
"The law is written in believers' hearts,
"And well impress'd upon their inmost parts:
"A God in Christ becomes their sure defence,
"Good works the necessary consequence.
"These flow from principles of faith and love,
"The soul in a new element does move,
"And hence to glory it does forward press,
"This world's esteem'd a dreary wilderness.
These are the marks by MERCER pointed out,
To place the saving change beyond a doubt:
Our *Herald* trumpet's out a Saviour meet,

One free and large, and ev'ry way complete;
One, who most strictly to his trust is true,
The *Alpha*—Yes, and the *Omega* too.
While thus a dear Redeemer he proclaims,
Believers are enwrapt in heavenly flames;
While guilty sinners loud for mercy cry,
As being at the very point to die;
Despairing, downcast mourners are built up,
The weak and wav'ring are confirm'd in hope;
Ignorant souls instructed below how to place,
The list of duties, on the scheme of grace;
Proud, haughty rebels, who have long withstood, [God!
Now how their necks, behold they worship
Zion, rejoice! Your hero plays the man,
To vindicate the evangelic plan;
For this he pushes, we can say no less,
By words, and works, and pamphlets from the press.
Without cessation, truth is marching forth
Tow'rd every quarter, east, west, south and north;
Against delusion, all its force it bends,
While MERCER, in the cause, himself extends:
In state, as well as church, he's much engag'd,
Most firm he stands, while many are enrag'd;
In freedom's happy cause his heart grows big,
He's justly view'd a most illustr'ous whig.
Be calm ye saints, let ev'ry tear be dry,
Bid fear depart, your champion's standing by,
With ev'ry danger he will manly cope,
He'll never rest till he's dethron'd the Pope;
By arguments both solid and profound,
He'll face the foe, and will maintain the ground;
Behold what numbers fall before him slain,
He bears the sword, and bears it not in vain.
Push on ye saints, fear not your foes attack,
This champion follows close upon your back;
Nay, too in front, it may be said, he stands,
And cries to God for you with lifted hands.
Amen, the happy day is drawing near,

When glorious things the world at large shall hear;
Babylon falls, she falls to rise no more,
The saints transported wonder and adore—
What sound is that which doth my ears assault!
Like rumbling thunder, pushing thro' the vault,
Preparing peals to fill our minds with dread,
The thunder cracks, proclaiming MERCER'S dead.
Sad dispensation! Dark without a gleam!
Surprising! Is it so? Or do I dream?
Is SILAS MERCER dead? Oh! Yes 'tis true!
To all terrestrial things he's bid adieu.
He's gone! He's gone! whither we all must go;
He's gone! and will be seen no more below;
No more he'll stand the truth to testify,
And say ye must be born again or die. [eyes,
Let tears run down from both my weeping
Let Zion's sighs before her God arise;
The man is gone! in whom we took delight,
Alas! how soon his day is turn'd to night!
Let all, by whom his works were understood,
Now join the weeping widow and her brood;
Let *Salem** too be clad in mourning weeds,
Reflecting on his beneficial deeds.
I would not fail in this to bear my part,
I feel the stroke it settles at my heart;
My brother I am much distress'd for thee!
For very pleasant hast thou been to me
Stop, O my soul here pause and make a stand,
Be still! and know 'tis the divine command;
Things may appear mysterious at first view,
And afterwards be found both just and true.
As I reflect, I find 'twas hardly right,
To say his day was turned into night;
I would correct myself, and choose to say,
His night is turn'd to an immortal day.
We must believe he's enter'd into rest,
If so the change for him is surely best.
'Tis now he knows his darling topic grace,
By which he's lifted to a heavenly place,
Great things take place upon his seeming fall,
He bids adieu to trials, dangers, all;

Hymn Texts From *The Cluster*

His death has put an end to all the strife,
He, Samson-like, slew more in death than life.
Could he now only whisper thro' the veil,
And tell us all the animating tale;
What tidings then across the ear would roll!
*I perfect am, yet do not know my soul.**
Well then ye saints, let us be reconcil'd,
A father often frowns upon his child;
He often frowns, but then he frowns in love:
So doth our heavenly Father from above,
Such dispensations oftentimes are sent,
Design'd for trial, or for chastisement;
To say the worst they're but a Father's rod,
We've lost our *man;* but have not lost our God.
Our hope remains, remains both firm and sure,
It shall remain when time shall be no more.
In all distress, this consolation gives,
Silas is dead, but lo! our Jesus lives
Now let the faithful watchmen be awake,
Nor hold their peace, but cry for Zion's sake:
Young Jesse, rise, your father's dead and gone;
Be strong in faith, and act like *Jesse's* son.
Let all incessant be, by fervent pray'r,
For the important change let all prepare:
Our Lord has said he'll quickly come, and then
All saints shall join, and say aloud, *Amen.*

* Job, ix. 21.

THE END.

* The Salem Academy.

APPENDIX

1. (L. M.)
The Lord will come.

1 THE Lord will come! the earth shall quake,
  The hills their fixed seat forsake;
  And, withering, from the vault of night
  The stars withdraw their feeble light.

2 The Lord will come! but not the same
  As once in lowly form he came,
  A silent lamb to slaughter led,
  The bruis'd, the suffering, and the dead.

3 The Lord will come! a dreadful form,
  With wreath of flame, and robe of storm,
  On cherub wings, and wings of wind,
  Anointed Judge of human kind!

4 Can this be He who wont to stray
  A pilgrim on the world's highway!
  By power oppress'd, and mock'd by pride.
  Oh God! is this the crucified?

5 Go, tyrants! to the rocks complain!
  Go, seek the mountain's cleft in vain!
  But Faith, victorious o'er the tomb,
  Shall sing for joy—the Lord is come!

2. (7's.)
The Judgment Solemnity.

1 IN the sun and moon and stars
    Signs and wonders there shall be;
  Earth shall quake with inward wars,
    Nations with perplexity.

2 Soon shall ocean's hoary deep,
    Toss'd with stronger tempests, rise;
  Darker storms the mountain sweep,
    Redder lightning rend the skies.

3 Evil thoughts shall shake the proud,
    Racking doubt and restless fear;
  And, amid the thunder–cloud,
    Shall the Judge of men appear.

4 But though from that awful face
    Heaven shall fade and earth shall fly,
  Fear not ye, his chosen race,
    Your redemption draweth nigh!

3. (7's.) 5S./4L.
Star in the East

1 SONS of men, behold from far,

4. (11, 10.)
The Same.

1 BRIGHTEST and best of the sons of the morning!
  Dawn on our darkness and lend us thine aid!
  Star of the East, the horizon adorning,
  Guide where our infant Redeemer is laid!

2 Cold on his cradle the dew-drops are shining,
  Low lies his head with the beasts of the stall,
  Angels adore him in slumber reclining,
  Maker and Monarch and Saviour of all!

3 Say, shall we yield him, in costly devotion,
  Odours of Edom and offerings divine?
  Gems of the mountain and pearls of the ocean,
  Myrrh from the forest or gold from the mine?

4 Vainly we offer each ample oblation;
  Vainly with gifts would his favour secure:
  Richer by far is the heart's adoration;
  Dearer to God are the prayers of the poor.

5 Brightest and best of the sons of the morning!
  Dawn on our darkness and lend us thine aid!
  Star of the East, the horizon adorning,
  Guide where our infant Redeemer is laid!

5. (C. M.)
A Missionary Hymn.

1 BEHOLD the mountain of the Lord
  In latter days shall rise,
  Shall tower above the meaner hills,
  And draw the wondering eyes

2 To this the joyful nations round,
  All tribes and tongues, shall flow!
  "Ascend the hill of God," they say,
  "And to his temple go!"

3 The beam that shines on Sion hill
  Shall lighten every land,
  The King that reigns in Sion's towers
  Shall all the world command.

4 No strife shall vex Messiah's reign,
  Or mar the peaceful years;
  To ploughshares shall they beat their swords,
  To pruning-hooks their spears.

5 No longer host encountering host
  Their millions slain deplore;
  They hang the useless helm on high,
  And study war no more!

6 Come then, oh come from every land,
  To worship at his shrine;
  And walking in the light of God,
  With holy beauty shine.

6. (C. M.)
The Shepherd.

1 MY Shepherd is the living Lord,
  I therefore nothing need;
  In pastures fair, near pleasant streams
  He setteth me to feed.

2 He shall convert and glad my soul,
  And bring my mind in frame
  To walk in paths of righteousness,
  For His most holy name.

3 Yea, though I walk the vale of death,
  Yet will I fear no ill;
  Thy rod and staff they comfort me,
  And Thou art with me still.

4 And, in the presence of my foes,
  My table Thou shalt spread;
  Thou wilt fill full my cup, and Thou
  Annointed hast my head.

5 Through all my life Thy favour is
  So frankly shown to me,
  That in Thy house for evermore
  My dwelling-place shall be.

7. (7, 6.)
Missions.

1 FROM Greenland's icy mountains,
  From India's coral strand,
  Where Afric's sunny fountains
  Roll down their golden sand;
  From many an ancient river,
  From many a palmy plain,
  They call us to deliver
  Their land from error's chain!

2 What though the spicy breezes
  Blow soft o'er Java's isle,
  Though every prospect pleases,
  And only man is vile:
  In vain with lavish kindness
  The gifts of God are strown,
  The heathen, in his blindness,
  Bows down to wood and stone!

3 Can we, whose souls are lighted
  With Wisdom from on high,
  Can we to men benighted
  The lamp of life deny?

Hymn Texts From *The Cluster*

Salvation! oh, Salvation!
  The joyful sound proclaim,
  Till each remotest nation
  Has learn'd Messiah's name!
4 Waft, waft, ye winds, his story,
  And you, ye waters, roll,
  Till, like a sea of glory,
    It spreads from pole to pole;
  Till o'er our ransom'd nature,
  The Lamb for sinners slain,
  Redeemer, King, Creator,
    In bliss returns to reign!

8. (7's.)
Ask what I shall give thee.

1 COME, my soul, thy suit prepare,
    Jesus loves to answer pray'r;
  He himself has bid thee pray,
  Therefore will not say thee nay.

2 Thou art coming to a King,
  Large petitions with thee bring;
  For his grace and pow'r are such,
  None can ever ask too much.

3 With my burden I begin,
  Lord, remove this load of sin!
  Let thy blood, for sinners spilt,
  Set my conscience free from guilt.

4 Lord! I come to thee for rest,
  Take possession of my breast;
  There thy blood-bought right maintain,
  And without a rival reign.

5 As the image in the glass
  Answers the beholder's face;
  Thus unto my heart appear,
  Print thine own resemblance there.

6 While I am a pilgrim here,
  Let thy love my spirit cheer;
  As my guide, my guard, my friend,
  Lead me to my journey's end.

7 Show me what I have to do,
  Ev'ry hour my strength renew;
  Let me live a life of faith,
  Let me die thy people's death.

9. (S. M.) 8S./4L.
The Same.

1 BEHOLD the throne of grace!

10. (C. M.)
Oh that I were as in months past.

1 SWEET was the time when first I felt
    The Saviour's pard'ning blood
  Applied, to cleanse my soul from guilt,
    And bring me home to God.

2 Soon as the morn the light reveal'd,
    His praises tun'd my tongue;
  And when the ev'ning shades prevail'd,
    His love was all my song.

3 In vain the tempter spread his wiles,
    The world no more could charm;
  I liv'd upon my Saviour's smiles,
    And lean'd upon his arm.

4 In pray'r my soul drew near the Lord,
    And saw his glory shine:
  And when I read his holy word,
    I call'd each promise mine.

5 Then to his saints I often spoke
    Of what his love had done;
  But now my heart is almost broke,
    For all my joys are gone.

6 Now when the evening shade prevails,
    My soul in darkness mourns:
  And when the morn the light reveals,
    No light to me returns.

7 My pray'rs are now a chatt'ring noise,
    For Jesus hides his face;
  I read, the promise meets my eyes,
    But will not reach my case.

8 Now Satan threatens to prevail,
    And make my soul his prey;
  Yet, Lord thy mercies cannot fail,
    O come without delay.

11. (C. M.)
The name of Jesus is precious.

1 HOW sweet the name of Jesus sounds
    In a believer's ear!
  It soothes his sorrows, heals his wounds,
    And drives away his fear.

2 It makes the wounded spirit whole,
    And calms the troubled breast;
  'Tis manna to the hungry soul,
    And to the weary rest.

3 Dear name! the rock on which I build,
    My shield and hiding place;
  My never-failing treas'ry fill'd
    With boundless stores of grace.

4 By thee my pray'rs acceptance gain,
    Although with sin defil'd;
  Satan accuses me in vain,
    And I am own'd a child.

5 JESUS! my Shepherd, Husband, Friend,
    My Prophet, Priest, and King;
  My Lord, my Life, my Way, my End,
    Accept the praise I bring.

6 Weak is the effort of my heart,
   And cold my warmest thought;
But when I see thee as thou art,
   I'll praise thee as I ought.

7 Till then I would thy love proclaim
   With ev'ry fleeting breath;
And may the music of thy name
   Refresh my soul in death.

12. (C. M.)
The Prodigal Son.

1 AFFLICTIONS, though they seem severe,
   In mercy oft are sent;
They stopp'd the prodigal's career,
   And fore'd him to repent.

2 Although he no relenting felt
   Till he had spent his store;
His stubborn heart began to melt,
   When famine pinch'd him sore.

3 "What have I gain'd by sin," he said,
   But hunger, shame, and fear;
My father's house abounds with bread,
   While I am starving here.

4 "I'll go and tell him all I've done,
   And fall before his face;
Unworthy to be call'd his son,
   I'll seek a servant's place."

5 His father saw him coming back,
   He saw, and ran, and smil'd;
And threw his arms around the neck
   Of his rebellious child.

6 "Father, I've sinn'd—but O forgive!"—
   "I've heard enough," he said,
Rejoice my house, my son's alive,
   For whom I mourn'd as dead.

7 "Now let the fatted calf be slain,
   And spread the news around;
My son was dead, but lives again,
   Was lost, but now is found."

8 'Tis thus the Lord his love reveals,
   To call poor sinners home;
More than a father's love he feels,
   And welcomes all that come.

13. (C. M.)
Looking at the Cross.

1 IN evil long I took delight,
   Unawed by shame or fear;
Till a new object struck my sight,
   And stopp'd my wild career.

2 I saw one hanging on a tree,
   In agonies and blood;
Who fix'd his languid eyes on me,
   As near his cross I stood.

3 Sure, never to my latest breath
   Can I forget that look;
It seem'd to charge me with his death,
   Though not a word he spoke.

4 My conscience felt, and own'd the guilt,
   And plung'd me in despair;
I saw my sins his blood had spilt,
   And help'd to nail him there.

5 Alas! I knew not what I did,
   But now my tears are vain;
Where shall my trembling soul be hid?
   For I the Lord have slain.

6 A second look he gave, which said,
   "I freely all forgive;
This blood is for thy ransom paid;
   I'll die, that thou may'st live.

7 Thus, while his death my sin displays
   In all its blackest hue,
(Such is the mystery of grace)
   It seals my pardon too.

8 With pleasing grief and mournful joy,
   My spirit now is fill'd;
That I should such a life destroy,
   Yet live by him I kill'd.

14. (C. M.)
The Same.

1 ALAS, and did my Saviour bleed!
   And did my Sovereign die!
Would he devote that sacred head
   For such a worm as I?

2 Thy body slain, dear Jesus, thine,
   And bathed in its own blood,
While all exposed to wrath divine,
   The glorious Sufferer stood.

3 Was it for crimes that I had done,
   He groan'd upon the tree?
Amazing pity! grace unknown!
   And love beyond degree!

4 Well might the sun in darkness hide,
   And shut his glories in,
When Christ, the mighty Saviour, died,
   For man, the rebel's sin.

5 Thus might I hide my blushing face,
   While his dear cross appears,
Dissolve my heart in thankfulness,
   And melt my eyes to tears.

6 But drops of grief can ne'er repay
   The debt of love I owe:
Here, Lord, I give myself away:
   'Tis all that I can do.

THE END.

DISCARDED TEXTS FROM THE 1810 *CLUSTER*

D-3
APPENDIX
SONG 2

Cf. O THOU, in whose presence my soul takes delight, Hymn 281 (1823 ed.).

SECOND PART

1. BUT armed with vengeance in terror he comes,
The nations rebellious to tame,
The reins of omnipotent power assumes,
And rides in a chariot of flame.

2. A two-edged sword from his mouth issues forth,
Bright quivers of fire are his eyes,
He speaks—the black tempests are seen in the north;
And storms from their caverns arise.

3. Ten thousand destructions, which wait for his word,
And ride on the wings of his breath,
Fly swift as the wind at the nod of their Lord,
And deal out the arrows of death.

4. His cloud bursting thunders their voices resound,
Thro' all the vast regions on high,
'Till from the deep centre loud echoes rebound,
And meet the quick flames in the sky.

5. The portals of heaven his bidding obey,
And expand e'er his banners appear,
Earth trembles beneath till her mountains give way,
And hell shakes her fetters with fear.

6. When he treads on the clouds as the dust of his feet
And grasps the big storms in his hand
What eye the fierce glance of his anger shall meet,
Or who in his presence shall stand?

D-6
SONG 17

1. HOSTS first rebellious muster'd in the eternal world,
The heavenly realms invaded, but thence were quickly hurl'd,
Down to the lower regions, to gnaw their iron bands,
And fill'd with foaming fury they prowl throughout our lands.

2. An easy prey was first made, of our unhappy race,
Who quickly join'd with them, to run rebellion's race,
And thus both men and devils, with foaming fury flood,
Menacing of destruction, to all who join'd with God.

3. T' oppose these mighty forces behold the Lamb of God,
Tho' meedkly in his nature, yet is a man of blood;
He comes array'd in glory his name is on his thigh,
The KING of kings most holy and Lord of Lords most high.

4. In regular batalia he musters all his host,
To fire well their passions he breaths the Holy Ghost,
In battle array thus placed, he charges on the foe,
A deadly wound infixing at every single blow.

5. With consternation filled, amazement seiz'd their souls,
To see what devastation, what blood and carnage rolls,
Thro' evry tent and dwelling, and not a place is free,
The terror still increasing; so they prepare to flee.

6. Behold the combin'd forces of hell, the world, and sin,
Are flying o'er the mountain's (sic) before our conquering king,
They lick the dust for terror, and yell a hideous noise,
While seeking for a shelter, from his tremendous voice.

7. Then the bright CHIEFTAN orders, a standard to the slain,
He pours salvation on them, and bids them live again,
And come to him for pardon, and never be afraid,
For he has lov'd them freely, and never will upbraid.

8. Grace, flying on the pinions of everlasting love,
Pursues the dying convicts, their bleeding wounds to soothe,

Instead of wrath deserved, he mercy shows
    thro' blood;
In lieu of pain and anguish, he seals their
    peace with God.

9 Repairing to his standard, instead of death
    and hell,
They find their sins forgiven, and they be-
    loved well;
Their nature being changed, they fight
    with hell by faith,
They triumph over devils, and hope they
    have in death.

10 Rejoice in this my brethren, that Christ is
    on our side,
When tribulation rises we'll run to him and
    hide,
We'll tell him all our sorrows, he'll grant us
    our request,
He'll lead us thro' our troubles, and takes
    us home to rest.

11 O dearest friends, and neighbors, and chil-
    dren of our love,
It grieves us much to see you, in sinful
    courses move,
To stumble on dark mountains, and sink
    forever down,
In fiery volcanoes, forever there to burn.

12 O that the Lord may turn to you, from
    folly's dangerous race,
And give you much to mourn o'er, your
    sad and ruin'd case,
To fly to him for shelter amid the general
    wreck,
Who only can relieve you, for his own
    mercy's sake.

13 Thus tho' we can't but mourn you, while
    you are Satan's aids
We shall be much delighted, when you are
    Jesus' babes,
And join to shout and praise him, as long
    as we have breath,
And when we've fought his battles, we'll
    praise him after death.

D-7

SONG 59

1 IT grieves me Lord, it grieves me sore,
   That I have liv'd to thee no more,
   And wasted half my days;
My inward pow'rs shall burn and flame,
With inward passions to thy name
I would not speak, but for my God,
   Nor move, but to his praise.

2 What are my eyes, but aids to see,
   The glories of the Deity,
     Inscrib'd with beams of light,
On flowers and stars, Lord, I behold,
The shining azure, green and gold;
But when I try to read thy name,
   A dimness veils my sight.

3 My ears are rais'd when *Virgil* sings,
Sicilian swains or *Trojan* kings,
     And drink the music in;
Why should the trumpet's brazen voice,
Or, *Oaten* reed awake my joys,
And yet my heart so stupid lie,
   When sacred hymns begin.

4 Change me, O God; my flesh shall be,
An instrument of song to thee,
     And thou the notes inspire;
My tongue shall keep the heavenly rhyme,
My cheerful pulse shall beat the time,
And sweet variety of sounds,
   Shall in thy praise conspire.

5 The dearest nerve about my heart,
Should it refuse to bear a part,
     With my melodious breath;
I'd tear away the vital chord,
A bloody victim to my Lord,
And live without that impious string,
   Or, shew my zeal in death.

CHAPTER FOUR

A SAMPLE OF TUNES FOR *THE CLUSTER*

William Rabun, while serving as governor of Georgia at Louisville, led the singing at Mercer's Powelton church. They had been boyhood friends. As to Mercer's own musical ability, we have no reports. Mallary does tell of his preaching voice, but it would be precarious to infer any judgment about singing voice from so scanty a source of evidence. An accomplished musician (a Lowell Mason for instance) would not have included numerous hymns which are included in *The Cluster*; but Mercer was guided as much by the content and theology of the hymns as by any poetic eloquence and musical standard, perhaps more so. *The Cluster* reflects some of the staid and conventional types and the experimental new. Congregational participation in the revivals by singing has become a hallmark characteristic for the Evangelicals, from the Wesleys through the lifetime of Mercer. Noteworthy in *The Cluster* are the chorused hymns or even the repetitive phrases where the people join in.

The metrical variety is wide in Mercer's collection, as our charts will show. "P.M." stands for particular or peculiar meter, and these have been delineated. The roughness of beat and rhyme indicate the unpolished and rugged character of colonial America, while most of the tunes and texts from the British Isles convey a style of regularity and polish. There are exceptions of course, and the works of George Pullen Jackson are fascinating studies in this regard. Irish jigs, bawdy house ditties, broadside shoutings of London drummers and hucksterers ("Come all ye. . ."), fife and drum airs, and sea chanties punctuate the melodies of the spiritual songs and divine hymns among Mercer's selections. Tunes show family connections in variant renderings (Captain Kidd, Lord Lovel, Barbara Allen, Go tell Aunt Rhoda, for example). *The Cluster* is a significant piece of Americana in that it keeps and passes on to later generations early religious ballads and spiritual folksongs, which in their beginnings were individually sung and then "communalized" into hymns for group participation. The research of George Pullen Jackson testifies to a high number of ballads and folksongs that have found their way into *The Cluster*. He knew the importance of Mercer's *Cluster*.

Most probably the hymns, during Mercer's time, were sung without instrumental accompaniment. Searching the Scripture, Mercer reached the conclusion that while the Old Testament did speak of the use of musical instruments, nowhere did the New Testament (Cf. 113). He argued that violins were not allowable in church worship services because they had associations with secular parties and carryings on. We have not been able to determine if everyone sang in unison or in parts. Some of the old hymnbooks of the time which did include the music supply soprano, tenor, and bass parts; and it is not without significance that the shaped-notes or "buck-wheat notes" were coming into use during the same period as Mercer's hymnbooks. Revivals, camp-meetings, and singing schools went along with the impact of the nearness of Christ to the people of Kentucky, Tennessee and Georgia in early U.S. history. The freshness of new experiences were actively sought, as the works of Billings show us.

Mainly for illustrative purposes do we offer in this volume twenty-seven tunes which are related to texts of *The Cluster*. Occasionally, specific tune names are given in the heading of an individual hymn (Bray, Repentance, Mere, America, etc.); but these are limited to only about forty different tunes. "Lenox" is the most popular and is listed eighteen times, informing us that at least this many texts were sung to this one tune. The tune names are derived from towns and countries, Biblical themes and stories, and other sources such as the association with the authors of the hymns. The meter is always given, but Mercer did not supply in his hymnbooks a metrical index (which we have chosen to add in our book). Not the names of the composers, not the names of the tunes, not other musical indications are to be found. It is similar with the Biblical psalms. The realities being sung about took precedence over all else. Arrogance as to singing ability and flourishes of a flamboyant nature as well as pride of authorship were to be avoided. Praise to God was the end, not any sort of ego-trip.

The tunes here selected were chosen from among a wider grouping because most seemed likely to have been old enough and popular enough to have been the tunes sung with the texts of *The Cluster*. Those great preservers of hymn tunes, the "Sacred Harp" people, have accomplished an outstanding feat by collecting and publishing the music with the texts. Even of greater significance is the continuation of the "fasola" and sacred harp singings still carried on today, witnessing to the moving of the Spirit in a live and highly committed following. The 1971 revision

A Sample Of Tunes For *The Cluster*

of the *Original Sacred Harp* (with the kind permission of Hugh McGraw) has been our source for all twenty-seven hymn tunes. We refer the reader to all of the rich books of George Pullen Jackson for further development in this area.

In this selection it is the tenor part that gives the melody; however if parts were sung in the family circles and church congregations where Mercer preached or led devotions, we can say reliably that the sounds reaching the ear will cause the modern hearer a rewarding satisfaction, even a shock, that may set into motion a reviving action of the human spirit. Folkways Records and groups of the Old Sturbridge Village and Harvard University singers recently have sought to reenact this sort of singing. In regions of the South one may attend the "all-day singings" of the Sacred Harp folks, who are very friendly and generous toward all who come to visit.

Of interest to some readers may be the fact that twenty-three hymns are presently to be found in today's hymnals, though not all are limited to Baptist hymnbooks.* The oldest of all is probably Hymn 110 by Nahum Tate, "While shepherds watch'd their flocks." Closest to our own times may be Bishop Heber's missionary hymn, "From Greenland's icy mountains (#A-7). Most of the twenty-three, five in number, come from the man designated by George Pullen Jackson as "the favorite of the rural singers," John Newton, the same infidel slave-trader who became pastor of St. Mary Woolnoth, London (#23, #287, #347, #464, #A-11). With the exception of "What wondrous love is this" (#673), which is claimed for America, all the others come from the British Isles. Three come from Baptists: "Come thou fount of every blessing" (#349) by Robert Robinson, "Father, whate'er of earthly bliss" (#419) by Anne Steele, and "On Jordan's stormy banks I stand" (#294) by S. Stennett.

Most hymnals today include a metrical index. It is helpful for a number of reasons: tunes and texts have a way of becoming bound to each

---

*Alas, and did my Saviour bleed (A-4); Am I a soldier of the cross (#318); Amazing Grace (#23); Blow ye the trumpet, blow (#197); Brightest and best of the sons (A-14); Come thou fount of every blessing (#349); Come ye sinners, poor and wretched (#192); Father, whate'er of earthly bliss (#419); From Greenland's icy mountains (A-7); Glorious things of Thee are spoken (#287); God moves in a mysterious way (#588); Guide me, O thou great Jehovah (#395); How firm a foundation (#566); How sweet the name of Jesus sounds (A-11); How tedious and tasteless the hours (#347); Jesus lover of my soul (#351); Love divine, all loves excelling (#350); May the grace of Christ our Saviour (#464); O for a closer walk with God (#381); On Jordan's stormy banks I stand (#294); Rock of Ages, shelter me (#123); What wondrous love is this (#673); While shepherds watch'd their flocks (#110).

other, and many would like to know this; the unusual or experimental forms become easily identifiable; linkage of one hymn with one or several others may be found with facility; the balance between the standard or conventional forms, COMMON METER, LONG METER, SHORT METER, may be compared with the new or irregular tunes.

Numerous linkages among hymns in Mercer's *Cluster* are evident through use of this metrical index, e.g., #4 and #189; #255 and #302; #667 and #673; #11 and #548; #192 and #654; and #619, #620, #659. Sixteen hymn tunes are bound together under the meter of "7,6." While we have selected only half the hymns to be printed in full, interested persons may consult one of the *Clusters* in Stetson Library, Mercer University, for fuller research purposes. Fortunately the pagination and hymn numbers remain constant from the 1823 to the 1835 editions.

For our present purpose, which deals mainly with the texts, one may observe that Mercer's time brought new spontaneity and experimentation in trying out rather strange meters and including choruses in which audiences took part, with emphasis on communal singing; there are ballad types but not for solo presentations. The tunes mark the sentiment of Hymn 60, "I'm tir'd of visits, modes and forms," i.e., the same old meters of the standard kind; yet Mercer's *Cluster* is a combination of the "standard" and the "new."

A Sample Of Tunes For *The Cluster*

METRICAL INDEX

C.M.	Total Hymns	=	210	
C.M.	Double	=	6	(#1, #187. #270, #285, #348, #494)
C.M.	Chorus 8's	=	1	(#273)
C.M.	Chorused	=	1	(#284)
L.M.	Total Hymns	=	178	
L.M.	Double	=	2	(#229, #346)
S.M.	Total Hymns	=	40	
S.M.	Double	=	4	(#243, #467, #571, #572)
P.M.	(Peculiar or Particular Meter)			

Hymns	Meter
#4	8.7.8.7.8.7.8.7.8.8.8.8.8.8.7.
#11	7.6.7.6.7.8.7.6.
#12	5.5.5.5.6.5.6.5.
#60	8.8.6.8.8.8.6.
#67	5.5.11.5.6.12. with variations
#68	8.8.8.6.8.8.8.6.
#105	10.7.14.9.
#115	6.6.8.6.6.6.8.6.
#159	11.10.11.11.6.6.10.6.6.9.
#160	7.7.7.7.7.7.7.7.
#165	5.5.5.11.
#181	7.7.7.7. Chorus: 7.7.7.7.
#186	11.11.11.11.
#188	7.6.7.6.7.7.7.6. Chorus: 8.7.7.6.
#189	8.7.8.7.8.7.8.7.8.8.8.8.8.8.7.
#192	8.7.8.7.4.7.
#195	8.8.8.8.6.
#224	8.8.6.8.8.8.6.
#255	8.8.8.7.8.8.4.3.3.3.8.7.
#267	8.8.8.7.
#302	8.8.8.7.8.8.4.3.3.3.8.7.
#501	8.8.8.8.6.6.
#532	6.6.10.6.6.10.
#548	7.6.7.6.7.8.7.6.
#556	5.7.8.6.6.9. with peculiar variations
#564	8.8.8.8.8.4.
#619	11.11.11.5.
#627	7.7.8.8.7.8. 7.7.7.7.7.8. 8.8.6.8.8.6.
#653	8.7.8.7.11.
#654	8.7.8.7.4.7.
#664	11.11.6.6.7.6.

Tune: BUNKER'S HILL

#620	11.11.11.5.
#659	11.11.11.5.
#667	6.6.6.3.6.6.6.6.6.3.
#673	6.6.6.3.6.6.6.6.6.3.

Meter	Hymns
4 M Chorus'd 8.8.8.8.	#8.
5's.	#64, 201, 226.
6's.	#63.
6,4.	#107, 120, 152, 507.
6,5.	#172, 353, 566, 567, 575.
6.6.6.6.8.8. (Lenox)	#658.
6's, 8's (Lenox)	#58.
6,8.	#17, 109, 119, 173, 193, 197, 203, 244, 256, 257, 280, 383, 463, 492, 505, 568, 601.
7's	#9, 28, 29, 62, 123, 147, 200, 217, 218, 315, 351, 357, 387, 425, 441, 450, 469, 477, 527, 529, 530, 542, 543, 569, 596, 604, A-2, A-3, A-8.
7's Double	#496.
7,6.	#6, 59, 66, 114, 124, 227, 288, 484, 491, 495, 497, 560, 597, A-7.
7.7.7.6.	#303, 304.
8's	#10, 13, 15, 70, 116, 118, 121, 122, 158, 171, 252, 301, 347, 385, 434, 470, 472, 475, 493, 558, 576, 577, 578, 591, 595, 599, 600, 603, 616, 670, 671.
8's, 11's.	#473.
8,6.	#61, 190.
8,7.	#5, 16, 20, 26, 65, 71, 74, 75, 108, 113, 117, 191, 225, 253, 269, 287, 306, 349, 350, 352, 464, 465, 545, 562, 563, 570, 602, 605, 674.
8,7,4.	#19, 162, 198, 199, 283, 395, 462, 466, 474, 476.
8,7,7.	#279.
8,8,6.	#3, 18, 25, 57, 72, 76, 156, 223, 231, 232, 254, 275, 276, 345, 655, 656.
9,7.	#196.
9,8.	#69, 183, 546, 568, 649.
10's.	#182, 286, 561, 574, 598, 606, 617, 666, 668, 669.
10,8.	#621.
10,11.	#251.
11's.	#7, 125, 164, 184, 185, 230, 274, 277, 278, 305, 549, 555, 557, 650.
11,8.	#2, 163, 281, 608, 618.
11,9.	#672 N.B. #233 is in error; in reality, 11,8. meter.
11,10.	A-4.
12,11.	#282.

A Sample Of Tunes For *The Cluster* 167

A NOTE ON HYMN TUNES IN *THE CLUSTER*

Tune names explicitly mentioned in the headings of particular tunes are as follows:

LENOX   17, 58, 109, 119, 120, 173, 193, 187, 244, 256, 257, 280, 383, 492, 505, 568, 601, 658.
DELIGHT   107, 463.
BUNKER'S HILL   620, 659.
PSALM   25: 382.
PSALM   34: 509.
MAJESTY 24, REPENTANCE 92, WARREN 93, LEBANON 94, CRUCIFIXION 105, SHERBURN 110, AMERICA 141, MIDDLETOWN 160, WINDHAM 220, GREENWICH 221, EXHORTATION 220, NORWICH 238, WILLIAMSTOWN 250, NEW JORDAN 294, ROCHESTER 340, OCEAN 341, LITTLE MARLBORO 342, NEWBURG 343, NEW JERUSALEM 344, PORTUGAL 354, RUSSIA 490, BETHESDA (duplicated with DELIGHT) 507, GREENFIELD 508, MONTGOMERY 520, BRIDGEWATER 521, WALSALL 522, FLORIDA 526, MERE 554, BRAY 594, MARTYRS' 642, NEW DURHAM 643, MORTALITY 644.

HYMNS IN MERCER'S *CLUSTER* WITH CHORUSES OR SEMI-CHORUSES

CHORUSES		SEMI-CHORUSES or REPETITIVE WORDS
#8	4 M. Chorus'd.	#11
#181	P.M.	#14
#188	P.M.	#20
#196	9,7.	#36
#197	6,8.	#48
#268	L.M.	#62
#271	L.M.	#66
#273	Chorus 8's.	#76
#283	8,7,4.	#83
#284	C.M. Chorused.	#96
#465	8,7,4.	#112
#501	P.M.	#120
#544	C.M. Double.	#122
#545	8,7.	#125
#547	L.M.	#133
#548	P.M.	#145
#604	7's.	#146
#652	7,6.	#159
#660	L.M. Chorused.	#186
		#186
		#195
		#212
		#228
		#267
		#308
		#358
		#474
		#496
		#553
		#561
		#564
		#578
		#592
		#628
		#673

In the early years of the nineteenth century the use of choruses indicated greater group or congregational participation.

A Sample Of Tunes For *The Cluster* 169

(OSH, 52)

Mercer's *CLUSTER* Hymn 352

CHARLESTOWN. 8s, 7s.

JOHN NEWTON. "Jesus, thou Son of David, have mercy on me. And many charged him that he should hold his peace."—MARK 10: 47, 48. STEPHEN JENKS, 1806.
Key of F Major.

1. "Mer-cy, O Thou Son of Da-vid," Thus blind Bar-ti-me-us prayed, "Oth-ers by Thy word are sav-ed, Now to me af-ford Thine aid."
2. Ma-ny for his cry-ing chid him, But he called the loud-er still, Till the gra-cious Sav-iour bid him,"Come and ask me what you will."

Stephen Jenks, New Canaan, Conn., published the "Delights of Harmony" in 1805. Twenty-six of the tunes in that book were composed by him, and it was published on subscription. He removed to Thompson, and died there in 1856. He was a ready composer.

170 The Cluster Of Jesse Mercer

Mercer's CLUSTER Hymn 300

(OSH, 77)

THE CHILD OF GRACE. C. M. D.

CHARLES WESLEY, 1759. Key of A Minor.
In whom we have redemption through his blood, even the forgiveness of sins."—Col. 1:14.
Mercer's "Cluster," page 246.   E. J. KING, 1844.

1. { How happy's every child of grace, Who feels his sins forgiv'n; A country far from mortal sight, The land of rest, the saints' delight,
     This world, he cries is not my place, I seek a place in heaven.   Yet, oh! by faith I see   A heaven prepared for me.

2. { Oh, what a blessed hope is ours, While here on earth we stay, We feel the ressurrection near, And with His glorious presence here
     We more than taste the heav'nly powers And antedate that day.   Our life in Christ concealed,   Our earthen vessels filled.

This is one of Charles Wesley's best hymns, first published in 1759. It was considered by John Wesley to be one of the best hymns his brother ever composed. See sketch of Charles Wesley under tune "Arnold," page 285. Sketches about E. J. King appear on different pages of this book.

A Sample Of Tunes For *The Cluster* 171

(OSH, 44)

Mercer's *CLUSTER* Hymn 37

THE CONVERTED THIEF. C. M. D.

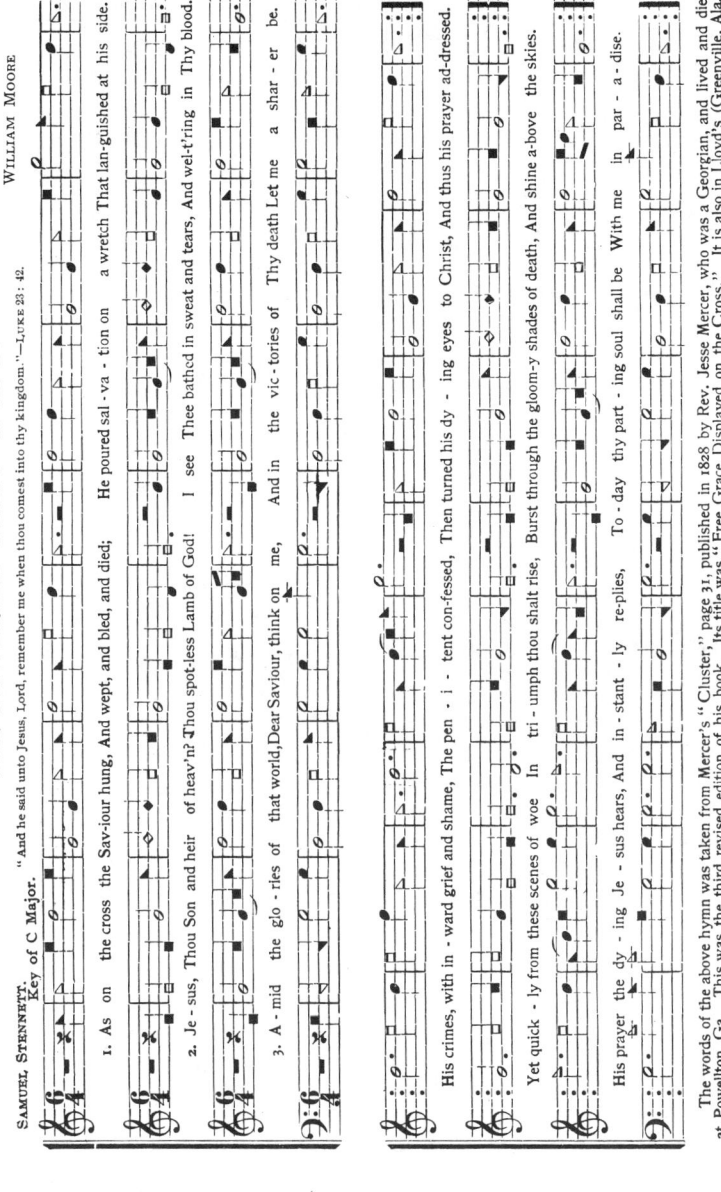

SAMUEL STENNETT.
Key of C Major.

WILLIAM MOORE

"And he said unto Jesus, Lord, remember me when thou comest into thy kingdom."—LUKE 23 : 42.

1. As on the cross the Sav-iour hung, And wept, and bled, and died; He poured sal-va-tion on a wretch That lan-guished at his side.
2. Je-sus, Thou Son and heir of heav'n? Thou spot-less Lamb of God! I see Thee bathed in sweat and tears, And wel-t'ring in Thy blood.
3. A-mid the glo-ries of that world, Dear Saviour, think on me, And in the vic-to-ries of Thy death Let me a shar-er be.

His crimes, with in-ward grief and shame, The pen-i-tent con-fessed, Then turned his dy-ing eyes to Christ, And thus his prayer ad-dressed.
Yet quick-ly from these scenes of woe In tri-umph thou shalt rise, Burst through the gloom-y shades of death, And shine a-bove the skies.
His prayer the dy-ing Je-sus hears, And in-stant-ly re-plies, To-day thy part-ing soul shall be With me in par-a-dise.

The words of the above hymn was taken from Mercer's "Cluster," page 31, published in 1828 by Rev. Jesse Mercer, who was a Georgian, and lived and died at Powellton, Ga. This was the third revised edition of his book. Its title was "Free Grace Displayed on the Cross." It is also in Lloyd's (Greenville, Ala.) hymn book, page 4. We have not been able to obtain the name of the author of the words.
The music to the above tune is of long standing, but none of the books we have consulted give the name of the author. It appears in "Southern Harmony," by William Walker, 1835, page 5, and in tune books of an earlier date than this.

(OSH, 123)

THE DYING CHRISTIAN. 11, 8.

"Dying, and, behold, we live."—2 Cor. 6, 9.
Original tune by Edward Harwood, 1760. Re-arranged by E. J. King, 1844.

Benjamin Francis   Key of A Major.

1. Ye objects of sense, and enjoyments of time, Which oft have delighted my heart, I soon shall exchange you for views more sublime, For joys that shall never depart.
2. Thou, Lord of the day, and thou, Queen of the night, I soon shall behold, with increasing delight, A sun that shall never go down. To me ye no longer are known;
3. Ye mountains and valleys, groves, rivers and plains, More permanent regions where righteousness reigns, Thou earth and thou ocean, adieu; Present their bright hills to my view.

"The Dying Christian" is an old melody—much older than the "Sacred Harp" by White and King, in 1844; yet Mr. King made some valuable improvements in it in 1844. Hence we give him credit for the tune.

A Sample Of Tunes For *The Cluster* 173

(OSH, 29) Mercer's *CLUSTER* Hymn 235

FAIRFIELD. C. M.

"And so I will go in unto the king, . . . and if I perish, I perish. When the king saw Esther the queen standing in the court, that she obtained favor: In his sight; and the king held out to Esther the golden sceptre that was in his hand."—ESTHER 4: 16; 5: 2.

EDMUND JONES, 1750. Key of A Minor. Hitchcock.

1. Come, humble sinner, in whose breast A thousand thoughts revolve, Come, with your guilt and fear oppressed,
And make this last resolve, Come, with your guilt and fear oppressed, And make this last resolve, solve.

2. I'll go to Jesus, though my sin hath like a mountain rose; I know his courts, I'll enter in,
What ever may oppose, I know his courts I'll enter in, Whatever may oppose, pose.

3. I can but perish if I go, I am resolved to try, For if I stay away I know I must forever die,
For if I stay away I know I must forever die, die.

"Fairfield" is in most of the earlier publications of this country. In Andrew Law's books, Oliver Holden's works, "Missouri Harmony," 1837, page 43; "Southern Harmony," 1835, page 48, and in 1849; "Temple Harp," 1872, and earlier books; Little & Smith's publications of 1830, as well as many others of the earlier editions of the earlier composers. Edmund Jones was an English Baptist minister, born in 1721 and died in 1765. He composed several important hymns, one of his best is the above. Nothing is known of the author of the music. After a search through many books we fail to find the author's name. It is one of the old church tunes.

Copyright, 1909, by J. S. James.

174 The Cluster Of Jesse Mercer

Mercer's CLUSTER Hymn 526

(OSH, 203)

FLORIDA. S. M.

Isaac Watts

"And it shall come to pass, that whosoever shall call on the name of the Lord shall be saved."—Acts, 2–21
Psalmist, 761st Hymn. Truman S. Wetmore, about 1808.

Key of E. Minor.

1. Let sin-ners take their course, And choose the road to death, But in the wor-ship of my God, I'll spend my dai-ly breath,
2. My thoughts ad-dress his throne, When morning brings the light; I seek his blessings ev'-ry noon, And pay my vows at night.

(OSH, 127) Mercer's *CLUSTER* Hymn 347

GREENFIELD. 8s.

JOHN NEWTON, 1779. Key of G. "Whom have I in heaven but thee? and there is none upon earth I desire beside thee." Psa. 73: 25.

This widely-popular hymn, on "Delights in Christ," was taken from "Olney Hymns," in 1779. John Newton was one of the best English hymn writers. Born 1725 and died 1807; belonged to the Church of England.

(OSH, 183)

Mercer's *CLUSTER* Hymn 221

GREENWICH L. M.

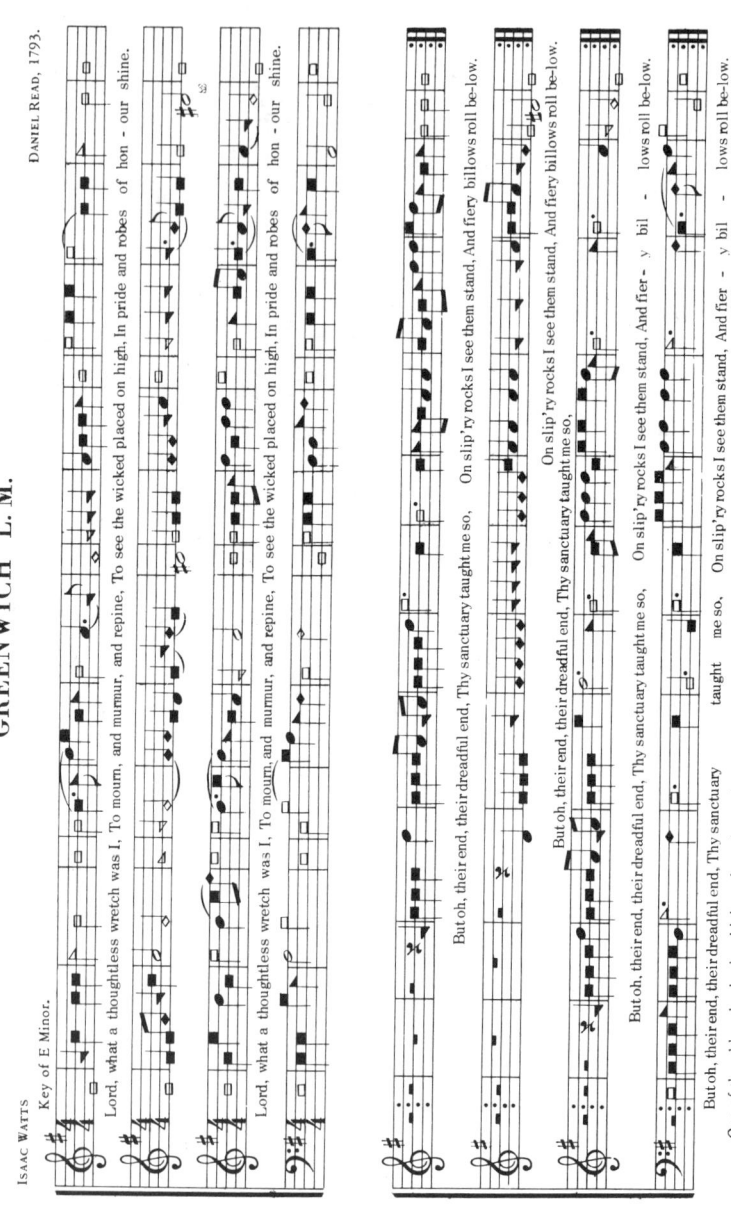

Isaac Watts

Daniel Read, 1793.

Key of E Minor.

Lord, what a thoughtless wretch was I, To mourn, and murmur, and repine, To see the wicked placed on high, In pride and robes of hon-our shine. But oh, their end, their dreadful end, Thy sanctuary taught me so, On slip'ry rocks I see them stand, And fiery billows roll be-low.

One of the oldest books in which we have been able to find the tune "Greenwich" is the "Presbyterian Psalmist," page 364. This book was printed very early in the 19th century, and perhaps even an earlier date than this; it is highly probable in the 18th century. We gather from the remarks on page 364 of this old book that the tune had been of long standing at the time of this "Presbyterian Psalmist." Also see John Wyeth's "Repository of Sacred Music, 1810, page 108. We find the words "A few tunes embraced in the Assembly's list," so imperfect in their structure that any effort toward appropriate correction would have destroyed the identity. These tunes the editor has thought fit to throw together at the close of this volume without the slightest revision. See "Sacred Harp," by White and King, 1844 to 1869. Same words in all the books. It was first published in the author's book, 1793, "Columbian Harmony."

A Sample Of Tunes For *The Cluster* 177

(OSH, 317)

Mercer's *CLUSTER* Hymn 468

JACKSON. L. M.

M. F. McWhorter, 1908.

Jesse Mercer, 1825. Key of G Major.

"They were strangers and pilgrims on the earth."—Heb. 11: 13.

1. I am a stranger here below, And what I am is hard to know, I am so vile, so prone to sin, I fear that I'm not born again.
2. When I experience call to mind, My understanding is so blind, All feeling sense seems to be gone, Which makes me think that I am wrong, wrong.
3. I find my self out of the way, My thoughts are often gone astray, Like one alone I seem to be, Oh, is there any one like me?

178 *The Cluster* Of Jesse Mercer

(OSH, 53)

Mercer's *CLUSTER* Hymn 139

JERUSALEM. L. M.

"Hope of eternal life, which God, that cannot lie, promised before the world began."—TITUS 1:2.

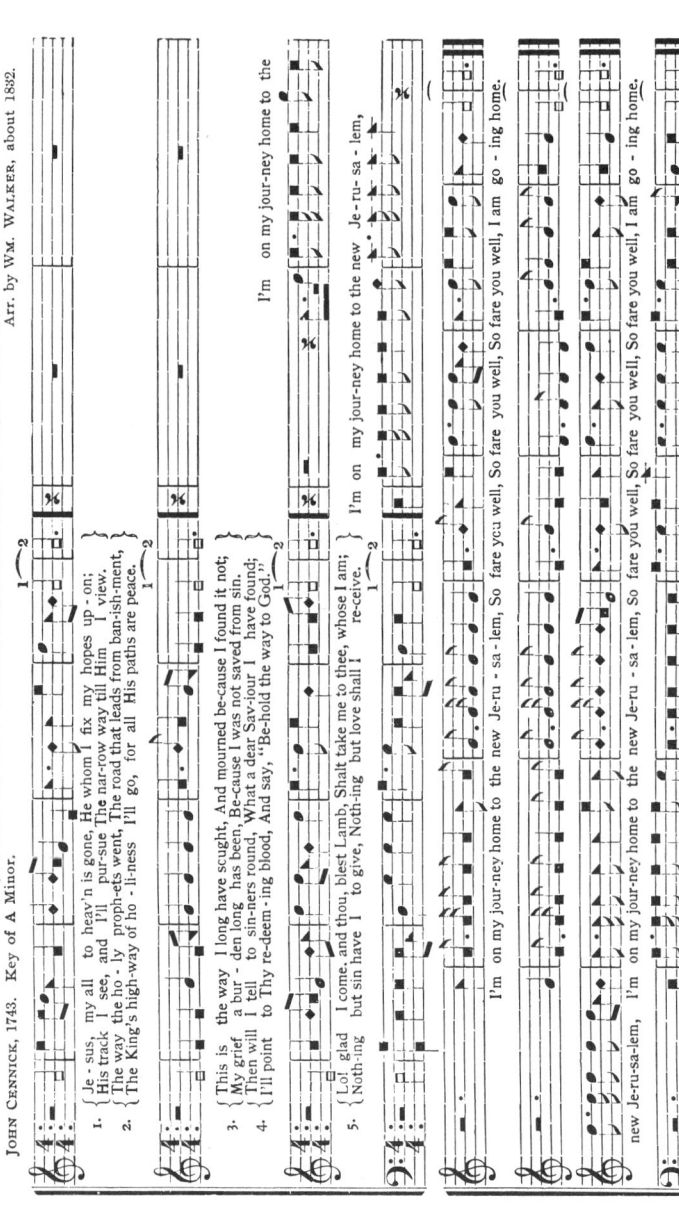

JOHN CENNICK, 1743. Key of A Minor. Arr. by WM. WALKER, about 1832.

1. Je-sus, my all to heav'n is gone, He whom I fix my hopes up-on;
   His track I see, and I'll pur-sue The nar-row way till Him I view.
2. The way the ho-ly proph-ets went, The road that leads from ban-ish-ment,
   The King's high-way of ho-li-ness I'll go, for all His paths are peace.
3. This is the way I long have sought, And mourned be-cause I found it not;
   My grief a bur-den long has been, Be-cause I was not saved from sin.
4. Then will I tell to sin-ners round, What a dear Sav-iour I have found;
   I'll point to Thy re-deem-ing blood, And say, "Be-hold the way to God;"
5. Lo! glad I come, and thou, blest Lamb, Shalt take me to thee, whose I am;
   Noth-ing but sin have I to give, Nothing but love shall I re-ceive.

I'm on my jour-ney home to the new Je-ru-sa-lem, So fare you well, So fare you well, I am go-ing home,
I'm on my jour-ney home to the new Je-ru-sa-lem, So fare you well, So fare you well, I am go-ing home.

The original title to this hymn was "Christ, the Sinner's Way to God." John Cennick was born in England in 1718. He joined the Methodist societies of the Wesley's when he was seventeen years old, and afterward became a preacher. A dispute arose in the church, and he afterward founded an independent church of his own, which was gathered into the Whitfield and Huntingdon connection.

A Sample Of Tunes For *The Cluster* 179

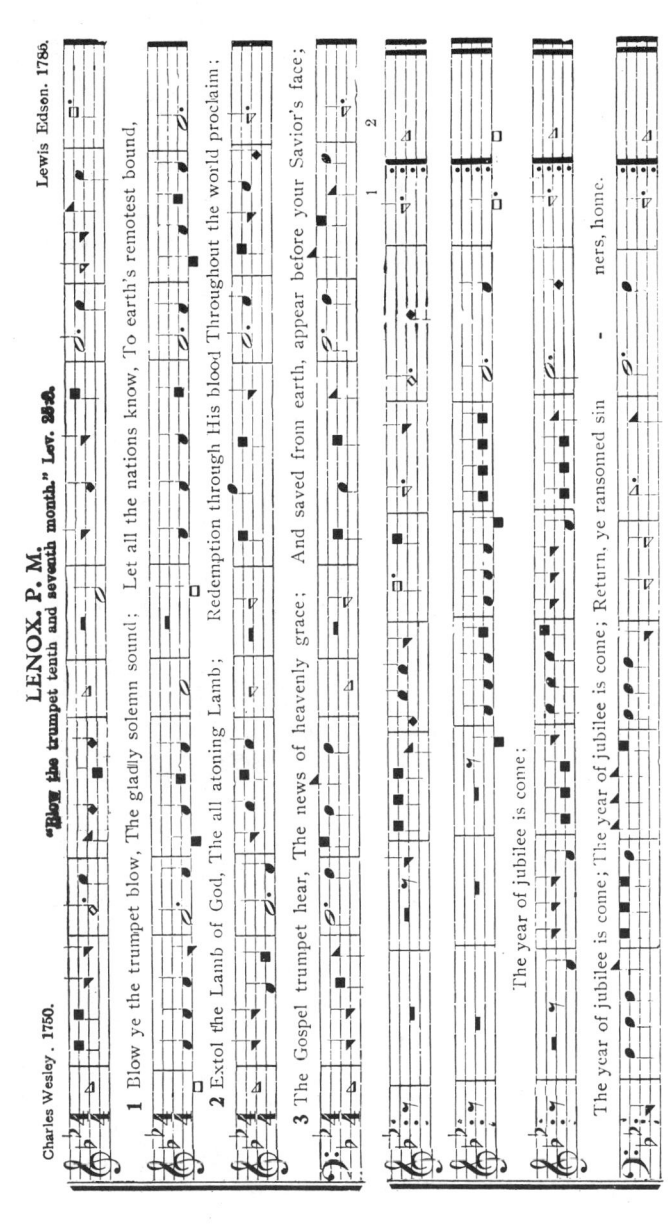

180 *The Cluster* Of Jesse Mercer

(OSH, 37)

Mercer's *CLUSTER* Hymn 187

LIVERPOOL. C. M.

M. C. H. DAVIS.

"Remember now thy Creator in the days of thy youth."—Eccl. 12:1.

1. Young peo-ple all, at-ten-tion give, And hear what I shall say; I wish your souls with Christ to live In ev - er-last - ing day.
2. Re-mem-ber you are hast'ning on To death's dark, gloom-y shade; Your joys on earth will soon be gone, Your flesh in dust be laid.

The above hymn was found in "Mercer's Cluster," page 146, headed "Solemn Addresses to Young People." This is the third revised edition of said book. Rev. Jesse Mercer of Powellton, Ga., was the editor in 1823. The hymn has appeared in several hymn books, but none of them give the author's name or date of the hymn. "Liverpool," is credited to M. C. H. Davis. It is probably an English production.

A Sample Of Tunes For *The Cluster* 181

(OSH, 189–190)

Mercer's *CLUSTER* Hymn 520

MONTGOMERY.   C. M.   Psalmist, 18th Hymn.

"Remember now thy Creator in the days of thy youth, while the evil days come not, nor the years draw nigh, when thou shalt say, I have no pleasure in them."—Ecc. 12:1.
Isaac Watts, 1719.   Key of C Major.
Rev. David Morgan, about 1805.

Ear - ly my God, without de - lay, I haste to seek thy face; My thirs-ty spi - rit faints a - way......... With

Ear - ly my God, without de - lay, I haste to seek thy face; My thirs-ty spi - rit faints a - way......... With

Ear - ly my God, without de - lay, I haste to seek thy face; My thirs-ty spi - rit faints a - way, With

Ear - ly my God, without de - lay, I haste to seek thy face; My thirs-ty spi - rit faints a - way, With

There are two sources laying claim to this tune. One is that of "Moore;" the other by David Morgan, a Presbyterian minister. We are satisfied that Morgan is the author of the tune

MONTGOMERY. Concluded.

(OSH, 299)

Mercer's *CLUSTER* Hymn 344

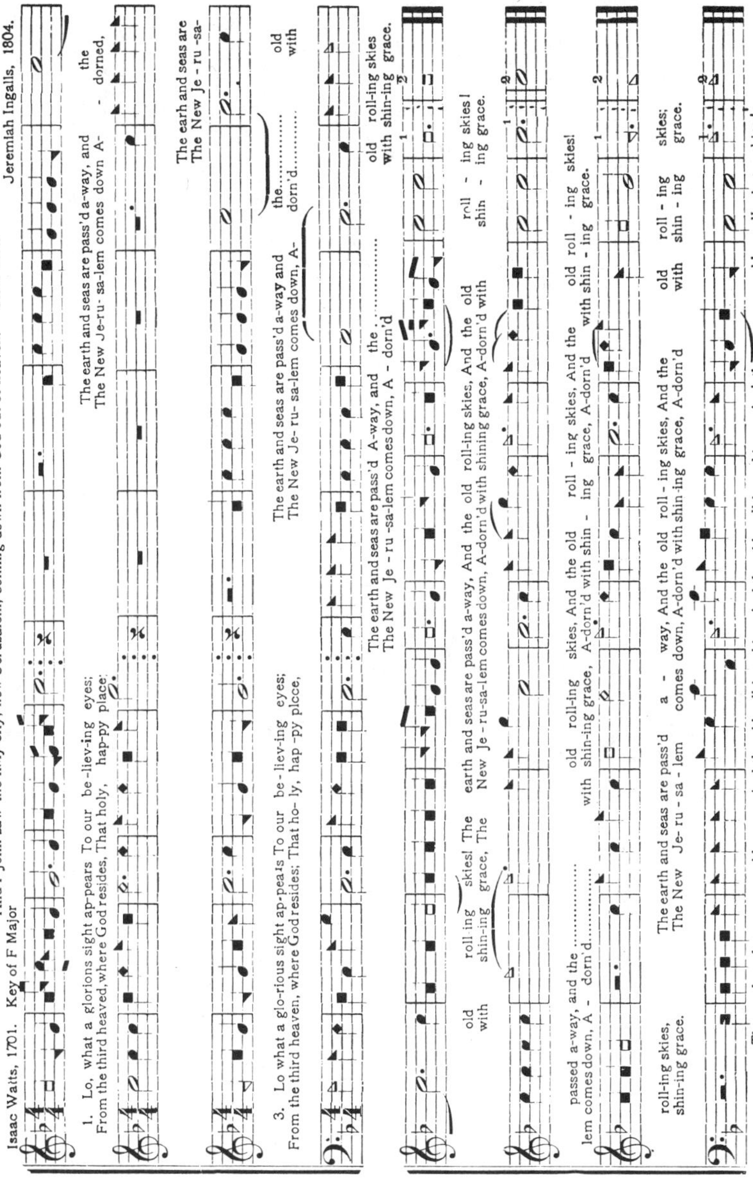

184 The Cluster Of Jesse Mercer

(OSH, 442–443) Mercer's CLUSTER Hymn 294

NEW JORDAN. C. M. D.

Samuel Stennett. "Thine eyes shall behold the King in his beauty; they shall behold the land that is very far off."—Isa. 33:17.
Key of C Sharp Minor. Remodeled by S. M. Denson and J. S. James, April 29, 1911.

1. On Jor-dan's storm-y banks I stand, And cast a wish-ful eye, To Ca-naan's fair and hap-py land,
3. There gen-'rous fruits that nev - er fail, On trees Im - mor - tal grow; There rocks, and hills, and brooks, and vales,
Where my po - ses - sions lie
With milk and hon - ey flow. O the trans - port - ing rapt' - rous scene That ri - ses to my
All o'er those wide ex - tend - ed plains Shines one e - ter - nal
With milk and hon - ey flow. O the trans - port - ing rapt' - rous scene That ri - ses to my sight!
All o'er those wide ex - tend - ed plains Shines one e - ter - nal day!

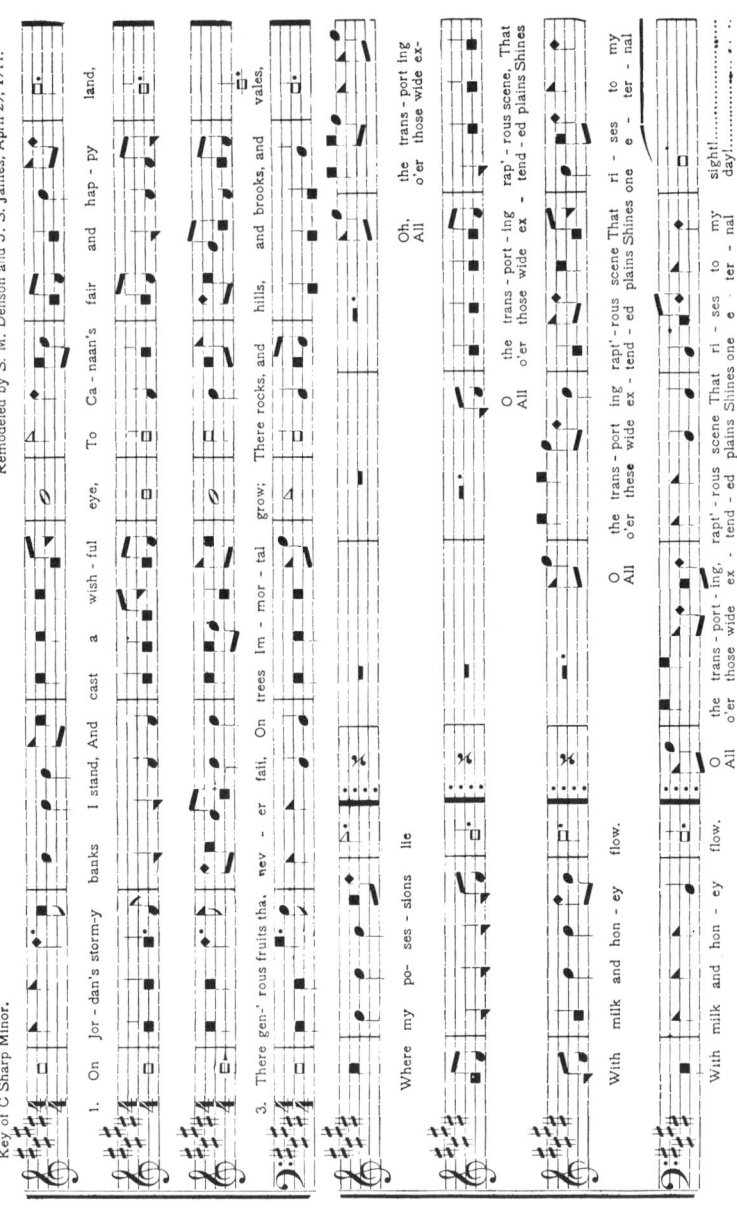

The title of the above Hymn is "Christ's Message." It is considered Doddridge's masterpiece. It is taken from the Author's Hymn Book of 1755, and is published in all the leading hymn books of the world. The hymn has five verses, but only two of them are in this tune.

A Sample Of Tunes For *The Cluster*   185

(OSH, 182)

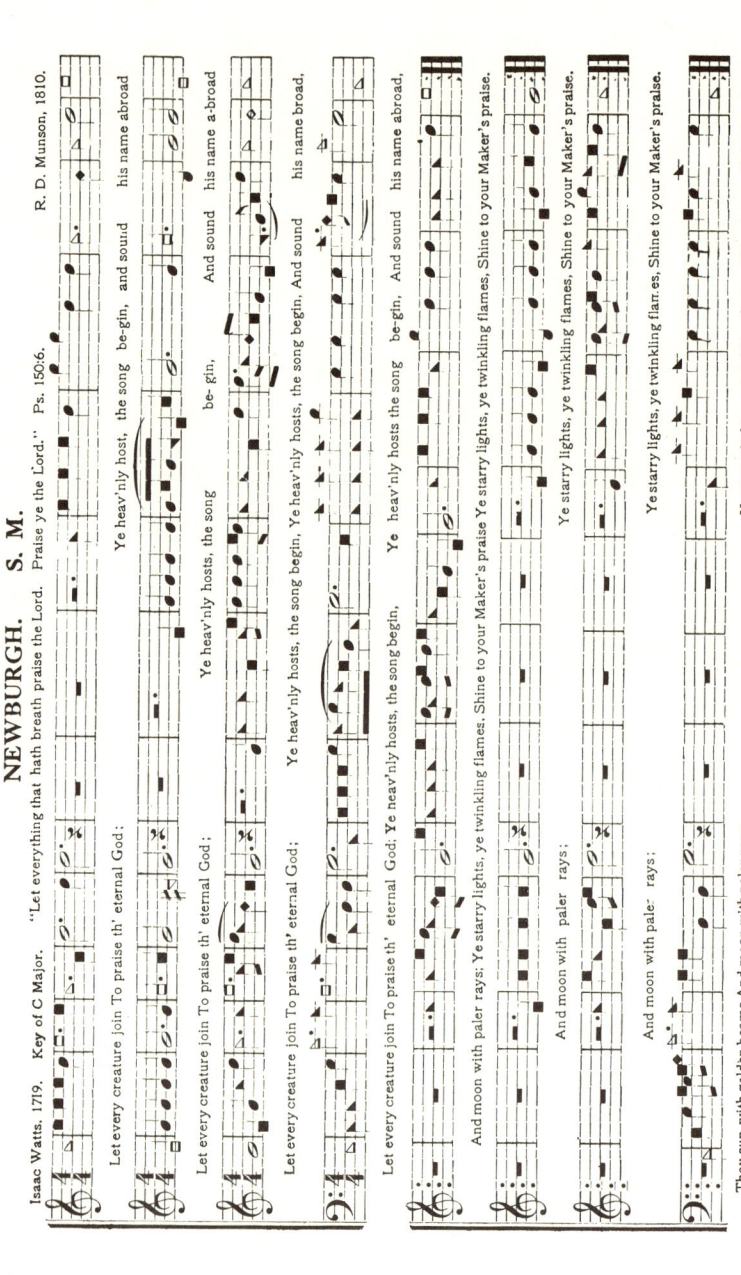

186   *The Cluster* Of Jesse Mercer

Mercer's *CLUSTER* Hymn 343

NEWBURGH.   S. M.

Isaac Watts, 1719.   Key of C Major.   "Let everything that hath breath praise the Lord.   Praise ye the Lord."   Ps. 150:6.   R. D. Munson, 1810.

Let every creature join To praise th' eternal God; Ye heav'nly host, the song be-gin, and sound his name abroad

Let every creature join To praise th' eternal God; Ye heav'nly hosts, the song be-gin, And sound his name a-broad

Let every creature join To praise th' eternal God; Ye heav'nly hosts, the song begin, Ye heav'nly hosts, the song begin, And sound his name broad,

Let every creature join To praise th' eternal God: Ye heav'nly hosts, the song be-gin, And sound his name abroad,

And moon with paler rays; Ye starry lights, ye twinkling flames, Shine to your Maker's praise Ye starry lights, ye twinkling flames, Shine to your Maker's praise.

And moon with paler rays; Ye starry lights, ye twinkling flames, Shine to your Maker's praise.

And moon with paler rays; Ye starry lights, ye twinkling flames, Shine to your Maker's praise.

Thou sun with golden beams And moon with paler rays; Ye starry lights, ye twinkling flames, Shine to your Maker's praise.

Newburg appears in "The Southern Harmony," by William Walker, 1835, "Missouri Harmony," 1827, 1837 by Allen D. Carden, supplement. It is credited to Munson in "Southern Harmony," also see Christian Harmony" by Walker, 1866, page 52. The tune is credited to Munson in the "Chistian Harmony" Also see "Lute of Zion," by T. B. Woodbury, 1856, page 361. The oldest book we can find this tune in is "Wyeth's Repository of sacred music," 1810, page 41. In this book R. D. Munson is put down as its author.

A Sample Of Tunes For *The Cluster* 187

(OSH, 31) Mercer's CLUSTER Hymn 49

NINETY-THIRD PSALM. S. M.
"By grace ye are saved."—EPH. 2:6.

PHILIP DODDRIDGE, 1785. Key of C Major. JEREMIAH INGALLS, 1805.

1. Grace! 'tis a charm-ing sound, Har-mo-nious to the ear; Heav'n with the ech - o shall re - sound, And all the earth shall hear.
2. Grace first con-trived the way To save re - bel - lious man; And all the steps that grace dis - play, Which drew the won-drous plan.
3. Grace taught my wan-d'ring feet To tread the heav'n-ly road; And new sup - plies each hour I meet, While press-ing on to God.
4. Grace all the work shall crown Through ev-er-last - ing days; It lays in heav'n the top - most stone, And well de - serves our praise.

This hymn is on "Salvation by Grace," from the author's hymns, 1755. The original name of this tune was "Kentucky." Philip Doddridge, D. D., the author of the hymn, was born in London, 1702, over two hundred years ago. He was a scholar of high attainments; was ordained to the Nonconformist ministry; was an English Congregationalist, and for many years pastor of one of these churches, from 1829 to the time of his death, 1852. He was a great pulpit orator and theologian. He composed many standard hymns and high-class sacred music.
See sketch of Jeremiah Ingalls under the tune "Northfield." He is the author of some of the best music of those who composed in his day, and many of his tunes are still popular with the church people, especially in the United States, and many of his best productions are in the leading tune and hymn books of to-day.
This tune appears in Jeremiah Ingall's "Song Books," beginning 1805 to 1820; also in the "Southern Harmony," by Walker, 1835 and 1849, by same author; in the "Christian Harmony," 1866 and 1901. See "Missouri Harmony," page 31, 1837, and many other publications.
Copyright, 1909, by J. S. James.

188 *The Cluster* Of Jesse Mercer

(OSH, 222)

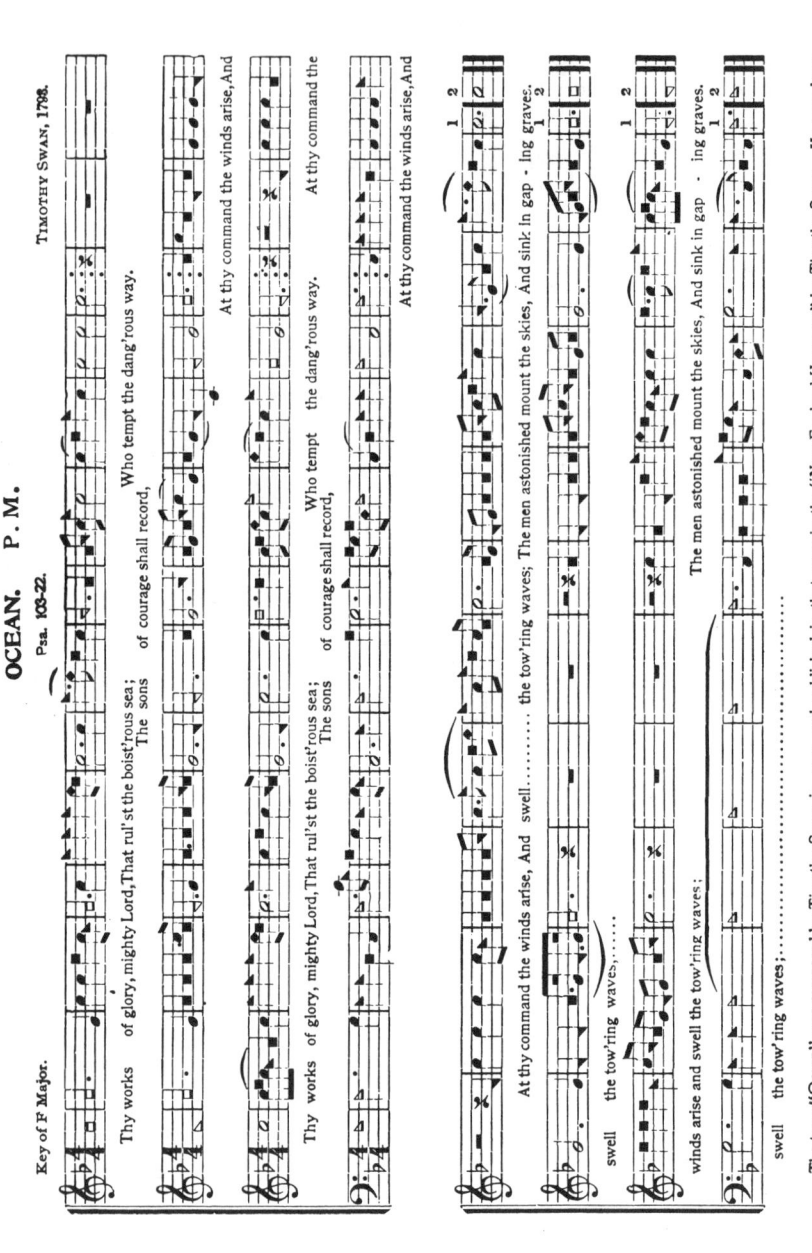

Mercer's *CLUSTER* Hymn 341

OCEAN. P. M.

Psa. 103-22.

Timothy Swan, 1798.

Key of F Major.

Thy works of glory, mighty Lord, That rul'st the boist'rous sea; Who tempt the dang'rous way.
The sons of courage shall record, At thy command the winds arise, And

Thy works of glory, mighty Lord, That rul'st the boist'rous sea; Who tempt the dang'rous way.
The sons of courage shall record, At thy command the winds arise, And

At thy command the winds arise, And swell......... the tow'ring waves; The men astonished mount the skies, And sink in gap - ing graves.
swell the tow'ring waves,......

At thy command the winds arise, Who tempt the dang'rous way. The men astonished mount the skies, And sink in gap - ing graves.
winds arise and swell the tow'ring waves;
swell the tow'ring waves;............

The tune "Ocean" was composed by Timothy Swan in 1793, and published in that year in the "New England Harmony" by Timothy Swan. He was born 1760 at Sheffield, Conn. See other remarks about him in different sketches in this book. Tune has appeared in different books.

A Sample Of Tunes For *The Cluster* 189

190   *The Cluster* Of Jesse Mercer

(OSH, 30)   Mercer's CLUSTER Hymn 639

PROSPECT. L. M.

"Blessed is the dead who die in the Lord."—REV. 14:13.

ISAAC WATTS, 1707. Key of C Major.   GRAHAM.

1. Why should we start and fear to die? What tim'rous worms we mortals are! Death is the gate to end-less joy, And yet we dread to en-ter there.

2. The pains, the groans, the dying strife, Fright our approaching souls away; And we shrink back a-gain to life, Fond of our pris-on and our day.

3. O if my Lord would come and meet, My soul would stretch her wings in haste, Fly fearless through death's iron gate, Nor feel the terrors as she passed.

4. Je-sus can make a dy-ing bed Feel soft as down-y pil-lows are, While on His breast I lean my head, And breathe my life out sweetly there.

The original title to this hymn was "Christ's Presence Makes Death Easy." Full sketch of Dr. Watts is given in other parts of this book. He was born in 1674, and died in 1748. He was one of the greatest ministers in the world. "Prospect" is one of the older melodies. It appears in "Southern Harmony," by Walker, page 92. In 1835; also "Christian Harmony," and many other books.

Copyright, 1909, by J. S. James.

A Sample Of Tunes For *The Cluster* 191

(OSH, 214)

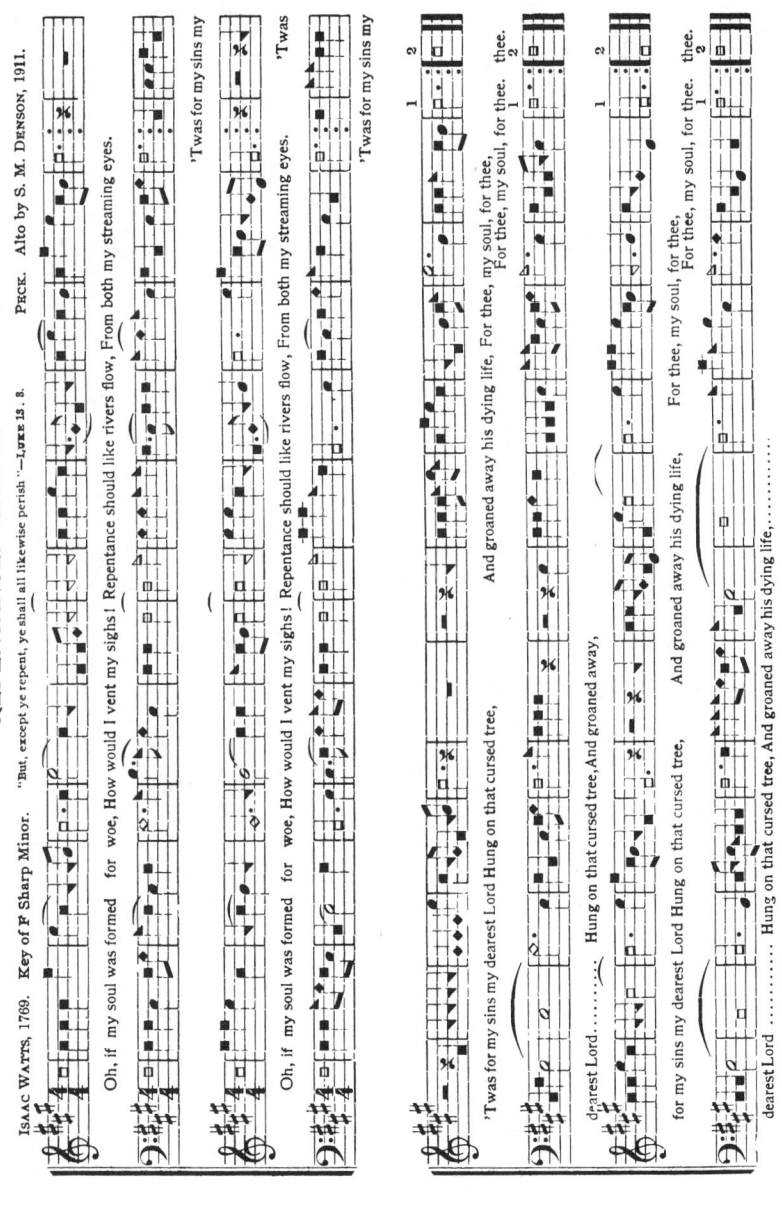

Mercer's *CLUSTER* Hymn 92

REPENTANCE. C. M. D.

Isaac Watts, 1769. Key of F Sharp Minor. "But, except ye repent, ye shall all likewise perish."—Luke 13. 3. Peck. Alto by S. M. Denson, 1911.

Oh, if my soul was formed for woe, How would I vent my sighs! Repentance should like rivers flow, From both my streaming eyes. 'Twas for my sins my dearest Lord Hung on that cursed tree, And groaned away his dying life, For thee, my soul, for thee.

192   *The Cluster* Of Jesse Mercer

(OSH, 107)   Mercer's *CLUSTER* Hymn 490

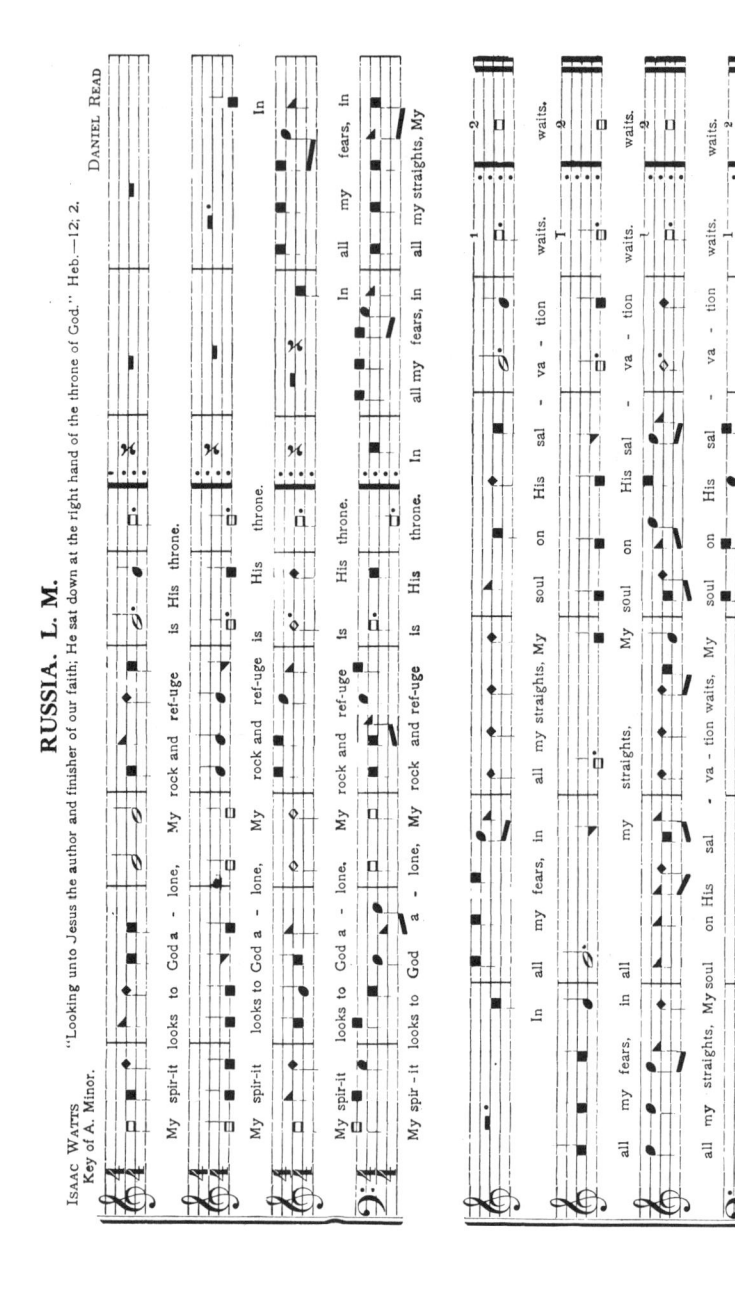

RUSSIA. L. M.

ISAAC WATTS   "Looking unto Jesus the author and finisher of our faith; He sat down at the right hand of the throne of God.". Heb.—12; 2.
Key of A. Minor.   DANIEL READ

My spir-it looks to God a - lone, My rock and ref-uge is His throne. In all my fears, in all my straights, My soul on His sal - va - tion waits.

The above tune was once in the Sacred Harp page 274, and was removed and "Golden Harp and Baldwin," inserted in its place, see page 274. It was first published in Daniel Reeds book, The Columbian Harmony, 1793. See history of Daniel Reed under tune **W**indham page 38. several of his tunes appear in these pages.

A Sample Of Tunes For *The Cluster* 193

(OSH, 186)

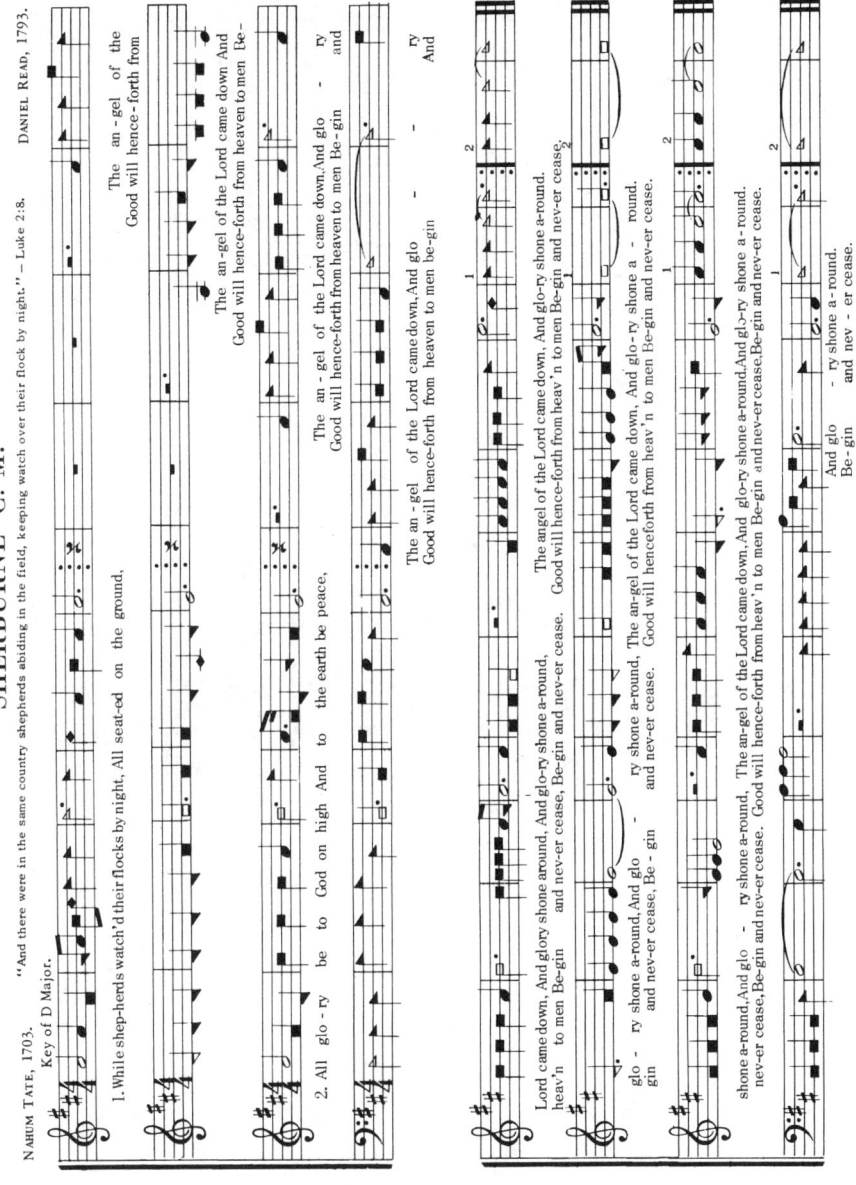

Mercer's *CLUSTER* Hymn 110

SHERBURNE C. M.

Nahum Tate, 1703. "And there were in the same country shepherds abiding in the field, keeping watch over their flock by night." – Luke 2:8. Daniel Read, 1793.

Key of D Major.

194   The *Cluster* Of Jesse Mercer

Mercer's *CLUSTER* Hymn 474

SWEET AFFLICTION. 8s, 7s.

"In the world ye shall have tribulation, but be of good cheer, I have overcome the world."—JOHN 16:33.

(OSH, 145)

SAMUEL PEARCE   Key of F.   JOHN J. ROSSEAU, 1752. Alto S. M. DENSON.

1. In the floods of trib-u-la-tion, While the bil-lows o'er me roll,
Je-sus whispers con-so-la-tion, And sup-ports my faint-ing soul,
Hal-le-lu-jah, Hal-le-lu-jah, Hal-le-lu-jah, Hal-le-lu-jah, praise the Lord.

2. Wear-ing there a weight of glo-ry, Still the path I'll ne'er for-get,
But ex-ult-ing cry it led me To my bless-ed Sav-iour's feet.
Hal-le-lu-jah, Hal-le-lu-jah, Hal-le-lu-jah, Hal-le-lu-jah, praise the Lord.

A Sample Of Tunes For *The Cluster* 195

(OSH, 160)

Mercer's *CLUSTER* Hymn 164

WAR DEPARTMENT. 11s.

Num. 14-8.

Mercer's Cluster   Key of E Minor.

No more shall the sound of the war-whoop be heard,
The ambush and slaughter no longer be feared,
The tomahawk, buried, shall rest in the ground,
And peace and good-will to the nations abound.

The above song was composed, it is believed, soon after one of the wars with the Indians. The words indicate this. The tune is supposed to have been composed about 1835, but the author of the tune is not given in any of the books so far as we can find. It was first published in the "Southern Harmony," by William Walker, 1835, see page 94. Nothing further is known of the tune and words. See "Social Harp," by McCurry, 1853, page 167.

196   *The Cluster* Of Jesse Mercer

(OSH, 38)   Mercer's *CLUSTER* Hymn 220

WINDHAM. L. M.

"Wide is the gate, broad is the way that leadeth to destruction. Straight is the gate, narrow is the way that leadeth unto life."—MATT. 7:13,14.

ISAAC WATT, 1709. Key of E♭ Minor.   DANIEL READ 1785.

1. Broad is the road that leads to death And thou-sands walk to-geth-er there; But wisdom shows a nar-row path, With here and there a trav-'ler.
2. "De-ny thy-self, and take thy cross," Is the Re-deem-er's great command; Na-ture must count her gold but dross, If she would gain this heav'nly land.
3. The fear-ful soul that tires and faints, And walks the ways of God no more, Is but es-teem-ed al-most a saint, And makes his own destruc-tion sure.
4. Lord, let not all my hopes be vain, Cre-ate my heart en-tire-ly new, Which hy-po-crites could ne'er at-tain, Which false apostates nev-er knew.

Daniel Read, the author of the music, was born 1757. He published the "American Song Book," in 1785, "Columbia Harmony," 1793. He also compiled and published several other selections. He died at New Haven, Conn., 1836. The music first appeared in the "American Singing Book." He is the author of a number of standard tunes, "Sherburn," "Russia," "Stafford," and other psalmodies. He is an American composer.

A Sample Of Tunes For *The Cluster* 197

CHAPTER FIVE

A GENERAL INDEX OF *THE CLUSTER*

A GENERAL INDEX OF
CLUSTER HYMNS
LISTED ALPHABETICALLY

To this basic indexing of "first lines" are added two additional indexes: (1) fourteen hymns which Mercer himself added in later editions, and (2) seventeen hymns found in the 1810 *Cluster* edition, but which Mercer discarded and did not use in later editions. The total number of hymns in this general index is, therefore, 708. The reader is reminded that meter indications are to be found by consulting the earlier section where hymn texts are given (or omitted).

The hymn number is given in Arabic numerals, for the convenience of modern readers, instead of the Roman numerals as found in the *Cluster* editions. It is well to note that page numbers, which Mercer employed in his indexes, have been dropped.

One hundred and sixty-six of the hymns that Jesse Mercer selected for the 1810 edition of *The Cluster* were carried over into later editions; and the use of the asterisk beside the first line of each hymn indicates this title is to be found in the 1810 edition. Seventeen hymns from the 1810 edition were discarded by Mercer.

A.

	Hymn Numbers
A debtor to mercy alone	591
* A fulness resides in *Jesus* our head	606
A heavenly flame creates my song	293
A sight of Jesus with his eyes	33
* A story most lovely I'll tell	70
A thousand promises are wrote	503
* A union rare divinely shines	308
* A worldling spent each day	193
Afflicted saint, to Christ draw near	611
Again, indulgent Lord, return	454
* Ah! lovely appearance of death	616
Ah, wretched souls, who strive in vain	421
Ah! wretched, vile, ungrateful heart	552
All glory to God in the sky	158
* All thanks be to God	165
Almighty Maker, God!	513
Aloud we sing the wond'rous grace	27
Altho' the righteous man may fall	610
Am I a soldier of the cross	318
Amazing grace! how sweet the sound	23

Amid the dark, the dismal scene	502
* And am I born to die	467
And art thou with us, gracious Lord	386
And have I, Christ, no love for thee	314
And is thy lovely shadow fled?	624
And let this feeble body fail	648
And must I part with all I have	411
And will th' eternal King	417
Approach, my soul, the mercy-seat	384
"Arise and be baptiz'd"	263
* Arise, and shine, O Zion fair	651
* As near to Calvary I pass	57
As on the cross the Saviour hung	37
Ascend thy throne, Almighty King	169
Astonish'd and distress'd	480
At anchor laid, remote from home	400
At thy command, our dearest Lord	89
Awake, awake, arise	109
Awake my heart, arise my tongue	594
Awake my soul in joyful lays	36
Awake, my tongue, thy tribute bring	359
* Awak'd by Sinai's awful sound	223
* Away my unbelieving fear	472

B.

Backsliders, who your mis'ry feel	553
Begin, my soul, thy morning song	514
* Begone, unbelief, my Saviour is near	598
Behold a sinner, dearest Lord	240
Behold, the blind their sight receive	98

Behold th' expected time draws near	178
Behold the gift of God	100
Behold the gloomy vale	634
Behold the love, the gen'rous love	94
Behold the perfect man	129
Behold the Saviour at thy door	214
Behold the Saviour of mankind	79
* Behold the war-like trumpets blow	140
Beset with snares on every hand	416
Beside the gospel pool	241
* Blessed are the sons of God	604
Bless'd Jesus! source of grace divine	398
Blest Jesus, when my soaring thoughts	330
Blow ye the trumpet, blow	197
Brethren, while we sojourn here	496
* Bright scenes of glory strike my sense	269
Broad is the road that leads to death	220
* By whom was David taught	280

end B.

C.

* Children of the heav'nly King	307
Christ, as our great physician, heals	143
* Christ is the eternal rock	115
Christ is the way to heav'nly bliss	135
Christ plans the temple of the Lord	145
* Come all who fear the Lord, and see	224
Come all ye chosen saints of God	14
* Come all ye Christian soldiers	560

A General Index Of *The Cluster*

* Come all ye poor sinners who from Adam came   185
* Come all ye skillful souls in weeping   69
* Come all ye weary Pilgrims   227
* Come Christians, be wise   556

Come Christians dear, of every name   647

Come, dearest Lord, and bless this day   517

Come dearest Lord, who reigns above   48

* Come ev'ry pious heart   119
* Come friends and relations, let's join heart in hand   186

Come guilty souls, and flee away   208

Come, Holy Spirit, come (with energy divine)   399

Come Holy Spirit, come (let thy bright beams arise)   458

* Come humble sinner, in whose breast   235-A

Come humble souls, ye mourners, come   504

* Come in this cold declining day   657

Come let our hearts and voices join   329

Come, let us join in sweet accord   518

Come, let us join our cheerful songs   340

Come, let us lift our voices high   531

* Come, my soul, and let us try   497

Come, O my soul, look up and see   629

* Come saints and sinners hear me tell   267
* Come sinners all, attend the call   191
* Come sinners attend, and make no delay   182

Come, thou desire of all thy saints   326

* Come thou fount of ev'ry blessing   349
* Come, ye Christians, sing the praises   562
* Come ye sinners, poor and wretched   192

Come, ye that love the Saviour's name   150

Come ye weary souls opprest   218

* Come ye who know the Lord indeed   559
* Commit thou all thy griefs   571

Convinc'd as a sinner, to Jesus I come   125

D.

* Day of Judgment, day of wonders   653
* Dear Jesus here comes   226

Dear Jesus, when, when shall it be   487

Dear Lord, and will thy pard'ning love   258

Dear Lord, my best desires fulfil   379

Dear Lord! though bitter is the cup   388

Dear refuge of my weary soul   443

Dear Saviour, will thy pard'ning love   362

Death and the grave are doleful themes   622

Death cannot make our souls afraid   638

Descend, celestial Dove   256

Despise me not, my carnal friends   261

Did Christ o'er sinners weep   141

Didst thou, dear Jesus, suffer shame   377

Diffuse thy beams, and teach my heart   43

Do not I love thee, O my Lord   289

Do we not know that solemn word   266

Dost thou my profit seek   392

Dread Sov'reign, let my ev'ning song   537

* Dress'd uniform the soldiers are   589

end D.

E.

Early, my God, without delay	520
* Earth has engross'd my love too long	73
Election! 'tis a joyful sound	45
Encompass'd with clouds of distress	475
* Encourag'd by thy word	492
Eternal God, I bless thy name	371
Eternal God, now smile on those	264
Eternal life! how sweet the sound	334
Eternal Spirit! we confess	41
Eternity is just at hand	372
Exert thy pow'r, thy rights maintain	176
Expand my soul, arise and sing	44

end E.

F.

Fain would my soul with wonder trace	299
Far beyond all comprehension	26
Farewell, dear Friends, I must be gone	501
* Farewell, my brethren in the Lord	171
Father divine, thy piercing eye	420
* Father of light, from whom proceeds	385
Father, whate'er of earthly bliss	419
Fatigu'd in spirit, and void of merit	672
Firmly I stand on Zion's hill	365
For a season call'd to part	441
Forbear, my friends, forbear, and ask no more	621
Forever shall my fainting soul	550
Frequent the day of God returns	541
From realms where the day her first dawning extends	164
* From whence this fear and unbelief	61

end F.

G.

* Gird thy loins up, Christian soldier	565
Give me thy Spirit, O my God	404
Give thanks to God, invoke his name	675
* Give to the winds thy fears	572
* Glorious things of thee are spoken	287
Glory to thee, my God, this night	536
Go, Missionaries, and proclaim	167
God hath bereav'd me of my child	628
God is our refuge in distress	508
God moves in a mysterious way	588
God of my life, my morning song	515
God of the morning, at whose voice	512
God with us! O glorious name	147
Good morning, brother Pilgrim	288
Grace! 'tis a charming sound	49
Gracious Father, gracious Lord	450
Great God of providence! thy ways	50
* Great God of wonders! all thy ways	8
Great God, though from myself conceal'd	247
Great God! to thee I make	505
Great God, to thee my ev'ning song	535
Great God, we now surround thy board	83
Great high priest, we view thee stooping	71

A General Index Of *The Cluster*

Great Spirit of immortal love 433
Great Sun of righteousness,
  arise 457
Guide me, O thou great
  Jehovah 395

end G.

H.

Hail, Father! hail, eternal
  Son! 464
* Hail! God the Father, eternal
  light 112
Hail, mighty Jesus, how divine 31
Hail! my ever blessed Jesus 20
Hail sacred Saviour! Prince of
  light 255
* Hail sov'reign *love* which first
  began 228
Hail, the day that sees him
  rise 160
Hail to the Lamb! that in
  triumph advances 159
Hail, ye sighing sons of
  sorrow 674
Hark! from the tombs a doleful
  sound 643
* Hark how the gospel-trumpet
  sounds! 564
* Hark, my soul! It is the
  Lord 596
Hark, the glad sound, the
  Saviour comes 296
* Hark! the voice of love and
  mercy 65
Hark! 'tis our heav'nly leader's
  voice 215
Hark! 'tis the Saviour's voice I
  hear 157
He lives, the great Redeemer
  lives 149
Hear what the voice from heav'n
  proclaims 637
High on his Father's royal
  seat 148
High on a throne my Lord doth
  sit 80
* Hosannah to Jesus! my soul's
  fill'd with praises 282

How bless'd is ev'ry child of
  grace 302
How bright is the prospect
  the saint has in view 608
How condescending and how
  kind 87
* How firm a foundation 566
How great, how terrible that
  God 661
How happy are the souls
  above 631
* How happy's every child of
  grace 300
* How happy is the Pilgrim's
  lot 276
How hard and rugged is the
  way 489
How long and tedious are the
  days 479
How long, thou faithful God,
  shall I 245
How lost was my condition 124
How lovely, how divinely
  sweet 354
How much the hearts of those
  revive 335
How precious is the book
  divine 310
How sad and awful is my
  state 485
* How shall I my Saviour set
  forth 121
How shall the sons of men
  appear 210
How sweet and awful is the
  place 88
How sweet, how heav'nly is the
  sight 585
* How tedious and tasteless the
  hours 347
How vast the benefits divine 47
* Humble souls who seek
  salvation 253
Hungry, and faint, and poor 394

end H.

I.

* I am a stranger here below 468
I am, saith Christ, *the Way* 132

I cannot bear thine absence, Lord	439
* I have no leisure to bestow	665
* "I know that my Redeemer lives,"	126
I lift my soul to God	382
* I now consider, O my God	189
* I set myself against the Lord	231
I sing my Saviour's wond'rous death	77
I thirst, but not as once I did	431
I walk'd abroad one morning fair	234
I would, but cannot sing	488
* If dust and ashes might presume	348
* If ever it could come to pass	599
If, Lord, in thy fair book of life	613
If secret fraud should dwell	412
* If to Jesus for relief	597
* I'll praise my Maker while I've breath	13
* I'll sing my Saviour's grace	532
* I'm tir'd of visits, modes and forms	60
In all my Lord's appointed ways	262
In Christ alone all fulness dwells	336
In darkest hours and greatest grief	478
In the floods of tribulation	474
* In Jordan's tide the Baptist stands	252
In one harmonious cheerful song	333
In Sharon's lovely Rose	138
In sin's howling waste, my poor soul was forlorn	233
In songs of sublime adoration and praise	2
* In th' house of King David, a fountain did spring	184
In the morning let us pray	529
In the morning of the day	530
* In thunder once Jehovah spoke	194
In thy great name, O Lord, we come	449
In vain Apollo's silver tongue	51
Indulgent God! how kind	17
Infinite excellence is thine	328
Infinite grace! and can it be	42
* Innumerable foes	573
Inquiring souls who long to find	211
Inspire our souls, thou heavenly Dove	146
Is any thing too hard for God?	587
Is Jesus mine! I'm now prepar'd	142
Is this my Jesus, this my God	76
* Israel in ancient days	58
I've found the pearl of greatest price	137

end I.

J.

Jehovah is a God of might	358
Jehovah's grace, how full, how free	34
* Jerusalem, my happy home	284
* Jesus! and shall it ever be	127
* Jesus, at thy command	383
Jesus, dear name, how sweet it sounds!	592
* Jesus drinks the bitter cup	59
Jesus, engrave it on my heart	153
Jesus for us with nails was torn	86
* Jesus how precious is thy name	122
Jesus, I sing thy matchless grace	130
Jesus, immutably the same	155
Jesus! in thy transporting name	103
Jesus is all I wish or want	154
* Jesus is our great salvation	605

* Jesus, let thy pitying eye	548
Jesus, lover of my soul	351
Jesus, my all, to heaven is gone	139
Jesus, my Lord, my soul's delight	361
Jesus, our soul's delightful choice	391
Jesus' precious name excels	200
Jesus, since thou art still to-day	131
Jesus, the mighty Saviour, lives	623
Jesus, thou art the sinner's friend	438
* Jesus, thy blood and righteousness	590
Jesus, to multitudes unknown	355
Jesus, what shall I do to show	297

end J.

K.

Kindred in Christ, for his dear sake	291
King of Salem, bless my soul	357

end K.

L.

Laid by Jehovah's mighty hands	134
* Legion was my name by nature	5
Let all our tongues be one	93
Let ev'ry creature join	343
Let not your hearts within you grieve	499
* Let others boast their ancient line	603
Let sinners take their course	526
* Let the world their virtue boast	11
* Let us all with grateful praises	108
* Let us ask th' important question	570
Let us awake our joys	152
* Listed into the cause of sin	113
Lo, he comes array'd in vengeance	663
* Lo! he comes with clouds descending	654
Lo, what a glorious sight appears	344
Long ere the sun began his days	54
* Long have I view'd, long have I tho't	493
Look from on high, great God, and see	424
Look up my soul, with cheerful eye	360
Lord at thy feet in dust I lie	248
Lord, at thy table I behold	104
Lord, before we leave thy temple	461
Lord, didst thou die, but not for me?	500
Lord, dismiss us with thy blessing	465
Lord, dost thou say, "ask what thou wilt?"	444
Lord God, omnipotent to bless	428
Lord, hast thou call'd me by thy grace	380
Lord, hear a burden'd sinner mourn	460
Lord, how delightful 'tis to see	540
Lord, how divine thy comforts are	78
Lord, how large thy bounties are	217
Lord, I commit my soul to thee—	633
Lord, if thou thy grace impart	387
Lord, in the morning thou shalt hear	522
Lord, in thy courts we now appear	448

Lord! let me see thy beauteous face	418	M.	
Lord, must I die? O let me die	625	Many woes had Christ endur'd	62
Lord, must thy gospel fly away?	551	May the grace of Christ, our Saviour	463
Lord, send thy word, and let it fly	180	Mercer, Rev. Silas, Character, Death	677
Lord, shall we part with gold for dross	246	"Mercy, O thou Son of David,"	352
Lord, thou hast made me know thy ways!	609	Methinks the last great day is come	662
Lord, thou hast won, at length I yield	25	Mighty God! while angels bless thee	283
Lord, thou wilt hear me when I pray	538	Mixtures of joy and sorrow	484
Lord, to this fountain we repair	260	Mortals awake, with angels join	106
Lord, 'twas a time of wond'rous love	312	My brethren, and my sisters dear	645
Lord, vouchsafe to us thy blessing	466	My Father God! and may these lips	337
Lord, we adore thy matchless ways	32	My God, accept my early vows	524
Lord, we adore thy vast designs	389	My God!-how cheerful is the sound!	612
Lord, we come before thee now	425	My God, how endless is thy love!	525
Lord, what a barren heart is mine	406	* My God, my heart with love inflame	346
Lord, what a thoughtless wretch was I	221	My God, the cov'nant of thy love	22
Lord, what a wretched land is this	481	My grace so weak, my sin so strong	401
Lord, when I count thy mercies o'er	539	* My gracious Redeemer I love	301
Lord, when together here we meet	456	My heart and my tongue shall unite in the praise	305
Lord, when we cast our eyes abroad	179	* My Lord, my Saviour died	63
Lord! with a griev'd and aching heart	239	My rising soul with strong desires	409
* Love divine, all loves excelling	350	My Saviour, let me hear thy voice	408
Love divine, how sweet the sound	28	My sisters, hear, and I'll relate	646
		My sorrows like a flood	238
end L.		* My soul doth magnify the Lord	270
		* My soul forever stand and wonder	183

My soul now arise, my passions take wing	574	O for a glance of heav'nly day	459
* My soul with Zion claims salvation	546	O for an overcoming faith	636
* My span of life will soon be done	494	O God, my Sun, thy blissful rays	432
My spirit looks to God alone	490	* O God of all grace	67
* My thoughts are inditing of some solemn theme	549	* O give me, Lord, my sins to mourn	236
My waking dreams are best conceal'd	670	* O glorious hope of perfect love	275
		* O great Jehovah, God of love!	547
N.		* O how I have long'd for the coming of God	277
Nightly to the list'ning ear	542	* O how shall I myself assure	471
* No prophet, no dreamer of dreams	558	O Lord, behold thy people bow	403
Not unto us, but thee alone	316	O Lord, my God! whose sovereign love	407
Now for a hymn of praise to God	18	O Lord, thy mourning people bow	402
Now I have found the ground wherein	15	* O may I worthy prove to see	268
Now in the heat of youthful blood	222	* O my distrustful heart	601
Now in thy praise, eternal King	369	* O my Lord, what must I do	9
Now is th' accepted time	216	O my soul, what means this sadness?	476
Now let our voices join	321	* O now, my dear brethren	172
Now, Lord, the heav'nly seed is sown	427	O save me, save me! O my God	405
Now may the God of peace and love	429	* O Sir, we would see Jesus	114
* Now may the Lord reveal his face	1	* O tell me no more of this world's vain store	286
Now the gloomy night comes on	543	O the sweet love of Jesus	304
Now, while the gospel net is cast	426	O thou, at whose almighty word	447
		O thou eternal glorious Lord	373
O.		O thou, from whom all goodness flows	455
* O brethren we are going on	271	* O thou, in whose presence my soul takes delight	281
O could I speak the matchless worth	156	* O 'tis a glorious mystery	272
O for a closer walk with God	381	O were my heart but form'd for wo,	453
		O what amazing words of grace	207

* O when shall I see Jesus	491
O with what pleasure we behold	436
* O ye immortal throng	107
O Zion afflicted with wave upon wave	555
O'er the gloomy hills of darkness	162
Oh, if my soul was form'd for woe	92
Oh! let me run the Christian race	415
Oh, may my heart, by grace renew'd	413
* Oh! once I had a glorious view	544
On Jordan's stormy banks I stand	294
On the brink of fi'ry ruin	16
Once more, my soul, the rising day	523
Once on a time a paper kite	670
One there is above all others	117
* Our souls by love together knit	273

P.

Peace, by his cross, hath Jesus made	581
Pity a helpless sinner, Lord	237
* Poor mourning soul! in deep distress	225
Poor, weak, and worthless tho' I am	311
Praise to thy name, eternal God	363
Pray'r makes the darken'd cloud withdraw	396
Pray'r was appointed to convey	397
Precious Bible! what a treasure	306
Prepare me, gracious God	437
Proud Babylon yet waits her doom	166

Q.

* Quite weary, near to faint	243

R.

Ransom'd sinners, sing the praises	279
* Rejoice the Lord is King	120
Rejoice, ye nations of the world	175
Religion's form is vain	451
Remember, Lord, our mortal state	641
Renew'd by grace, we love the word	435
* Resolving thus, I entered in	235-B
Rise, O my soul, pursue the path	374
* Rock of ages, shelter me	123

S.

Salvation, through our dying God	313
Saviour of men, and Lord of love	295
* Saviour, visit thy plantation	545
Saw ye my Saviour? saw ye my Saviour?	105
Scarce in this cold declining day	580
See a poor sinner, dearest Lord	506
See how the mounting sun	511
See, on the mount of Calvary	97
See! see in the east a new glory ascends	163
See the fountain open'd wide	181
Self-righteous souls on works rely	38
Shall mortals aim at themes so great	338
Shepherds! rejoice, lift up your eyes	111
Shew pity, Lord; O Lord forgive;	250
Sin, in ten thousand treach'rous ways	440
Sin, like a raging fever, reigns	202
Sinful, and blind, and poor,	244

Sing the dear Saviour's glorious fame	144	The blessed Spirit, like the wind	40
Sinner, O why so thoughtless grown?	219	The blest memorials of thy grief	84
Sinners, awake to know	206	The busy scene of life is clos'd	635
Sinners, away to Sinai fly	593	The cause that is for me too hard	367
Sinners, this solemn truth regard	212	The day is past and gone	533
Sinners, will you scorn the message	199	The day of the Lord—the day of salvation!	664
Sinners, you are now addressed	198	The finest flow'r that ever blow'd	35
Sitting around our Father's board	90	The food on which thy children live	339
Some author (no great matter who)	671	* The fountain of Christ	64
* Sons we are, through God's election	602	The glorious plan of man's Redemption	196
Sov'reign grace has pow'r alone	29	* The great tremendous day's approaching	649
Sov'reign grace o'er sin abounding	19	The intercession of our Lord	586
Sov'reign of worlds display thy pow'r	168	The King of heaven his table spreads	101
Stoop down my thoughts, that us'd to rise	644	The Lord, descending from above	24
* Stop poor sinner, stop and think	188	* The Lord into his garden's come	345
* Strange and mysterious is my life	470	* The Lord is my protector	495
Strange that so much of heaven and hell	483	* The Lord is my Shepherd	575
Submissive to thy will, my God	378	* The Lord my pasture shall prepare	576
* Supported by thy word	568	The Lord of Sabbaths let us praise	519
Sweet is the work, my God, my King	521	The Lord, the God of glory reigns	322
* Sweet rivers of redeeming love	285	The Lord, who truly knows	446
Sweet singers of Israel, begin your sweet strains	278	The peace which God alone reveals	430
Sweet the moments, rich in blessing	74	* The reason Christians persevere	607
		* The Saviour comes to set you free	595

T.

Temptations, trials, doubts, and fears	390	The Saviour meets his flock to-day	434
* That glorious day is drawing nigh	161	The Saviour! O what endless charms	356
* The Bible is justly esteem'd	118	* The sinner that truly believes	600
		* The Son of man they did betray	68

The soul that's truly born of God	56	Thus far the Lord hath led me on	534
The table spread, my soul there spies	72	* Thus it became the Prince of grace	254
The time is short! the season near	626	Thus saith the Shepherd of the sheep	327
* The toiling ocean groans, the stars grow pale	666	Thus was the great Redeemer plung'd	259
The Tree of Life my soul hath seen	133	Thy goodness, Lord, our souls confess	323
The wond'rous love of Jesus	303	* Thy mercy, my God, is the theme of my song	7
Thee we adore eternal name!	642	Thy people, Lord, have ever found	498
* Thee will I love, my strength, my tower	10	Thy people, Lord, who trust thy word	177
There is a God, all nature speaks	516	Thy presence, everlasting God	442
There is a period known to God	46	Thy promise, Lord, and thy command	393
This is the feast of heav'nly wine	91	Thy way O God, is in the sea	21
This is the field, the world below	660	Thy ways, O God, with wise design	376
This morning let my praise arise	510	Thy works of glory, mighty Lord	341
Thou dear Redeemer, dying Lamb	95	* 'Tis a point I long to know	469
* Thou God of glorious majesty!	655	* 'Tis finish'd! 'tis done! the spirit is fled	617
Thou God of Jabez, hear	452	'Tis life to know the dying Lamb	136
Thou lovely source of true delight	290	'Tis my happiness below	477
* Thou Shepherd of Israel and mine	577	'Tis not the nat'ral birth of man	39
Thou, who for sinners once was slain	99	'Tis religion that can give	315
Tho' I am poor and needy too	445	To distant lands thy Gospel send	170
* Though the morn may be serene	569	To God who lives and reigns on high	370
* Though troubles assail, and dangers affright	561	To him who on the fatal tree	82
Thro' all the changing scenes of life	509	To keep the lamp alive	52
Thro' the wisdom of the skies	527	To our Redeemer's glorious name	331
Through all the downward tracts of time	366	To thee, my Shepherd and my Lord	332
Through all the world below	667	To thee our wants are known	462

A General Index Of *The Cluster*

To-day, if you will hear his voice — 204
To-day the saint with time-things has to do — 668
To-day the sinners state is much admir'd — 669
* Transporting news, the Saviour's come — 4
'Twas not to make Jehovah's love — 324
'Twas on that dark, that doleful night — 85
'Twas the commission of our Lord — 265

U.

* Unclean! unclean! and full of sin — 232
Unto thine altar, Lord — 422
Up! haste to Calvary — 81
Upward I lift mine eyes — 507

V.

* Vain, delusive world, adieu — 66
Vital spark of heav'nly flame — 627

W.

* Wand'ring pilgrims, mourning Christians — 563
Warm was his heart, his faith was strong — 96
We seek a rest beyond the skies — 320
Welcome, sweet day of rest — 342
Welcome, thou well-belov'd of God — 298
* Were oceans, rivers, floods, and lakes — 3
* What contradictions meet — 173
What makes mistaken men afraid — 53
What poor despised company — 482
* What solemn signal's that which daunts my courage — 619
* What think you of Christ? is the test, — 116
What wond'rous love is this — 673
* When Christ the Lord was here below — 579
When converts first begin to sing — 292
When death appears before my sight — 632
When, descending from the sky — 652
When faith presents the Saviour's death — 364
When first the God of boundless grace — 55
When from the precepts to the cross — 242
When heaven does grant at certain times — 486
When in his earthly courts we view — 151
When in the cloud, with colours fair — 582
When Jesus for his people died — 309
When marshall'd on the nightly plain — 676
* When my Saviour, my Shepherd, is near — 578
When Noah, with his favour'd few — 615
When Paul was parted from his friends — 174
When pity prompts me to look round — 205
When the chosen tribes debated — 75
* When the fierce north-wind with his airy forces — 659
When the wounded spirit hears — 6
* When Thou my rightesous Judge shall shall come — 656
Where from thy Spirit shall I stretch — 325
"Where two or three with sweet accord — 423

* While angels strike their tuneful strings	195
While carnal men with all thy might	414
While here on earth I'm call'd to stay	30
While poets, in exalted strains of verse	677
While shepherds watch'd their flocks by night	110
While sinners, who presume to bear	583
* While sorrows encompass me round	473
Who is the trembling sinner, who	209
Why do we mourn departing friends?	640
Why, mourning soul, why flow these tears?	249
Why, O my soul, these anxious cares?	368
Why, O my soul! why weepest thou?	410
Why should the dread of sinful man	375
Why should vain mortals tremble at the sight of	620
Why should we start, and fear to die?	639
"Why tarriest thou, arise	257
Will God forever cast us off?	554
* With gladness, dear brethren	353
With Israel's God who can compare	319
With morning light let us rejoice	528

Y.

* Ye brethren and sisters	567
Ye burden'd souls to Jesus come	213
* Ye children of God	12
* Ye children of Zion who're bound for the kingdom	274
Ye fleeting charms of earth farewell!	630
Ye little flock, whom Jesus feeds	614
* Ye objects of sense, and enjoyments of time	618
* Ye people who wonder at me and my ways	230
* Ye Pilgrims who often look up for the train	650
* Ye pris'ners of hope	201
Ye saints of ev'ry rank, with joy	317
* Ye scarlet-colour'd sinners, come	190
Ye sin-sick souls draw near	203
* Ye soldiers of Jesus, awake from your sleep	557
Ye virgin souls arise!	658
Ye worlds of light, that roll so near	128
Ye wretched, hungry, starving poor	102
* You captives restor'd and saints of the Lord	251
* Young people all attention give	187
* Young women all I pray draw near	229
Your harps, ye trembling saints	584

FOURTEEN MORE HYMNS IN *THE CLUSTER*
(Added by Mercer but not indexed in earlier editions)

A-12	Afflictions, though they seem severe	(C. M.) 8S./4L.
A-14	Alas, and did my Saviour bleed!	(C. M.) 6S./4L.
A-5	Behold the mountain of the Lord	(C. M.) 6S./4L.
A-9	Behold the throne of grace!	(S. M.) 8S./4L.
A-4	Brightest and best of the sons of the morning!	(11,10.) 5S./4L.
A-8	Come, my soul, thy suit prepare	(7's.) 7S./4L.
A-7	From Greenland's icy mountains	(7.6.) 4S./8L.
A-11	How sweet the name of Jesus sounds	(C. M.) 7S./4L.
A-13	In evil long I took delight	(C. M.) 8S./4L.
A-2	In the sun and moon and stars	(7's.) 4S./4L.
A-6	My shepherd is the living Lord	(C. M.) 5S./4L.
A-3	Sons of men, behold from far	(7's.) 5S./4L.
A-10	Sweet was the time when first I felt	(C. M.) 8S./4L.
A-1	The Lord will come! the earth shall quake	(L. M.) 5S./4L.

SEVENTEEN ADDITIONAL HYMNS FROM THE 1810 *CLUSTER*
(but discarded by Mercer and not carried over into later editions)

The asterisk indicates the 1810 edition. The letter "D" symbolizes "the Duke edition," i.e., the 1810 *CLUSTER*. The hymn number, as indexed according to the 1810 edition, follows the "D" designation. Meter and the number of stanzas and lines follow the "first line" listing.

* D-1,	Hymn 79.	Ah! how dismay'd the gardner sees (8.8.6.8.8.6) 5S./6L.
* D-2,	Hymn 61.	Almighty love inspire our souls with sacred fire (P. M.) 6S./4L.
* D-3,	Hymn 2, Appendix.	But armed with vengeance in terror he comes (P. M.) 6S./4L. Compare with Hymn 281, 1823 edition, to which this was added.
* D-4,	Hymn 104.	Come all ye mourning Pilgrims, dear (C. M.) 10S./8L.
* D-5,	Hymn 135.	Courage! my dear brethren, who trust in the Lord (11's.) 8S./4L.
* D-6,	Hymn 17.	Hosts first rebellious muster'd in the eternal world (13's.) 13S./4L.
* D-7,	Hymn 59.	It grieves me Lord, it grieves me sore (P. M.) 5S./7L.
* D-8,	Hymn 34.	Let Christ the glorious lover, have everlasting praise (13's.) 15S./4L.

* D-9, Hymn 172.	Lo! behold how unexpected (P. M.) 6S./8L.
* D-10, Hymn 175.	O! Christians are you ready now (C. M.) 5S./8L. Compare with Hymn 651, 1823 edition, to which this was added.
* D-11, Hymn 83.	O Christians pray beware of error (9. 8.) 13S./8L.
* D-12, Hymn 7. Appendix	O come my son, and let us take 8.8.10.9 15S./4L.
* D-13, Hymn 101.	Shall *Jesus* descend from the skies (8's.) 9S./4L.
* D-14, Hymn 2.	The voice of free grace cries escape to the mountain Chorused. 12.12.12.12. + 13.12. 5S./4L.
* D-15, Hymn 71,	There is a heaven above with God Chorused. 8.8.8.8. + 8.16. 10S./4L.
* D-16, Hymn 151.	What think you my friends of the preaching of *John*? (11's.) 15S./4L.
* D-17, Hymn 86.	Ye trav'llers to Paradise (7.6.) 8S./8L.

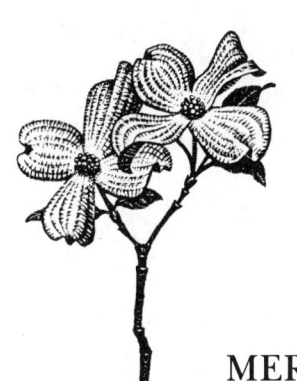

CHAPTER SIX

A LIST OF MERCER'S WRITINGS

(CDM = Mallary's *Memoirs of Elder Jesse Mercer*)

I. *LETTERS.*

- 1803 Aug. 19. Original manuscript (Duke University). To Nancy F. Anthony. Introducing a possible suitor.
- 1805 Mar. 5. Original manuscript (Duke University). To Nancy F. Anthony. Counsel on religious matters.
- 1813 Apr. 24. Original manuscript (Mercer University). To Rev. Thomas Polhill.
- 1815 May 17. "My dear Sir," Religious counsel to a friend, written from Grantsville, Green Co., Ga. CDM: 87–92.
- 1815 n.d. "Dear Madam . . ." On inward anxiety. CDM: 93–95.
- 1819 July 6. To Mrs. T. of (Orange ?) Va, "My dear Sister . . ." Comforting words for times of affliction. CDM: 96–97.
- 1821 Sept. 13. Original manuscript (Mercer University). To Rev. David Benedict of Pawtuckett, R. Island.
- 1825 Nov. 13. To Rev. B. Manly, "My very Dear Brother . . ." On Mercer's illness, cooperation between conventions in Ga. and in S.C., written from Powelton, Ga. CDM: 97–98.
- 1826 Oct. 4. To Dr. Lucius Bolles of Salem, Mass. Concerning the death of Sabrina, Mercer's wife, written from Powelton. CDM: 103.
- 1827 Jan. 14. To "My very dear Sister in the Lord" (at Countyline), written from "Sister L----'s." Concerning death of Sabrina. CDM: 104–105.
- 1827 Sept. 24. Re.: Tinsawattee School (Indians). *The American Baptist Magazine.*
- 1827 Sept. 27. Original manuscript (Mercer University). To Rev. David Benedict.
- 1829 Sept. 19. Re.: dispute over "cogniac brandy," in *Columbian Star and Christian Index.* CDM: 224–226.

1829	Sept. 30. To Mrs. C, "Dear Sister C . . ." On sufferings after deaths in the family, written from Washington, Ga. CDM: 114.
1830	Feb. 21. "Dear Sister C . . ." Concerning the afflictions of Mr. C., written from Washington, Ga. CDM: 115.
1830	Apr. 26. "Dear Sister C . . ." Concerning death of Mr. C., written from Washington, Ga. CDM: 115–116.
1830	Apr. 27. "My dear Brother Bolles . . ." Re.: History-Log-Town," written from Washington, Ga. *The American Baptist Magazine*, June, 1830.
1830	May 3. To Sister C, Dear Sister . . ." Consolations, written from Washington, Ga. CDM: 116–117.
1830	Aug. 2. Original manuscript (Mercer University). To James Carter.
1831	Mar. 11. "My dear Brother . . ." Concerning feasibility of a union educational institution for Ga. and S.C. CDM: 163–164.
1832	Jan. 9. To Sister C. Concerning revivals. CDM: 117.
1832	Apr. To *The Christian Index*. "Brother Brantly . . ." Concerning "Imprisonment of the Missionaries to the Cherokees." CDM: 216–223.
1832	Dec. 26. "Dear Sister S." (Same as "Sister C." after a remarriage). Re.: feelings of woe. CDM: 118.
1832	Dec. 26. To the Rev. Lucius Bolles, Boston, written from Washington. Concerning the rising of a manual labor school (Mercer Inst.) and foreign missions. CDM: 118–120.
1833	June 22. "My dear Sister S." Concerning death of Mr. S., written from Washington, Ga. CDM: 120–121.
1834	n.d. *The Christian Index*. "Dear Sister in the Lord . . ." On doctrinal questions and Brantly's third sermon. CDM: 121–128.
1835	Sept. 25. To President Wayland, Brown University, "Rev. and Dear Sir . . ." Acceptance of doctorate by Mercer. CDM: 113.
1836	(early). *The Christian Index*. "Dear Brother A . . ." Re.: Bible, Tract, Sunday School, and Temperance Societies." CDM: 193–197.
1836	(early). "Dear Brother A . . ." Re.: "new schemes." CDM: 197–203.
1836	Feb. 23. To Mrs. S, "Dear Sister D." (Dolly). Concerning the work of editing *The Christian Index*, written from Washington, Ga. CDM: 130–131.
1836	May 14. "Dear Brother Bolles . . ." On forming a Bible Society and publishing a Burman Bible, written from Washington, Ga. CDM: 131–133.
1836	Sept. 26. "Dear Brother B . . ." Re.: article on Election, written from Washington, Ga. CDM: 271–273.
1838	Apr. 6. "Dear Brother Shuck . . ." (Macao. Concerning mission field in China, written from Washington, Ga. CDM: 204–207.
1838	June 28. "Dear Brother B. . . ." Concerning divisions in the Associations. CDM: 274–275.
1838	Oct. 19. "Dear Brother Bolles . . ." Concerning foreign missions and the *Christian Review*, written from Washington, Ga. CDM: 133–136.
1838	Nov. 14. "My Dear Brother and Longed For . . ." Re.: divisions among Baptists, Missionary Baptists, etc., Washington, Ga. CDM: 275–277.

1838	Dec. 8. "My Dear Brother L..." Concerning personal development after a revival, written from Washington, Ga. CDM: 277–280.
1839	Mar. 27. "Dear Sister Dolly..." Concerning her recent marriage, written from Washington, Ga. CDM: 332–334.
1840	*The Christian Index.* "To the Patrons of the *Christian Index*, signed "Jesse Mercer, the aged." CDM: 335–338.
1840	Oct. 6. "To the Georgia Association, at Bethesda." Mercer's inability to attend the meeting on account of his wife's illness. CDM: 338–351.
1840	Oct. 21. "Dear Brother Bolles..." Re.: Anti-slavery Convention held in N.Y., written from Washington, Ga. CDM: 208–210.
1840	Nov. 19. *The Christian Index*, "Communication." Re. "unkind treatment from Bro. Hartwell," pp. 741–742.
1841	Jan. To an anonymous minister. On Mercer's facing of death. CDM: 372–373.
1841	Feb. 26. "My dear Sister Dolly..." Re.: afflictions of Jesse and Nancy Mercer. CDM: 342–343.
1841	Mar. Cover letter to Bro. Stokes, *The Christian Index.* Re.: "Hear what the Spirit saith unto the Churches." CDM: 355–356.
1841	Apr. 11. To Mr. Heman Lincoln, of Boston, "My very dear Brother Lincoln..." On resigning from the presidency of the American Foreign Mission Board, written from Washington, Ga. CDM: 343–345.
1841	n.d. *The Christian Index.* Communication concerning possible split of American Baptists. CDM: 210–212.
1841	May 23. "My Dear Brother M..." Re.: "the vexed question" (slavery) at Baltimore meeting, written from Washington, Ga. CDM: 346–347.
1841	June 8. "My dear Brother Curtis..." On afflictions, written from Washington, Ga. CDM: 349–351.
1841	June 23. To Mr. Heman Lincoln. On the death of Nancy, his wife, written from Washington, Ga. CDM: 352–353.
1841	July 18. "My dear Brother Sturgis..." On crops, his health, religious activities, etc., written from Penfield, Ga. CDM: 380–384.
1841	July 20. Cover letter to Bro. Stokes, *The Christian Index.* Re.: "Hear what the Spirit saith unto the Churches." CDM: 372.
1841	Aug. 12. Original manuscript (Mercer University). To Col. Absalom Janes.

II. HYMNBOOKS. THE CLUSTER

N.B.   CDM: 85. "Whilst attending the General Convention, in 1817, in Philadelphia, he (Jesse Mercer) published a revised edition of two thousand five hundred copies, and had the copyright secured. Editions were also published in 1820, 1826, and 1835." Also, "This work was first published, unbound, in Augusta (Ga.): subsequently two more editions were published in the same place, which were bound..."

| 1810 | Original "3rd Edition, Improved." Augusta: Hobby & Bunce. Located |

in the Rare Book Room, Duke University. 183 hymn texts, without music. "The Cluster of Spiritual Songs."

1817 n.d. (supra).
1820 n.d. (supra).
1823 Original "3rd Edition Philadelphia: W. W. Woodward. Located in Special Collections, Stetson Library, Mercer University. 664 hymn texts with miscellaneous poems and an appendix of hymn texts, without music. Title: "The Cluster of Spiritual Songs, Divine Hymns, and Sacred Poems."
1826 n.d. (supra).
1828 Original "4th Edition, Revised." Philadelphia: Published for the Proprietor, By J. J. Woodward. Located in the Georgia Room, Wesleyan College. Title: "The Cluster of Spiritual Songs, Divine Hymns, and Sacred Hymns."
1829 Original "5th Edition, Corrected." Philadelphia: Printed for the Proprietor, By J. J. Woodward, 1829. Located in Special Collections, Stetson Library, Mercer University, (in bad repair). Title: "The Cluster of Spiritual Songs, Divine Hymns, and Sacred Poems."
1835 Original "5th Edition Corrected, and Enlarged by an Appendix." Philadelphia: Thomas, Cowperthwaite, and Co. New York: Collins and Brother. Located in Special Collections, Stetson Library, Mercer University. Title: "The Cluster of Spiritual Songs, Divine Hymns, and Sacred Poems."

III. *BOOKS*. (Cf. CDM: 331–332)

1836 *History of the Georgia Association*. Published with W. H. Stokes, Junior Editor of *The Christian Index*.

IV. *SERMONS, CIRCULARS, AND DISCOURSES*. (Cf. CDM: 331–332)

1797 Oct. 14. Introductory Sermon: Isaiah 13: 14 (sic) (Isiah 13:4). "The Lord of hosts mustereth the host of the battle.:
1801 Circular Letter of the Georgia Association.
1806 Circular Letter of the Georgia Association.
1811 Circular Letter of the Georgia Association.
1813 Oct. Introductory Sermon: Genesis 24:56. "Send me away, that I may go to my master."
1816 Circular Letter of the Georgia Association. Christian Duties.
1819 Nov. 24. Milledgeville, Ga. Funeral Oration for Governor William Rabun. Cf. *Georgia Pulpit*, Vol. 1.
1821 Circular Letter of the Georgia Association. "Unity and Dependence of the Churches."
1823 June 26. Powelton. Discourse: 1 Thessalonians 2:3. "Finally, brethren, pray for us, that the word of God may have free course and be glorified even as it is among you."

1825	Read to the Convention at Eatonton. "An Exposition of the first seventeen verses of the 12th chapter of Revelation."
1826	May. Sermon: Matthew 28: 19. Triennial Convention of Foreign Missions at Oliver St. church, New York.
1829	Dissertation on the Prerequisites to Ordination. To the Baptist Convention, Milledgeville.
1830	On the Atonement: Ten letters addressed to Cyrus White. CDM: 285.
1830	"Essay on the Scriptural Meaning and Manner of Ordination." Circular letter in Convention Minutes, pp. 31–38. Dated April 8, 1830, Washington, Ga.
1831	Buckhead. Circular Address of the Baptist State Convention. "On the importance of a more elevated standard of christian morality, among the churches and ministers of our denomination."
1833	"A dissertation on the resemblances and differences between church authority and that of an Association." Read at McDonough in lieu of the Circular Address.
1833	"Essay on the independence of the Churches." (Republished in *The Christian Index*, Dec. 10, 1833.
1833	An essay on the Lord's Supper, being an attempt to run the analogy between it and the Passover."
1834	Aug. 15. "The Prefatory Notice" to Rev. John Sladen's *The Doctrine of Particular Election*.
1834	"Knowledge indispensable to a Minister of God." A discourse before the Baptist Convention of Ga., at Indian Creek Meeting House, Morgan Co., Ga.
1836	Feb. 11-Apr. 21. Five replies to "H". *The Christian Index*, Feb. 11, Feb. 18, Feb. 25, Apr. 7, Apr. 21.
1836	Committee Report for Ministers' Meeting. Covington, Ga. Oct. 29-Nov. 1. By Jesse Mercer, et al.
1836	(or, 1837) "The Nature and Importance of Christian Unity, and the means by which it may be promoted," by Jesse Mercer, C. D. Mallary, and A. T. Holmes. *The Christian Index*, publishers, Jan. 1, 1837 printing.
1837	Review of a certain Committee's Report on Church and Associational Difficulties. *The Primitive Baptist*, No. 12/Vol. 1.
1838	Oct. Eatonton. Discourse on "the importance of union amongst ministers of the gospel." Based on John 17: 11. CDM: 265.
1839	Sermon on the Excellency of the Knowledge of Christ. *Georgia Pulpit*, Vol. 1.
1839	Nov. An essay on "The Cause of Missionary Societies the Cause of God." Cf. *The Christian Index*, Dec. 5, 1839.
1841	Essay on the Forgiveness of Sins.
1841	"Hear what the Spirit saith unto the Churches."
n.d.	Manuscript sermon on Baptism, founded on Acts 10: 47.
n.d.	Manuscript sermon on Missions, from Matt. 28: 19.
N.B.	Numerous editorial comments are made in *The Christian Index* by Jesse Mercer as Senior Editor, 1833–1840, but these are not listed in this bibliography.

HYMNBOOKS FROM MERCER'S TIME

1769 Bayley, Daniel. The American Harmony. Newburyport.
1770 Billings, William. The New-England psalm-singer; or, American chorister. Boston.
1779 Law, Andrew. Select harmony. New Haven.
1782 Jocelin, Simeon and Amos Doolittle. The Chorister's companion. New Haven.
1783 Law, Andrew. A Collection of hymns, for social worship. Cheshire, Conn.
1784 Billings, William. The Massachusetts Harmony. Boston.
1784 Harrison, Ralph. Sacred Harmony. London.
1784 Bayley, Daniel. A Collection of anthems and hymn tunes. Newburyport.
1784 Smith, Joshua. Divine Hymns, or Spiritual Songs, Norwich, N.H.
1785 Swan, Timothy. The Federal Harmony.
1785 Read, Daniel. The American Singing Book. New Haven.
1786 Thomas, Isaiah. Worcester Collection of Sacred Harmony.
1786 Billings, William. The Suffolk Harmony. Boston.
1787 Adgate, Andrew. Select Psalms and Hymns. Philadelphia.
1787 Rippon, John. A Selection of Hymns.
1787 Read, Daniel. Supplement to the American Singing Book. New Haven.
1788 A Selection of Sacred Harmony. Philadelphia.
1789 Adgate, Andrew. Philadelphia Harmony.
1789 Wood, Abraham. Divine Songs. Boston.
1790 Benham, Asahel. Federal Harmony. New Haven.
1790 Philadelphia Collection.
1791 Smith, Joshua. Divine hymns, or spiritual songs for the use of religious assemblies and private Christians. Exeter, N.H.
1791 Holyoke, Samuel. Harmonia Americana. Boston.
1791 Adgate, Andrew. Philadelphia Harmony: Part II.
1792 Jocelin, Simeon. Supplrement to the Chorister's companion.
1792 Holden, Oliver. The American Harmony. Boston.
1793 Holden, Oliver. The Union Harmony. Boston.
1793 Shumway, Nehemiah. The American Harmony. Philadelphia.
1793 Read, Daniel. The Columbian Harmonist. No. 1. New Haven.
1794 Billings, William. The Continental Harmony. Boston.
1794 Law, Andrew. The Christian Harmony. Cheshire, Conn.
1794 A Choice Collection of Hymns and Spiritual Songs. Richmond, Va.
1795 Billings, William. The Republican Harmony.
1795 The Village Harmony. Exeter, N.H.
1798 Benham, Asahel. Social Harmony. New Haven.
1798 Broadus, Andrew. A Selection of hymns and spiritual songs from the best authors.

A List Of Mercer's Writings

1798 (?) The Boston Collection.
1799 Pillsbury, Amos. The United States' Sacred Harmony. Boston.
1799 (?) Goddard, Josiah. A New and beautiful collection of select hymns and spiritual songs. Walpole, N.H.
1800 Edson, Lewis, Jr. Social Harmonist.
1800 Jenks, Stephen. The New England Harmony.
1801 Little, William and William Smith. The Easy Instructor; or, a New Method of Teaching Sacred Harmony.
1804 Ingalls, Jeremiah. Christian Harmony; or, Songster's Companion. Exeter, N.H.
1804 Smith, Joshua. The Christian Harmonist.
1804 Smith, Elias. Hymns.
1805 Jenks, Stephen. The Delights of Harmony.
1805 Mintz, David. Spiritual Song Book.
1807 Adgate, Andrew. Philadelphia Harmony. Philadelphia.
1807 Woodward, Charles. Ecclesia Harmonia. Philadelphia.
1808 Chapin, Nathan and Joseph L. Dickerson. Musical Instructor.
1808 Read, John. The New England Selection.
1808 Boston Collection.
1809 Smith, William. The Churchman's Choral Companion. New York.
1809 Forbes, Azariah. The Delaware Harmony.
1810 Wyeth, John. Repository of Sacred Music. Harrisonburg, Pa.
1812 Dupuy, Starke. Hymns and Spiritual Songs.
1812 Newton, John and William Cowper. O? Hymns in Three Books.
1813 Wyeth, John. Repository of Saved Music. Part Second. Harrisonburg, Pa.
1815 (?) Davisson, Ananias. Kentucky Harmony. Harrisonburg, Va.
1817 Winchell's Watts. (Arrangement of Watts with a supplement).
1818 Jenks, Stephen. Laus Deo, the Harmony of Zion, or the Union Compiler.
1818 Boyd, James M. The Virginia Sacred Musical Repository.
1820 Carden, Allen D. The Missouri Harmony. Cincinnati.
1820 Davisson, Ananias. Supplement to the Kentucky Harmony. Harrisonburg, Va.
1823 Baltimore. Public, Parlour and Cottage Hymns.
1824 Carden, Allen D., et. al. The Western Harmony.
1825 Moore, William. The Columbian Harmony.
1825 Zion's Harp.
1830 Leavitt, Joshua. Christian Lyre. New York.
1831 Carrell, James P. and David S. Clayton. Virginia Harmony. Winchester, Va.
1832 Funk, Joseph. Genuine Church Music. Winchester, Va.
1832 Wakefield, Samuel. The Christian's Harp.
1834 Smith, Henry. Church Harmony.

1835 Walker, William. The Southern Harmony.
1836 Linsley and Davis. Select Hymns.
1837 Caldwell, William. The Union Harmony.
1838 Jackson, John B. Knoxville Harmony. Madisonville and Pumpkintown.

Three sources have been invaluable for this selection: (1) George P. Jackson, Spiritual Folk-Songs of Early America (New York: J. J. Augustin, 1937); (2) Irving Lowens, Music and Musicians in Early America (New York: W. W. Norton and Co., 1964); and (3) Donald L. Hixon, Music in Early America: A Bibliography of Music in Evans, (Metuchen, N.J. The Scarecrow Press, Inc., 1970). It is to be noted above that the selection of hymnbooks is almost totally limited to American printings and compilations and that the time span coincides with the life of Jesse Mercer, 1769–1841.

FOOTNOTES

1. *The Columbian Star*, August 8, 1829, p. 93.
2. Spright Dowell, *A History of Mercer University, 1833–1953* (Macon: Mercer University, 1958), p. 68.
3. In this essay, the analysis will use the numbers of the individual hymn texts instead of page numbers, and Roman numerals will be changed to Arabic. Thus, DCLXXVII becomes 677.
4. John Julian, *A Dictionary of Hymnology* (London: J. Murray, 1907).
5. The only reference to Mercer's *Cluster* found in Julian's *Dictionary* is on p. 58, an erroneous entry made by the Rev. F. M. Bird of Lehigh University. It is called "Mercer's *Chester*."
6. Index of Mercer's *Cluster*:

Topic		No. of Hymns
On Free Grace		56
Christ Crucified		49
The Glories of Christ		55
Missions		20
Warning & Invitation		42
Conviction & Conversion		28
Believers' Baptism		16
Christian Exercises		288
Joy and Praise	79	
Prayer and Praise	18	
Faith and Prayer	20	
Prayer	83	
Conflict	23	
Hope & Encouragement	20	
Morning Devotions	22	
Evening Devotions	12	
Backslidings Lamented	11	
Christians Encouraged		34
Imputed Righteousness		6
Perseverance in Grace		21
Death		33
Judgment		16

Of the hymns, 43.37 percent are devoted to Christian Exercises. The four largest categories are Prayer, Joy and Praise, On Free Grace, and The Glories of Christ.

7. C. M. Mallary, *The Memoirs of Elder Jesse Mercer* (New York: Printed by John Gray, 1844), p. 408.
8. Northrop Frye, *The Great Code* (New York: Harcourt, Brace and Jovanovich, 1982).
9. B. L. Manning, *The Hymns of Wesley and Watts* (London: Epworth Press, 1954), p. 80.
10. Mercer's account book for 1822–1824 is located in Special Collections, Stetson Library, Mercer University, Macon, Georgia. Entered with ink or pencil are sales of books, receipts paid, subscriptions, and other personal transactions which list persons and dates. On p. 9 he recorded: "Left with Brother Barrow Nov. 8th 88 plain Clusters at 75, 35 gilt—1.00, 27 Calf Ex. gilt—2.00, 3 best

Mo.—2.25." Ten fowls cost $1, and 7 dozen eggs brought 87½ cents. On June 14, 1823, Mercer paid $6 to a Sister Thompson for 2 shirts and 2 overalls; for preaching at Crooked Creek he received $6.12½.

11. Mallary, *Memoirs of Elder Jesse Mercer.*

APPENDIX

Index of Hymns by Authors

Watts, Isaac (1674–1748): 24, 41, 73, 76, 78, 85, 87, 88, 89, 90, 92, 93, 98, 111, 220, 222, 250, 266, 318, 340, 342, 343, 389, 439, 457, 481, 507, 512, 513, 518, 520, 521, 522, 523, 526, 531, 534, 538, 540, 559, 592, 594, 636, 638, 640, 641, 642, 643, 644, 675, A-14.

Wesley, Charles (1707–1788), Wesley, John (1703–1791), Wesley, Samuel (1662–1735): 9, 10, 11, 15, 59, 66, 67, 79, 120, 158, 165, 197, 275, 276, 350, 351, 385, 387, 467, 518, 519, 548, 571, 572, 577, 616, 648, 654, 655, 658, A-3.

Newton, John (1725–1807): 5, 23, 29, 117, 124, 173, 188, 291, 311, 319, 320, 347, 352, 384, 393, 394, 430, 441, 463, 464, 469, 506, 545, 561, 569, 598, 653, A-8, A-9, A-10, A-11, A-13.

Steele, Anne (1716–1778): 102, 103, 149, 150, 290, 326, 354, 356, 360, 372, 389, 419, 421, 443, 515, 516, 535, 552, 632.

Beddome, Benjamin (1717–1795): 50, 51, 82, 128, 141, 169, 239, 317, 361, 388, 392, 399, 409, 410, 411, 480, 505, 625.

Doddridge, Philip (1702–1751): 22, 49, 101, 289, 295, 296, 321, 363, 386, 398, 415, 417, 420, 433, 634.

Hart, Joseph (1712–1768): 14, 64, 71, 84, 108, 115, 192, 397, 458, 459, 565, 599, 600.

Medley, Samuel (1738–1799): 36, 106, 126, 144, 153, 156, 207, 506, 564.

Fawcett, John (c.1739–1817): 21, 310, 328, 413, 476, 606, 611.

Stennett, Samuel (c.1727–1795): 37, 55, 119, 210, 294, 314, 423.

Toplady, Augustus Montague (1740–1778): 47, 61, 123, 155, 400, 475, 584, 591.

Cowper, William (1731–1800): 91, 381, 477, 588, 596.

Cennick, John (1718-1755): 95, 139, 307, 316.

Fellows, John (?–1785): 253, 256, 257, 258.

Heber, Reginald (1783–1826): A-1, A-2, A-4, A-7.

Mercer, Jesse (1769–1841): 233, 235, 364, 468, 471.

Davies, Samuel (1723–1761): 8, 122, 661.

Gibbons, Thomas (1720–1785): 180, 334, 429.

Heginbothom, Ottiwell (1744–1768): 330, 332, 504.

Keen, _____(?): 2, 118, 566.

Leland, John (1754–1841): 231, 491, 533.

Needham, John (?-c. 1786): 109, 427, 662.

Cruttendon, Robert (c.1691–c.1764): 500, 603.

Dobell, John (1757–1840): 216, 517.

Francis, Benjamin (1734–1799): 301, 630.

Grigg, Joseph (1728–1768): 127, 214.

Haweis, Thomas (1732–1820): 378, 455.

Humphreys, Joseph (1720–?): 208, 604.
Kent, John (1766–1843): 17, 19.
Montgomery, James (1771–1854): 284, 575.
Robinson, Robert (1735–1790): 283, 349.
Swain, Joseph (1761–1796): 496, 585.
Tate, Nahum (1652–1715): 110, 509.
Vokes, Mrs. (unknown but about end of 18th century): 166, 178.
Williams, William (1717–1791): 162, 395.

Each of the following contributed at least one hymn: Adams, John (1751–1835): 605; Addison, Joseph (1672–1719): 576; Allen, Jonathan (?): 199; Bourne, Hugh (1778–1843): 492; Brewer, Jehoiada (1752–1817): 228; Browne, Simon (c.1680–1732): 541; Bruce, Michael (1746–1767): A-5; Burnham, Richard (1749–1810): 438; Cole, Charles (1733–1813): 546; Crossman, Samuel (c.1624–1683): 501; Draper, Bourne Hall (1775–1843): 168; Evans, Jonathan (c.1748–1809): 65; Fountain, John (1767–1800): 198; Gambold, John (1711–1771): 286; Grant, James (?–1785): 555; Hammond, William (1719–1783): 425; Hegenwalt, Erhart (J. C. Jacobi, tr.) (16th century): 250; Hinchsliffe, Joseph (1760–1807): 660; Hoskins, Joseph (1745–1818): 449; Jones, Edmund (1722–1765): 435; Ken, Thomas (1637–c.1710): 536; Kingsbury, William (1744–1818): 152; Knight, Joel A. (1754–1809): 299; Maxwell, James (1720–1800): 377; Norris, John (1657–1711): 493; Occum, Samson (1723–1792): 223; Pearce, Samuel (1766–1799): 474; Pope, Alexander (1688–1744): 627; Rowley, Henry (1786–?): 508; Ryland, John (1753–1825): 262; Scott, Elizabeth Shirley (c.1708–1776): 511; Shirley, Walter (1725–1786): 74; Slinn, Sarah (18th century): 147; Stennett, Joseph (1663–1713): 104; Sternhold, Thomas (?–1549): A-6; Stocker, John (18th century): 7; Wallin, Benjamin (1711–1782): 31; White, Henry Kirke (1785–1806): 676; Wingrove, John (1720–1793): 20.

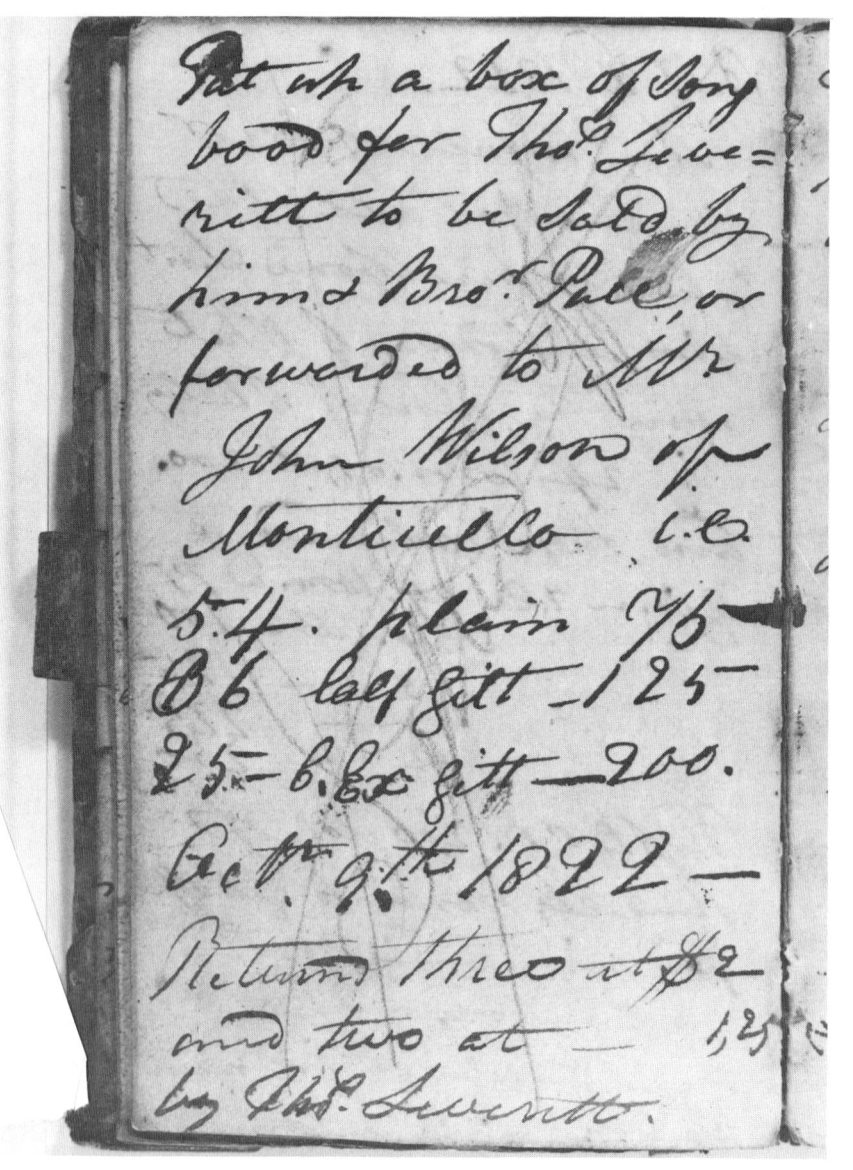

Put up a box of song book for Thos Leveritt to be sold by him & Bro^r Pace, or forwarded to Mr John Wilson of Monticello i.e.

54 plain   75
? 6 calf gilt   125
25- C. Ex gilt   200
by Thos Leveritt.

Octr 9th 1822
Returned three at $2
and two at   1,25
by Thos Leveritt.

A page from Jesse Mercer's "Accounts book."